Players and Teams of
the National Association,
1871–1875

ALSO BY PAUL BATESEL

*Major League Baseball Players of 1884:
A Biographical Dictionary* (McFarland, 2011)

*Major League Baseball Players of 1916:
A Biographical Dictionary* (McFarland, 2007)

Players and Teams of the National Association, 1871–1875

PAUL BATESEL

McFarland & Company, Inc., Publishers
Jefferson, North Carolina, and London

LIBRARY OF CONGRESS CATALOGUING-IN-PUBLICATION DATA

Batesel, Paul, 1938–
Players and teams of the National Association, 1871–1875 /
Paul Batesel.
Includes bibliographical references and index.

ISBN 978-0-7864-7012-9
softcover : acid free paper ∞

1. National Association of Base Ball Players (U.S.)—History.
2. Baseball players—United States—Biography—Dictionaries.
3. Baseball players—United States—Statistics.
I. Title.
GV870.N18B38 2012   796.357097309034—dc23   2012034632

BRITISH LIBRARY CATALOGUING DATA ARE AVAILABLE

© 2012 Paul Batesel. All rights reserved

*No part of this book may be reproduced or transmitted in any form
or by any means, electronic or mechanical, including photocopying
or recording, or by any information storage and retrieval system,
without permission in writing from the publisher.*

Front cover: The Philadelphia Athletics, *Harper's Weekly*,
July 25, 1874, photographs by Suddards and Fennemore,
Philadelphia (Library of Congress)

Manufactured in the United States of America

*McFarland & Company, Inc., Publishers
Box 611, Jefferson, North Carolina 28640
www.mcfarlandpub.com*

Acknowledgments

A book, like a child, is the product of a community. Perhaps this can best be illustrated by an image in this book. A university librarian in Maine scanned an image from a defunct Philadelphia magazine and sent it to me in North Dakota. Being pictorially challenged, I sent the image to a SABR Pictorial Committee member in the state of Washington for cleaning and repair. I, in turn, sent it to a publishing house in North Carolina.

A baseball book requires a baseball community. The author relies on the work of hundreds who came before: the sportswriters who filed the original stories; the statisticians who (since the days of *Beadle's Dime Base Ball Player* in 1860) have compiled the records; and the researchers who, having assessed the statistics and game accounts, have given them meaning.

Since 1971 the Society for American Baseball Research has collected, preserved and edited materials as a commons we all can claim. In providing the materials used in this book, two committees stand out. The Biographical Research Committee deserves praise for its on-going work in correcting errors in biographical records and in locating information about former players. The latest finding about Jim Clinton, for example, came to light just before this book left my hands. And, as indicated above, I am much indebted to the Pictorial Committee for its assistance with the photographs found on these pages.

Being married to a librarian, I love all the collectors and guardians of information—whether formal libraries, museums, websites or blogs. I owe a great deal to Eric Miklich, Jeffrey Kittel, and Brian McKenna, not only for the information they maintain on their websites but also for generously allowing me to borrow from them. And like many who appreciate nineteenth-century baseball images, I am indebted to the auction houses that see and evaluate baseball treasures and kindly allow us to borrow images from their catalogues.

Here in North Dakota, Mayville State University continues to provide technical assistance and support for my writing. Dr. Delbert Hlavinka serves as my medical advisor for those—to me—strange nineteenth-century death-inducing illnesses such as phthisis pulmonalis.

I have not formally met T. Scott Brandon, but for the second time he has been a pictorial advisor for one of my books by providing images, cleaning, editing, and identifying images. While I would gladly list him as photo editor on the title page, I fear my shortcomings as researcher and writer might be laid to his account. Suffice it to say that without him, the number, quality, and accuracy of images would be considerably lower.

Table of Contents

Acknowledgments v

Preface 1

Introduction 5

BIOGRAPHICAL DICTIONARY 13

CLUB DICTIONARY 139

Bibliography 215

Index 219

Preface

Unlike its two predecessors, *Major League Baseball Players of 1916* and *Major League Baseball Players of 1884*, which focused on a single season, *National Association Players and Clubs* is centered on the life of a league. It is both a player dictionary of the 325 men who played during the 1871–75 period and a club dictionary of the 25 teams for which they played. However, like its predecessors, this study includes all participants. A one-game player named "Hellings" is, I hope, treated with the same courtesy as Hall of Fame player and manager Cap Anson, and the Maryland Base Ball Club that left the league with an 0–6 record receives the respect accorded the four-time league champion Boston Red Stockings.

Based on the notion that every player who wears a major league uniform and every club that is awarded a major franchise represents some piece of the American dream, I have once again chosen as my model the most inclusive of studies. *Baseball Players of the 1950s* by Richard Marazzi and Len Fiorito includes a sketch of all 1,560 players of that decade. Two SABR committees on whose research I depend—the Biographical Research Committee and the Pictorial Committee—both maintain checklists as they work toward all-inclusive lists of major league players. Of course, the mammoth SABR BioProject has as its goal a biographical sketch of "every player who ever played in the major leagues." That work as now is moving toward 1,700 biographies.

Why another book on the National Association? My admiration of the works of such pioneer National Association researchers as Marshall Wright, William J. Ryczek, and the late Preston Orem is boundless. Their research, shown in the information they bring to their pages, is vital to understanding the history of baseball. Wright put together the records and rosters for NA clubs, even for the 15 years of Organized Baseball history preceding the league; Ryczek analyzed the history of the league, the individual pennant races and the problems the league encountered, laying a foundation for much of the scholarship that followed. Preston Orem painstakingly put together the newspaper accounts of baseball for more than a quarter century, showing the development of baseball as viewed by the sportswriters. Among others, David Nemec, Eric Miklich (*19th Century Baseball*), Jeffrey Kittel (*This Game of Games*), and Brian McKenna (*Baseball History Blog*) continue to offer well-researched studies in nineteenth-century baseball.

National Association Players and Clubs is not competition for these studies. It is not a statistical study; it is not an analysis of pennant races or problems. The question I hear from people I know is a simple one: What were people like who played the game then? Where did they come from, and where did they go after their day in the sun was over? How different are they from those who wear a major league uniform today? These questions are what I hope to answer in the biographical dictionary. The baseball literature of my youth tended to be hagiography, focusing on character that allowed players to overcome obstacles and learn from mistakes. In my adult years, I began to see a literature that emphasized the warts of professional sport, showing that baseball players are often all too human. Either approach requires a carefully edited list of players and supporting materials. By chance, I researched Harry Berthrong and John Glenn on consecutive days, so I can see how a writer would be tempted to one approach or the other. Players in the National Association straddle a line between "gentleman" and "gun for hire." Given this, any account of the players would have to include both character and warts; I hope that I have accounted for both without exploiting either.

At a time when league membership could be had for $10, and $3,100 was considered a sufficient amount to build a franchise from scratch, it is not surprising that so many clubs attempted to become major league. The club dictionary shows that while many clubs tried to compete with the Yankees and Red Sox of the time, clubs whose payrolls alone were five times the threshold $3,000, none succeeded. What the books shows is that while as Americans we may believe in *Hoosiers* and decry the success of *Damn Yankees*, we basically know that when the American dream meets economic reality, reality wins. History shows that fourteen clubs were unable to complete so much as a single season in the National Association.

Why focus on the National Association? In 1990, the editors of the eighth edition of *Baseball Encyclopedia* judged that because of the "erratic schedule and procedures," the National Association "is not considered a major league." Therefore, NA records are relegated to the back of the volume in a separate section. Today it is not uncommon on websites to see a mention of an NA performance qualified with the phrase "for those who consider the National Association to be a major league."

However, the last twenty years has seen an increased interest in the National Association. The baseball researchers mentioned above have made us more aware of that phase of baseball history. At the same time, the different SABR committees—especially the Biographical Research Committee—have filled in many of the holes in the National Association records by correcting errors in the identity of players and in their playing records. For instance, we now know that playing records formerly assigned to Dan Patterson really belong to Tom Patterson and that a player named Kavanagh is really James Cavanagh. In this ongoing process of cleaning up records, formerly one-name players are being given their full identity. In this process, several researchers are moving ever backward to the very roots of the game.

Likewise, for me, baseball's center of gravity has settled backward. Though born in 1938, I consider myself a child of the 1950s and began a research project on 1952, my coming-to-knowledge-of-major league baseball year. I actually researched the Deadball Era, and then continued to look backward to the nineteenth century and now to the National Association. Perhaps there is always a sense that to understand a baseball age, one really needs to understand the preceding generation. The National League was not born full-blown from the brow of Jove; it was an evolutionary phase developed to solve some of the problems created by the NAPBBA. But the professional league was itself an evolutionary phase of the baseball organization called the NABBP (1857–1870), which was itself an evolution of the game that had been played by amateur clubs primarily in New York City and Brooklyn since 1845. But now we see that even the Knickerbocker game was merely an attempt to find a common ground among other earlier games involving a ball and a bat. Therefore, this look at National Association clubs and players is a way of developing a better understanding of the game we know today.

For the most part the same sources that were available to me for my two earlier books were still of use in researching the National Association. Once again *SABR Encyclopedia* and Baseball-Reference.com were the source for playing records. Two of the former sources that bear special mention are Ancestry.com and the newsletters from the SABR Biographical Research Committee. The ever-expanding Ancestry database provided invaluable research material from censuses, city directories, family trees, and military records. The Biographical Research Committee continues to make major strides in locating missing players from the nineteenth century, and the newsletter allows the baseball community to share in their findings each month. Two new sources that were very helpful were SABR's research report on Civil War veterans (a number of NA players were old enough to have served in the War) and Genealogy Bank. This indexed newspaper archive allowed me to read reports of National Association games, find references to players whose National Association experience was brief, and to discover useful pieces of information about players as they pursued other careers. The Library of Congress is surely not a new source, but the Geography and Maps Division, especially the Panoramic Maps, was very helpful as I attempted to locate nineteenth-century ballparks. In at least a dozen cases I was able to find a bird's eye view of grounds, showing the configuration of the ball field and often the presence of grandstands.

Basically the plan of organization for the book is this: the introduction brings forth two concepts. Players were in a juncture between "gentlemen" who played for "health and recreation only" and a more democratic group of players who saw baseball as a source of income. The second concept was that while many of the clubs were well-financed organizations, able to attract the players to be competitive, many others clubs saw major league baseball as an embodiment of the American dream. The biographical dictionary has entries for each of the players, showing league performance, any other baseball experience, and what we know of the player's post-baseball life. Surprisingly, we have photographs of 200 of these players. The club dictionary covers all teams giving what we know of their histories. Two clubs—Atlantic and Eckford—both formed in the 1850s, predate any formal baseball organization; two clubs—the Boston Red Stockings (Atlanta Braves) and the Chicago White Stockings (Chicago Cubs)—are still in existence today. For each club covered, the dictionary shows home grounds, management, uniforms and logos, and a detailed account of its experience in the league. Each club has up to three supporting photographs or illustrations.

Under a purely professional scenario—call it the Boston Red Stocking modus—the National Association would have involved fewer than ten teams and around one hundred players. However, because amateur players dream of becoming professionals and amateur teams dream of major league status—call it the St. Louis Red Stocking modus—the National Association actually involved 325 players and 25 teams.

Introduction

Baseball was originally a sport of gentleman. *Baseball: An Illustrated History* notes that members of the 1845 Knickerbocker Club were men "who were at leisure after 3 o'clock in the afternoon" and men who could afford to play baseball "for health and recreation merely" (Ward 4). In addition to writing the rules for playing baseball, the Knickerbocker Club wrote parameters of decorum for its members, emphasizing that baseball was a game for and played by gentlemen. Players on the club were assessed fines for behaviors such as the use of profane language, arguing with the umpire, or trying to influence an umpire's decision. Even the choice of material for uniforms reflected a cultural bias in favor of white collar and professional persons. The Baseball Hall of Fame article "Dressed to the Nines" states that while cotton would make more comfortable uniforms, it was associated with working class clothing; hence, early uniforms were made of wool or silk. The article also notes that Knickerbocker—like many of the later National Association clubs—chose blue as a "gentlemanly" uniform color, thereby setting themselves apart from the red-trimmed uniforms selected by "lower class, disorderly, juvenile or small-town clubs."

But change was not long in coming. First, there was a change in the cultural makeup of the large eastern cities with the arrival of a great number of immigrants, particularly from Ireland, England, and Germany. Answers.com notes that "by the 1850s–1860s, 28 percent of all people living in New York, 26 percent in Boston, and 16 percent in Philadelphia had been born in Ireland." Geoffrey Ward says that New York City was filled with "restless young men" looking for social outlets, which they increasingly began to find in baseball clubs (5–6). As a result, baseball began to move away from being a pastime for gentlemen toward being a sport for all. In 1855, ten years after the formation of the Knickerbocker club, a working-class baseball club was formed in Brooklyn. The Eckford club was composed almost entirely of shipyard workers. The Civil War advanced baseball's democratization process as men learned the game in camps and carried it back home to towns across the country.

Second, baseball itself was changing. What once were formally arranged contests often involving social components such as banquets and entertainment began to change with the formation of the National Association of Base Ball Players in 1857. By 1860 *Beadle's Dime Base Ball Player* began to show team records so that followers of baseball could see the relative strength of teams and increase the talk of championships. They also began to see lists of players, showing how well each performed in terms of runs scored and "hands lost." Once baseball reached this point, clubs began to seek the better players and to offer inducements to obtain them. While claims have been made for several players as being the first professional, it is clear that early on many key players were beneficiaries of financial arrangements of some nature. Harry Wright's contribution to baseball may be that in openly paying players, he merely regularized what was more or less a common practice.

In a period of less than a quarter century, baseball moved from an activity played by well-to-do men "for health and recreation merely" to one played by working-class men—many of them immigrants—to provide some portion of their livelihood. The players of the National Association of Professional Base Ball Players stand in that crossroads. Among the 325 players, there are representatives of both approaches to the game.

National Association Player Demographics

NA demographics reflect the "restless" population that produced the players. While the overwhelming majority of players were American born, twenty-five were foreign born, just a trickle of what was to come before the end of the century as waves of immigrants would find baseball to be a path to social belonging and financial security. Not surprisingly, eight NA players were born in Ireland. Tommy Bond, Fergy Malone and Andy Leonard head this list, which includes the Campbell brothers, Ed Duffy, "Fancy" O'Neil and Jimmy Hallinan. Harry Wright, Al Reach, George Hall and Dick Higham are the most distinguished of the group of eight English-born players, one that also includes Sam Jackson, Al Nichols, Al Thake, and Bobby Clack. George Heubel, Marty Swandell, and Joe Miller were born in Germany; Bob Addy and Tom Smith were Canadians; Steve Bellan hailed from Cuba, Larry Ressler from France, and Rynie Wolters from Holland.

Through the census we also have the parentage of 270 players. Of the 274 American-born players, 126—about 46 percent—were sons of American-born parents. This figure includes the Jewish American parents of Lip Pike and Nate Berkenstock and the Native American parents of Tom Oran. Almost as many—119—had at least one parent born outside the United States. Of these 69 were born in Ireland, 26 in England, 15 in Germany, and four in Scotland.

Of the 55 players whose parents we cannot determine, at least a third bore names such as Sullivan, McGee, O'Rourke, Kelly, Cavanagh, Malone, Quinlan, and Laughlin, names that suggest an Irish birth or an Irish father.

None of this is to suggest that native-born equates to gentility or wealth, but rather that the growing popularity of baseball caused it to draw players from every strata of a changing society. Some American-born players such as Count Sensenderfer can list their occupation in the census as "gentleman"; others such as Maurice "Mollie" Moore are referred to as "denizens of the Bowery."

The birthplace of NA players likewise reflects both tradition and change. One in four of the 299 players whose birthplace we know came from New York State, with the bulk from the metropolitan area. Three of four (222) were born in a 250-mile eastern corridor of states extending from Connecticut to Washington, D.C., reflecting both the cradle and the early spread of Organized Baseball. Pennsylvania produced 57 players (most from Philadelphia), Maryland 29 (most from Baltimore), Connecticut 16, New Jersey and the District of Columbia 11 each.

The spread of baseball is demonstrated by the number of league players either born in or developed in the West and South. St.

Louis, for example, was a hotbed of baseball even before the Empire club joined the NA in 1866. When the Red Stockings joined the league in 1875, they drew heavily on local talent, such as the Dillon brothers, Joe Blong, Trick McSorley, Pidge Morgan, Billy Redmon, Art Croft and Charlie Hautz. The city and the club also fostered the talents of Tom Oran from California, Dan Collins from Louisiana, and Joe Ellick from Ohio. Another St. Louis great, Pud Galvin, debuted with the Brown Stockings, one of the few local players with that club. Chicago's John Peters also came from the St. Louis area. In all, 11 NA players came from Missouri.

Another western outpost was the Rockford area of Illinois, which, more than Chicago, led in popularizing baseball in the region. The Forest City club spawned Al Spalding, George Bird, Gat Stires and Tom Foley, and fostered the develop of Midwesterners Cap Anson (Iowa), Scott Hastings (Ohio), and Al Barker (Indiana), as well as New Yorkers Joe Simmons and Ross Barnes and the Canadian Bob Addy. Foley's brother Will began in Chicago with the White Stockings, and Chicago natives Jimmy Hallinan and Paddy Quinn debuted with Kekionga. Not only did the amateur Aetna club of Chicago foster the talents of Hallinan and Quinn, it also prepared Ohio-born Hugh Reid for his chance with Lord Baltimore.

Cal McVey came from the small town of Montrose, Iowa, to the powerful Cincinnati Red Stockings while still a teenager; this club also brought to the fore George Wright, Asa Brainard, and Fred Waterman (all from New York) and Philadelphia native Doug Allison. Cincinnati native Charlie Gould began with the Buckeyes, another Cincinnati club, which sent along Charlie Sweasy (New Jersey), Lefty McMullin and Cherokee Fisher (both Philadelphia), and Irish-born Andy Leonard. Up north, Forest City of Cleveland nurtured New York State natives Deacon and Elmer White.

Collins, Charlie Mason, and Billy Barnie were the first of a half-dozen New Orleans players who would begin to appear in the majors in the 1880s.

Amateurs vs. Professionals

While by definition the NAPBBP was a professional league, some players clearly were throwbacks to an earlier age when baseball was a game played by those who didn't need the money. We can perhaps isolate three overlapping sub-groups of these players. One group would be composed of "drop by" major leaguers—generally short-term players for whom the major league experience was at most an interesting interlude before they began or continued their chosen careers. The best known player in this group is Martin Mullen. Although he was a much-sought-after baseball player, Mullen wanted nothing to do with professional baseball, according to his obituary in the *Cleveland Plain Dealer*. However, on August 17, 1872, when Forest City outfielder Rynie Wolters became deathly ill after swallowing his chaw of tobacco, the 19-year-old Mullen came out of the stands to fill his position. While the circumstances may be apocryphal—Wolters had a reputation for missing games (Ryczek 83)—that contest constituted Mullen's major league career. He went on to become a national amateur billiards champion and a millionaire Great Lake coal dealer.

Several other league players did not need major league baseball to make their lives complete. Frank Abercrombie, George Knight and Alex Nevin were college students on the brink of professional careers in engineering, medicine and finance, respectively. Jim Gilmore, Caleb Johnson and Count Sensenderfer were law students preparing to embark on careers in law or politics. Several players had already begun careers while or before playing. Yale-educated Lester Dole was about to start a career as a physical education instructor. Harry Berthrong, Dennis Coughlin, Jacob Doyle, Bill Yeatman, and Warren White obtained government appointments while playing and went on to become career government employees; Tom Foley (publishing), Jim Carleton (banking) and George Popplein (paint) had begun private business ventures; George Bird rejected a baseball contract to operate his farm. Frank Norton inherited a fortune, leaving both baseball and government service behind.

For some players, baseball was just one of the sports in which they won distinction. Mullen won more honors in billiards, as did Gene Kimball. Berthrong and William Rexter both were champions in rowing. Dole was a professional champion "pedestrian."

A second group—including some of the above—would be composed of pick-up players. Clubs carried few substitutes and occasionally had to dip into the amateur and semi-pro ranks to field a team. Twenty-two of 325 players have no known first name, surely an indicator of pick-up status. Another likely index is one-game status; 92 players—more than one-fourth—appeared in only one game during a given season. The 1874 Atlantic club used no fewer than 14 one-game players; Maryland in 1873 used eight in only six games; Lord Baltimore in 1874 used five, and National in 1872 needed four in 11 games.

The most egregious example of needing local help was Atlantic in July of 1875. The club arrived in Philadelphia to play Athletic, bringing only five players. A raid of the sandlots turned up four amateurs who took part in a 23–3 shellacking by Athletic. Of these, 18-year-old Doc Bushong, a dental student, went on to a distinguished stint catching with St. Louis and Brooklyn before undertaking his real career. Starting pitcher Harry Arundel later twirled for Providence and Pittsburgh; 35-year-old third baseman Washington Fulmer, brother of Chick Fulmer, played his only major league game that day; likewise, a second baseman named Hellings made his only major league appearance.

A final group would be composed of the members of the amateur clubs that entered the league. Mansfield, Resolute and the St. Louis Red Stockings had operated as amateur clubs long before determining to test themselves against professionals. Resolute was able to add five veterans to their amateur core; the Red Stockings and Mansfields added only one each. Other clubs, such as Centennial, Western, and Maryland, dipped heavily into the amateur ranks to fill out teams. Maryland used 15 players with no previous league experience, while Centennial, like Resolute, used eight; Western employed four.

Of course, many of these players were not—strictly speaking—amateurs, as they shared in the gate receipts and any prize money their clubs earned. But even when these clubs became "professional," they invariably operated as cooperatives, providing little income for the players.

On the other hand, competition for good players led to salaries that promised a future when baseball would provide a livelihood of sorts for most and a very lucrative one for some. The published salary schedule for Rockford in 1871 shows future Hall of Fame player Cap Anson making the princely sum of $66.67 per month during the season—less than $500 total. Some comparisons are perhaps in order. According to ehow.com, the average worker in manufacturing made roughly $345 annually in 1880; at the same period male teachers were paid $71.40 for the school year. Skilled workers such as carpenters earned $2 to $2.50 per day and perhaps as much as $750 annually if they were able to work the year round. As low as Anson's salary seems, it would have been better than or comparable to what most males earned at the time.

Some NA players were faring very well. According to the *Springfield Republican* of November 11, 1873, Boston was paying four players—Harry Wright, George Wright, Al Spalding, and Ross Barnes—a salary of $1,800. Four other players—Deacon White ($1,500), Andy Leonard ($1,400), Harry Schafer ($1,200) and Dave Birdsall ($1,000)—all exceeded a thousand dollars. The *Cleveland Plain Dealer* on February 20, 1874, reported that four clubs with published salary schedules—Chicago, Boston, Philadelphia and Athletic—were together paying out more than $57,000 in salaries to 46 players, all of whom were earning at least $1,000. Three Chicago players—Fergy Malone, Jimmy Wood and George Zettlein—had salaries exceeding $2,000. Lord Baltimore supposedly offered Bobby Mathews $2,500 for 1874. Chicago captain Fergy Malone reportedly demanded that his salary be increased to $2,800 for 1875; however, the club determined that a .248 batting average was not worthy of that salary.

Additionally, a number of players enjoyed extended playing tenures, suggesting that baseball could indeed be seen as a career. While 197 players did not play major league baseball beyond the NA, 128 played on into the National League; 69 were still active in 1882 when the American Association was founded; 58 NA players saw the Union Association formed in 1884. Fifteen took part in the next three-league experiment, with the Players League in 1890. Jim Keenan, Doc Bushong, Jim Holdsworth, Pop Snyder, Jack Burdock, and Paul Hines all lasted into 1891; Pud Galvin and Lou Say played in 1892; Cap Anson toiled through 1897; Jim O'Rourke played occasionally into the twentieth century.

Baseball was also starting to provide spin-off career opportunities related to the sport. For example, Al Reach, Al Spalding, and George Wright cashed in on the demand for baseball equipment by manufacturing and selling it. Reach, Spalding, Tim Murnane, and Harry Wright were involved in baseball at the executive level. Murnane's thirty-year career in sportswriting earned him in place in the Hall of Fame's Honor Rolls of Baseball in 1946. Charlie Mason had a brief major league playing experience—21 games—but spent the next 55 years in baseball as a minor league player, manager, club owner, operator, and ballpark manager.

One unfortunate effect of higher salaries and the competition for players was the destabilization of clubs, a trend that predated the league. At that time before the institution of the reserve clause, players were free to change clubs whenever they saw opportunities for higher pay. And while those players who indulged in the practice were given the derogatory term "revolvers," the clubs were hardly innocent. Harry Wright's great Cincinnati Red Stocking club was an all-star team, drawn to the Queen City by a guaranteed salary schedule. In the same way, Chicago (1870), Boston (1871), Lord Baltimore (1872), Philadelphia (1873), Hartford (1874), Chicago (1874), and St. Louis (1875) began operation by raiding players from other clubs in order to become instant contenders. Each of these clubs was in turn victimized by the next club with deeper pockets. For example, while Philadelphia was blowing an eight-game lead in the final months of the 1873 season, six of their regulars—Jimmy Wood, Fred Treacey, Ned Cuthbert, Fergy Malone, George Zettlein and Jim Devlin—had already signed with Chicago for 1874.

Loyalty did exist among some players: Joe Start and John Hatfield for Mutual; Dick McBride, Wes Fisler and Al Reach for Athletic; Harry and George Wright, Ross Barnes, Al Spalding and Harry Schafer for Boston all played throughout the NA with one club. More players, however, seized any opportunity to better themselves economically. Fourteen five-year NA men changed clubs each year. Shortstop Davy Force began 1871 with Olympic, 1872 with Troy, 1873 with Lord Baltimore, 1874 with Chicago and 1875 with Athletic. Hard-throwing Cherokee Fisher pitched for Rockford in 1871, for Lord Baltimore in 1872, for Athletic in 1873, for Hartford in 1874 and for Philadelphia in 1875. Five players—Doug Allison, Frank Fleet, Charlie Sweasy, Fred Treacey and George Zettlein—managed to play for six clubs in five seasons. Such instability continued until 1876 when the new league ended both poaching and revolving.

A considerably worse consequence regarding the amount of money surrounding professional baseball was the aura of dishonesty that began to envelop the game. In most grounds (Boston and Hartford were exceptions), gamblers openly set up shop to accept wagers not only on the outcome of the game, but of innings and even individual at-bats. In some grounds these wagers were laid within the hearing of the players involved. William J. Ryczek notes that outside of Capitoline Grounds in Brooklyn there was a saloon where gamblers and players drank together. It should come as no surprise that the proximity of gamblers and players led to a general sense that often the outcome of a game was tainted. As early as May 27, 1872, the *Washington Critic-Record* complained that "young men who once played for sport and exercise now play as the hired tool of gamblers." William J. Ryczek concludes, "Accepting bribes was likely to be a safe, steady source of income for a professional ballplayer" (214).

Among NA clubs, Mutual, Philadelphia and Chicago seemed to have the most questionable games. Mutual in particular was believed to be controlled by gambling interests. The *Chicago Tribune* noted of one game involving Mutual, "There is ample reason to believe that at least four [players] were hired to throw the game and had no intention of winning at any stage" (Oran 195). Ryczek noted that the Philadelphia players who lost the 1873 pennant race under clouded circumstances simply continued their practices in Chicago (214).

Among players, many were suspected of "hippodroming"; that is, working with the gamblers to ensure the outcome of games. In *The Fix Is In*, Daniel Ginsburg cites the *Brooklyn Eagle* "all star" team of "rogues," selected from those players whose names came up most often in connection with fixing games: "George Zettlein, pitcher; Dick Higham, catcher; Bill Craver, first base; Mike McGeary, second base; John Radcliff, shortstop; Davy Force, third base; Fred Treacy, left field; George Bechtel, center field; Joe Blong, right field; and Dickey Pearce and Frank Fleet, substitutes" (30).

On the other hand, few players were actually disciplined in any lasting way. Jeffrey Kittel cites an October 1875 *St. Louis Globe-Democrat* complaint that

> although numerous players were accused of dishonesty, desertion and unfaithful conduct during the season, not a single member was expelled from the association. On the contrary, they were all released from their engagements; and, by being at once hired by some rival club to the one which they had left, were tempted still further to sell out and "revolve." Higham left Chicago, and the Mutuals received him with open arms. Blong was expelled from the Reds and Stars, to be affectionately received in the Brown Stocking fold. Latham went from Boston to New Haven, and thence to Canada. Fields skipped the Washingtons for the Ludlows, and others too numerous to mention skipped from one club to another with perfect impunity.

It was not until 1877 that the National League actually banned four Louisville players—former NA players Jim Devlin, George Hall, Al Nichols and Bill Craver—for life for fixing games.

National Association Clubs

The earliest base ball clubs were metropolitan and local. Sixteen New York City and Brooklyn clubs met to organize the National Association of Base Ball Players in 1857. A year later the Liberty club of New Brunswick, New Jersey, appeared in the list of 25 NA members, the first club from outside metropolitan New York City. In 1859 the Niagara club from Buffalo was among 50 members; in 1860 five clubs from New Haven, Washington, Boston, Baltimore, and Detroit were included in the 59 members. At the outbreak of the Civil War, six Philadelphia clubs were among the 55 members. After the Civil War the number of clubs mushroomed to 202 in 1866, featuring teams from as far away as Tennessee and Kansas. When the National club of Washington, D.C., made the first western tour in 1867, it played teams in Columbus, Cincinnati, Louisville, Indianapolis, St. Louis, Rockford and Chicago. In that year membership in the NA exceeded 400.

The year 1869 was a watershed time for baseball clubs. In that year Harry Wright established a salary schedule for his Cincinnati club and recruited top players from outside the region. The NA sanctioned the payment of players, which meant that what had previously been done under the table had become the principle of baseball. Other clubs were not slow to see the advantage of recruiting and paying the best players. The result was a split between those dozen or so clubs with the means to follow the Red Stockings' example and the hundreds of other clubs without the ambition or the means to do so.

The American Dream vs. Economic Reality

When ten of the top members of the NA met in March of 1871 to form the National Association of Professional Base Ball Players and establish a league of professional clubs playing a schedule to culminate in the pennant, this should have established a pattern and a principle for inclusion in the group. The league would be composed of those strong and stable clubs with the means to compete. That was the way it was supposed to be. However, this is America where dreams of success abound. And so the story of the NAPBBP—now simply called the NA—is the story of a contest between reality and those dreams. The story shows that however strong the dreams, clubs without the means to survive did not.

Seven of the nine clubs that contested the 1871 pennant were of the strong and stable pattern. But from the beginning, clubs entered the league with little more to offer than some scenario of the American dream. Despite a strong baseball tradition, Rockford had a population of roughly 11,000—one-thirtieth the size of Chicago—and a payroll less than half that of Boston, allowing Harry Wright to pluck three of their greatest stars in Al Spalding, Ross Barnes and Fred Cone. Because of its western location, Rockford also had the highest travel costs and arguably the worst grounds in the league. None of these factors prevented the Forest City club from believing it could replicate its past glories. And in an 1871 version of "If you build it, they will come," Kekionga of Fort Wayne tried to jump from the amateur ranks to the top professional level, their case strengthened by the construction of an elaborate grandstand, called the Grand Duchess. However, fans did not come, and the group of Maryland players, disgruntled over their share of the gate receipts, returned to Baltimore.

The failure of these clubs did not prevent the small-town amateur Mansfield club from entering the league in 1872; as with the Rockford club, supporters believed the Middletown population base of around 10,000 was sufficient to support a team competing against clubs from Philadelphia, Boston and New York. That same season four big-city clubs in Washington and Brooklyn entered the league, spurred on by the faith that gate receipts alone would allow them to put competitive teams on the field. Mansfield, Atlantic, Eckford, Olympic and National combined to post a 19–91 record.

Even the loss of six clubs from the league in 1872 did not prevent amateur teams Resolute of Elizabeth, New Jersey, and Maryland of Baltimore from trying their hand in 1873. Both faced the same problems of attempting to move directly from the amateur ranks and depending strictly on gate receipts for player salaries and operating expenses. Resolute was further hampered by Elizabeth's modest population base. Another under-funded Washington club—a combination of the two losing clubs of 1872—also entered the pennant race. The three teams combined for a 10–58 record.

The stability that had marked the 1874 season, when all eight clubs more or less finished the season, did not last into 1875. The ranks that final season were swollen by the addition of six new clubs, five of whom existed far to the left of hopeful. Two St. Louis clubs represented the difference between the haves and have nots. The Brown Stockings were a club of professionals, recruited from the East and funded by local business interests as a corporate entity. The Red Stockings were a popular local amateur club dependent on fan support for their existence in the professional arena.

Western of Keokuk was a most compelling story in the pursuit of the American dream. Like other clubs before them, the Westerns believed that they could successfully compete with professionals. But their move into the NA was a piece of an even larger dream—that Keokuk (population 12,000) was destined to replace Chicago as the cultural, economic and political center of the Midwest. And if it could be the leader in the Midwest, then surely it could be of the nation as well. Elm City of New Haven came into existence on the belief that for an initial investment of a mere $3,100, a city could build a competitive major league team from scratch and operate it throughout a season. (The Chicago White Stockings had a payroll of more than $17,000.) Centennial was created on the premise that since Philadelphia was able to support two clubs, an investor only had to bring another in existence and the fans would show up to support it. Finally, yet one more Washington club came into being on the principle that the city "should not be behind her sister cities." The Red Stockings, Western, Elm City, Centennial, and Washington combined for a 19–102 record.

History writes that only three clubs—Athletic, Boston and Mutual—competed for all five NA pennants. Chicago likely would have done so had the Great Fire not siphoned off money and personnel. But the lessons were clear: to enjoy even a modicum of success, clubs needed solid financial and fan support. Successful new clubs such as Lord Baltimore in 1872, Philadelphia in 1873 and the Brown Stockings in 1875 had these in place before a team took the field. As clubs lost these supports, they slid into mediocrity and then passed into history as did Troy and Cleveland in 1872, Lord Baltimore in 1874 and Philadelphia in 1875.

Biographical Dictionary

John Abadie began with the Keystone club of Philadelphia. He came to Centennial in 1875 from the powerful Easton semi-pro team—one of nine past or future major league players on the club. A six-foot, 190-pounder, Abadie was the regular first baseman for Centennial before the club disbanded in late May. On June 10, he filled in at first base for Atlantic in a game in Philadelphia. Between the two clubs, he hit .224 in 13 games. Defensively, he fielded .910, 28 points under the league average. The *Inquirer* said of his defensive ability that "there are boys of 12 in amateur clubs far his superior." Later in the season he played for the Ludlow club of Kentucky, and in 1877 he played for Auburn, New York, in the League Alliance. His name is spelled "Aubidy" in the 1860 census for Philadelphia. He appears in the 1880 census and the 1881 Philadelphia city directory as a married laborer. The 1900 census shows him living in New Jersey, working as a hostler. Abadie died in Pemberton, New Jersey, on May 17, 1905, at age 54. Census data show him born in 1850 rather than the 1854 listed in baseball records. *(Baseball-Reference.com; U.S. Federal Census; Sporting Life; Philadelphia Inquirer; Philadelphia City Directory; SABR Baseball Encyclopedia)*

Frank Abercrombie played shortstop for Troy on October 21, 1871, in a home game against Chicago. The 19-year-old went hitless at the plate and committed two errors on six fielding chances. Until recently his records were assigned to the Scottish-born David Abercrombie. Frank Abercrombie played baseball at Rensselaer Polytechnic Institute in Troy, New York, so it is probable that the Haymakers borrowed him from the

Frank Abercrombie (*History of the Pennsylvania Railroad*, William Bender Wilson, 1895).

college team for the game against Chicago. Born into a military family, Abercrombie first appears in the 1850 census for San Antonio as an infant born in Arkansas, though his birth is officially listed as Fort Towson, Oklahoma. Both the 1891 Williamsport city directory and the 1930 federal census for Philadelphia list him as a civil engineer; *Burke's American Families with British Ancestry* lists him as a civil engineer and former superintendent of the New York Division of the Pennsylvania Railroad. Frank Abercrombie died in Philadelphia on Veterans Day, 1939, at age 87. *(Baseball-Reference.com; U.S. Federal Census; Boyd's Williamsport City Directory; Descendants of John Joseph Abercrombie and Sarah Denormandie; Burke's American Families with British Ancestry)*

Bob Addy was 29 years old when the NA was formed. He had played for Rockford as early as 1868, when he allegedly invented the slide. In 1869 he had the highest hits-per-game average among professional players. For the NA Forest City club he hit .271 as the regular second baseman in 1871. After sitting out 1872 to pursue business interests in Rockford, Addy joined the Philadelphia White Stockings in 1873 but finished the season with Boston prior to playing with Hartford (1874) and Philadelphia (1875) in the NA. In 1876 he hit .282 for the National League champion Chicago White Stockings before finishing with Cincinnati in 1877. For his career he hit .277 in 274 games; statistically, he was a superior second baseman and a below-average outfielder. He served as playing manager at both Philadelphia and Cincinnati, his teams posting a combined 8–23 record. Born in Port Hope, Ontario, Addy became a resident of Rockford, where he is listed as a "tinner" in his 1863 draft registration and as a tinsmith in the 1870 census. After moving to Pocatello, Idaho, he married for a second time in 1892 when he was almost 50 years old. The 1900 census for Pocatello lists him as a hardware merchant. Addy died at Pocatello on May 9, 1910, at age 67 or 68. *(Baseball-Reference.com; Robert Edward Addy Family Tree; National Association of Base Ball Players, 1857–1870; Sporting Life; Chicago Republic; U.S. Civil War Draft Registration Records, 1863–65)*

Frank E. "Ham" Allen played in 17 games for Mansfield in 1872, hitting .271 with 11 RBIs. He fielded at the league average in nine games at shortstop and also played nine games in the outfield. He had joined Mansfield in 1870, coming from the Fairmount club of Marlboro, Massachusetts, where he was the regular catcher in 1869. David Arcidiacono believes Allen later played in the International Association. Born in Maine, Allen was a farmer in Milford, Massachusetts, at the outbreak of the Civil War. Enlisting on August 18, 1862, Allen served in the Thirty-sixth Massachusetts Infantry until he received a disability discharge on October 21, 1863. He was listed in the 1880 census for Natick, Massachusetts, as a railroad worker. Allen died at Natick on February 6, 1881, at age 34. While the consensus among sources is that this is the correct "Ham" Allen, *Total Baseball* is one of the sources suggesting the ball player is actually Homer S. Allen, a slightly younger Connecticut resident who also appears in the 1880 census as a railroad worker and who died at Hamden in 1892. *(Baseball-Reference.com; U.S. Federal Census; National Association of Base Ball Players, 1857–1870; Total Baseball; Civil War Veterans Who Played Major League Baseball Research Project; Major League Baseball in Gilded Age Connecticut)*

Andy Allison joined the Eckford club as a first baseman in 1867 and continued through 1872. Earlier he had played for the Marions of Bushwick, Long Island. When Eckford joined the NA in 1872, Allison, the team captain, hit .163 in 22 games and fielded

.930, the league average. He did not return to the team for 1873. The 1870 census and the 1888 Brooklyn city directory both list Allison as a printer. The 1880 census shows him as a clerk in a printing office. Born into a Scots family in New York City in 1848, he died in Brooklyn on March 21, 1897, at age 49. Initially listed as a brother of Doug and Art Allison, he was not "found" until 2008. His last name is spelled "Ellison" on the death certificate. His brother Bill also played for Eckford. *(Baseball-Reference.com; U.S. Federal Census; Lain's Brooklyn City Directory; National Association of Base Ball Players, 1857–1870; SABR Biographical Research Committee Newsletter)*

Art Allison led NA outfielders with 17 assists in 1875. The Philadelphia native began his baseball career in 1868 with the Geary club in his hometown. In 1869 he joined Forest City of Cleveland, moving into the NA in 1871 with that club, though newspapers reported he had signed with Indianapolis. A .259 career hitter, he reached .292 with Forest City and hit a career-high .320 in 1873 with Resolute. Away from the majors in 1874, he was one of nine major leaguers on the Easton semi-pro team. Back in the NA, he played for Washington and Hartford in 1875, finishing in the National League with Louisville in 1876. Allison is listed as a printer in the 1870 census. Later he worked as a typesetter and proofreader in the government printing office in Washington, D.C. The 67-year-old died there on February 25, 1916, when he was struck by a truck during a blinding snowstorm. Allison was a brother of Doug Allison. *(Baseball-Reference.com; U.S. Federal Census; Sporting Life; Rockford Weekly Gazette; National Association of Base Ball Players, 1857–1870)*

Bill Allison was the younger brother of Andy Allison. His only Organized Baseball experience may be five games he played with the Eckford club between May and July of 1872. In those five games he had three hits for a .158 batting average. He played two games as a first baseman, two as an outfielder, and one as a second baseman. The supposition is that his brother, as team captain, called on him when Eckford was short of players. William J. Ryczek says that Bill Allison also played in five games for Eckford in 1870. Both the 1870 and 1880 censuses list Bill Allison as a ship joiner. He served one term as a Brooklyn city alderman but was defeated for re-election by ten votes. Allison also was appointed an appraiser for the Customs House. He died in Brooklyn on January 25, 1887, at about the age of 37. *(Baseball-Reference.com; U.S. Federal Census; SABR Biographical Research Committee Newsletter; New York Herald-Tribune; When Johnny Came Sliding Home)*

Doug Allison was a part of four movements in professional baseball. He caught for the Cincinnati Red Stockings in 1868–70 before the formation of the league. When the NA opened, he caught for Olympic, and then moved on to Troy (1872), Eckford (1872), Resolute (1873), Mutual (1873) and Hartford (1874–75). Allison entered the National

Art Allison, from Cleveland team photograph (courtesy T. Scott Brandon).

Doug Allison (image courtesy www.oldcardboard.com).

League with the Dark Blues and later played with Providence. In 1883 he finished his major league career by playing a game with the American Association Baltimore Orioles. After batting .331 with Olympic, he saw his hitting fall to a career .271 mark over ten seasons, including six of which he was a regular. In 279 games as a catcher, he fielded far above the league average. Born in Philadelphia in 1845, Allison served as a private in the 192nd Pennsylvania Infantry during the Civil War. The 1870 and 1880 censuses list Allison as a stone cutter. The 1891 Washington city directory and 1900 census show him as a clerk in the Dead Letter Office. Allison died on December 19, 1916, at age 70. He was a brother of Art Allison. (*Baseball-Reference.com; U.S. Federal Census; Boyd's Directory of the District of Columbia; Sporting Life; National Association of Base Ball Players, 1857–1870; Civil War Veterans Who Played Major League Baseball Soldiers Research Project*)

Adrian "Cap" Anson played major league baseball for 27 seasons, beginning with Rockford (1871) and Athletic (1872–75) of the National Association. When the National League was formed in 1876, he began a 22-year career with the Chicago White Stockings, helping them win the initial NL championship. Beginning in 1879, he also managed the team, winning five league titles. During his playing career he hit .329 with four batting crowns, reaching .399 in 1881. He was the first member of the 3,000-hit club and finished with 3,435. A 200-plus pounder, he also hit with power, winning three slugging titles and leading the league in RBIs eight times. He led the NL in fielding five times—four as a first baseman. As manager he ran his club with an iron hand, enforcing a no-drinking rule. Anson had been enrolled in college prep classes at Notre

Cap Anson (LC-DIG-bbc-0102f Library of Congress Prints and Photographs Division).

Dame, and after leaving the playing ranks in 1897 he was involved in running a billiards parlor, managing a touring all-star baseball team, acting in vaudeville, working in Democratic Party politics and managing a golf course. He was a native of Marshalltown, Iowa—the first white baby born in the town, he said—but became a Chicago resident. He died in Chicago on April 14, 1922, and was elected to the Baseball Hall of Fame in 1939. *(New York Times; Rockford Republic; Baseball-Reference.com; Total Baseball; National Baseball Hall of Fame; SABR BioProject)*

Bob Armstrong joined Kekionga for a game at New York on June 26, 1871, and started their last 12 games of the season, including 11 in center field. The tall, slim Armstrong fielded .816 in those barehanded days, committing seven errors in 38 chances. Statistically, he was average for the league in both percentage and range. As a batter, he hit .234 with one triple and two doubles among his 11 hits. Earlier listed as Sam Armstrong, he had played for the Maryland club of Baltimore in 1868–70. When Kekionga disbanded in late August, Armstrong left the majors. There is a Robert Armstrong listed in the 1850 census for Baltimore as a one-year-old. The son of a farmer from New York, Armstrong appears in each census through 1880 as a resident of Baltimore. A "clerk" in 1870, he was still living at home and working as a store clerk in 1880. There is no Baltimore city census for 1890, and the Federal census for that year was lost in a fire. The Maryland-born Robert L. Armstrong who appears in the 1900 and 1910 censuses as an abstract clerk living in Ft. Worth, Texas, is likely the ball player. His death date, December 3, 1917, is the same as that given by Peter Morris for the ball player. *(Baseball-Reference.com; U.S. Federal Census; SABR Baseball Encyclopedia; National Association of Base Ball Players, 1857–1870; Petermorrisbooks.com; Fort Worth Star-Telegram)*

Willis S. "Billy" Arnold began his career in 1869 with the amateur Mansfield team in his hometown of Middletown, Connecticut. When Mansfield entered the NA in 1872, he played two games in right field. He had one hit for a .143 batting average and handled two fielding chances without error. In 1875 he was the organizer, secretary, and manager of the Elm City club in New Haven. However, he resigned before the season began, probably because of conflicts with team captain Charlie Gould. Arnold later managed successfully in the minors at Auburn, Springfield, and Albany, and became president of the New York State League in 1885. The 1880 census shows him living in Middletown, working as a grocer. In 1896 *Sporting Life* reported that Arnold had suffered a paralytic stroke and that a benefit baseball game would be played for him. The 47-year-old Arnold died of apoplexy at Albany County Almshouse Hospital in New York on January 17, 1899. *(Baseball-Reference.com; U.S. Federal Census; National Association of Base Ball Players, 1857–1870; Major League Baseball in Gilded Age Connecticut; Sporting Life)*

Harry Arundel, a right-handed pitcher from Philadelphia, made his NA debut on July 19, 1875, without leaving town. He was one of four local amateurs recruited by the short-handed Brooklyn Atlantics for a game against Athletic. Arundel gave up six hits and six runs—two earned—in 2.1 innings and was the losing pitcher in a 23–3 game. Seven years later he made fourteen starts for the American Association Pittsburgh Alleghenys, compiling a 4–10 record. In 1884, pitching the last game of the season for the Providence Grays, Arundel gave up only one earned run in a win, allowing him to leave the majors with a 5–11 career record and a 4.40 ERA career record from three leagues. He pitched in the minors until 1885 with stops at Janesville, Binghamton, Grand Rapids, East Liberty, Franklin, Milwaukee, St. Paul, Spring-

Harry Arundel (Wikimedia Commons).

field and Oswego. In 1891 *Sporting Life* noted that he had become an agent for a book company in Cleveland. The 1900 census for Cleveland lists Arundel as an insurance agent. Suffering from Bright's disease, he died at Cleveland on March 25, 1904, at age 49. *(Total Baseball; Baseball-Reference.com; Sporting Life; U.S. Federal Census; DeadballEra.com; Cleveland Plain Dealer)*

Ed Atkinson played right field for Washington in the last two games of the 1873 season. The 22-year-old Baltimore native was hitless in eight at-bats but scored two runs. He handled his only fielding chance cleanly. The best candidate was born to English parents in Baltimore in December of 1850. That Atkinson appears in the 1870 census for Baltimore as a day laborer, living at home. The 1900 and 1910 censuses show him married with a family, still listed as a laborer. The 80-year-old Atkinson is still listed in the 1930 census, living with a younger son. According to Peter Morris, this Ed Adkinson died on March 8, 1931. *(Baseball-Reference.com; U.S. Federal Census; Total Baseball; Petermorrisbooks.com)*

Henry Austin first appears on team rosters in 1865 with Union of Morrisania. He continued to play with Union through 1870. In 1871 he joined the amateur Resolute club and moved with them into the league in 1873. Playing center field, he appeared in all 23 games before the club disbanded. Austin hit .248 but fielded .722, one hundred points under the league average. In 1877 he also played for Elizabeth in the League Alliance. A New York City product, Austin was a Civil War veteran. One Henry C. Austin enlisted in the New York Eighty-second Infantry Regiment in 1861 and was mustered out on July 10, 1864. Another Henry C. Austin of the same age enlisted in the Fourteenth New York Heavy Artillery Regiment on November 1863 and was mustered out in August 1865. A SABR committee determined that the ball player clearly was a

Henry Austin, from Union of Morrisania team photograph (courtesy www.19cbaseball.com).

veteran even though his service record was not clear. The 25-year-old Austin is in the 1870 census for Morrisania; he is married and listed as a weaver. In the 1900 census for Amityville, New York, he has remarried and is living on a pension. He died at Amityville on August 7, 1904. *(Baseball-Reference.com; U.S. Federal Census; Civil War Veterans Who Played Major League Baseball Research Project; National Association of Base Ball Players, 1857–1870; U.S. Civil War Soldiers, 1861–1865)*

John "Studs" Bancker played in 19 games for Elm City in 1875. According to *Sporting Life*, Bancker was one of nine future major league players on the powerful Easton semipro team in 1874. Like most of the Elm City team, Bancker didn't hit well, managing just 11 hits for a .153 average. Fourteen of his games were as catcher, where he fielded .796, 34 points under the league average. Bancker finished that season at Providence. Born in Philadelphia, he was the son of a Civil War veteran. The 1880 census and the 1881 Philadelphia city directory both list John V. Bancker as a "segarmaker," living at home. By 1887 he is listed as a roofer. The *SABR Biographical Research Committee Newsletter* identified the ball player as having died in Philadelphia on October 7, 1888. He would have been approximately 34 years of age. *(Baseball-Reference.com; Major League Baseball in Gilded Age Connecticut; Sporting Life; SABR Biographical Research Committee Newsletter; Gopsill's Philadelphia City Directory; U.S. Federal Census)*

Al Barker played left field for Rockford in a road game in New York on June 1, 1871. The 32-year-old had a single and a base on balls, driving in two runs. In the field he handled two chances cleanly. Barker had played with Rockford, from 1868 to 1870. *Sporting Life* notes that he had lost a distance throwing contest in 1867 to Archie McFadden of Milwaukee. Born in Lost Creek, Indiana,

Al Barker (courtesy T. Scott Brandon).

Barker grew up in Rockford. He had enlisted for the Civil War and was commissioned a second lieutenant in the Illinois Seventy-fourth Infantry Regiment before mustering out in March of 1863. In the 1870 census Barker is listed as a paper hanger, living in Rockford; in 1881 he was a substitute umpire in the National League; in the 1910 census the 71-year-old Barker is listed as a dancing teacher. His obituary notes that he had been a popular clothing salesman and a musician of note. Barker died at Rockford on September 15, 1912, at age 74. *(Baseball-Reference.com; U.S. Federal Census; Sporting Life; American Civil War Soldiers; Civil War Veterans Who Played Major League Baseball Research Project; National Association of Base Ball Players, 1857–1870; Rockford Morning Star)*

Tommy Barlow hit .316 as the regular catcher for Atlantic as a 20-year-old. At this time he is credited with inventing the bunt as a means of taking advantage of fair-foul rules. After two years of catching, leading in assists both seasons but also committing the most errors and passed balls once each, he shifted to shortstop for Hartford in 1874. For the

Dark Blues he hit .297 and led the NA in stolen bases. "No George Wright at shortstop," Barlow finished well above the league average in percentage and range factors. However, his baseball career effectively came to a close in 1874. In 1877 when he was arrested for shoplifting, he claimed he had been injured in 1874 by a pitch from Cherokee Fisher and had been given morphine. As a result, he had developed an addiction to morphine. Barlow signed with both Atlantic and Elm City in 1875 but played in only two games—one with each team—before dropping from the majors and ultimately from sight. Modern scholarship shows that while his story has little validity in terms of specific details, he did become an addict, costing him his baseball career. After three seasons as a regular, he was still only 22 years of age. The time and place of his death are not known. Born to Irish parents in New York in 1852, he appears in the 1880 census as a baseball player. In 1888 he was reported dead by a former teammate. *(Baseball-Reference.com; U.S. Federal Census; Petermorrisbooks.com; Major League Baseball in Gilded Age Connecticut; Sporting Life; The Curious Case of Tommy Barlow)*

Charles Roscoe "Ross" Barnes is considered to be one of the greatest players of the 1870s. As a batter he led the NA or the National League in hitting three times in five seasons, batting higher than .400 four times. He was considered a master of fair-foul hitting, a practice of chopping down on the ball to impart "English," causing it to hit in fair territory and spin out into foul territory. After three years with the Forest City club of Rockford, Barnes went to Boston in 1871, helping the Red Stockings to four consecutive NA titles. In 1876 he shifted to Chicago, where he helped the White Stockings win the initial National League crown. However, in 1877 he contracted the ague, limiting him to 22 games, in which he hit only .272. Robert T. Schaefer argues that Barnes never fully recovered from the illness and was never more than an average player after 1876. He played with the Tecumsehs of the International League in 1878 and with Cincinnati in 1879 before finishing with Boston in 1881. The three sub-.300 seasons pulled his career

Tom Barlow (Wikimedia Commons).

Ross Barnes, from "Chicago Champions" (LC-DIG-pga-18390 Library of Congress Prints and Photographs Division).

average down to .360. A very strong second baseman whose percentage and range exceeded the league average, he became a more average shortstop later in his career. Born in Mount Morris, New York, Barnes appears in the 1870 census for Rockford as a clerk living at home. His obituary in *Sporting Life* notes that Barnes "went to the Board of Trade" and later entered "the hotel business." His obituary in the *Rockford Republic* says that at the time of his death, he was an accountant in the Peoples Gas, Light and Coke Company. He died in Chicago on February 5, 1915. *(Baseball-Reference.com; SABR Baseball Encyclopedia; Sporting Life; "The Lost Art of Fair-Foul Hitting"; Baseball Necrology; U.S. Federal Census; Rockford Register)*

Billy Barnie struck out a league-leading 13 times as a rookie in 1874, when he hit .184 with Hartford. A year later he hit .129 between Mutual and Keokuk before dropping into the minors with Columbus. In 1883 he became manager of the American Association Baltimore Orioles, for whom he played 17 games in 1883 and two games in 1886. As a player he hit .171 in 83 career games. Neither as a catcher nor as an outfielder did he have fielding statistics approaching the league average. He managed in the majors for 14 seasons with Baltimore (1883–91), Washington (1892), Louisville (1893–94) and Brooklyn (1897–98). Four of his teams finished with winning records, with his 1887 club placing third in the AA. Overall, his teams had a won-lost record of 632–810 for a .438 percentage. The *Baltimore Sun* noted that Barnie was not a success as a manager because his "kind-hearted and easy-going ways caus[ed] players to impose on him." Barnie also managed in the minors at Baltimore, Milwaukee, Scranton and Hartford. Born to Scots parents in New York City, he is listed in the Brooklyn census of 1900 as a base ball manager. He died of pneumonia at Hartford on July 15, 1900, at age 46. At the time of his death, he was manager and part-owner of the Hartford club. *(Baseball-Reference.com; U.S. Federal Census; Bullpen; Total Baseball; Sporting Life; Baltimore Sun)*

Billy Barnie (LC-DIG-bbc-0399f Library of Congress Prints and Photographs Division).

William Barrett played in three NA games for three teams in three years. On July 8, 1871, he played third base and caught for Kekionga in a game at Washington. Errorless in the field, he had a single in three at-bats. A year later he caught a game for Olympic, going hitless with four passed balls and three errors. In 1873 he played shortstop and outfield for Lord Baltimore in his hometown. His hit that day allowed him to leave the majors with a .154 batting average. It is likely that this is the same "Barrett" who played third base for Olympic in 1869 and caught for Pastime of Baltimore in 1870. The Baltimore William Barrett who would qualify to be the ball player was born in 1850 to native Maryland parents. The 1880 census shows him married and living in Baltimore, working as a store clerk. Twenty years later he had moved to Chicago, had fathered five children, and was working as an office clerk. His family tree on Ancestry.com shows that he died on February 18, 1909, at age 58. The SABR committee investigating Civil War involvement of major league players determined that Barrett was possibly a veteran, but "the evidence ... remains very weak." *(Baseball-Reference.com; U.S. Federal Census; National Association of Base Ball Players, 1857–1870; William Thomas Barrett Family Tree; Civil War Veterans Who Played Major League Baseball Research Project)*

Frank Barrows came to the Boston Red Stockings in 1871 from the Boston Tri Mountain club, where he had played 1867–70. That season the 26-year-old split playing time in left field with Fred Cone. The light-hitting Barrows managed only a .151 batting average in 18 games; statistically he was an average fielder. He is listed as a substitute umpire in the 1872 season and also played a non-league game with Mansfield. And in 1897, when he was 52 years old, he played right field and scored a run for the "Old Bostons" in an exhibition game against an Australian all-star team. Born in Hudson, Ohio, to a college professor, Barrows entered the wool trade after leaving the playing ranks. The Boston city directory of 1880 lists his occupation as "wool broker." The 1900, 1910, and 1920 censuses list him as a wool buyer, a wool sorter and an overseer in a worsted mill. Barrows died at Fitchburg, Massachusetts, on February 6, 1922, at age 77. *(Baseball-Reference.com; U.S. Federal Census; Sporting Life; Boston Journal; City Directory of Boston; Middletown Daily Constitution)*

John Bass led the NA with ten triples in the inaugural season. With three homers, the 23-year-old Cleveland shortstop finished third in slugging while hitting .303. In 22 games at shortstop, he fielded just under the league average of .782. After this start, Bass played little in the majors—two games for Atlantic in 1872 and one game for Hartford in 1877. Cleveland had acquired him after he had played for Union of Morrisania in 1870. Born in Charleston, South Carolina, and the son of a minister, Bass appears in the 1870 census for Brooklyn as a store clerk. The census shows his family as mulatto. In the 1880 census for Brooklyn, he is still listed as a store clerk living at home; this time the family is listed as white. In January of 1888 *Sporting Life* noted that Bass had applied for an umpire's position. Suffering from consumption, he traveled to Denver to recuperate. He died on September 25, 1888, at age 40. His obituary in the *Brooklyn Eagle* says that Bass had served in the Civil War with the First New York Lincoln Cavalry, though a SABR committee found no evidence to support this claim. *(Baseball-Reference.com; Brooklyn Eagle; The National Association of Base Ball Players, 1857–1870; Sporting Life; Civil War Veterans Who Played Major League Baseball Research Committee)*

Joe Battin played through four movements of professional baseball and was influenced by a fifth. He debuted with Forest City of Cleveland in 1871 when he was 19 years old. He also played with Athletic and the St. Louis Brown Stockings in the NA, moving with the St. Louis club into the National League in 1876. In that first NL season he hit .300 and led NL third basemen in fielding. On August 25, 1877, he and Joe Blong were named by gamblers as "willing partners" in a St. Louis loss and as a result were "eased" out of the league. In 1882 he returned to the majors with the American Association Pittsburgh Alleghenys, whom he managed in 1883. Released in 1884, he played for and managed the Union Association

Joe Battin (courtesy Nigel Ayres).

Pittsburgh Stogies prior to finishing that season with the Baltimore Monumentals. Battin made a 29-game return to the majors in 1890 with the AA Syracuse Stars, an opportunity created in part by the Players League. In ten seasons—six in the NL or AA—he hit .218. He later played and umpired in the minors for a number of years. Battin died in Akron, Ohio, on December 10, 1937, at age 86. Bill Lee called Battin a "retired bricklayer." Lee's finding is confirmed by the 1920 U.S. Federal Census for Akron. His obituary claims that he was the highest-paid player of his day, making $700 per month. *(Baseball Encyclopedia; Total Baseball; Baseball Necrology; Baseball Chronology; Sporting Life; U.S. Federal Census; Cleveland Plain Dealer)*

Tommy Beals was an infield regular for Olympic in 1872 (.306 in nine games) and for Washington in 1873 (.272 in 37 games). He had joined Olympic in 1871, coming from Union of Morrisania. Beals played with the champion Red Stockings in 1874–75, and with the National League champion White Stockings in 1880. Between engagements, he played in the California League with Oakland and San Francisco in 1879. A career .243 hitter, he had three seasons under .200. Although Beals was an above-average second baseman, 60 of his 123 games were as an outfielder. Born in New York City, he appears in the 1870 census as a resident of Gold Hill, Nevada. The 1900 census shows him living in San Francisco, working as a photographer, as his father had done. By 1910 he was working as a railroad conductor, still living in San Francisco. He died in San Francisco on October 2, 1915, at age 65. *(Baseball-Reference.com; U.S. Federal Census; National Association of Base Ball Players, 1857–1870)*

Tommy Beals, from Union of Morrisania team photograph (courtesy www.19cbaseball.com).

Edward Beavens (E.P. Bevens) played in three games as a second baseman for Troy in 1871. The following season he played ten games—again primarily as a second baseman—with Atlantic. In the two trials he had 15 hits for a .259 average. In the field he had a .720 percentage against a league average of .849. Before the league, he had played in Brooklyn for Peconic, Powhatan, and Star. Beavens presents several problems for a researcher. The variant spellings of the name in the census make an accurate search difficult. The most likely candidate in the census is Edward P. Bevan or Bevans, a Brooklyn resident in 1860, 1870, and 1880. The son of a Welsh paper hanger, he is listed as a painter in 1880. While official sources list Beavens as a Troy native, born in 1848, Peter Morris believes he was born in Brooklyn three years earlier and that he died in Brooklyn on December 28, 1920. *(Baseball-Reference.com; U.S. Federal Census; petermorrisbooks.com; National Association of Base Ball Players, 1857–1870)*

George Bechtel was the first player to be sold from one team to another and the first to be permanently blacklisted from baseball. Prior to the formation of the league, the Philadelphia native played Organized Baseball with West Philadelphia, Geary, Keystone and Athletic, moving with Athletic into the NA. In 1871 he hit .351 as the regular right fielder, helping Athletic to the championship. In 1872 he hit .300 for Mutual; thereafter his hitting fell off as a member of the Philadelphia White Stockings (1873–74), Centennial (1875), and Athletic (1875), and in the National League with Mutual (1876) and Louisville (1876). He finally settled for a .277 average. As an outfielder, he was an .812 fielder—right at the league average. With Centennial he was the starting pitcher, going 2–12 (2.71 ERA), which is part of a career 7–20 record (3.19 ERA). On May 26, 1875, he and Bill Craver were sold to Athletic for $1,500, the first such transaction in history. When the NL opened, Bechtel played poorly for Louisville and was suspended in May for making errors on crucial plays. In June he was suspended for offering pitcher Jim Devlin $500 to throw a game. Though he played two late-season games for Mutual, he was suspended by the NL at the end of the campaign and was never reinstated. Census searches for Bechtel are difficult because of the number of George Bechtels of the right age born in Pennsylvania. In 1893 *Sporting Life* identified Bechtel as an "ex-professional ball player residing in Philadelphia." Peter Morris believes that the George Bechtel who appears in the 1910 census for Philadelphia, listed as a "stock sorter" for a sporting goods company, is the former ball player. This George Bechtel died on April 3 1921. *(Baseball-Reference.com; U.S. Federal Census; Petermorrisbooks.com; Sporting Life; National Association of Base Ball Players, 1857–1870)*

Esteban "Steve" Bellan was the first Cuban-born player in the majors. Born in Havana to a Cuban father and an Irish mother, Bellan was sent to the United States in 1863 to be educated. After attending and playing baseball at Fordham University, Bellan played for Union of Morrisania, New York, (1868–69) and Union of Lansingburgh, New York (1870), and moved with that club into the NA. The regular third baseman in 1871, Bellan split time between third, shortstop and the outfield for the Haymakers in 1872, before finishing with Mutual in 1873. Overall, in 60 games he hit .251. At none of his regular positions—third base, shortstop, or the outfield—did he field at or near the league average. Although Bellan became a naturalized U.S. citizen in 1874, he returned to Cuba and is regarded as a pioneer in the development of Cuban baseball. He organized, played for, and managed a Havana team until 1885. According to his SABR

Steve Bellan (courtesy Fordham University Archives).

BioProject entry, his life after this is a mystery. He died in Havana on August 8, 1932, at age 83. *(Baseball-Reference.com; Baseball Fever; National Association of Base Ball Players, 1857–1870; Sporting Life; SABR BioProject)*

Clytus "Cy" Bentley began pitching for the amateur Mansfield club in 1869 and moved with the club into the NA in 1872. The local newspaper described him as "swift but a little wild" but felt that with "hard training" he would turn out all right. The team captain, Bentley started 17 of the 24 Mansfield games and compiled a 2–15 record with a 6.06 ERA for a 5–19 team. He also played seven games in the outfield, hitting .219. Born in East Haven, Connecticut, Bentley appears in the 1870 census for Middletown, Connecticut, working as an iron moulder. During the course of the 1872 season, he lost both his mother and an infant son. He died of consumption on February 26, 1873, only 22 years of age. *(Baseball-Reference.com; U.S. Federal Census; National Association of Base Ball Players, 1857–1870; Major League Baseball in Gilded Age Connecticut; DeadballEra.com; Middletown Daily Constitution)*

Nate Berkenstock was the first major league player to be born and the first Jewish major leaguer. The *SABR Baseball Encyclopedia* and Baseball-Reference.com give him an 1831 birthdate. One of the co-founders of the Athletic Baseball Club, Berkenstock played first base from 1863 to 1866 and served as a club officer. On the last day of the 1871 season, the 40-year-old Berkenstock played right field in Athletic's championship game with Chicago, replacing the injured Count Sensenderfer. Berkenstock struck out three times but fielded three chances cleanly, including the final put out in Athletic's 4–1 victory. In 1862 Berkenstock had volunteered for the Seventh Pennsylvania Infantry but was mustered out after two weeks. In the 1860 census he is listed as a salesman; thereafter, he becomes a dealer in hats and straw goods. *Sporting Life* called him a "wholesale hat dealer." Berkenstock died in Philadelphia on February 2, 1900, "in his 68th year." *(Baseball-Reference.com; National Association of Base Ball Players, 1857–1870; Civil War Veterans Who Played Major League Baseball Research Project; U.S. Federal Census; Baseball Chronology; Sporting Life)*

Tom Berry played in only one game for Athletic in 1871. "The Mayor of Chester" played right field in a home win over Mutual on September 2, collecting a single in four at-bats but making an error in his only fielding chance. He had been a regular for Athletic from 1867, playing on the championship team that season; in fact, the 1870 census for Philadelphia lists Berry as a professional baseball player. The Chester, Pennsylvania, native appears in the 1880 census as a "postal clerk (mail agent)." By 1900 he had become a chief of police. In 1910 the 67-year-old Berry is listed as a county detective. In 1912 he was appointed an alderman in Chester. His obituary in *Sporting Life* describes him as a Civil War veteran. Military records do show a Thomas H. Berry who served as a second lieutenant for 100 days in the 197th Pennsylvania Infantry in 1864. Berry died at Chester on June 6, 1915, at age 72. *(U.S. Civil War Soldiers, 1861–65; U.S. Federal Census; Baseball-Reference.com; Sporting Life; National Association of Base Ball Players, 1857–1870; Philadelphia Inquirer; Civil War Veterans Who Played Major League Baseball Research Project)*

Harry Berthrong, a 27-year-old outfielder/catcher, hit .233 for Olympic in 1871. He started with National in 1865 and continued with that club until he shifted to Olympic in 1870. Undefeated as a sprinter, he had outstanding range as the team's regular left fielder. In July 1868 he set a record by circling the bases in 14¼ seconds. Born at Mumford, New York, Berthrong enlisted in the 140th New York Volunteers in 1862 and served until July of 1865. He then spent 54 years in government service as a clerk in the War Department, as an appraiser at the Boston Customs House, as a liquidating clerk, and as an advisor to the Cuban government on revenue collection. He finished his career back in the Boston Customs House, retiring in 1924. Berthrong was also a portrait painter of note with his own studio, specializing in campaign portraits of presidential candidates. Among other athletic skills, he was a top-flight bowler and pulled an oar on the national champion rowing team. Berthrong died at the Old Soldiers' Home at Chelsea, Massachusetts, on April 24, 1928, at age 84. *(Baseball-Reference.com; U.S. Federal Census; Sporting Life; U.S. Civil War Soldiers; National Association of Base Ball Players, 1857–1870; Civil War Veterans Who Played Major League Baseball Research Project)*

William Bestick caught in four games for Eckford in late June and early July 1872, coming from the Flyaway club of New York, where he played in 1871 and was regarded as one of the "first class ball tossers." He hit well, batting .286, but fielded at .760, more than 100 points below the league average. Born around 1849 in New York City to Irish parents, Bestick appears in the 1870 and 1880 censuses as a printer. A William *Bostick* with the same occupation and address is in the 1890 New York City directory. The same person, this time referred to as William Bestick, is in the 1900 census, listed as a teamster. Peter Morris says that the only known William Bestick died in New York City on July 28, 1911. *(Baseball-Reference.com; U.S. Federal Census; Petermorrisbooks.com; New York City Directory; National Association of Base Ball Players, 1857–1870; New York Herald)*

Oscar Bielaski was the right fielder in National's winless 1872 venture into the league. In ten games he hit .174. A year later he en-

Harry Berthrong, from 1871 Olympic team composite (Wikimedia Commons).

joyed his best season, hitting .283 in 38 games with Washington. He played with Lord Baltimore in 1874 and with Chicago in 1875–76, seeing his average fall to .209 against National League pitching in 1876. This caused him to settle for a .240 average over five seasons. He is likely the same Bielaski who played for Capitol (1867) and Union (1868) in Washington. Though he was a resident of Washington, D.C., born to a Polish father, Bielaski enlisted in the Eleventh New York Cavalry Regiment in September 1864, giving his occupation as printer. On October 10, he was discharged as being underage. In 1866 he enlisted in the navy. The 1880 and 1900 censuses show Bielaski as a clerk in the treasury department. He died on the street of a heart attack in Washington, D.C., on November 8, 1911. At the time he was employed at the navy yard. In 2005 Bielaski was inducted into the National Polish-American Sports Hall of Fame. *(Baseball-Reference.com; Bullpen; National Association of Base Ball Players, 1857–1870; Civil War Veterans Who Played Major League Baseball Research Project; Rockford Republic; U.S. Federal Census)*

Charles Bierman played first base for Kekionga in a game at Boston on June 21, 1871. Drawing a walk in three plate appearances, he committed two errors in 11 fielding chances. He may be the Charley Bearman who played for Mutual (1867–68), Union of Lansingburg (1868–69), Union of Morrisania (1870) and Maryland (1870). Born in Hoboken, New Jersey, in 1845 or 1846, Bierman died at Hudson, New Jersey of phthisis pulmonalis on August 4, 1879. The *Jersey Journal* notes that the death was the result of "late hours, bad associates and whiskey," and describes him as a "complete wreck" at the time of death. The *U.S. Federal Census Mortality Schedule 1850–1880* lists him as 34 years of age, single, and a musician. In the 1850 census the family name is spelled Bearman; by 1870 it had become Beerman. In that census, the 25-year-old Charles is listed as a having "no occupation." The SABR committee reported that it is "likely, but by no means certain" that he is the Charles Bierman who served in the Ninety-fifth New York Infantry during the Civil War. *(Baseball-Reference.com; Total Baseball; U.S. Federal Census Mortality Schedule 1850–1880; U.S. Federal Census; Civil War Veterans Who Played Major League Baseball Research Project; National Association of Base Ball Players, 1857–1870)*

George Bird was a 20-year-old local player when the Rockford Forest City team entered the National Association in 1871. In introducing him, the local newspaper noted that "though he has never played in its 'nine,' [Bird] is a good fielder, batter and runner." In 25 games as the regular center fielder, Bird hit .264 and grounded into a league-leading three double plays. He had a .756 fielding percentage, more than 90 points below the league average. According to the *Rockford Republic*, Bird was offered a position with Athletic for 1872 but rejected the con-

George Bird (courtesy T. Scott Brandon).

tract offered. Born into a farm family at Stillman Valley, just below Rockford, Bird became a successful farmer in Ogle County and is listed as a farmer in the 1900 census. Some time before 1910 he became a resident of Rockford, and the census shows that he had his own income. He died at Rockford on November 9, 1940, at age 90. His son, Homer, pitched in the minors in the Northern League. *(Baseball-Reference.com; U.S. Federal Census; Rockford Republic; Rockford Weekly Register-Gazette)*

Dave Birdsall, a New York City native, played Organized Baseball before the Civil War, starting with Metropolitan in 1858. During the war he served with the New York Eighty-seventh Infantry from June 1861 to July 1865. He still found time to play with Harlem (1862) and Union of Morrisania (1863–65). After the war, he continued with Union before joining National of Washington (1869) and the Cincinnati Red Stockings (1870), and was already 32 years old when the league was formed. As the regular right fielder for Boston, he hit .303 in 1871, but played only 16 games in 1872 and three in 1873, mostly as a substitute catcher. *Sporting Life* judged that Birdsall's 126-pound frame was too slight for the rigors of catching and his bat was too light for regular outfield duty. Also, his .720 fielding average was more than 130 points below the league average for outfielders. After leaving baseball he "was a billiard room keeper." In 1896 *Sporting Life* reported that Birdsall "hobbles around with the aid of a stick," the result of an operation. He died on December 30, 1896, at age 58. His death was reported to be a result of the operation. *(Baseball-Reference.com; U.S. Federal Census; Sporting Life; U.S. Civil War Soldiers; Civil War Veterans Who Played Major League Baseball Research Project; Boston Journal)*

Dave Birdsall (courtesy T. Scott Brandon).

Joe Blong came from Notre Dame to pitch for the St. Louis Red Stockings in 1875. After going 3–12 with a 3.07 ERA for the hapless Red Stockings, he left the team in late June, signing a contract with the Covington Stars of Kentucky. The *Globe-Democrat* reported that he had been kicked off the Red Stockings for "hippodroming." Blong also left the Stars before the end of the season, again under suspicion for crooked play. Signed by the Brown Stockings, Blong entered the National League as an outfielder in 1876. In 1877 he started 21 games as a pitcher while seeing regular duty in the outfield. As a pitcher he had a 13–21 record and a 2.84 ERA for teams with losing records. He hit only .216, but he was a very sure-handed outfielder, with a percentage 25 points higher than the league average. However, in 1877 he and Joe Battin were named as "willing partners" by Chicago gamblers. The result was that Blong, Battin, Davy Force and Mike McGeary were blacklisted. Blong never played major league baseball again, though according to his death notice in *Sporting Life*, he had an "engagement"

Joe Blong, from 1876 St. Louis team photograph (courtesy T. Scott Brandon).

with the St. Louis Maroons. He appears in the St. Louis census in both 1870 and 1880 as a house painter. He died of gastritis on September 17, 1892—his birthday—at age 39. His brother, Andrew, played with the amateur Red Stockings, managing the 1874 team. *(Baseball-Reference.com; Missouri Death Records; This Game of Games; U.S. Federal Census; Sporting Life)*

Fred Boardman played right field for Lord Baltimore on August 29, 1874, in a road loss to Chicago. Boardman, a Chicago resident, had a single in four at-bats and had no fielding chances. His name frequently appeared as an umpire during that season. He is likely the same Boardman who played for Chicago clubs Atlantic and Athletic in 1868–69. Born in Missouri, Boardman appears in the 1870 census for Chicago. The 19-year-old was listed as a bookkeeper. Peter Morris says that after marrying a much younger woman, Boardman pulled up stakes in Chicago around 1916 and was never seen again. However, a Missouri-born Frederick S. Boardman—possibly the same person—appears in the 1930 census for Indianapolis, with the 79-year-old working as a buyer for a wholesale clothing store. He was 47 years old when he married; his wife, Minnie, was 17. Morris recently found that Boardman died in Indianapolis on April 12, 1941. *(Baseball-Reference.com; U.S. Federal Census; National Association of Base Ball Players, 1857–1870; petermorrisbooks.com; SABR Biographical Research Committee Newsletter; Daily Inter Ocean)*

Boland played third base for Atlantic on September 4, 1875. In a 13–4 loss to Mutual, Boland went hitless in four at-bats. In the field he handled three of four chances, about par for a third baseman of the time. *(Baseball-Reference.com; New York Times)*

Tommy Bond was only 18 years old when he pitched 55 complete games for Atlantic in 1874. One of the great pitchers of the 1870s, the Irish-born right-hander had 195 victories in the decade, putting together 31–13, 40–17, 40–19 and 43–19 records for the Hartford Dark Blues and Boston in the 1876–79 period. In the same years, he posted ERAs of 1.68, 2.11, 2.06, and 1.96.

Tommy Bond, from 1875 Hartford team photograph (courtesy Robert Edward Auctions).

He led the National League twice in wins, winning percentage, strikeouts and in ERA. Bond also pitched for Hartford in the National Association, posting a 1.56 ERA in 1875. His effective pitching concluded by age 24, Bond made token appearances with Boston in 1881 and Worcester in 1882, and sat out 1883 before joining the Boston Reds in 1884. After a 13-win valedictory season with the Reds and Indianapolis that season, the 28-year-old Bond retired from the playing ranks with 234 victories. He briefly umpired in the National League and coached at Harvard before going to work in the Boston assessor's office. Bond died in Boston on January 24, 1941, at age 84. *Sporting Life* lists him as a Holy Cross man. *(Total Baseball; Baseball-Reference.com; New York Times; Sporting Life; Sporting News)*

Booth played shortstop for New Haven on May 1, 1875, as a replacement for Sam Wright. In a 12–5 home loss to Centennial, Booth went hitless in two at-bats and committed one error in two fielding chances. He may have been borrowed for the day from the Bridgeport amateur Friendly United Social Baseball Club. *(Baseball-Reference.com; Major League Baseball in Gilded Age Connecticut)*

Eddie Booth began 1872 as the regular second baseman with Mansfield, then shifted to Atlantic when Mansfield disbanded. Between the two clubs he hit .318 in 39 games. He split 1873 between Elizabeth City and Atlantic, but his hitting began to fall off. Becoming an outfielder, he was a regular with Atlantic in 1874, and with Mutual in 1875–76, hitting .239 overall. Booth was a much better outfielder than second baseman, where his .787 percentage was more than 50 points below the league average. A *Sporting Life* note says that he had played right field for the Buckeye club of Cincinnati in 1867. It can be assumed that he is the same Booth who played second base for Atlantic in 1870. A local article on the Mansfield team in 1872 indicates that Booth had formerly played for Excelsior and the Stars of Brooklyn and had played second base for the Athletics of Brooklyn in 1871 before joining Mansfield in August. In 1890 *Sporting Life* says that Booth was last seen "working on the Third Avenue Elevated in New York City." Peter Morris believes—but is not certain—that the Booth who died in New York City on December 21, 1928, is the ball player. *(Baseball-Reference.com; Sporting Life; Petermorrisbooks.com; National Association of Base Ball Players, 1857–1870; Baseball Fever; Middletown Daily Constitution)*

Joe Borden (Josephs or Nedrob) had a 1.50 ERA in seven starts for Philadelphia in 1875. The following year Boston gave him a contract for $2,000 over three years to pitch for them. After winning the first game in National League history, Borden led the NL in walks while compiling an 11–12 record. He may have thrown the first no-hitter in NL history, allowing two walks that were recorded as hits at the time. When his pitch-

Joe Borden (Wikimedia Commons).

ing deteriorated to the point that he could not be used, Boston made him a groundskeeper and ticket taker before finally buying out his contract. Between NA and NL service, Borden left the playing ranks with a 13–16 record and a 2.56 ERA. Born in Jacobstown, New Jersey, he made his home in the Philadelphia suburb of Yeadon, where he is listed in the 1900 census as a clerk in an investment company and in the 1910 census as a banker. In 1889 *Sporting Life* erroneously reported that Borden had been swept away in the Johnstown flood; he actually died in Yeadon on October 14, 1929, at age 75. His name changes were supposedly to prevent his father from learning of his involvement in baseball. *(Baseball-Reference.com; U.S. Federal Census; Sporting Life; Wikipedia)*

Bill Boyd was a 19-year-old third baseman for Mutual in 1872, hitting .268 in 35 games. In a four-year career, the 250-pound Boyd also played with Atlantic (1873 and 1875) and Hartford (1874). He hit as high as .350 for Hartford, giving him a .288 career mark. Whether as a third baseman (76 games) or as a right fielder (57 games), he was a mediocre defender, with percentages 70 or more points under the league average. Brooklyn did not field a team in the National League in 1876, and Boyd was out of the majors at age 23. He was born in New York City to Irish parents around 1853. The most likely William J. Boyd in the 1880 census kept a liquor store. The same person appears in the 1910 census as a resident of Queens, working as a bookkeeper in the city treasurer's office. The ballplayer died at Jamaica, New York, on August 1, 1912, at age 59. *(Baseball-Reference.com; U.S. Federal Census)*

George Bradley was one of the great pitchers in the inaugural National League season. In 1876, as a one-man pitching staff, he led the NL in shutouts (16) and ERA (1.23) while compiling a 45–19 record for the St. Louis Brown Stockings. He also pitched the first official no-hitter in NL history. Bradley

Bill Boyd (Wikimedia Commons).

George Bradley, from "Chicago Champions" (LC-DIG-pga-18390 Library of Congress Prints and Photographs Division).

had gone 33–26 with St. Louis in the final year of the National Association, coming from Easton. After 1876 his number began to decline to 18–23 (Chicago, 1877), to 18–40 (Troy, 1879), to 13–8 (Providence, 1880), to 2–4 (Cleveland, 1881). He rebounded with 16 wins for the Philadelphia A's in 1883, and closed with a 25–15 record for the Cincinnati Outlaw Reds in 1884. In 1885, when the NL allowed pitchers to throw overhand, *Sporting life* noted that "Poor George Bradley would make a great pitcher under the new League rule." Overall, he won 171 games in nine seasons in four leagues. He was also a position player, appearing in 170 games as a third baseman and 93 games at other positions, hitting .228. In fact, he made appearances as a shortstop for the Athletics (13 games in 1886), Detroit (one game in 1881) and the Orioles (one game in 1888). He continued to play in the minors until 1890. Born in Reading, Pennsylvania, Bradley became a Philadelphia policeman after leaving baseball, retiring in 1930. The U.S. censuses for Philadelphia verify his occupation. Bradley died in Philadelphia on October 2, 1931, at age 79. *(Baseball Necrology; Baseball-Reference.com; U.S. Federal Census; Sporting Life; BaseballLibrary.com)*

Michael "Spike" Brady played center field in one game for Chicago on September 25, 1875. In a 15–6 loss to Philadelphia, Brady hit a triple and scored a run. In the field, he had errors on three of eight chances. Born in Chicago to Irish parents, Brady had played for the local Emmetts and the amateur St. Louis Red Stockings in 1874. A Spike Brady also played for Syracuse as late as 1888. Brady appears in the 1900 census for Chicago as a clerk. The 1910 census shows Brady and his wife and seven children living in Chicago, where he worked as a factory watchman. Peter Morris says that Brady disappeared around 1910; the 1920 census shows his wife and seven children still living in Chicago with her brother. *(Baseball-Reference.com; U.S. Federal Census; Chicago Daily Inter Ocean; Sporting Life; petermorrisbooks.com)*

Steve Brady began his career in the NA with Hartford in 1874, "secured" from the Hartford amateur club. He also played in the league with Washington in 1875. After playing semi-pro ball with Providence, Rochester, and Worcester, he came to the New York

Steve Brady, from "Metropolitan baseball nine 1882" (LC-DIG-ppmsca-18773 Library of Congress Prints and Photographs Division).

Metropolitans in 1881, and re-entered the majors with that club in 1883. The team captain, he shifted from first base to the outfield, helping the Mets win the American Association pennant in 1884 and playing in the first "World Series" against NL champion Providence. Since Brady had been in Organized Baseball from the middle 1870s, he was rumored to have played with Methuselah. A .264 career hitter, he reached .295 in 1885. When he left the Mets after 1886, he played at Newark and managed Jersey City until he left baseball in 1895. As early as 1891 Brady is described as a "prosperous saloon keeper" in Jersey City. From an Irish family living in Hartford, Brady was still living at home in 1910. The federal census that year lists Brady and two of his brothers as bottlers with their "own place." He died at Hartford on November 1, 1917, at age 66. *(Total Baseball; Baseball-Reference.com; Sporting Life; National Police Gazette; Washington Post; New York Times; Boston Daily Globe; U.S. Federal Census)*

Asahel "Asa" Brainard was the greatest pitcher of the late 1860s when he pitched for the Cincinnati Red Stockings (1868–70). Brainard had played amateur ball for Excelsior of Brooklyn as early as 1860. Cincinnati had obtained him from National of Washington by offering a salary of $1,200. When the League opened, the 30-year-old Brainard joined Olympic. Starting 30 games, he had a 12–15 record with a 4.40 ERA. With Olympic and Mansfield in 1872, Brainard finished with Lord Baltimore in 1873–74; in four seasons in the league, he compiled a record of 24–53 and a 3.71 ERA. Born in Albany, New York, he grew up in Brooklyn and is listed as a clerk in the 1860 census. Bullpen says that he held government jobs before becoming superintendent of the Markham Hotel billiards room in Denver, Colorado. Brainard died of pneumonia in Denver on December 29, 1888, at age 47.

Asa Brainard, from "First Nine of the Cincinnati (Red Stockings) Baseball Club" (LC-USZC4-1291 Library of Congress Prints and Photographs Division).

An Asahel Brainard enlisted in the New York 144th Infantry in November 1864, serving until June of 1865. This could be the ball player, though the soldier's age isn't quite right, and the SABR committee does not include Brainard among Civil War veterans. *Baseball Digest* says that the term "ace" to designate the top pitcher came from Asa's name. *(Baseball-Reference.com; U.S. Federal Census; National Association of Base Ball Players, 1857–1870; Sporting Life; U.S. Civil War Soldiers, 1861–1865; Civil War Veterans Who Played Major League Baseball Research Project; Baseball Digest)*

Mike Brannock played third base for the Chicago White Stockings for the last three games of 1871 and for two games in 1875. For the five games he hit .087. In the field he committed errors on eight of 16 fielding chances. In 1872–74, Brannock played in Chicago with the Blue Stockings and was being tried as a pitcher by the White Stockings. The *SABR Baseball Encyclopedia* shows that Brannock played in the League Alliance with Ludlow, Champion City and Minneapolis in 1877. *Notre Dame Baseball Greats* says that Brannock attended Notre Dame in 1869, pitching and playing shortstop for the high school-age team Star of the West. *Baseball Without Borders* says that Brannock was a Canadian who played for the Guelph Stars, Canada's national semi-pro champions in 1870. And in 2009 Brannock was elected to the Guelph Sports Hall of Fame. However, the 1860 and 1870 censuses for Chicago show him to have been born to Irish parents in Massachusetts. Baseball-Fever says that Brannock played for the Actives of Clinton, Iowa, in 1871 before joining the White Stockings. Only 29 years of age, Brannock died in Chicago on October 7, 1881. *(Baseball-Reference.com; Notre Dame Baseball Greats: From Anson to Yaz; Baseball-Fever. com; U.S. Federal Census; Baseball Without Borders; SABR Baseball Encyclopedia; Daily Inter Ocean)*

Jim Britt started (and completed) every game for the 1872 Atlantic club at age 16. The Brooklyn-born Britt almost duplicated the feat in 1873 when he started 54 of Atlantic's 55 games. His 51 complete games led the league. Unfortunately, Atlantic was not up to league competition, contributing to Britt's records of 9–28 and 17–36. Before the 1874 season Atlantic acquired Tommy Bond, so at age 17, Britt was out of the majors. He continued to pitch around Brooklyn for the Flyaway and Nameless clubs in 1874. He was listed as a change pitcher for Elm City in 1875 but did not play with the club. Born in Brooklyn to Irish parents, Britt was already earning a paycheck by working in a printing office at age 14. By 1880 he was living in San Francisco, working as a plumber, and was shown to be doing the same in the 1910 census. He died in San Francisco on February 28, 1923, at age 77. His death certificate lists him as a plumbing inspector for the San Francisco Board of Health. *(Baseball-Reference.com; U.S. Federal Census; Middletown Daily Constitution; New York Herald)*

Oliver Brown enlisted in the First New Jersey Cavalry in the fall of 1864, though he was only 14 years old at the time. He was mustered out in May of 1865 and began playing baseball in Brooklyn, playing with Atlantic as early as 1869. In 1872 he appeared in four league games for the team, collecting two hits. In 1875 he played in an additional three games, going hitless. His two hits gave him an .080 average. In six games in the outfield he fielded .846, well above the league average. Born in Brooklyn, he appears in the 1900 census as a machinist, living with his wife and mother. By the 1920 census he has become a watchman for government property. He died on September 23, 1932, at age 83. While neither the SABR committee nor DeadballEra.com includes Brown in the list of Civil War veterans, his death notice in the *New York Times* referred to him as Captain Oliver Brown, cited his Civil War record, and stated that he had played professional baseball with Brooklyn. *(Baseball-Reference.com; U.S. Federal Census; National Association of Base Ball Players, 1857–1870; New York Times; Civil War Veterans Who Played in the Major Leagues Research Project; DeadballEra.com)*

Robert Brown now has a first name, but other details of his life are missing. He played shortstop for Lord Baltimore in July and August 1874. In two games he was hitless in nine at-bats and committed three errors in 11 fielding chances. The *Baltimore Sun* gives his name as "Locke" and describes him as the "new shortstop." After his first game, the *Sun* noted that he "made several fine plays" but that his hitting "is of the fair-foul order." A William Locke is listed as the umpire in two semi-pro games played in Baltimore in the summer/fall of 1874. *Baseball Encyclopedia* credited these games to

Marshall Locke. *(Baseball-Reference.com; U.S. Federal Census; Baltimore Sun)*

John "Black Jack" Burdock was a 20-year-old shortstop for Atlantic in 1872. When the National League was formed in 1876, he was already a four-year veteran, having played with Mutual (1874) and the Dark Blues (1875). With Hartford in 1876, Burdock moved on to Boston two years later. Shifting to second base, he led the NL in fielding five times. Only a career .244 hitter, he hit .330 for the NL champions in 1883. As a second baseman, he fielded almost twenty points above the league average. However, an 1885 note in *Sporting Life* stated that he had been "suspended indefinitely for dissipation." Boston wanted to unload him, but according to the *National Police Gazette*, no distillery owner also owned a baseball franchise. In 1888 Burdock is described as being quite an artist but that his painting activity was detrimental to the team. Burdock finished his major league career with Brooklyn clubs—the American Association Bridegrooms in 1888 and the NL Bridegrooms in 1891. The 1910 and 1920 censuses show him living in Brooklyn, employed as a painter. He is listed as an inspector for an oil corporation in the 1930 census. Born in Brooklyn to English and Irish parents, Burdock died in Brooklyn on November 27, 1931, at age 79. *(Total Baseball; Baseball-Reference.com; Boston Daily Globe; New York Times; National Police Gazette; U.S. Federal Census; Sporting Life)*

Henry Burroughs was a utility player for Olympic in 1871–72. In 1871 he had 15 hits in 12 games; six of his hits were for extra bases, and he drove in 14 runs. A solid third baseman for five games, he was a mediocre outfielder. Burroughs had been a regular with the club in 1870. The *Cincinnati Daily Gazette* said that he came from the Eurekas

Jack Burdock (LC-DIG-bbc-0074f, Library of Congress Prints and Photographs Division).

Henry Burroughs, from 1871 Olympic composite photograph (Wikimedia Commons).

of Newark. A Burroughs pitched and played shortstop for Eureka in 1864. In *Early Baseball in Michigan,* Peter Morris says that Burroughs was a star pitcher for Detroit in 1865, one who was being paid under the table, but that he returned to New Jersey and played professionally for Irvington. Burroughs was from Newark, and died there of pneumonia on March 31, 1878, at age 33. *(Baseball-Reference.com; Baseball-Fever: Early Baseball in Michigan; U.S. Federal Census; National Association of Base Ball Players, 1857–1870; Sporting Life; Cincinnati Daily Gazette)*

Albert "Doc" Bushong helped five teams win league championships in a six-year period. On July 19, 1875, he was one of four Philadelphia amateurs signed for the day by Atlantic for a game with Athletic. A year later he caught five games for the Athletics in the National League. Bushong then attended the University of Pennsylvania Dental School before joining Worcester in 1880. After three seasons with the Ruby Legs, he spent two seasons with Cleveland, three with the American Association champion St. Louis Browns, and three with the Brooklyn Bridegrooms, helping that club win championships in both the AA (1889) and the NL (1890). Only a .214 hitter over his career (.167 in 24 World Series games), he hit .267 for the Browns in 1885 and led AA catchers in fielding in 1886. In 668 career games as a catcher, he fielded .916, thirteen points above the league average. When Bushong left baseball after the 1890 season, he became a dentist in Brooklyn, practicing there until his death from kidney disease on August 19, 1908, at age 52. *(New York Times; Baseball-Reference.com; SABR Collegiate Database; Total Baseball; U.S. Federal Census; Sporting Life; DeadballEra.com)*

Frank Buttery was the change pitcher for Mansfield in 1872 while also filling in at third base and the outfield. In eight games as a pitcher he had a 3–2 record and a 4.27 ERA. In 18 games he hit .215. As a third baseman, he fielded at the league average; as an outfielder he had errors in four of nine chances. When Mansfield disbanded, Buttery's major league career ended. The book *Orator O'Rourke* says that Buttery had played for Osceola of Stratford and Liberty of Nor-

Doc Bushong (LC-DIG-bbc-0578f Library of Congress Prints and Photographs Division).

Frank Buttery (Wikimedia Commons).

walk before joining Mansfield. It states that he was college educated and that he became a minister. A native of Silvermine, Connecticut, Buttery appears in the 1880 and 1900 censuses for Norwalk and in the 1887 Norwalk city directory, listed each time as a grocer. He died of erysipelas at Norwalk on December 16, 1902, at age 51. David Arcidiacono says that his death was the result of complications from a hunting accident. (*Baseball-Reference.com; U.S. Federal Census; Major League Baseball in Gilded Age Connecticut; Connecticut Certificate of Death; Orator O'Rourke*)

Hugh Campbell played for Newark in 1865 and then joined his brother, Mat, with Irvington (1865–69) and Resolute, starting in 1870. He began pitching at Irvington and by 1873 was the main pitcher for Resolute. Starting 18 games, he won two—Resolute's only wins—while compiling a very respectable 2.95 ERA. When Resolute disbanded, Campbell was out of the majors. The 1870 census shows that Campbell had been born in Ireland in 1846, and that he was a resident of Elizabeth, New Jersey, working as a laborer. The Elizabeth city directory for 1872 lists his occupation as "scroll work." Later directories show him as a machinist. His death certificate calls him a "rule maker." Campbell died of phthisis pulmonalis at Newark, New Jersey, on March 1, 1881, at age 34. (*Baseball-Reference.com; U.S. Federal Census; Elizabeth City Directory; National Association of Base Ball Players, 1857–1870; New Jersey Certificate of Death*)

Michael "Mat" Campbell played first base for Irvington (1866–69) before moving to the Resolute club of Elizabeth. In Resolute's foray into the NA in 1873, Campbell managed only 12 hits in 21 games for a .143 batting average. However, he was an excellent first baseman; his .938 average and his range factors exceeded the league average. Like his brother, Hugh, he played in no major league games following the demise of Resolute. Born in Ireland, Mat Campbell arrived in the United States in 1863 or 1865 and learned baseball quickly. Listed as a farm laborer in the 1870 census, he had become a clerk in the express office by 1880 and was described as an "express man" by 1900. Elizabeth city directories show Michael Campbell and Hugh Campbell living at the same address. Michael Campbell died at Scotch Plains, New Jersey, on January 12, 1926, at age 75. (*Baseball-Reference.com; U.S. Federal Census; National Association of Base Ball Players, 1857–1870; Elizabeth City Directory*)

John Carbine played first base in ten of Western's games in 1875, after coming from the Franklins. The 19-year-old Syracuse native had only three hits for an .083 average. A year later he played in seven games for the NL Louisville Grays, hitting .160. Carbine fielded well, his .921 percentage being just under the league average and his range factors being higher. By August 1876 the *Cincinnati Daily Enquirer* said that he was playing for Mutual of Jackson, Michigan. In December of 1876 he is on the list of disen-

Jack Carbine (Wikimedia Commons).

gaged players. Carbine played amateur ball in Chicago for the Franklins before and after his major league trials. He appears in the box scores for the Franklins up to 1889. Born to Irish parents, Carbine appears in the 1880 and 1910 censuses for Chicago as a pressman for a newspaper, apparently the *Tribune*. His death certificate lists his occupation as saloon keeper. He died of liver cancer in the Chicago suburb of Forest Park on September 11, 1915, at age 59. *(Baseball-Reference.com; U.S. Federal Census; Chicago Sunday Times; Illinois Certificate and Record of Death; Chicago Daily Inter Ocean; Cincinnati Daily Enquirer)*

Tom Carey (J.J. Norton) was a nine-year regular infielder in the NA and National League. After playing for Maryland in 1870, he became the regular second baseman for Fort Wayne in 1871. Returning to Baltimore, he played with Lord Baltimore in 1872–73 before moving on to Mutual in 1874 and Hartford in 1875. He played in the National League with the Dark Blues in 1876–77, before finishing with Providence in 1878 and Cleveland in 1879. In nine seasons he hit .277, dropping from .287 in the NA to .250 in the NL. Defensively, he fielded .814 as a shortstop and .862 as a second baseman, both at the league average for the time. He served as playing manager at Baltimore in 1873 and for Mutual. Once thought to have been born in 1849, he is now believed to have been born in 1846. He was a Civil War veteran, having served with the Seventeenth New York Infantry, and was part of the Presidio guard in California prior to his major league debut. He umpired in 1882 and then returned to California. The 1900 census shows him as an "inmate" in the California Veteran's hospital. He was discharged from the hospital in 1905 for "non-compliance with hospital rules" and died in San Francisco on August 16, 1906. *(SABR Biographical Research Committee Newsletter; U.S. Fed-

Tom Carey, from Hartford team photograph (courtesy Robert Edward Auctions).

eral Census; Baseball-Reference.com; Civil War Veterans Who Played Major League Baseball Research Project; National Association of Base Ball Players, 1857–1870)*

Lewis (Louis) Carl played in one game for Lord Baltimore on September 9, 1874, drafted into service became the Lords were a player short. The 38-year-old Carl went hitless in three at-bats and had three errors in four fielding chances as catcher. Born in 1836, he enlisted in the Civil War as a captain in the Maryland Fourth Infantry Regiment on October 4, 1862. He is listed as a shipping clerk at the time. Carl served until the end of the war, mustering out on May 31, 1865. Apparently he learned baseball while in the service and began playing amateur ball around Baltimore in 1867—primarily with the Enterprise club—playing until he was 44 years of age. He appears in the 1870 Baltimore census as a clerk in the Customs House. Carl applied for an invalid's pension in 1884 and died in Newark, New Jersey, the following year at age 49. Brian McKenna argues that Carl was born in 1832, which would make him 42 years old when he debuted with Lord Baltimore. Therefore, he may have been the first-born major league baseball player, born even before Nate Berkenstock. McKenna also notes that Carl had numerous run-ins with the law through the years, twice for attempted murder. *(Baseball-Reference.com; U.S. Federal Census; Civil War Veterans Who Played Major League Baseball Research Project; American Civil War Soldiers; Early Baltimore Baseball, Part 9; SABR Biographical Research Committee Newsletter)*

Jim Carleton played first base for the Forest City club of Cleveland during 1871 and part of 1872. In 36 games he hit .267 and fielded just below the league average. From Clinton, Connecticut, Carleton had played with Mutual and Forest City prior to the opening of the league. Apparently he remained in Cleveland, for he is listed as a resident in the 1880 census, his occupation given as "speculator." Moving to Detroit, he is listed in the 1892 Detroit city directory as a partner in Delano and Carleton, a firm dealing in stocks, bonds and commercial paper. The 1900 and 1910 censuses also show him as an investment broker and a broker in stocks and bonds. He died of pneumonia in Detroit on April 25, 1910, at age 61. *(Baseball-Reference.com; U.S. Federal Census; National Association of Base Ball Players, 1857–1870; Detroit City Directory; Michigan Certificate of Death)*

John Cassidy played every position in his eleven major league seasons, in eight of which he held regular status. After playing for the amateur Nassau club of Brooklyn, Cassidy, at age 18, pitched for Atlantic in 1875, going 1–21 with a 3.03 ERA before finishing the season as a first baseman at New Haven. In the National League he played with the Hartford Dark Blues (1876–77) and the Chicago White Stockings (1878). After playing part of 1879 at Springfield, he returned to the NL with the Troy Trojans (1879–82) and the Providence Grays (1883) before finishing in the American Association with the Brooklyn Trolley Dodgers (1884–85), for whom he served as team captain. A career .246 hitter, he batted .378 in the inflated 1877 season. The majority of his games were played in the outfield, but across all positions his fielding percentage of .845 was well below the league average. Born in Brooklyn to Irish parents, Cassidy died of dropsy at his home in Brooklyn on July 2, 1891, at age 36. His death notice says that he organized the Long Island Athletic League. *(Total Baseball; Baseball-Reference.*

Jim Carleton, from Cleveland team photograph (courtesy T. Scott Brandon).

John Cassidy (courtesy T. Scott Brandon).

com; *Sporting News; U.S. Federal Census; Sporting Life; New York Times*)

James Cavanagh played in five games for Eckford in September of 1872. In the five games he hit .261 and drove in four runs. Four of his games were at first base, where he fielded .921, roughly the league average. Cavanagh had previously been listed as Kavanaugh, a no-first-name player. Research by Richard Malatsky has recently shown that Cavanagh was a member of the semi-pro Burnsides club of Brooklyn. He was apparently borrowed by the short-handed Eckfords for late-season games. There are both Irish-born and New York-born James Cavanagh's of the right age living in Brooklyn, making research difficult. *(Baseball-Reference.com; SABR Biographical Research Committee Newsletter)*

Jack Chapman began playing with the Enterprise club of Brooklyn in 1860 when he was 17 years old. Shifting to Atlantic in 1862, he played with the championship teams of 1864–65, finishing third in the NA in runs in 1864. Chapman played for Quaker City in 1867 before returning to Atlantic in 1868, when he finished second in the NA in hits. In 1874, at age 30, he finished second in outfield assists while hitting .264 for Atlantic. He played for the Brown Stockings in 1875 before finishing as player-manager for Louisville 1876. In three major league seasons he hit .246 in 113 games, but his .739 fielding percentage was 90 points below the league average. He continued to manage Louisville through 1877, when the club folded following a bribery scandal. In all, Chapman managed for 11 seasons at Milwaukee (1878), Worcester (1882), Detroit (1883–84), Buffalo (1885) and Louisville (1889–92). His teams compiled a 351–502 record, winning an American Association pennant in 1890. Born to an English father in Brooklyn, Chapman is listed as a store clerk in 1870. His death notice in *Sporting Life* says that he became a traveling salesman for a commercial house. Chapman died in Brooklyn on June 10, 1916, at age 73. *(Baseball-Reference.com; U.S. Federal Census; Sporting Life; Complete New York Clipper Baseball Biographies; National Association of Base Ball Players, 1857–1870)*

Jack Chapman (*Sporting Life*, 1916).

Bobby Clack may have been the first pinch-hitter in major league history. The English-born Clack played center field for Atlantic in 1874, coming from the amateur Chelsea club. After hitting .170 that season, he returned to hit .102 in 1875. When the National League opened, he played 32 games in a utility role for the hapless Cincinnati Red Stockings. On May 13 of that year, he entered the game to hit for an injured Dave Pearson. Overall, Clack hit .161 in three seasons. Sixty-five of his career 82 games were as an outfielder, but he fielded 37 points under the league average. He played in the International League with Syracuse in 1878. After becoming a naturalized citizen in 1884, Clack is listed in the 1900 census as a hotel proprietor residing in the Boston sub-

Bobby Clack (courtesy Nigel Ayres).

urb of Medford. *Sporting Life* notes that he was a "high roller in one of the local leagues." By the time of the 1910 census, Clack was living in Revere, Massachusetts, and was listed as a restaurant owner. He died at Danvers, Massachusetts, on October 22, 1933. (*Baseball Research Journal; Baseball-Reference.com; U.S. Federal Census; Sporting Life; New York Herald-Tribune*)

John Clapp spent 11 seasons in the major leagues, including ten as a regular catcher. The Ithaca, New York, product jumped from the amateur Ilion Clippers to Mansfield as playing manager in 1872, entered the National League with St. Louis in 1876, and closed as playing manager with the New York Gothams in 1883. In between he played with Athletic and served as playing manager at Indianapolis, Buffalo, Cincinnati and Cleveland. A career .283 hitter, he reached .318 in the inflated 1877 season and batted higher than .300 four times. As a catcher he fielded .877, 22 points above the league average. As a manager he led teams to a 174–237 record. For a while he operated a restaurant in New York City with Metropolitan pitcher Jack Lynch. In 1890 he returned to Ithaca and became a night sergeant

John Clapp, from "Metropolitan baseball nine 1882" (LC-DIG-ppmsca-18773 Library of Congress Prints and Photographs Division).

of the police force, a position he held for 14 years. Clapp died of a stroke on December 18, 1904, at age 53. At the time he was assisting a fellow officer in making an arrest. The *Philadelphia Inquirer* credits Clapp with having begun the use of a heavy rubber mouthpiece, employed by catchers before the development of the mask. (*Baseball-Reference.com; Major League Baseball in Gilded Age Connecticut; Baseball Necrology; Complete New York Clipper Baseball Biographies; Sporting Life; Philadelphia Inquirer*)

Denny Clare played infield for Atlantic on September 14 and 16, 1872. The 19-year-old singled and scored a run in seven at-bats for a .143 average. A successful second baseman, he had errors on four of five fielding chances at shortstop. He had played for the Amity Junior team of Brooklyn in 1871. Apparently he returned to Amity, for he represented the club in an 1874 all-star game of Brooklyn amateurs versus New York amateurs. Born in Brooklyn to Irish parents, Clare appeared in every census from 1870 through 1920. Throughout his adult life he worked as a government clerk in Brooklyn. He died on November 26, 1928, at age 75. *(Baseball-Reference.com; U.S. Federal Census; New York Times; New York Herald-Tribune)*

James "Big Jim" Clinton began in the majors as a player and manager for Eckford in 1872, hitting .234 in 25 games. The 5'8", 174-pound Clinton had played for Mutual as early as 1869. He later played for Resolute (1873) and Atlantic (1874–75) in the NA. Making fourteen starts as a pitcher for Atlantic in 1875, he went 1–13 for a 2–42 team. When the National League was formed, Clinton played 16 games for the Louisville Grays and was then out of the majors until 1882, playing in the International Association with Syracuse, Pittsburgh, Hartford and New Haven. He returned to the majors with the Worcester Ruby Legs and then became the regular left fielder for the American Association Baltimore Orioles (1883–84) and Cincinnati Red Stockings (1885). He finished his major league career as a utility player with Baltimore in 1886. In ten seasons in three leagues, he hit .256 but reached .313 for the Orioles in 1883. Clinton later played with and managed Jersey City, Birmingham, Nashville, and Manchester. The 1900 and 1910 censuses show Clinton living in Brooklyn and tending bar in a hotel. The latest findings from SABR's Biographical Research Committee show that Clinton was an inmate of the Kings Park State Hospital for the Insane at Smithtown, New York, in 1920. He died there in September of 1921 at age 71. *(Total Baseball; Baseball-Reference.com; U.S. Federal Census; Sporting Life; Complete New York Clipper Baseball Biographies)*

Dan Collins hit .125 in 10 major league games—three NA games with Chicago in 1874 and seven National League games with Louisville in 1876. He had a 1–1 record in two starts with the White Stockings and fielded a solid .909 as an outfielder with the Grays. According to the *New Orleans Times*, Collins pitched for the R.E. Lee club of New Orleans in 1873, shifted to the Empire club of St. Louis, and then accepted a professional engagement with Chicago before returning to New Orleans. He pitched for the St. Louis Red Stockings in 1875, playing there until he joined Louisville. Sources say that he was born July 12, 1854, in St. Louis and died in New Orleans on September 21, 1883, at age 29. There may be problems with this record. Ancestry.com shows a Daniel Collins with that birth date, but that Daniel Collins, who died in 1918, is not the ball player. The ball player actually did die on September 21, 1883, and according to his obituary, he "didn't leave much to support his wife and three children." *(Baseball-Reference.com; New Orleans Times-Picayune; Cincinnati Daily Gazette; U.S. Federal Census; This Game of Games)*

Fred Cone was the regular left fielder for the Boston Red Stockings in 1871, his only season in the majors. In 19 games he hit .260, the lowest average on the team. But at Fort Wayne on July 12, he had five hits to help Boston defeat Kekionga, 30–9. Both his fielding percentage (.854) and range factors were far greater than the league averages for outfielders. Born in Rockford, Illinois, he

Jim Clinton (Wikimedia Commons).

Fred Cone (Wikimedia Commons).

Terry Connell (Wikimedia Commons).

played first base and later the outfield for Forest City (1868–70) before being signed for the Red Stockings. Cone left baseball at age 23; the *Boston Journal* noted in 1872 that Cone "is now engaged in business in this city." The 1870 census for Rockford lists him as a baseball player, while the 1880 census for Chicago lists him as a hotel clerk. His obituary in *Sporting Life* notes that he worked as a clerk for the Grand Pacific, Wellington and Great Northern hotels. Cone died of apoplexy in Chicago on April 13, 1909. He was 61 years of age. *(Baseball-Reference.com; U.S. Federal Census; Sporting Life; Deadball Era.com; National Association of Base Ball Players, 1857–1870; Rockford Morning Star; Boston Journal)*

Terry Connell caught one game for the Chicago White Stockings on June 20, 1874. In a road loss to Atlantic, Connell went hitless in four at-bats and committed four errors in seven fielding chances. The newspaper reported "a man named Connell" caught "fairly" in place of Fergy Malone, who had sore hands. In 1881 Connell worked as an Eastern League umpire. In 1889 he is described as "late of the Lancaster club," looking for a league umpiring position. Deadball Era.com lists him as an American Association umpire for 1884 and 1890. His death notice says that he developed the two-umpire system of officiating. Connell was a Philadelphia native, born to an Irish carpenter. In the 1900 census he is listed as a ticket agent for a theatre. In the 1910 census he has become a doorman at a theatre, and the 1920 census calls him a theatre custodian. Connell died at Narberth, Pennsylvania, on 1924 at age 68. *(Baseball-Reference.com; U.S. Federal Census; Philadelphia Inquirer; Harrisburg Patriot; Chicago Daily Inter Ocean)*

Ned Connor played in seven games as a first baseman and outfielder for the Haymakers in 1871. The 21-year-old stroked seven hits for a .212 average. In a non-league loss to Eckford on August 6, he recorded 20 putouts. A first baseman with an .878 fielding percentage, Connor committed four errors on nine fielding chances in the outfield. Born in Philadelphia, he played for the Keystone club in 1867 and 1868. He died suddenly of a hemorrhage of the lungs at the Philadelphia City Hall on January 28, 1898, at age

47. His death certificate states that he was married but gives no occupation. His death notice states that he was a plasterer by trade and that he was active in Philadelphia politics. *(Baseball-Reference.com; Baseball Chronology; National Association of Base Ball Players, 1857–1870; Gopsill's Philadelphia City Directory; Pennsylvania Certificate of Death; Philadelphia Inquirer)*

William Coon played for his hometown Athletic club in both the NA and the National League. Described as an amateur catcher, he had a four-game trial in 1875 and became a regular in 1876. For his career he hit .224 in 58 games, playing 30 games as a right fielder and 22 games as a catcher. In neither case was his fielding percentage within one hundred points of the league average. Born in 1855, he was just 20 years old when he made his debut. By 1890 he had moved to Burlington, New Jersey, where the city directory listed him as a clerk. His death certificate called him a mail clerk for the Railway Mail Service. Coon died of carcinoma of the liver in Burlington on August 30, 1915, at age 60. *(Baseball-Reference.com; Burlington City Directory; Trenton Evening Times; New Jersey Certificate of Death; New York Morning Telegraph; Boston Daily Advertiser)*

Dennis Coughlin has the most distinguished military record of any NA player. As an 18-year-old private, he enlisted in the 140th Infantry Regiment of New York and served until the end of the war. Wounded at Petersburg, he also fought at Gettysburg and the Wilderness. Before being mustered out in 1865, he had been promoted to corporal and then to full sergeant. Peter Morris believes that Coughlin played with the Excelsior club of Rochester after the war. In 1868 he moved to Washington, D.C., where he began a career with the Treasury Department and signed with the National club. In 1872 Coughlin played in eight of National's 11 games in the NA, five as a very good center fielder with a .941 fielding percentage. He also hit .297. This constituted his major league experience, as National disbanded. Coughlin worked at the Treasury almost 45 years before dying at Washington, D.C., on May 14, 1913, at age 69. *(Baseball-Reference.com; SABR BioProject.com; Civil War Veterans Who Played Major League Baseball Research Project; Washington Post; U.S. Civil War Soldier Records and Profiles; U.S. Federal Census)*

Fred Crane joined the Enterprise club of Brooklyn in 1861, which means he had a long career in Brooklyn baseball prior to the opening of the league. He played with Atlantic (1862–69), including the great teams of 1864–65. In 1865 he finished second to teammate Joe Start in runs scored. By 1870 he had moved to the Alpha club. Already 32 years of age, he played one game for Resolute

Fred Crane (courtesy T. Scott Brandon).

in 1873, and two years later he returned to Atlantic, playing first base on one of the worst teams in major league history. He hit only .210 in 21 games but played an excellent first base. A minister's son from Saybrook, Connecticut, Crane appeared in the 1884 Brooklyn city directory as a clerk. The 1910 census for Brooklyn shows him working as an accountant for a printing company. He died on April 27, 1925, in Brooklyn at age 85. Peter Morris believes that the 1873 records with Resolute and the 1875 records with Atlantic likely belong to a different player. *(Baseball-Reference.com; U.S. Federal Census; National Association of Base Ball Players, 1857–1870; Sporting Life; Lain's Brooklyn City Directory; petermorrisbooks.com)*

Bill Craver played with and managed his hometown Troy Haymakers in the inaugural NA season. A Civil War veteran with the Thirteenth New York Heavy Artillery Battalion (January 1864 to April 1865), he began his baseball career with the local Union club of Lansingburgh in 1867, a club he also managed. Chicago discovered that Craver's $2,500 salary demand was too much for their budget, so he remained in Lansingburgh, hitting .322 in 1871. In 1872 Craver moved on to Lord Baltimore and then to Philadelphia for a stint with the Pearls (1874), Centennial (1875) and Athletic (1875). When the National League opened, he played with Mutual in 1876 and Louisville in 1877. William J. Ryzcek points out that while Craver had a "prominent role" in every allegation of scandal from 1870 on, he was not disciplined until 1877. He was one of the players banned after the 1877 season because of his refusal to cooperate with the NL investigation into fixed games. Overall, Craver hit .290 for seven seasons, with a high of .343 in 1874. Statistically he was a better-than-average catcher and shortstop and an average second baseman. His 70–66 record as manager was pulled down by a 2–12 mark with Centennial. In 1886 Craver became a policeman at Troy, a position he held until his death from heart disease on June 17, 1901. He was 57 years old. *(Baseball-Reference.com; Sporting Life; U.S. Civil War Soldiers; U.S. Federal Census; Civil War Veterans Who Played Major League Baseball; New York Times; Blackguards and Red Stockings)*

Art Croft was the regular left fielder for the St. Louis Red Stockings in 1875; he went on to play two more seasons in the National League for St. Louis (1877) and Indianapolis (1878). In 133 games, he hit only .195, the .232 mark with the Brown Stockings being his only season over .200. In 79 games as a first baseman, he fielded .965, eleven points above the league average. Born in St. Louis to an English father and Irish mother, he was already in the work force at age 15 as a "laborer." He appeared in the 1880 census as a store clerk. Croft died of typhoid pneumonia in St. Louis on March 16, 1884, at age 29. His obituary notes that Croft had played with the St. Louis Browns before their entry into the American Association and with Troy. In *Missouri Death Records 1834–1910*, his name is spelled "Kroft," and his occupation is given as teamster. *(Baseball-Reference.com; U.S. Federal Census; New York Times; Missouri Death Records 1834–1910)*

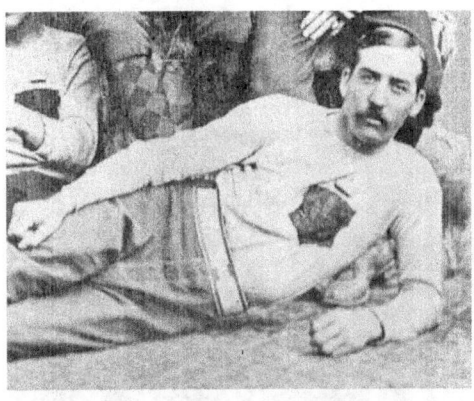

Bill Craver, from 1872 Lord Baltimore team photograph (*The Home Team* by James H. Bready).

Bill Crowley began his career as an 18-year-old first baseman and outfielder with the Philadelphia Base Ball Club in 1875, hitting .081 in nine games. He was a regular National League outfielder for Louisville (1877), Buffalo (1879–80 and 1885) and Boston (1881 and 1884). On September 29, 1881, he was placed on the NL "black list." Reinstated in 1883, he split that season between two American Association clubs—the Philadelphia Athletics and the Cleveland Blues. A career .266 hitter, he reached .287 with Buffalo in 1879. Statistically, he was an average outfielder for the time; however, he was considered to be a "model right fielder." His death notice described him as "one of the best-known catchers in the country." In 1881 he twice had four assists in a game, the only player ever to do so. Born in Philadelphia, the son of Irish immigrants, Crowley worked in a print factory in Gloucester, New Jersey, when he began his baseball career. He was listed as a base ball player as late as 1888–89 in the Gloucester city directory. Only 34 years old, Crowley died of Bright's disease at Gloucester on July 14, 1891. *(Total Baseball; Boston Globe; Baseball-Reference.com; DeadballEra.com; U.S. Federal Census; Gloucester City Directory; Sporting Life; Philadelphia Inquirer)*

William Arthur "Candy" Cummings had developed a curveball some time before he began pitching for the Excelsior senior team in 1866. Shifting to the Star club of Brooklyn in 1868, he continued as an amateur until 1872, when he joined Mutual. In four NA seasons with Mutual, Lord Baltimore, the Philadelphia White Stockings and Hartford, he won 124 games. In 1872 he led the NA in complete games, innings, and shutouts, but he had his best year in 1875 when he compiled a 35–12 record, leading the NA with 82 strikeouts and seven shutouts while walking only four batters in 416 innings. He moved into the National League with Hartford, but he was no longer an effective pitcher. Ten years of throwing the curveball had worn down his 120-pound frame, and he was out of the majors at age 29. By 1884

Bill Crowley, from 1878 Buffalo team photograph (courtesy Mearsonlineauctions.com).

Candy Cummings (courtesy T. Scott Brandon).

he was in the paint and wallpaper business in Athol, Massachusetts. During the final years of his life, he lived with his son in Toledo, Ohio. Cummings died in Toledo on May 16, 1924, at age 75. He was named to the Baseball Hall of Fame in 1939 as a pioneer of the game. *(Baseball-Reference.com; SABR BioProject; U.S. Federal Census; National Association of Base Ball Players, 1857–1870; Complete New York Clipper Baseball Biographies; Cleveland Plain Dealer; Baseball Necrology)*

Edgar "Ned" Cuthbert is alleged to have stolen the first base in baseball history in 1865 while a member of Philadelphia Keystone. Until the formation of the league, he played with Keystone, West Philadelphia, Athletic, and the Chicago White Stockings. Already 26 years old in 1871, he entered the National Association with Athletic, for whom he hit a career-high .338 in 1872. He also played with the Philadelphia White Stockings, the Chicago White Stockings, and the St. Louis Brown Stockings. In 1876 Cuthbert entered the National League with the Brown Stockings, and played for the Cincinnati Red Stockings in 1877. When St. Louis placed a club in the American Association in 1882, Cuthbert managed it and played outfield before jumping to the Union Association in 1884. At age 39 he was the regular right fielder for the Baltimore Monumentals. In ten seasons he hit .254 and fielded .841, much higher than the league average for outfielders. Bill Lee says that Cuthbert was "superintendent of the original Sportsman's Park before he opened a saloon in St. Louis." Cuthbert died of endocarditis in St. Louis on February 5, 1905, at age 59. *(Total Baseball; Baseball-Reference.com; Baseball Necrology; U.S. Federal Census; Sporting Life; DeadballEra.com)*

John Dailey, a Brooklyn-born infielder, played in 29 games, split between Washington and Atlantic in 1875. In these games he hit .178. Used primarily at shortstop, the 22-year-old showed superior range but fielded 23 points under the league average. He also played for Louisville that year, for Manchester, New Hampshire, in 1877–78, and for Utica, Albany and Rochester in 1879. A John J. Dailey umpired in the National League in 1882 and in the American Association in 1884. When Dutch Dehlman died in March of 1885, Dailey succeeded him as manager of Wilkes-Barre. He later umpired in the Texas League, the New England League and the New York State League. That John J. Dailey was also from Brooklyn and is described as a former professional player. But *Sporting Life* demonstrates the problem Dailey presents for a researcher, spelling his name "Daily" in some issues and "Dailey" in others. Peter Morris says that Dailey was living in Brooklyn in 1897, working as a printer. Details of his death are unknown. *(Baseball-reference.com; Sporting Life; Petermorrisbooks.com; DeadballEra.com; Quincy Whig)*

John Henry "Harry" Deane joined Fort Wayne on July 12, 1871. The 25-year-old

Ned Cuthbert (Wikimedia Commons).

outfielder played in six games, hitting .182. He replaced Bill Lennon as manager on July 26, leading Kekionga to a 2–3 record. When Kekionga disbanded in August, Deane was out of the majors until 1874, when he returned as a regular center fielder for Lord Baltimore, hitting .246. Statistically a better-than-average outfielder, he fielded .850, 52 points above the league average. The "Bullpen" section of Baseball-Reference.com says that Harry Deane is the same person as the "Dean" who played outfield and caught for the Cincinnati Red Stockings in 1869. Born in Trenton, New Jersey, Deane lived his adult life in Indianapolis, where he is listed as a surveyor in the 1870 census. The 1900 and 1910 censuses list him as a civil engineer, employed by the city. Deane died in Indianapolis on May 31, 1925, at age 79. *(Baseball-Reference.com; National Association of Base Ball Players, 1857–1870; U.S. Federal Census)*

Herman "Dutch" Dehlman, a Brooklyn product, joined his hometown Atlantic club in 1872, coming from the Warren club. The 20-year-old became the regular first baseman but hit only .226. He remained a regular with Atlantic and the St. Louis Brown Stockings through the formation of the National League, finishing as a reserve in 1877. In his best year as a batter, he hit .237 in 1873, but finished with a .215 mark. However, as a first baseman he was one of the best, having a much higher fielding percentage and range factors than the league average and leading the league three times in put-outs. He participated in the second triple play in NL history on June 29, 1876. Dehlman managed Allentown of the Eastern League in 1884. According to his obituary, he died of typhoid fever on March 13, 1885, only two days after arriving at Wilkes-Barre to take over the management of that club. He was 33 years of age. *(Baseball-Reference.com; Sporting Life; New York Times; Encyclopedia of Minor League Baseball)*

Jim Devlin moved from Easton to the Philadelphia White Stockings in 1873 as a reserve first baseman. Over the next two years, he played in Chicago for the White Stockings, becoming the club's regular first baseman in 1875. Having developed an almost unhittable down-shoot pitch, Devlin became a starting pitcher for the Louisville

Dutch Dehlman, from 1876 St. Louis team photograph (courtesy T. Scott Brandon).

Jim Devlin (Wikimedia Commons).

Grays when the National League opened. He pitched every inning in 1877 and 1,405 innings over the two-year period, leading the NL in games, complete games and innings both seasons. Though he also led the NL in losses both seasons, he paced the circuit in strikeouts in 1877 and compiled ERAs of 1.56 and 2.25. However, in 1877 he was accused of—and later admitted to—accepting bribes to lose games. As a result, he was banned from baseball at age 28. In addition to his 72–76, 1.90 ERA career pitching record, he hit .288 in 266 games as a position player. Although he continued to apply for reinstatement, he was repeatedly denied. He tried pitching in the minors for Trenton but had to withdraw because other teams refused to play against him. For the last fifteen months of his life, Devlin served as a policeman in his native Philadelphia. He died of consumption on October 10, 1883, at age 34, leaving a family in "straitened circumstances." *(Baseball-Reference.com; Sporting Life; DeadballEra.com; Trenton Evening News)*

John Dillon played shortstop for the St. Louis Red Stockings on May 8, 1875. In a 6–1 victory at Keokuk, he had no fielding chances and went hitless in his only at-bat. Dillon had played outfield for the amateur Red Stockings in 1874. He was the older brother of Patrick "Packy" Dillon, and appears in the 1860 census as a 10-year-old, the son of an Irish-born butcher. *(Baseball-Reference.com; U.S. Federal Census; Chicago Daily Inter Ocean)*

Patrick Henry "Packy" Dillon caught three games for the St. Louis Red Stockings in 1875. The 22-year-old had three hits—one a double—for a .231 average. He was a better-than-average catcher with only one error for a .923 percentage. Dillon was a native of St. Louis, and played baseball around the city during the late 1860s and early

Packy Dillon (courtesy of the Dillon family).

1870s. He enrolled in Notre Dame in a commercial course but did not graduate. When the Red Stockings withdrew from the NA in 1875, Dillon, along with Joe Blong and Tricky Nichols, moved on to the Stars of Covington, Kentucky, and back to the Reds—now an independent team—in 1876. He left baseball in 1876 and, like his father, became a butcher. He is listed in the 1880 census as a "produce Hucster." Bill Carle noted that Dillon later became a farmer. Dillon died in Mehlville, Missouri, on July 27, 1902. *(Baseball-Reference.com; U.S. Federal Census; SABR Biographical Research Society Newsletter; Baseball Necrology; Chicago Daily Inter Ocean)*

Lester Dole played center field for New Haven on May 17, 1875, in a home game against Washington. The 19-year-old had two hits and scored a run in a 10–7 loss. He handled three of four fielding chances successfully. Dole was the son of a professor and athletic trainer at Yale and was a gymnastics instructor at the club where the New Haven club trained. In 1877 the *New York Herald* described Lester Dole as a "professional pedestrian" who had won a $500 prize by defeating the English champion over a four-

Lester Dole, from St. Paul School yearbook (courtesy T. Scott Brandon).

mile walking course. In the same year he won a $500 American championship match over a seven-mile course at Providence. Dole first appeared in the 1880 census as teacher of athletics at New Haven, Connecticut. He also owned a small sporting goods store, supplying imported rugby balls for college teams. For forty years he worked as an instructor of gymnastics at St. Paul's School in Millville, New Hampshire,. Axel Bundgaard notes that Dole was one of the first instructors hired at a private school, whose responsibilities included the coaching of sports. He died at Concord, NH on December 10, 1918, at age 63. *(Baseball-Reference. com; U.S. Federal Census; Concord City Directory; New York Herald; New York Times; Axel Bundgaard)*

Pete Donnelly joined Kekionga at the onset of 1871, coming from the Champion club of Jersey City. After nine games as a utility outfielder/infielder, hitting .206, the 21-year-old left the team, along with Ed Mincher, after drawing advance pay. After being blacklisted, he returned to the majors with Washington in 1873, the *Boston Globe* judging him to "still have his reputation to make." Playing in thirty games, Donnelly hit .255. In 1874 he finished in the majors by playing six games with the Philadelphia White Stockings. Overall he hit .251 in 45 games. The Washington and Philadelphia records had previously been credited to John Donnelly. Pete Donnelly's death certificate shows that he was born to Irish parents and that his post-baseball occupation was as a plumber. According to his *Jersey Journal* obituary, he was a leader of the Democratic Party, served on the Board of Alderman, and was a member of the County Board of Freeholders. Donnelly died at Jersey City, New Jersey on October 1, 1890, at age 40. Peter Morris believes that the Kekionga Pete Donnelly was actually a Philadelphia player who died on December 8, 1878, and that the Washington and Philadelphia records may belong to his brother, John. *(Baseball-Reference.com; U.S. Federal Census; DeadballEra.com; Washington Post; Jersey Journal; National Association of Base Ball Players, 1857–1870; Cleveland Plain Dealer; petermorrisbooks.com)*

John Henry "Herm" Doscher played in 109 major league games over an 11-year period. The 19-year-old New York City product first played with Atlantic in 1872, coming from Chester. After playing with Nassau, he also played with Washington (1875) in the NA and Troy (1879), Chicago (1879) and Cleveland (1881–82) in the National League. He hit only .225 but was a competent third baseman with at least average numbers when given the opportunity to play, as he did in 1879. Doscher played in the minors for the Tecumsehs (1877–78), umpired in the National League (1880–81 and 1888) and in the American Association (1888 and 1890), and managed at Binghamton in 1894. His first name became Herman in later censuses. Doscher is listed as a baseball umpire in 1910, as an assistant foreman for the city of Buffalo in 1920, and as a professional athlete in 1930. Bill Lee found that Doscher operated a restaurant in Buffalo. Doscher died in Buffalo on March 20, 1934. Doscher's son, Jack, pitched for Chicago, Brooklyn and Cincinnati between 1903 and 1910, making the Doschers the first father/son major league pair. *(Baseball-Reference.com; Ancestry.com; Baseball Necrology; Sporting Life; Encyclopedia of Minor League Baseball)*

Jacob Doyle was earlier listed as Joseph Doyle. He was only 16 years old in 1872 when he became the regular shortstop for the winless National club. Playing in nine of the club's 11 games, he hit .268. However, in 54 fielding chances, he committed 18 errors for a .667 percentage. When National disbanded, Doyle was out of the majors. The 1880 census for Washington, D.C., shows him working as a government clerk. The 1888–89 city directories for Washington, D.C., show him as a member of the U.S. Navy. He served as an ensign during the Spanish-American War. Federal censuses after 1900 show him living in Lake County, Illinois, still associated with the U.S. Navy. During World War I he was paymaster at Great Lakes Naval Training Station. Doyle died at Lake Bluff, Illinois, on August 15, 1941, at age 85. *(Baseball Reference.com; U.S. Federal Census; Washington City Directory; DeadballEra.com)*

Ed Duffy, an Irish-born shortstop, was one of the first players to be banned from baseball. Playing for Mutual in 1865, Duffy accepted a $30 bribe to throw a game against Eckford. He confessed and was banned until 1870. Duffy had begun his career as early as 1860 with the Eagle club of New York. He played with Eckford both before and after his ban, coming to Chicago in 1870. In the

Ed Duffy, from Chicago composite photograph (courtesy Robert Edward Auctions).

1871 season, Duffy was the regular shortstop for the White Stockings but hit only .231 while fielding 40 points below the league average. His family tree on Ancestry.com shows him to be living in Philadelphia in 1880, working as a laborer. Suffering from chronic nephritis, he died in Brooklyn on June 21, 1889, at age 44. *(Baseball-Reference.com; U.S. Federal Census; Edward Duffy Family Tree)*

Edwards started a game for Atlantic against Elm City on September 11, 1875. He pitched two innings in the 13–6 loss, giving up four hits and six runs, only one of which was earned. Shifted to center field, he handled his only fielding chance. At the plate he went one-for-five and scored a run. Bullpen notes that there is a possibility that Wisconsin-born Charles Edwards, listed as a baseball player in the 1880 census for San Francisco, might at least be a candidate for the Atlantic player. Charles Edwards would have been 20 in 1875. *(Baseball-Reference.com; U.S. Federal Census)*

Dave Eggler began with Eckford in 1868, shifted to Mutual in 1869, and moved with the club into the NA in 1871. After playing with Philadelphia in 1874, he joined Athletic

Eland played right field for Maryland on Opening Day 1872. He went hitless in three at-bats and committed one error in three fielding chances. No player named Eland appears on the rosters prior to 1870. A landowning family named Eland held property in Ann Arundel County in Maryland in 1878. However, there is no person named Eland in the 1880 Baltimore city directory. Peter Morris believes that the Maryland player was actually named Ehlan, one of a group of baseball-playing brothers. *(Baseball-Reference.com; U.S. Federal Census; Woods' Baltimore City Directory; petermorris books.com)*

Dave Eggler (courtesy Nigel Ayres).

and moved with them into the National League in 1876. Eggler also playing with NL clubs in Buffalo and Chicago, and with the American Association Baltimore Orioles. A strong National Association hitter (.323 average for five seasons), he tailed off to .224 in six seasons in the NL and AA. He led NA outfielders three times in fielding, and it was later said of him that he "could get under long drives as well as the modern stars." For his career he fielded .900, 69 points over the league average. Toward the end of his career with Buffalo, he was "released at the end of each week and signed at the beginning of the next to fill some hole in the team." Born in Brooklyn to German parents, he lived in Buffalo, where, for the last eighteen years of his life, he was employed by American Express. He died after being run over by a train in Buffalo on April 5, 1902, at age 50. *(Total Baseball; Baseball-Reference.com; Chicago Daily Tribune; Washington Post; U.S. Federal Census)*

Joe Ellick debuted in 1875 with the St. Louis Red Stockings, hitting .222 in seven games, before jumping to Louisville. Trials with the Milwaukee Cream Citys (1878) and Worcester Ruby Legs (1880) added only eight games. When the Union Association was formed in 1884, the 30-year-old Ellick became the regular right fielder for Chicago, hitting .236, and managing the team for twelve games, in which it went 6–6. He finished that season and his major league career with the Kansas City Unions and the Baltimore Monumentals. Overall, he hit .218 in 116 games and fielded above the league average both as an outfielder and a shortstop. Ellick was an NL umpire (1886) and an AA umpire (1888–89). Between times he managed the Kansas City Western League team. The 1910 and 1920 censuses show Ellick living in Kansas City, Kansas, working as a bookkeeper for a cigar factory. He died at Kansas City on April 21, 1923, at age 69. Before his death, Ellick expressed great regret over his 1875 contract jumping. *(Total Baseball; Baseball-Reference.com; U.S. Federal Census; Baseball Necrology; Sporting Life)*

Evans played left field for Elm City in at game at Washington on June 1, 1875. In an

8–7 loss, Evans had two hits in four at-bats, scored a run and drove in one. He had no fielding chances. Since he never played in the majors again, there is a strong likelihood that he was a local Washington player who was recruited for the day. *(Baseball-Reference.com; Major League Baseball in Gilded Age Connecticut)*

George Ewell played right field for Cleveland on June 26, 1871, in a game at Washington. He went hitless in three at-bats but had a putout on his only fielding chance. A player named Ewell caught and played first base with Philadelphia Keystone in 1868–69 and with Washington Olympic in 1870; this could be the same player. George Ewell was born in Philadelphia and is listed in the 1870 census as a "baseballist." The 1880 census lists him as a sailor. His father was an oyster dealer, and Ewell appeared in the 1900 and 1910 Philadelphia censuses as an "oysterman" and an "oyster opener." His death certificate confirms the oyster opener occupation. Ewell died of Uremia and acute Bright's disease on October 20, 1910, just before his 60th birthday. *(Baseball-Reference.com; U.S. Federal Census; DeadballEra.com; Philadelphia Inquirer; Commonwealth of Pennsylvania Death Certificate)*

Jack Farrell, called "Hartford Jack" to distinguish him from a contemporary Jack Farrell from Providence, played center field for Hartford for three games at the end of 1874. He hit .385 and handled six fielding chances without error. Only 18 years of age, he never played another major league game. In the 1880s he played minor league ball for Harrisburg, Bridgeport, and Waterbury before finishing for his hometown Hartford club in 1887. Born to Irish parents in Hartford, he is listed as a store clerk in the 1880 census. The 1900 census called him a salon keeper— a "successful liquor dealer," according to *Sporting Life*. This Jack Farrell died in Hartford on November 15, 1916, at age 60. He is surely the same Jack Farrell, "a veteran Hartford player," who organized a benefit for Bobby Mathews in 1897 and who paid the funeral expenses for former major league pitcher "Big Bill" Taylor in 1900. *(Baseball-Reference.com; U.S. Federal Census; Sporting Life; Major League Baseball in Gilded Age Connecticut)*

Jack Farrow began his major league career with Resolute in 1873, having played with the club in 1872 as an amateur. The 19-year-old catcher played in 12 games, hitting .167. The following season he played in 27 games for Atlantic. The Verplanck, New York, native was then out of the majors until 1884, when he played in 16 games with Brooklyn of the American Association, leaving the majors with a .197 average for 55 games. He managed briefly for Newark of the Eastern League in 1885. In the 1880 census Farrow, the son of an English father and an Irish mother, is shown as a retail milk dealer. In 1910 Farrow and his son were listed as proprietors of a saloon. Bill Lee describes Farrow as a retired hotel keeper. After a long illness, Farrow died at Perth Amboy, New Jersey, on December 31, 1914, at age 61. *(Total Baseball; Baseball-Reference.com; New York Times; Encyclopedia of Minor League Baseball; U.S. Federal Census; Baseball Necrology)*

Bob Ferguson was the first switch-hitter in professional baseball. He played "amateur" baseball with the Enterprise club of Brooklyn as early as 1865, before beginning a five-year stint with Atlantic. He became player/manager with Mutual at the inauguration of the NA but returned to Atlantic (1872–74) before going to the Hartford Dark Blues (1875) and moving with them to the National League. In the NL he was a playing manager for Chicago, Troy and Philadelphia, in addition to Hartford. After finishing

Bob Ferguson, from 1875 Hartford team photograph (courtesy Robert Edward Auctions).

Sam Field (Wikimedia Commons).

as a player with Pittsburgh early in 1884, he resigned to take up umpiring. Ferguson umpired until 1891 with time out to manage New York in 1886–87. At that time, "being well fixed financially," he retired from baseball. As a player he was a regular at third base or second base for thirteen seasons in a 14-season career. Ferguson hit .351 for Chicago in 1878, much above his career .265 mark. His fielding statistics in both percentage and range far exceed those of third basemen of his era; those for second base are at the league average. Born in Brooklyn to Irish parents, Ferguson died there of an attack of apoplexy on May 3, 1894. He was 49 years old. *(Baseball Encyclopedia; Baseball-Reference.com; Sporting Life; U.S. Federal Census; National Association of Base Ball Players, 1857–1870)*

Sam Field played in eight games in 1875—three with his hometown Centennial club and five with Washington. A year later he played in four games with the hapless Cincinnati Red Stockings of the National League. In his 12 major league games, he hit only .146. Nine of his games were as a catcher, a position in which he committed 15 errors for a .717 percentage. His obituary notes that he began playing baseball in Philadelphia in 1865 and that he gained fame as a catcher of hard-throwing Cherokee Fisher. After his major league career, he played for the Actives of Reading and served as a "prominent fireman" in the area. In the 1880 census and the 1890 Reading city directory, Field is identified as a hotel keeper. At the time of his death he was a hotel keeper in Sinking Springs, Pennsylvania. He died at Sinking Springs on October 28, 1904, at age 56. During the Civil War Field served in the U.S. Navy aboard the *U.S.S. Richmond* from May 1864 to November 1865. *(Baseball-Reference.com; U.S. Federal Census; Reading City Directory; Sporting Life; Pennsylvania Veterans Burial Cards, 1777–1999)*

George Fields played shortstop for the amateur Mansfield club in 1870 and 1871. When the club entered the NA in 1872, he shifted to third base. In 18 games he hit .221, lowest among the Mansfield regulars. Third base was not kind to him, as he committed 23 errors in 12 games there for a .629 percentage. When Mansfield left the NA, Fields' major league career was over. A native of Waterbury, Connecticut, he worked at the clock factory in various capacities throughout his adult life. He is variously listed in the censuses as a brass turner, a foreman and a bench boss. Fields died at Waterbury on September 22, 1933, at age 80. *(Baseball-Reference.com; U.S. Federal Census; National Association of Base Ball Players, 1857–1870; Major League Base Ball in Gilded Age Connecticut)*

William "Cherokee" Fisher pitched for seven major league teams in seven seasons. Debuting with Rockford in 1871, he went 4–16 that season. Previous to the formation of the league he played for West Philadelphia (1867), Buckeye (1868) and Union of Lansingburgh (1869–70). In both 1872 (with Lord Baltimore) and 1873 (with his hometown Athletic) he led the NA in ERA. In his most productive season he won 22 games for Philadelphia in 1875, this coming on the heels of a 23-loss season with Hartford. In the National League he was 4–20 for the last-place Reds in 1876 and 0–1 for Providence in 1877, causing him to leave the majors with a 56–84 record. A.G. Spalding later said of Fisher that he "could send them in like lightning," but that he never changed pitches. Fisher also played 93 games as an outfielder and 26 as a third baseman, hitting

Cherokee Fisher, from 1872 Lord Baltimore team photograph (*The Home Team* by James H. Bready).

.236 and fielding well below the league average at both positions. Born in Philadelphia to a German father, Fisher is described in *Sporting Life* in 1886 as "a pressman living in Chicago." He appeared in the 1900 census for Chicago as a city fireman. Fisher died in New York City on September 26, 1912, at age 67 or 68. *(Baseball-Reference.com; U.S. Federal Census; National Association of Base Ball Players, 1857–1870; Sporting Life; Rockford Morning Star)*

Wes Fisler, "one of the most graceful players that ever handled a ball," joined Athletic in 1866. When the league was formed, the 26-year-old Fisler had been a club regular for five seasons. He continued as a regular for Athletic through 1876. In 1868 he finished third among Association batters using the scoring system in place at the time. In 1872 he hit .348 and was second in the NA with 48 runs batted in. Overall, in both the NA and National League, he hit .310. Fisler led NA first basemen in fielding in 1871 and second basemen in fielding in 1873. In both positions, he fielded above the league average. In 1874 he made the European tour with Athletic and Boston. His obituary notes that he was known as "the dandy of the diamond" because of his white cuffs, collar and necktie. The son of a physician, Fisler appeared in the 1870 census for Camden, New Jersey, as a clerk. Bill Lee notes that later Fisler opened a haberdashery store and still later served as a clerk to an attorney. Fisler died in Philadelphia on Christmas Day 1922. He was 78 years old. *(Baseball-Reference.com; Baseball Necrology; Sporting Life; U.S. Federal Census; Jersey Journal)*

Frank Fleet pitched the last game of the 1871 season for Mutual, giving up 20 hits and ten earned runs to champion Athletic. With Eckford in 1872, Resolute in 1873, Atlantic in 1874–75 and the St. Louis Brown Stockings in 1875, he played every position, hitting .228 and going 2–6 as a pitcher. He was a better fielder at shortstop and third base than he was in other positions. However, he was judged to be "without a superior as a second baseman." In 1877 he played "middle garden" on the Columbus Buckeyes team that included King Kelly and Charlie Pabor. In 1878 he was back in Brooklyn playing third base for the Flyaway club. Born in New York City, he enlisted in the New York Eighth Infantry Regiment in May of 1862 as a 14-year-old but was mustered out in September of that year. However, he is not listed in SABR's Civil War veterans project. He well may be the "Fleet" listed as a member of Eagle Baseball Club of New York in 1869. Frank Fleet died of heart disease in New York City on June 13, 1900, at age 51. He is not included in any of the city directories for New York City. *(Baseball-Reference.com; U.S. Civil War Soldier Records and Profiles; Sporting Life; New York Herald; New York City Deaths 1892–1902)*

George Fletcher played in two games as a right fielder for Eckford on June 21 and 22, 1872. In road losses to Mansfield, he had two hits in eight at bats with a run scored and a run batted in. In the field he had two errors in five fielding chances. Born in Brooklyn to a real estate dealer, Fletcher began playing with Excelsior in 1864. By 1867 he had moved to the National club of Washington, D.C., and made the western tour with that club. In the 1870 census, Fletcher is living in Washington, D.C., and, like many National players, is a clerk in the Treasury Department. Fletcher died in Brooklyn on June 18, 1879. *(Baseball-Reference.com; U.S. Federal Census; National Association of Base Ball Players, 1857–1870)*

Frank "Silver" Flint played for the St. Louis Red Stockings as a teenager in 1875. Like several of the Red Stockings, he went to Covington; from there he went to Indi-

Silver Flint (courtesy Nigel Ayres).

anapolis in 1876 and moved with the club into the National League in 1878. He joined the Chicago White Stockings in 1879, remained with them until 1889, and helped them win five league championships in seven years (1880–82 and 1885–86). Flint hit .310 in 1881 but only .239 for his career and .118 in five World Series games. Twice leading the National League in fielding, he was described as having "few equals and no superiors" as a catcher. For his career he fielded .911, some thirteen points over the league average at the time. In 1888 he contacted consumption, limiting his play to just 37 games in his last two seasons with Chicago. The years of catching with little protection also took their toll: "His fingers, owing to all the breaks and bruises, pointed in all directions." The Philadelphia native lived most of his life in St. Louis. Only 36 years of age, Flint died in Chicago on January 14, 1892. *(New York Times; National Police Gazette; Baseball-Reference.com; Chicago Daily Tribune)*

Charles "Dickie" Flowers hit .314 as the regular shortstop for the Haymakers in 1871.

Six of his 33 hits came in one game—a 37–16 victory over New York on July 3. He had begun playing with his hometown Quaker City club in 1867, continuing with Keystone in 1868–69. In 1870 he played with Union of Lansingburgh, entering the NA with that name-changed club. In 1872 he returned to Philadelphia and finished his major league experience with Athletic. In 24 career games he hit .308 but his fielding was below the league average. The 1880 census shows him residing in Philadelphia employed by the fire department. Flowers "dropped dead of heart disease" on October 6, 1892, at age 42. (*Baseball-Reference.com; Sporting Life; Ancestry.com; National Association of Base Ball Players, 1857–1870; Baseball Chronology*)

William "Clipper" Flynn, a local boy, played for the Haymakers in the 1871 season, hitting .338 and leading NA first basemen in assists. He had begun with Union of Lansingburgh as an 18-year-old in 1866. But in 1870 he was one of a group of Troy-area players who had migrated west to play for Chicago. In 1872 Flynn went to Washington to play for Olympic, but the team disbanded after nine games, ending his major league career. In 37 career games he hit .313 and fielded .934, a superior figure for the time. Born at Lansingburgh to Irish parents, Flynn is listed in the 1880 census as a resident of Lansingburgh with a wife and four young children, working in a brush factory. He died on November 5, 1881, at age 32. (*Baseball-Reference.com; U.S. Federal Census; National Association of Base Ball Players, 1857–1870*)

Tom Foley played in 18 games as an outfielder and catcher for the Chicago White Stockings in 1871. The 24-year-old Foley hit .262, fielding poorly as an outfielder or as a catcher. Born in Chicago in 1847, Foley played third base for Chicago Excelsior (1867–68) and Rockford Forest City prior

Tom Foley, from 1870 Rockford composite photograph (courtesy T. Scott Brandon).

to joining the White Stockings. He retired from baseball after that season. For a time after leaving the White Stockings, Foley operated a business manufacturing blank books, ledgers and journals. In fact, the 1870 census lists him as a bookbinder. In 1874 he accepted a position as a letter carrier, a position he held for 22 years. The 1880 census for Chicago lists him as such. *Sporting Life* points out that in this position, he was a "guardian of registered mail," transferring thousands of dollars each day among the banks and large business houses in downtown Chicago. Foley fell dead of heart disease at his home in suburban La Grange, Illinois, on January 4, 1896. He was 49 years old. (*Baseball-Reference.com; U.S. Federal Census; Sporting Life; Rockford Morning Star*)

Will Foley played in three games for the Chicago White Stockings as a 19-year-old in 1875. He became the regular third baseman for Cincinnati when the National League was formed, moving on to Milwaukee (1878) and back to Cincinnati (1879). Foley played briefly with Detroit in 1881

Will Foley, from Franklins team photograph (courtesy T. Scott Brandon).

before finishing with the Chicago Browns in 1884. In seven seasons, four as a regular, he hit as high as .271 with Milwaukee, considerably above his career norm of .226. However, his fielding statistics were below the league average. He later played at Omaha (1890–92). Born in Chicago to English parents, Foley worked as a railroad agent while playing baseball. DeadballEra.com lists his post-baseball occupation as clerk. He died in Chicago, found dead in the loft of his brother's barn, watched over by his dog on November 12, 1916, at age 60. The *Rockford Morning Star* says that he was the younger brother of former Rockford player Tom Foley, and the 1870 census seems to confirm this. *(Baseball Necrology; Total Baseball; Baseball-Reference.com; U.S. Federal Census; DeadballEra.com; Rockford Morning Star)*

Jim Foran was the leading hitter for Kekionga in 1871 with a .348 average. He had played third base for Athletic in 1869 and in the outfield for Union of Lansingburgh in 1870. For Kekionga Foran played 16 games as a first baseman, fielding more than 50 points below the league average, and four as an outfielder. When Kekionga disbanded in September, Foran finished the season playing for teams in the Baltimore area, and he never again played major league baseball. In 1888 *Sporting Life* printed a story that Foran had been a late-night person early in his career and that he had slept across the streetcar tracks so that the first train in the morning would wake him in time to get to the ballpark. Born in Ireland or in New York State to Irish parents, Foran appeared in the 1880 census for San Francisco, working as a machinist. *The SABR Encyclopedia* shows him playing for San Francisco and Oakland teams from 1877 through 1881. The 1910 census for Los Angeles shows him working as an engineer in a machine shop. Foran died in Los Angeles on January 30, 1928, at around age 80. *(Baseball-Reference.com; Sporting Life; U.S. Federal Census; Philadelphia Inquirer; SABR Encyclopedia)*

David "Wee Davy" Force was another player whose career spanned three manifestations of professional baseball. The New York City product played for Olympic of Washington beginning in 1867 and then moving with the club into the league. He also played for Troy, Lord Baltimore, Chicago and Athletic, moving with Athletic into the National League when it was formed in 1876. In the NL, Force also played for the Mutuals, St. Louis and Buffalo, before finishing with Washington in 1886.

Davy Force, from 1878 Buffalo team photograph (courtesy Mearsonlineauctions.com).

Only 5' 4" and 130 pounds, he was one of the best fielding shortstops of his time, leading his league in fielding seven times. His overall fielding percentage (.896) was forty-eight points higher than the league average. A strong National Association hitter (.336), he did not find National League pitching congenial, finishing with a .211 average for 10 seasons. When he retired from baseball, he received a position with Otis Elevator, which he held for 25 years. Force died on June 21, 1918, in Englewood, New Jersey, at age 68. (*Total Baseball; Baseball-Reference.com; Sporting News; U.S. Federal Census; Complete Clipper Baseball Biographies*)

Bill French hit .222 in five games with Maryland in 1873. He played two games at first base, fielding .905, but in two games in right field his percentage dropped to .600. On April 15 in Washington he pitched a complete game against the Blue Legs, giving up 30 hits and 27 runs, 12 of which were earned. Two men of the right age named William French appear in the 1870 census for Baltimore—a butcher and an apprentice blacksmith. Peter Morris has recently traced French through California newspaper and voter registration records. The player was the butcher, and he played baseball for the Californias in 1878–80. Born in Baltimore in 1849, French died in Baltimore on May 31, 1893. (*Woods' Baltimore City Directory; Baseball-Reference.com; U.S. Federal Census; SABR Biographical Research Committee Newsletter*)

Charles "Chick" Fulmer hit .270 as a 20-year-old shortstop for Rockford in 1871. Previously he had played with Olympic (1868) and Keystone (1869) of Philadelphia and Forest City of Cleveland (1870). After playing with Mutual and his hometown Philadelphia Base Ball Club, Fulmer joined Louisville when the National League began in 1876. He also played with Buffalo (1879–

Chick Fulmer, from 1878 Buffalo team photograph (courtesy Mearsonlineauctions.com).

80) before joining Cincinnati of the American Association. In 1882 he hit .281 and led AA shortstops in fielding to help the Red Stockings win the league championship. Fulmer finished his major league career in 1884 with the St. Louis Browns. Overall, he hit .266 in five seasons in the NA and .257 in six NL/AA seasons. His fielding average at shortstop (.839) was fifteen points above that of the league. He umpired in the NL in 1886; *Sporting Life* judged that he had a very poor sense of balls and strikes. The son of a butcher, Fulmer appears in the 1880 census as a butcher as well. Philadelphia censuses for 1900 and 1910 show him as retired. In 1916 *Sporting Life* says that Fulmer "became a magistrate in the Quaker City." In 1920 he is employed as a watchman for a publishing company. When Fulmer died in Philadelphia on February 15, 1940, he was the oldest major league player. His older brother, Washington, played for the Atlantics in 1875. (*Total Baseball; New York Times; Sporting News; U.S. Federal Census; Philadelphia City Directory; Baseball-Reference.com; U.S. Federal Census; National Association of Base Ball Players, 1857–1870*)

Washington Fulmer, a 35-year-old resident of Philadelphia, played third base for Atlantic on July 19, 1875, in a game at Athletic. He was one of the four local amateur players picked up by the short-handed Atlantic team for the game. In a 23–3 loss, Fulmer had two hits, scored a run and drove in one. In the field he had one error in four fielding chances. Fulmer was a Civil War veteran, having served in the Seventy-first Pennsylvania Infantry Regiment. In the 1880 census he is listed as a butcher; the 1890 city directory says he was an engineer; the 1900 census shows him as a watchman. His death certificate and DeadballEra.com say that he was a fireman for the Philadelphia Water Department. Fulmer died in Philadelphia on December 8, 1907, at age 67. (*U.S. Federal Census; Baseball-Reference.com; DeadballEra.com; Philadelphia City Directory; Pennsylvania Certificate of Death*)

James "Pud" Galvin, as an 18-year-old, pitched for his hometown Brown Stockings of the National Association in 1875. With a fastball that turned batters into pudding, hence the nickname, Galvin won 361 games in 15 seasons, sixth on the all-time list. He had back-to-back 46-win seasons in 1883–84, in which he completed 143 of 147 starts while working 1,292-plus innings. He also enjoyed a 37-win season and seven other 20-win seasons. Galvin did his best work for the Buffalo Bisons (1879–85), and later played for Pittsburgh teams in three different leagues; he finished back in St. Louis with the Browns in 1892. Second behind Cy Young in career innings pitched and complete games, Galvin is also second in losses (308). Listed at 5' 8" tall and 190 pounds, he ballooned to 300 pounds at points in his career. Galvin managed Buffalo for 24 games in 1885 and umpired briefly after leaving the playing ranks. When "Old Man Galvin" retired in 1892, *Sporting Life* reported that he "thinks of going into the laundry business." He actually opened a saloon in Pittsburgh but lost money even though the place was

Pud Galvin, from 1878 Buffalo team photograph (courtesy Mearsonlineauctions.com).

always packed. He died penniless. Born in St. Louis to Irish parents, Galvin died at Pittsburgh of catarrah of the stomach on March 7, 1902. He was 47 years old. Galvin was elected to the Baseball Hall of Fame in 1965. *(Sporting News; Total Baseball; Baseball Encyclopedia; Baseball-Reference.com; BaseballLibrary.com; U.S. Federal Census; Sporting Life)*

John Galvin played second base for Atlantic on Opening Day 1872. After going hitless and committing four errors in five fielding chances, he left the majors. However, he had a long history in Brooklyn and New York City baseball, going back to 1861 when he played with the Exercise club. He played with the great Atlantic teams of 1863–65, finishing second in run average in 1864. He played with Mutual in 1868 and was rumored to have dropped out of baseball in 1870. Born in Brooklyn in 1842, he volunteered for the Fifty-first New York Infantry in September 1861 and was mustered out at the end of October that same year. In the 1870 and 1900 censuses he is listed as a Brooklyn resident, working as a sewer inspector. In 1880 he was keeper of a truants home. Galvin died in Brooklyn on April 20, 1904, at age 61. *(Baseball-Reference.com; U.S. Federal Census; U.S. Civil War Soldier Records and Profiles; National Association of Base Ball Players, 1857–1870; Cincinnati Daily Gazette)*

Gavern played second base for Atlantic on June 15, 1874. In a home loss to Boston, Gavern scored a run but went hitless. He had a busy day in the field, handing 12 chances, nine cleanly. The *New York Herald* reported the player's name as "McGovern." In 1869 the *New York Times* reported that a third baseman named "McGovern," who played on the *Times* team, made "several 'stinging' catches," "like a professional." *(Baseball-Reference.com; SABR Encyclopedia of Baseball; New York Herald; New York Times)*

Alfred "Count" Gedney played outfield for Union of Morrisania in 1870 and for Eckford in 1871. He started the 1872 season with Troy; in ten games he hit .412 with three home runs. When Troy disbanded in July, Gedney moved back to Eckford, becoming the regular left fielder but hitting only .153. He played for Mutual in 1873, for Athletic in 1874 and for Mutual again in 1875. "In his day one of the finest of outfielders," he had a .846 percentage, but his hitting settled at .251. As a member of Athletic, he was part of the 1874 world tour. Continuing in baseball below the major league level, he played for a town team in Hackensack, New Jersey, as late as 1890. A New York City native, Gedney is listed as a student in the 1870 census; in 1880 he was a clerk in a produce store. The 1892 city directory gives his occupation as "oils"; in 1900 he is listed as an accountant. Gedney died at Hackensack on March 26, 1922, at age 72. *(U.S. Federal Census; Baseball-Reference.com; Sporting Life; National Association of Base Ball Players, 1857–1870; Trenton Evening Times; Cincinnati Daily Enquirer)*

William H. "Billy" Geer had seven major league trials with seven different teams in four leagues over a twelve-year period. He played two games for Mutual in 1874; in 1875 he was a regular for New Haven, hitting .244 in 37 games. Three years later he debuted in the National League as the regular shortstop for Cincinnati, also playing with Worcester in 1880. After six games in the Union Association with the Philadelphia Keystones in 1884, he became the regular shortstop for Brooklyn of the American Association, finishing his major league career with Louisville in 1885. All together he hit .214. As a shortstop he fielded .858, slightly below the league average but with above-

Billy Geer (Wikimedia Commons).

average range. Details of his life are often confusing. Some sources claim that he was only fourteen years old when he played with Mutual, giving an August 13, 1859, birth date. Even so, he would have been fifteen years old when he debuted in October 1874. SABR's Biographical Research Committee believes that an 1849 birth date is more likely and that he may have played at Manhattan College. Early in his career Geer was arrested for burglary of hotel rooms and later for passing bad checks. In 1897 *Sporting Life* refers to him as "the notorious ex-shortstop," who "is reported to be pursuing a criminal career in the West." That paper carefully separates him from another baseball-related Geer, George H. Some sources still list Billy Geer's birth name as George H. While SABR reports that Billy Geer lived for a while and married in Syracuse, the George H. Geer who appears in the Syracuse censuses for 1900, 1910 and 1920 may not be the ball player because of age. Peter Morris also shows that the family appears in three consecutive censuses using three different names, so Geer may have used the name Aiguier. *(Baseball Encyclopedia; Total Baseball; Baseball-Reference.com; Baseball Necrology; U.S. Federal Census; Sporting Life; SABR Biographical Research Committee Newsletter)*

Joe Gerhardt began his professional career as a teenage shortstop with his hometown Washington Blue Legs in 1873, also appearing with Lord Baltimore and Mutual in the NA. When the National League opened in 1876, he was the regular first baseman for the Louisville Grays before moving to Cincinnati in 1878. He also played with Detroit and the New York Giants in the NL. Disgruntled by his lack of playing time, he was released to the American Association New York Mets. After an exile to the minors, he returned to the majors with the Brooklyn Gladiators and the St. Louis Browns in 1890, leading AA second basemen in fielding that season. Gerhardt finished his major league career with Louisville in 1891. In fifteen seasons he hit .227 but reached .304 in the inflated 1877 season and

Joe Gerhardt (Wikimedia Commons).

was called a "lightning player" in the field. His fielding average and range factors were well above those for the league. He was also manager at Louisville in 1883 and for the Browns in 1890. After leaving baseball, Gerhardt became "manager of a café in the Columbia Theater Building, New York," from which he drew a "fat salary." He later operated hotels in New York City and in Tarrytown, New York, and for a while managed a bowling alley. Born in the District of Columbia to German parents, Gerhardt died at Middletown, New York, on March 11, 1922, at age 67. *(Total Baseball; Baseball-Reference.com; Washington Post; Chicago Daily Tribune; National Police Gazette; U.S. Federal Census)*

Barney Gilligan, a 130-pound catcher, lasted eleven seasons in the majors, including five as a regular. As an 18-year-old amateur, he caught two games for the Brooklyn Atlantics in 1875. In 1879 he joined Cleveland, coming from Clinton. He played for Cleveland (1879–80), Providence (1881–85), Washington (1886–87) and Detroit (1888). In all he batted .207, but he hit .245 for the National League champion Providence Grays in 1884, when he caught "Old Hoss" Radbourn, and hit .444 in the World Series that year. Gilligan is most often praised for not being "afraid of work"; his defensive statistics (.912 percentage, 6.78 range factor) are above the league average for the time. Born in Cambridge, Massachusetts to Irish parents, Gilligan moved to Lynn, Massachusetts, where he was described as "prospering in business." Bill Lee's research showed that Gilligan worked for the sanitation department, a fact confirmed by the 1930 U.S. Federal Census. Gilligan died in Lynn on April 1, 1934, at age 78. Peter Morris asserts that the 1875 record likely belongs to a man named Hugh Gilgan. *(Total Baseball; Washington Post; Boston Globe; New York Times; Baseball Necrology; U.S. Federal Census; Petermorrisbooks.com)*

Barney Gilligan (LC-DIG-bbc-0380f Library of Congress Prints and Photographs Division).

Jim Gilmore played in three games for Washington between April 26 and May 1, 1875. He had three hits for a .250 average. He caught two of the games, committing three errors and allowing two passed balls. He also filled in at third base and right field. Born in Baltimore to an Irish father, Gilmore is listed as a law student in the 1870 census. By 1880 he had married and "keeps a ducking shoot." He was listed as a farmer in 1900 and as a retired farmer in 1910. In his last census in 1920, the 67-year-old Gilmore was living with his son and working as a custodian at the Maryland Institute. Gilmore died in Baltimore on November 18, 1928. *(Baseball-Reference.com; U.S. Federal Census)*

Gilroy caught eight games for Chicago in September of 1874, hitting .211. The *Hartford Courant* describes him as being from the amateur Philadelphia Eurekas, recruited to replace an ill Fergy Malone. In 1875 he caught one game and played right field in another for Athletic. It seems likely, therefore, that he was from Philadelphia. Statistics show that he was an above-average catcher who hit .210 in ten games. In early 1876 the *Middletown Daily Constitution* reported that Gilroy, "formerly of the Athletics," had signed to catch for Cincinnati. Apparently, this did not happen. *(Baseball-Reference.com; Hartford Courant; Middletown Daily Constitution)*

John Glenn began his baseball career in Washington, D.C., in 1870, playing with both National and Olympic, and continuing with Olympic as the team entered the league in 1871. After hitting .308 that season, he again split 1872 between the two Washington clubs, before continuing with the Blue Legs in 1873. Glenn spent the remainder of his major league career in Chicago—first with the NA White Stockings and then with the National League White Stockings, hitting .304 with the NL champions of 1876. For his career he hit .267 with superior defensive numbers as an outfielder and mediocre statistics as a first baseman. Born in Rochester, New York, he is listed in the 1870 census as a ball player. In 1888 the 38-year-old Glenn was arrested for assaulting a ten-year-old girl and was accidentally shot and killed by a Sandy Hill, New York, policeman, who was trying to protect him from a lynch mob. *Sporting Life* reported that Glenn had a prison record for previous assaults on females, including his niece. The *Philadelphia Enquirer* indicated that Glenn had been employed at the iron and brass works. *(Baseball-Reference.com; U.S. Federal Census; Sporting Life; National Association of Base Ball Players, 1857–1870; Philadelphia Enquirer)*

John Glenn, from "Chicago Champions" (LC-DIG-pga-18390 Library of Congress Prints and Photographs Division).

Mike Golden pitched every inning for Keokuk in 1875, compiling a 1–12 record and a 1.86 ERA. After Western folded, Golden moved on to Chicago as a pitcher/outfielder, going 6–7 on the mound. After playing for Indianapolis of the League Alliance, Golden resurfaced in 1878 with the Milwaukee Cream City club in the National League. Hitting .354 as a part-time outfielder, he went 3–13, with a 4.14 ERA as a pitcher. Milwaukee folded, ending Golden's major league career. Overall, he compiled a 10–32 record with a 3.37 ERA. Born in Shirley, Massachusetts, to Irish parents, Golden and his brother appear in the 1870 census for Rockford, Illinois, with "none" as an occupation. Golden pitched for Keokuk in 1874, before the team entered the NA. Ralph Christian noted that despite Golden's "blinding speed," his wildness contributed to his lack of success as a pitcher. Both the 1900 and 1910 censuses show him living in Rockford, working as a city policeman, a position he held until he retired in 1914. He died in Rockford on January 11, 1929, at age 77. *(Baseball-Reference.com; U.S. Federal Census; Cleveland Plain Dealer; "High Expectations, Small Market, Regionalism and a Short-lived Season")*

Fred Goldsmith claimed to have been the inventor of the curveball, usually credited to Candy Cummings. He always kept a clipping from an 1870 *Brooklyn Eagle* article relating an experiment in which he proved that he could throw a baseball so that it curved around a pole. As a 19-year-old, he played one game as a second baseman for his hometown Elm City club in 1875. Then after pitching every game for the Tecumsehs of London, Ontario, for three seasons, he joined the NL Troy Trojans in 1879 and shifted to the Chicago White Stockings in 1880. Pitching beside Larry Corcoran, he won 98 games in a four-year period (1880–83) before injuring his arm. The NL leader in winning percentage (21–3, .875) in 1880, Goldsmith won 28 games in 1882. After a 9–11 start in 1884, he was released to the Baltimore Orioles and then became an umpire. The *Chicago Daily Tribune* later identified him as operating a truck farm. The 1910 U.S. Federal Census lists a Fred Goldsmith matching the pitcher's background working as a salesman in Detroit. According to Bill Lee, Goldsmith became a postmaster and operator of a general store in Berkeley, Michigan. He died there on March 28, 1939, at age 86. *(Baseball Necrology; Sporting News; Total Baseball; Chicago Daily Tribune; U.S. Federal Census)*

Warren "Wally" Goldsmith was one of a group of players to join Fort Wayne in 1870 from Maryland, a disbanded Baltimore club. Beginning with Enterprise in 1868, Goldsmith had moved on to Maryland in that same season. Starting every game for Kekionga in 1871, he hit .205 in 19 games. In 1872 he played as a middle infielder for Olympic until that club disbanded; a year later he played in one game for Maryland before finishing as a third baseman for Keokuk in 1875. Keokuk had obtained him from an amateur club in Quincy, Illinois. Overall, he hit .185 for 42 National Association games. Whether in percentage or range, Goldsmith was a mediocre shortstop and third baseman. The four NA teams for which he played had a combined 10–37 record. Born in Baltimore in 1848, Goldsmith appears in federal censuses from 1850. In 1900, he was living with his sister and brother-in-law in Washington, D.C., working as a hotel clerk. Goldsmith died in Washington on September 16, 1915. *(Baseball-Reference.com; U.S. Federal Census; Sporting Life; National Association of Base Ball*

Fred Goldsmith (courtesy Nigel Ayres).

Players, 1857–1870; "High Expectations, Small Market, Regionalism and a Short-lived Season")

Charlie Gould was the only local player on the 1869 Cincinnati Red Stockings. At 6'1" and 176 pounds, he was a giant for his day. In 1863 at age 16 he joined the Buckeye club of Cincinnati and played with them until 1869, when he joined the Red Stockings. In 1871 he went with the Wright brothers and Cal McVey to the new Boston Red Stockings. Called "the bushel basket" because of his range, Gould played first base as an amateur, as a pre–NA professional, as an NA player/manager, and finally as a National League player/manager—back with Cincinnati in 1876–77. He hit .285 in 1871, the high point of a career average of .257. He led the NA with eight triples for the champion Red Stockings in 1872. After missing 1873, he also played with Lord Baltimore and New Haven in the NA. The 1870 census lists him as a base ball player, though the *New York Clipper* said he worked as a bookkeeper for his father. Cincinnati censuses of 1900 and 1910 list him as a railway clerk. Gould died from a stroke of paralysis in Flushing, New York on April 9, 1917, at age 69. *(Complete New York Clipper Baseball Biographies; U.S. Federal Census; Baseball Necrology; Baseball-Reference.com; Sporting Life; National Association of Base Ball Players, 1857–1870)*

Jack Greason, a 22-year-old lefty, pitched in seven games for Washington in 1873. Making seven starts, he had a 1–6 record and a 5.86 ERA. Greason has only recently acquired a first name. An 1890 note in *Sporting Life* identifies him as one of the Washington-based players who had played at the White Lot with the amateur Astorias. Born into an Irish family in Washington, D.C., he appeared in the 1860 and 1880 censuses. In the last, the 30-year-old Greason is working as a clerk in his father's hotel. DeadballEra.com lists him as the proprietor of the hotel. The John "Greson" who appears in the 1870 census as a D.C.-born store clerk living in Wilson, North Carolina, may be the player. Greason died in Washington, D.C., on July 22, 1889, at age 37. *(Baseball-Reference.com; U.S. Federal Census; DeadballEra.com; SABR Baseball Encyclopedia; Sporting Life)*

Bill Hague (William L. Haug) was a "scientific" third baseman for the Brown Stockings in 1875 and for Louisville and Providence of the National League, helping Providence win the 1879 championship. In five seasons—all as a regular—he fielded .828, well above the league average of .819. In 1878 he fielded a league-leading .925 while also having the highest range factors. However, he was only a .237 hitter over his career, topping out at .266 in inflated 1877. In 1874 he was one of nine future major leaguers, including Brown Stockings teammates George Bradley, Joe Battin, and Reddy Miller, who played on the Easton team. Born in Philadelphia, Hague was still

Bill Hague (courtesy T. Scott Brandon).

playing well for Quaker City in 1885. He reportedly was a good umpire and was recommended for league work. In 1887 *Sporting Life* announced that Hague was living quietly in Philadelphia, looking for a managerial position. He died of uremia in Philadelphia on November 21, 1898, at age 49. His death certificate lists him as a ball player. *(Baseball-Reference.com; Sporting Life; Return of Death in the Philadelphia Almshouse and Hospital)*

George Hall hit .322 in seven major league seasons, all as a regular outfielder. In 1876 he hit .366 and led the National League in homers. The English-born Hall began with Brooklyn Enterprise in 1866 when he was 17 years old. Prior to the opening of the league, he also played for Excelsior, Star, and Atlantic in Brooklyn. One of the "revolver" players, he was with Olympic (1871), Lord Baltimore (1872–73), the Red Stockings (1874), Athletic (1875–76) and Louisville (1877). Not only did he hit well, he also played all outfield positions with a percentage and range well above the league averages. In 1877 he led NL outfielders in fielding percentage. But also in 1877 he, along with Louisville teammates Jim Devlin and Al Nichols, received money from gamblers to throw games. On December 2, 1877, they along with Bill Craver were banned from baseball. Hall was only 28 years of age at the time. The 1880 census showed Hall living in Brooklyn, working, like his father, as a steel engraver. This is confirmed by an 1894 *Sporting Life* note that Hall was an engraver in Brooklyn. He died at Ridgeway, New Jersey, on June 11, 1923, at age 74. *(Baseball-Reference.com; Sporting Life; U.S. Federal Census; National Association of Base Ball Players, 1857–1870)*

Jim Hall (Edwin Hall) played 13 games at second base for Atlantic in 1872. *Sporting Life* said that he had also played shortstop for Atlantic in 1871 before the club entered the league. Hall returned to Atlantic to play two games in 1874 and concluded his tenure in the majors by playing for Keokuk in a game in St. Louis in 1875. He hit well—a .316 average in 1872—but had difficulty in the field, committing 24 errors in 15 games as a second baseman. Hall died of consumption in Brooklyn on December 21, 1885. *Sporting Life* says he was a younger brother of George Hall, but George Hall did not have a younger brother named James. Recent research from the SABR Biographical Research Committee discovered that Hall's first name was actually Edwin. *(Baseball-Reference.com; Sporting Life; DeadballEra.com; SABR Biographical Research Committee Newsletter)*

Jimmy Hallinan, a left-handed middle infielder, joined Fort Wayne from the amateur Chicago Aetna club on July 26, 1871. He was a replacement player for Frank Sellman, who had been dismissed from the team. After playing five games for Kekionga, Hallinan returned to Aetna and played until 1875, when he joined Keokuk. When Keokuk

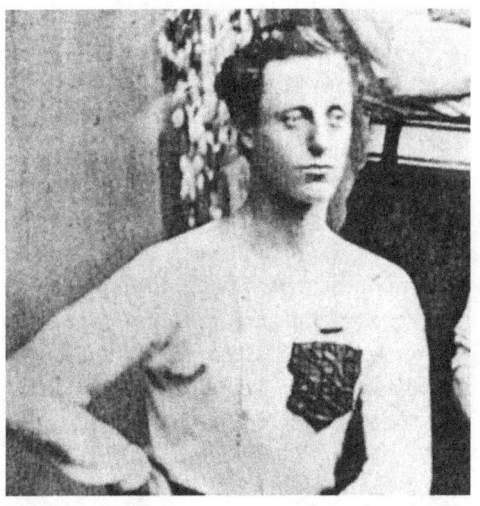

George Hall, from 1872 Lord Baltimore team photograph (*The Home Team* by James H. Bready).

disbanded, Hallinan moved on to Mutual, with whom he entered the National League in 1876. He also played with Cincinnati and Chicago, before finishing with Indianapolis in 1878. Overall, he hit .287 with a high of .321 in 1877. However, he was a very mediocre fielder. He led NL shortstops in errors in 1876, and in 111 career games at the position he fielded .744, more than 110 points below the league average. Born in Ireland in 1849, he is listed as a Chicago resident and a stone cutter in the 1870 census. He became ill during the 1878 season and died in Chicago of inflammation of the bowels on October 28, 1879. He was only 30 years of age. *(Baseball-Reference.com; New York Times; DeadballEra.com; BaseballFever.com; U.S. Federal Census)*

Ralph Ham, a 22-year-old Troy native, was the regular left fielder for Rockford in 1871, his only season in the majors. He came to Forest City from the amateur Putnam club of Troy. In 25 games, Ham hit .248 on a team that batted .264. In the field, he had a .723 percentage as an outfielder and 13 errors in seven games as a third baseman. However, Bullpen notes that the Rockford ballpark was not fielder friendly with trees in the outfield and third base atop a hill. The son of Irish immigrant parents, Ham returned to his home in Troy. He appeared in the censuses for 1850, 1860, and 1900. In the last census he was still living at home, and like his father, working as a stove moulder. City directories for Troy also show him as a moulder. Ham died at Troy on February 13, 1905, just short of his 56th birthday. *(Baseball-Reference.com; U.S. Federal Census; Troy City Directory; National Association of Base Ball Players, 1857–1870; Rockford Weekly Register-Gazette)*

Bill Harbidge (or Harbridge) played with the Expert club of Harrisburg in 1874. He began his major league career with Hartford in 1875 and moved with the club into the National League in 1876. He also played with Chicago, Troy and Philadelphia of the NL before finishing with the Cincinnati Outlaw Reds in 1884. He is supposed to be the first left-handed catcher in the NL when he caught Candy Cummings at Hartford. In a nine-year career spent mostly as a utility player, Harbidge hit .247, finishing with a .279 average as a regular with Cincinnati. Career statistics show that he was a slightly better-than-average outfielder and a slightly below-average catcher. Earliest census reports show that his name was Harbidge, later reported as "Harbridge." Born in Philadelphia to English parents, he remained a resident of that city, where he was employed as a government clerk and messenger and also worked in U.S. Customs. Harbidge died in Philadelphia on March 1, 1924, at age 68. *(U.S. Federal Census; Total Baseball; Baseball-Reference.com; Baseball Historian; Harrisburg Patriot)*

Ralph Ham from Rockford composite photograph (courtesy T. Scott Brandon).

Rit Harrison played for Elm City on May 20, 1875. In a home loss to Athletic, Harrison was a terror at the plate, going two-for-four with a double and a run batted in. However, he was woeful in the field. Starting at catcher, he had two errors in three chances and allowed two passed balls. Shifted to shortstop, he had one error in two fielding chances. Born in Haverstraw, New York, to an English mother and a painter from Connecticut, Harrison was listed as a painter's apprentice in the 1870 census. In 1880 he was living in Waterbury, Connecticut, and working as a brass turner. He died at Bridgeport, Connecticut, on November 7, 1888, at age 39. *(Baseball-Reference.com; U.S. Federal Census; Major League Baseball in Gilded Age Connecticut)*

Scott Hastings was a Rockford veteran by the time the NA opened, having played with Forest City as early as 1869. In that year he led all amateur players in runs, hits and scoring average. After debuting in the league with Rockford in 1871, he went on to play with Cleveland, Lord Baltimore, Hartford and Chicago of the National Association and with Louisville and Cincinnati of the National League. A regular for his first six seasons, he twice hit above .300, with a high of .362 in 1872. In 294 career games, he batted .279. Hastings was an average fielder as a catcher (177 games) and as an outfielder (144 games). Born in Hillsboro, Ohio, to a "wagon maker," Hastings was listed as a hotel clerk in the 1870 census for Rockford and as a laborer in a powder mill at Santa Cruz, California, in the 1900 census. Having volunteered for military service with the 145th Illinois Infantry in 1864 (and discharged for varicose veins), Hastings went into the Soldiers' Home at Sawtelle, California, in 1905, dying of stomach cancer in August 14, 1907. He was 60 years old. *(Baseball-Reference.com; U.S. Federal Census; Sporting Life; Civil War Veterans Who Played Major League Baseball Research Project; National Association of Base Ball Players, 1857–1870)*

John Hatfield threw a baseball 400 feet and seven inches in an exhibition in 1868, an unofficial record that stood for a quarter century. He began in organized ball in New York with Active and Gotham in 1865 and was with Active and Mutual in 1866 and Mutual in 1867. After playing with Cincinnati in 1868, he spent the remainder of his playing career with Mutual. He was a regular in the NA through 1874 and finished with one game in the National League in 1876. Whether he played outfield (74 games), second base (75 games) or third base (54 games), he performed well above the league average. A .280 career hitter, he reached .323 in 1872 and .302 in 1873. The 1850 census showed him living in Hoboken, New Jersey, the son of a merchant. In 1904 *Sporting Life* described him as a "prosperous bookmaker," married to a stage performer whom he was suing for divorce. His obituary says that he made a fortune easily and lost it easily, but his "striking personality" led to his success "as a seller of pools." Hatfield died in Long Island City on February 20, 1909, at age 61. *(Baseball-Reference.com; U.S. Federal Census;*

Scott Hastings (Wikimedia Commons).

Sporting Life; National Association of Base Ball Players, 1857–1870; Rockford Daily Register Gazette)

Charlie Hautz joined his hometown St. Louis Red Stockings in 1875. The 23-year-old first baseman hit .301 in 19 games before the club disbanded. In 1876 Hautz joined former St. Louis teammates Joe Blong, Trick McSorley, and Silver Flint at Indianapolis, helping the team win the League Alliance in 1877. After umpiring in the National League in 1876, 1879 and 1882, he returned to the majors as a player with the American Association Pittsburgh Alleghenys for seven games in 1884. In 26 major league games, he hit .280. Hautz was born in St. Louis to German immigrant parents. In the 1870 census he is listed as a nail cutter and in 1880 as a laborer. The *St. Louis City Directory* for 1899–1900 shows him to be a bartender. Writing in 1910, Alfred H. Spink says that Hautz was managing the Golden Lion in St. Louis. The 1920 census showed the 67-year-old Hautz to be retired and living with his brother-in-law. Hautz died in St. Louis on January 24, 1929, at age 76. *(Total Baseball; Baseball-Almanac; Baseball-Fever.com; DeadballEra.com; U.S. Federal Census; National Game; St. Louis City Directory)*

Frank Heifer joined the Boston Red Stockings in June of 1875 and played through September. In 11 games, primarily as a first baseman, the 22-year-old Heifer hit .280 with three triples. However, his .885 fielding percentage was 54 points below the league average for first basemen. His obituary in *Sporting Life* says that he played for and managed the Reading Actives in his hometown and that he also played for Providence and Oswego. He appears in the lineup for the Syracuse Stars in 1878. The son of a widow, Heifer held a factory job at age 16. The 1880 census and Reading city directory of 1889 show him as a moulder. His final appearance in the city directory of 1893 listed him as a contractor. Heifer died of typhoid in Reading on August 29, 1893, at age 39. *(Baseball-Reference.com; U.S. Federal Census; Sporting Life; Reading City Directory)*

Hellings, a Philadelphia amateur, played second base for Atlantic on July 19, 1875, in a game at Philadelphia. He, along with Washington Fulmer, Doc Bushong and Harry Arundel, were picked up by the short-handed Atlantic for the game. In a 23–3 loss to Athletic, Hellings went one-for-four at the plate and handled six of eight fielding chances. *(Baseball-Reference.com; SABR Baseball Encyclopedia; Philadelphia Enquirer)*

George Heubel played Organized Baseball in Philadelphia as early as 1866, toiling with National, Geary, and Athletic. With the opening of league play in 1871, he returned to Athletic from Cleveland. Appearing in 17 games as an outfield regular, he hit .307. Heubel finished his major league career with

George Heubel, from Cleveland team photograph (courtesy T. Scott Brandon).

Olympic (five games in 1872) and the New York Mutuals in the National League (one game in 1876). Overall, he hit .255 in 23 games. In 21 games as an outfielder, he had a .767 fielding percentage, 75 points below the league average. *Sporting Life* notes that Heubel was appointed a state umpire in 1887. In 1893 he reorganized the Philadelphia Athletics to serve as a developmental club. He served as superintendent of the Philadelphia Ball Park but was relieved of this position after an 1894 fire. Upon his death, *Sporting Life* referred to him as an "ex-groundskeeper." While his death certificate lists him as being born in Paterson, New Jersey, it is likely that he is the George Heubel who appears in the 1870 census for Philadelphia, born in Prussia, working as a garment cutter. The same person is listed in the 1887 and 1891 Philadelphia city directories, first as a clerk and then as a superintendent. Heubel died in Philadelphia on January 22, 1896, the result of injuries from a fall. He was 46 years of age. *(Baseball-Reference.com; SABR Baseball Encyclopedia; U.S. Federal Census; Gopsill's Philadelphia City Directory; Complete New York Clipper Baseball Biographies; Sporting Life; Return of Death for the City of Philadelphia)*

Nat Hicks (Wikimedia Commons).

Nat Hicks began with Eagle in 1866 and remained with that amateur Brooklyn club through 1869, also catching for the Harmonic and Star clubs. He caught professionally with National in 1870; the census shows that, like many National players, he had a position with the U.S. Treasury Department. He first played in the NA in 1872 with Mutual, catching Candy Cummings. Over the next four seasons he caught Bobby Mathews with Mutual and Cummings with Philadelphia. Hicks hit .307 in 1872 but settled for a .264 career mark over six seasons. He finished in 1877 by catching eight games for Cincinnati of the National League when he was 32 years old. In 252 career games behind the plate, he had an .812 fielding percentage, average for the time. He managed Mutual to a 30–38 record in 1875. He is credited with being the first catcher "to catch close up behind the bat." After leaving the playing ranks, he sang professionally and operated a billiard room in Naegell's Hotel in Hoboken, New Jersey. Hicks died at his room in the hotel on April 21, 1907, his death the result of "accidental asphyxiation from illuminating gas." *(Baseball-Reference.com; Complete New York Clipper Baseball Biographies; Baseball Necrology; U.S. Federal Census; Sporting Life; Baseball-Reference.com; Jersey Journal)*

Higby played right field for Atlantic on September 18, 1872. In the 13–4 home loss to Athletic, Higby went hitless in four at-bats and committed an error in three fielding chances. He does not appear on any of the rosters in *National Association of Base Ball Players, 1857–1870*. There were two men named Higby who played for the Burnside club of South Brooklyn in 1871 during games against Atlantic; "Higby" played left field and "R. Higby" played third base. The 1872 Atlantic is likely one of these. *(Baseball-Reference.com; National Association of Baseball Players, 1857–1870; New York Times)*

Dick Higham, an English-born outfielder, hit .307 in a career that covered five seasons in the NA and three in the National League. He began with Empire in 1869 and split 1870 between Union of Morrisania and Mutual. Still only 19 years old when the league opened, Higham hit .362 with Mutual in 1871, one of four seasons over .300. He led the NL in doubles while playing for Hartford in 1876 and in runs and doubles while playing for Providence in 1878. In a winding career, Higham played with Lord Baltimore in 1872, with Mutual in 1873–74 and part of 1875, with the White Stockings for part of 1875, Hartford in 1876, Providence in 1878, and Troy in 1880. In addition, he played in the minors for Syracuse in 1877 and Albany in 1879. A mediocre outfielder (66 points under the league average), he was a better-than-average catcher. After leaving the playing ranks at age 26, Higham served as an NL umpire in 1881 and 1882. Upon materials presented by the Detroit club, Higham was fired as a league umpire on June 22, 1882, for alleged collusion with gamblers. Two days later he became the only umpire ever banned from baseball. Larry R. Gerlach and Harold V. Higham argue that both the league procedure and the evidence against Higham are open to question today. His family tree lists him as a bookkeeper, though the 1900 census showed him as a bartender in Chicago. Higham died in Chicago on March 18, 1905, at age 54. *(Baseball-Reference.com; U.S. Federal Census; National Association of Base Ball Players, 1857–1870; Sporting Life; "Dick Higham—An Ump at the Bar of History")*

Dick Higham, from 1872 Lord Baltimore team photograph (*The Home Team* by James H. Bready).

Paul Hines, "the king of out-fielders," began his career as a twenty-year-old with National in 1872. He also played with the Washington Blue Legs and Chicago White Stockings, moving into the National League with the latter club in 1876. He helped them win the inaugural championship by hitting .331 with 21 doubles and leading the NL in fielding. Shifting to Providence in 1878, Hines hit .358, led the NL in homers, RBIs, and slugging, and was credited with an unassisted triple play. The following season he led the NL with 146 hits. For the 1884 NL champion Providence team that won the first World Series over the New York Mets, Hines had a league-leading 36 doubles. Before finishing in 1891 at age 39, Hines played with Washington, Indianapolis, Pittsburgh and Boston of the National League and Washington of the American Association. In addition to four seasons in the National Association, he played 16 seasons in the ma-

Paul Hines, from *Washington Base Ball Club* (LC-DIG-ppmsca-19675 Library of Congress Prints and Photographs Division).

jors, hitting .302. Both his fielding percentage and range were well above the league averages. His accomplishments are more remarkable because he was one of the first major league players to suffer from "a dramatic hearing loss." Born in the District of Columbia to Irish parents, Hines invested in Washington real estate, and after leaving baseball, he received a government position in the post office of the Department of Agriculture. Blind and deaf, he died at a nursing home at Hyattsville, Maryland, on July 10, 1935, at age 93. (*Boston Globe; Washington Post; Total Baseball; Baseball-Reference.com; U.S. Federal Census; Baseballhistoryblog.com*)

Charlie Hodes, a New York City product, went west to join the White Stockings in 1870. He started in Organized Baseball with Eckford in 1868–69. In the inaugural NA

Charlie Hodes (Wikimedia Commons).

season he served as the regular catcher for Chicago, hitting a career-high .277. Returning to the East, Hodes played thirteen games for Troy in 1872; he played 22 games with Atlantic in 1874 but became too ill to play at a professional level and finished his career with the Reliance amateurs. In 62 major league games, Hodes hit .231. In 26 games as a catcher, he fielded .781, more than 70 points below the league average. In 26 games in the outfield he posted average figures. Baseball-Fever.com notes that Hodes was one of a group of players known to have drinking problems. A benefit game was played for him in November of 1874. On February 14, 1875, Hodes died in Brooklyn. He was only 27 years old. (*Baseball-Reference.com; Baseball-Fever.com; New York Herald*)

James "Long Jim" Holdsworth played four seasons in the National Association before participating in the inaugural National League season in 1876. The 21-year-old Holdsworth played shortstop for Forest City of Cleveland and Eckford in 1872 and for Mutual in 1873. Shifted to third base, he played for Philadelphia in 1874 before returning to Mutual as an outfielder in 1875. In four seasons in the NA, Holdsworth hit .312, winning the Silver Slugger award when he hit .340 in 1874. He enjoyed two more seasons as a regular in the NL with the Mutuals (1876) and Hartford (1877). In 1882 Holdsworth played in one game for the Troy Trojans, and in 1884 he played in five games for Indianapolis of the American Association. In 1886 *Sporting Life* noted that Holdsworth had played for the Rochesters and was a candidate for State League umpire. Born in New York City with an English father, Holdsworth died there on March 22, 1918, at age 67. He appeared in the 1900 and 1910 censuses as a retired New York City resident. (*Baseball-Reference.com; Total Baseball; Retrosheet; U.S. Federal Census; Sporting Life*)

John "Holly" Hollingshead was a 19-year-old second baseman on the winless National club in 1872. His .318 batting average led the team. A year later he played center field for the Blue Legs, hitting .257. In 1875 he hit .247 for Washington, one of only two players to bat over .200. Still only 22 years old, he managed the team to a 4–16 record over the final 20 games. In 1884 he managed the American Association Washington team to a 12–50 record. Hollingshead had begun as early as 1868, playing with the Junior Nationals; in 1870 he played for both Olympic and National. Born in the District of Columbia, Hollingshead is listed in censuses through 1920 as a government clerk or accountant in the Treasury Department, apparently one of the perks for playing baseball in Washington. In 1887 the *Cleveland Plain Dealer* reported that Hollingshead—specifically identified as the ball player—had absconded with more than $1,000 from the Washington gas company, for which he worked as a clerk. He died in D.C. on October 6, 1926, at age 73. (*U.S. Federal Census; Baseball-Reference.com; National Association of Base Ball Players, 1857–1870; Sporting Life; Cleveland Plain Dealer*)

Mike Hooper played with the amateur Maryland club as early as 1868. In 1870 that club included Bobby Mathews and others who migrated to Kekionga in 1871. In 1873, when Maryland made a brief try at NA competition, Hooper played in three games, hitting .214 and committing only one error in six chances in left field. In that same season the *Baltimore Sun* called him the best umpire to work a game in Baltimore. He returned to the majors as a Union Association umpire in 1884. Michael H. Hooper appeared in Baltimore censuses from 1860 through 1910. A Michael Hooper, who, according to Brian McKenna, may have been the ball player's father or uncle, was general manager of the Maryland club in 1862. Different census years list the ball player as a car driver, a storekeeper and a clerk. The Baltimore city directory for 1879 lists him as a driver. Hooper died in Baltimore on December 2, 1917. (*Baseball-Reference.com; U.S. Federal Census; Woods' Baltimore City Directory; National Association of Base Ball Players, 1857–1870; DeadballEra.com; Early Baltimore Baseball; Baltimore Sun*)

Dick Hunt hit a robust .326 in 11 games for Eckford between May 7 and July 9, 1872. Less impressive on defense, he had ten errors, five each in right field and second base. Hunt had begun in Organized Baseball with Mutual in 1866, joining his brother, Charles. Both played in a game against Cincinnati on June 15, 1869, in which Mutual held the Red Stockings to a season-low of four runs. The Hunts shifted to Star in 1869 and Eckford in 1870–71. Born in New York City in 1845, Hunt and his brother both appeared in the censuses of 1850 and 1860, the sons of a butcher. In 1888 Henry Chadwick wrote that "the Hunt brothers are butchers in Fulton Market." The Richard M. Hunt who enlisted in the Forty-eighth New York Infantry in 1861 seems too old to be the ball player. The ball player died in New York City on November 20, 1895, at age 48. *(Baseball-Reference.com; U.S. Federal Census; U.S. Civil War Records and Profiles; National Association of Base Ball Players, 1857–1870; Old Battles on the Baseball Field)*

William H. "Dick" Hurley played right field in two games for Olympic in 1872, going hitless in seven at-bats and committing an error on one of three fielding chances. He had begun in Organized Baseball with Buckeye of Cincinnati in 1868 and was selected to play for the Red Stockings in 1869 but apparently did not play; instead, he played for Olympic, with whom he also played in 1870. Born in Honesdale, Pennsylvania, Hurley was the son of a blacksmith. He served in the Union Army from January 1864 to July 1865 and is listed as a blacksmith in his military record. Hurley appeared in the 1870 census for Philadelphia as a "horseshoer," in the 1880 census for Orbisonia, Pennsylvania, as a brick mason, and in the 1900 census for Harrisburg, Pennsylvania, as a stone mason. In 1905 he was admitted to the U.S. National Home for Disabled Volunteer Soldiers and was dismissed in 1909. The 72-year-old Hurley appeared in the 1920 census for Hummelstown, Pennsylvania. He is not included in the SABR list of Civil War veterans who played major league baseball. Peter Morris believes that the ball player was actually a Pennsylvanian named William F. Hurley, who dropped from sight after 1884. *(Baseball-Reference.com; U.S. Federal Census; U.S. National Home for Disabled Volunteers, 1868–1938; National Association of Base Ball Players, 1857–1870; Civil War Veterans Who Played Major League Baseball Research Project; petermorrisbooks.com)*

Sam Jackson, an English-born second baseman, played in 16 games for the Boston Red Stockings in 1871, coming from the Flour City club of Rochester, New York. Jackson got a chance to play at the beginning of the season when George Wright suffered a broken leg and Ross Barnes moved over to shortstop. An adequate fielder, Jackson carried a very light bat, averaging only .224. He

Sam Jackson (Wikimedia Commons).

had earlier played amateur ball with the Alert club of Rochester. In 1872 he played in four games for Brooklyn Atlantic but hit only .167. He may also be the Jackson who played shortstop for Canadian champion Maple Leaf of Guelph, Ontario, in 1872. Living his adult life in Manchester, New York, Jackson is listed as a miller in the 1910 and 1920 censuses. He died on August 4, 1930, in Clifton Springs, New York at age 81. *(Baseball-Reference.com; U.S. Federal Census; Cincinnati Times-Star; Philadelphia Enquirer)*

Nat Jewett caught two games for Eckford on July 4 and 6, 1872. He had one hit in eight at-bats and had three errors and nine passed balls in the field. Jewett had served in the Seventy-first Pennsylvania Infantry during the Civil War. In 1863 he began to appear on Organized Baseball club rosters in the metropolitan New York area—Henry Eckford (1863), Empire (1864–65), Mutual (1866–68) and Eckford (1869–70). He played on an amateur team in 1871. The censuses of 1860, 1900 and 1910 show him holding various clerical positions. In 1870 he is described as a letter carrier and in 1880 as a laborer. Jewett died in New York City on February 23, 1914, at age 69 or 71. *(Baseball-Reference.com; U.S. Federal Census; New York City Directory; Civil War Pension Index; National Association of Base Ball Players, 1857–1870; Civil War Veterans Who Played Major League Baseball Research Project)*

Tommy Johns played in one major league game on May 14, 1873. The Maryland left fielder went hitless in four at-bats and committed an error in his only fielding chance. Thomas P. Johns, who may be the ball player, is first listed in the 1870 census for Baltimore as a 19-year-old apprentice carpenter. He continued to be listed as a carpenter, builder, or contractor through the 1920 census, when he was 68 years old. Johns died in Baltimore on April 13, 1927, at age 75. *(Baseball-Reference.com; U.S. Federal Census; SABR Baseball Encyclopedia; Early Baseball in Baltimore)*

Caleb Johnson played 16 games in a utility role for the Forest City club of Cleveland in 1871. He hit only .224 and fielded .736 as a second baseman and .615 as a right fielder. He was 27 years old and apparently had not played professional baseball prior to 1871. However, his death notice claimed that he was "the oldest professional baseball player in the world." Born into a farm family in Whiteside County, Illinois, Johnson was living in Sterling, Illinois, and working as a lawyer by the time of the 1880 census. The

Caleb Johnson (*History of Whiteside County, IL*, by William W. Davis, 1908).

1900 and 1920 censuses showed the same residence and occupation. He was also involved in Democratic Party politics and held county office. Johnson died in Sterling on March 7, 1925, at age 81. *(Baseball-Reference.com; U.S. Federal Census; National Association of Base Ball Players, 1857–1870; Rockford Morning Star; Seattle Daily Times)*

Charles W. Jones (Benjamin Wesley Rippy) entered the majors with Western in 1875, also playing with Hartford after Keokuk disbanded. Born in North Carolina in 1850—the first major league player from the Tar Heel state—Jones toiled for the next three seasons for the Cincinnati Red Stockings in the National League, jumping to the White Stockings for two games in 1877. In 1879 with Boston he led the NL in runs, home runs, RBIs and fielding, one of six times he hit over .300. Blacklisted in 1880, he was forced to sit out 1881–82 and played independent ball before returning to Cincinnati. He played for the Red Stockings in the American Association from 1883 to 1887. Purchased and released by the New York

Mets in 1887, he finished his career with the Kansas City Cowboys in 1888. A career .299 hitter, he was a regular outfielder for 11 of his 12 major league seasons. In 1890 *National Police Gazette* stated that Jones had gone "into business for himself" in New York City. In 1900 the *Washington Post* noted that Jones "has a political job under the Tammany regime." Peter Morris found that Jones was "living in Staten Island in 1909 in very poor health; apparently still alive in December 1910." *(Total Baseball; Baseball-Reference.com; National Police Gazette; Washington Post; petermorrisbooks.com; U.S. Federal Census)*

Levin Jones had three hits and a run batted in as a center fielder for Maryland on May 14, 1873. In the field he handled four of five chances cleanly. A year later he played one game as a right fielder and one as a catcher for Lord Baltimore. Overall, his four hits gave him a .364 average. Levin Jones was a fairly common name around Baltimore at that time, with no fewer than four candidates born between 1849 and 1853. *(Baseball-Reference.com; U.S. Federal Census)*

Jim Keenan was barely seventeen years old when he played in five games for his hometown New Haven club in 1875. Over the next five seasons he played for Rhode Island, Auburn, Hornell and Albany of the League Alliance. He played briefly with Buffalo in 1880 and was blacklisted in 1881. Moving to the American Association, Keenan played twenty-five games for Pittsburgh in 1882 before becoming a regular with Indianapolis in 1884, leading the club with a .293 average. When Indianapolis folded at the end of the season, he signed with Detroit and then jumped to Cincinnati, where he played the remainder of his major league career, moving with the club into the National League in 1890. A .240 hitter over 11 seasons, he reached .287 in 1889. While generally sharing

Jim Keenan (Wikimedia Commons).

catching duties in Cincinnati and fielding 23 points over the league average, he also played about a fifth of his games at first base. Bill Lee says that Keenan operated a tavern in Cincinnati and once served on the city council. In the 1920 census Keenan is listed as a storekeeper. The second-generation Irishman died in Cincinnati on September 21, 1926, at age 68. *(Baseball-Reference.com; Baseball Encyclopedia; Baseball Necrology; Retrosheet; U.S. Federal Census)*

George Keerl played in six games for the Chicago White Stockings during May and June of 1875. In those games he had three singles for a .130 average. As a second baseman he fielded .815, 26 points under the league average. Born in Baltimore, Keerl was 28 years old when he played with Chicago. According to Brian McKenna, Keerl played with Maryland in 1866–69, Pastime in 1869, Chicago in 1870, and around Chicago in the early 1870s. Peter Morris says that Keerl also played with the Actives of Clinton, Iowa, in 1870. Keerl married a young woman from Michigan and appeared in the 1880, 1900, and 1910 federal censuses and the 1905 Wisconsin census as a resident of Marinette,

Wisconsin, across the border from Michigan. Each census shows him employed as a machinist except in 1900, when he is listed as a plumber. Keerl died in Menominee, Michigan, on September 9, 1923, at age 76. *(Baseball-Reference.com; U.S. Federal Census; Early Baltimore Baseball; Baseball-Fever.com)*

Bill Kelly was the regular right fielder for Kekionga in the inaugural 1871 season. Playing in 18 of 19 games, he hit .224. But he was an above-average outfielder, with a .833 fielding percentage. He is listed as possibly a New York product, but his birth date is unknown. The *Pictorial History of Fort Wayne, Indiana* lists a Kelly (no first name) as one of the disbanded Maryland players who had joined Kekionga in 1870. Kelly played in the majors only in the 1871 season, and his life beyond that is not known at this time. Kelly—with or without the second e—is a very difficult name to trace. *(Baseball-Reference.com; Pictorial History of Fort Wayne, Indiana)*

John Kenney played Organized Baseball for Atlantic as a regular outfielder in 1867. In 1868 he continued as a second baseman in 13 games, and in 1869 as a third baseman in nine games. In 1870 Kenney played outfield and third base for Union of Morrisania, getting 29 hits in 23 games. Between May 2 and May 20, 1872, Kenney played in five NA games for Atlantic. Hitless in 19 at-bats, he committed four errors in 13 chances at second and four errors in eight chances in the outfield. DeadballEra.com says that Kenney served as an NL umpire in 1877. Peter Morris points out that as John "Kenny," he appears in the 1880 Brooklyn census as a hydrant inspector. Kenney later became involved in Democrat Party politics. Morris found that Kenney had died on August 7, 1893. *(Baseball-Reference.com; National Association of Base Ball Players, 1857–1870; DeadballEra.com; petermorrisbooks.com; SABR Biographical Research Committee Newsletter; U.S. Federal Census)*

Joe Kernan played in two games for Maryland in 1873. He hit well, posting three hits, a run scored and one RBI. He played errorless ball in center field but committed three errors in his trial at second base. This is likely the same Kernan who played five games for Maryland in 1870. Listed as a Baltimore native, he was born in 1850 or 1851, the son of a "gentleman." In 1880 he boarded with a family in Baltimore while working as a collector for a book house. After marrying his landlady's daughter, he was listed as a street railroad conductor in 1900. He, his wife, and his mother-in-law were listed in the 1910 census. Peter Morris believes that Kernan died in Baltimore on February 16, 1911. *(Baseball-Reference.com; National Association of Base Ball Players, 1857–1870; U.S. Federal Census; petermorrisbooks.com)*

Henry Kessler played one game as a first baseman for Atlantic in 1873. Over the next two seasons, the Brooklyn-born Kessler caught and played outfield and third base for Atlantic. When the National League opened, he became the regular shortstop for Cincinnati, hitting .258. He finished his major league career with the Red Stockings in 1877 by catching in five games. Overall, he hit .253 in 105 games. In 64 games as a shortstop he fielded 71 points under the league average. *Sporting Life* notes that Kessler came to Franklin, Pennsylvania, in 1883 from the Colorado champion Leadville Blues and that he continued playing around Franklin. He "took to drink" and ultimately served time in the penitentiary for arson. Kessler finished his life in the county poor farm at Franklin, dying of heart failure on January 9, 1900. He was 53 years of age. *(Baseball-reference.com; Sporting Life; Cleveland Plain Dealer)*

Gene Kimball hit .191 in 29 games for Cleveland Forest City in 1871. He committed 29 errors in 17 games at second base and fared little better defensively in the outfield, at shortstop and at third base. As the second batter in the first major league game ever played, he hit a line drive to the second baseman, doubling up Deacon White, so is cred-

Gene Kimball, from Cleveland team photograph (courtesy T. Scott Brandon).

ited with hitting into the first double play. A native of Rochester, New York, Kimball played for his hometown Alert in 1869 and for Forest City in 1870. The 1880 Rochester city directory listed him as a resident, operating Kimball & Bronson Billiard Parlor. His obituary in the *New York Herald* identifies him as "the billiards player" and notes that he had been a professional billiards player for 18 years. On August 2, 1882, the 31-year-old Kimball died in Rochester of congestion of the lungs. *(Baseball-Reference.com; Rochester City Directory; National Association of Base Ball Players, 1857–1870; New York Herald)*

Marshall "Mart" King and his older brother, Steve, played with Union of Lansingburgh as early as 1867. In 1870 he, along with Bub McAtee and Clipper Flynn, came west to play for the new Chicago team. Re-

Mart King, from Chicago composite photograph (courtesy Robert Edward Auctions).

maining with the NA White Stockings in 1871, he filled in at five positions, hitting .208 in 20 games. In 1872 he returned to Troy, going hitless in two games, giving him a .188 average in 22 major league games. Fourteen of his games were as an outfielder and nine as a catcher; in neither position was his fielding up to the league average. One of nine children of a farm family, King is listed in the 1880 census as still living at home and working on the farm. The 1893 directory for Troy and Lansingburgh lists Marshall N. King as a laborer. The 62-year-old King died in Troy on October 19. 1911. *(Baseball-Reference.com; U.S. Federal Census; National Association of Base Ball Players, 1857–1870; Sporting Life; City Directory for Troy and Lansingburgh)*

Steve King played for his hometown club Union of Lansingburgh from 1867 until the club folded in 1872. In 1871 he hit a robust .396, fourth-best in the NA. He finished fifth in hits and total bases. On the negative side, his 15 errors led NA outfielders. In 1872 his average fell to .305, giving him a career figure of .353. His .807 fielding percentage was less than the league average, and his range figures were much lower. When Troy

Steve King (Wikimedia Commons).

disbanded, King left the majors. He is listed in the 1870 census as a ball player. In 1880 he is listed—like his brother, Mart—as a farm laborer, living at home. Like his brother he is in the 1893 Troy and Lansingburgh directory as a laborer. Steve King died on July 8, 1895, at age 53. *(Baseball-Reference.com; National Association of Base Ball Players, 1857–1870; U.S. Federal Census; City Directory for Troy and Lansingburgh)*

George Knight, a 19-year-old Yale student, pitched for New Haven on September 28, 1875. In a complete-game 8–6 victory over Mutual, Knight gave up 12 hits and six runs, including three earned. The son of a physician from Lakeville, Connecticut, Knight went on to receive his medical degree from New York University Medical College. He was superintendent of the Minnesota Institute for Deaf, Dumb and Blind at Fairbault before returning to Lakeville. In 1885 he was appointed superintendent of the Connecticut School for Imbeciles at Lakeville, a position he held until his death. Involved in Republican politics, he represented Salisbury in the Connecticut assemble for the last

George Knight (*Taylor's Legislative History and Souvenir of Connecticut, 190–*).

six years of his life. He was presiding at a Republican political rally in his hometown on October 4, 1916, when he fell dead on the stage. He was 56 years of age. *(Baseball-Reference.com; U.S. Federal Census; SABR Baseball Encyclopedia; Springfield Republican)*

Lon Knight (Alonzo Letti) played with Athletic in three leagues. He began with Athletic in 1875, continuing with the club into the National League in 1876. In 1880 he returned to the majors with Worcester before moving on to Detroit (1881–82). In 1883 he shifted to the American Association version of the Athletics before finishing with the Providence Grays in 1885. Primarily a pitcher early in his career, Knight made 32 starts with a 10–22 record and a 2.62 ERA in 1876; he was 16–28 with a 2.77 ERA for his career. As an outfield regular for four seasons, he hit .245, reaching .271 in both 1881 and 1884. His .887 fielding average was almost thirty points higher than the league average for outfielders. Knight managed the

Lon Knight (courtesy Nigel Ayres).

A's in both 1883 and 1884. After leaving the playing ranks, he umpired in all three major leagues through 1890. He "might have been one of the first Italian ball players in professional baseball." Knight had changed his name while attending Girard College, where he was trained as an accountant. His baseball career behind him, Knight worked for the city of Philadelphia as a highway inspector. On April 23, 1932, he died in Philadelphia of gas poisoning, the result of a gas line rupture. He was 78 years old. *(SABR BioProject; Total Baseball; Baseball Necrology; Baseball-Reference.com; U.S. Federal Census)*

Jake Knowdell, a Brooklyn product, caught for Atlantic in both 1874 and 1875 and for the National League Milwaukee Grays in 1878. In 71 games he hit .179 and fielded below the league average for a catcher. Knowdell played for the Tecumsehs of London, Ontario, in the first minor league world series in 1877. He also played with the semi-pro Colorado champion Leadville Blues in 1882. Newspapers reported that he played for Bay City in 1883 and for Harrisburg in 1884. Peter Morris and Alan Schwarz write that Knowdell was one of the catchers who suffered "precipitous emotional declines that began during or soon after their playing careers." In 1887 *Sporting Life* showed that Knowdell had been arraigned in Brooklyn for grand theft of his brother-in-law's wallet containing $188. Born in 1840, Knowdell is one of Morris' "Colder Cases." The variant spellings of his family name (Knodel, Nodel) make research difficult. Ancestry.com reports a death date of January 1, 1900. *(Baseball-Reference.com; Sporting Life; Petermorrisbooks.com; Harrisburg Patriot; New York Herald)*

Henry Kohler played his first game for Kekionga on July 12, 1871. The 19-year-old Baltimore native played in three games that season, hitting .167, before returning to his hometown. In 1873 he played in all six games of the Maryland club before it disbanded; he finished with two games for Lord Baltimore in 1874. Overall, he hit .122 in 11 games. Used primarily as a third baseman, he fielded .700, 45 points under the league average. Kohler appeared in the 1890 Baltimore city directory as a painter; the *U.S. Federal Census* later showed him as operator of a produce store and a dealer of produce. Kohler died in Baltimore on August 27, 1934, at age 82. *(Baseball-Reference.com; Baltimore City Directory; U.S. Federal Census)*

George "Juice" Latham began in 1875 with the Red Stockings and Elm City. Two years later he became the regular first baseman for the National League Louisville Grays, hitting .291. When the Philadelphia Athletics entered the American Association in 1882, he was a playing manager, hitting .285 and leading first basemen in fielding. Latham finished his major league career with the Louisville Eclipse in 1883–84 with a batting average of .248 for five seasons. His fielding percentage and range as a first baseman exceeded the league average. A notorious umpire baiter—described as "carrying his mouth around with him"—Latham twice served as a minor league umpire, in the American Association in 1880 and the Central League in 1888. He played with his hometown Utica team after leaving the majors and was last seen on the diamond playing for Richfield when he was well past forty years of age. In 1893 *Sporting Life* described him as having "gone into street car service." According to the 1900 census, Latham was a resident of Utica, working as a motorman for the railroad. He died at Utica on May 26, 1914, at age 61. His nickname apparently came from his high energy. *(National Police Gazette; New York Times; Chicago Daily Tribune; Baseball-Reference-com; U.S. Federal Census; Sporting Life; SABR BioProject)*

Ben Laughlin played second base for Elizabeth in 1872. In 12 games, he had 12 hits for a .235 batting average. In the field he committed 32 errors for only a .698 percentage, more than one hundred points below the league average. Laughlin does not appear on any roster in the *National Association of Base Ball Players, 1857–1870*. However, he played for the next two seasons in New York City for the amateur Flyaway club, and is twice singled out by the *New York Herald* for excellent play. Laughlin later played for the Chelsea club of Brooklyn in 1877, for another edition of Resolute in 1878, and for Newark as late as 1884. There are Benjamin Laughlins of the right age living in Beaver County, Pennsylvania, and in Albany, New York. *(Baseball-Reference.com; National Association of Base Ball Players, 1857–1870; U.S. Federal Census; Elizabeth City Directory; New York Herald)*

Michael Ledwith caught a game for Atlantic on August 19, 1874. In a 14–6 loss to the Pearls in Philadelphia, he had a hit, scored a run and drove in one in four at-bats. In the field he had two errors in five chances. For 1874 and 1875 Ledwith was the regular catcher for the Keystone club of New York City. In 1874 he was catcher on the picked New York nine for the annual game with a picked Brooklyn nine. That year he was the subject of a protest filed against the Lynn Live Oaks for paying him to catch a game against the Beacons while playing under the name of "Connerly." There are two Michael Ledwiths of the right age in New York City, both sons of Irish immigrants. In 2009 the SABR Biographical Research Committee made Ledwith the mystery of the month. The Michael Ledwith previously believed to be the ball player did not live in the United States in 1874. To complicate identification, the committee suggested that there is no proof that the player's first name was Michael. *(Baseball-Reference.com; SABR Biographical Research Committee Newsletter; U.S. Federal Census; New York Herald)*

Bill Lennon was Bobby Mathews' catcher for the amateur Maryland club before both joined Kekionga. Earlier he had played for Excelsior of Brooklyn. Lennon played in and managed Kekionga's first 12 games of the 1871 season. In those 12 games he hit .229 and managed the team to a 5–9 record. On July 25 he and teammate Frank Sellman were dismissed from Kekionga for desertion, insubordination and public drunkenness. In the following season he played for winless National before that club disbanded. In 1873 he played for winless Maryland before that club disbanded after six games. Overall, Lennon hit .215 in 28 games. In 24 games as a catcher, he fielded .817, more than 30 points below the league average. Born in Brooklyn to Irish parents, Lennon is listed in the 1880 census for Baltimore as a city clerk and in the 1900 census for New York City also as a city clerk. He died in Philadelphia of hemiplehia on August 19, 1910, at age 65. His death certificate lists his occupation as watchman. *(Baseball-Reference.com; U.S. Federal Census; SABR BioProject; National Association of Base Ball Players, 1857–1870; Cincinnati Commercial Tribune; Pennsylvania Certificate of Death)*

Andy Leonard played left field on the undefeated 1869 Red Stockings team. When the NA formed, he played second base for Olympic, hitting .291. He then rejoined the Red Stockings in Boston, playing for both the NA team (1872–75) and the National League club (1876–78), before finishing as a part-time player with Cincinnati in 1880. A career .299 hitter, he batted higher than

Andy Leonard, from "First Nine of the Cincinnati (Red Stockings) Baseball Club" (LC-USZC4-1291 Library of Congress Prints and Photographs Division).

.300 four times, with a high of .349 in 1872. In Boston he became primarily a left fielder (350 games), with 78 games at second base and 61 at shortstop. Overall, his fielding statistics are average for the league. Born in County Cavan, Ireland, Leonard immigrated at age two. He played amateur ball with Hudson River, Irvington and Buckeye of Cincinnati before joining the Red Stock-

ings. He lived his adult life in Boston, where he was listed as a "bass ballist" in the 1880 census and as a clerk in a sporting goods store in 1900—a store owned by former teammate George Wright. He died of stomach trouble in Boston on August 21, 1903. *(Baseball-Reference.com; Complete New York Clipper Baseball Biographies; Boston Journal)*

David Lenz caught four games for Eckford in May of 1872. The Prussian-born Lenz had one hit for a .083 average. Also, his .733 fielding average was more than 130 points under the league average. In September of that year he applied for naturalization status with no occupation listed. In baseball records his name was originally given as "Leutz" without a first name. The 1880 census shows David Lenz living in Brooklyn, driving an ice wagon. He died in Brooklyn of phthisis pulmonalis on May 21, 1886, at age 35. *(Baseball-Reference.com; U.S. Federal Census; Index to Petitions for Naturalization Filed in New York City, 1792–1989)*

Len Lovett pitched a game for Resolute on August 4, 1873, at Atlantic. Tagged for 22 hits and 16 runs (seven earned), he took the loss that day. In 1875 he played six games as an outfielder for Centennial, hitting .238 and fielding .700. In both 1875 and 1876 he pitched for the Reading Actives. He possibly is also the Lovett who pitched six games for Olympic of Philadelphia in 1869. The son of a farmer from Lancaster County, Pennsylvania, Lovett appeared in the 1870 census as an 18-year-old dentist when the family moved to Philadelphia. He lived most of his adult life in Newark, Delaware, appearing in the 1900 census as a furniture dealer and in the 1910 and 1920 censuses as a justice of the peace. Lovett died at Newark on November 18, 1922, at age 71. His death notice says that he had been a magistrate for 15 years. *(Baseball-Reference.com; National Association of Base Ball Players, 1857–1870; U.S.*

Federal Census; Springfield Republican; Harrisburg Patriot)

Charlie Lowe played second base for Atlantic for seven games in late September and October of 1872. He made five hits for a .161 average but fielded .828, above the league average. Sources say that he may have been born in Baltimore. A Charles Lowe, born in Baltimore in 1847, appears in the 1870 census for Baltimore working as a "marker in Custom House." The only Lowe in the rosters of the *National Association of Base Ball Player, 1857–1870* is from Ohio. However, Peter Morris believes that Lowe was a Brooklyn player and that his first name may have been Thomas. *(Baseball-Reference.com; U.S. Federal Census; National Association of Base Ball Players, 1857–1870; SABR Baseball Encyclopedia)*

John Lowry played in six games for Washington between June 26 and July 4, 1875. He managed three hits for a .136 average. As a center fielder he had three errors in 11 chances for a .727 percentage. Earlier sources listed him as a Baltimore native. However, Peter Morris says that the player was actually named John Lawrie, that he was from Washington, D.C., and that he died in 1879. That John W. Lawrie was born in Washington, D.C., to an English father, a stone cutter. The 1870 census lists the 22-year-old Lawrie as a dealer in wood and coal. *(Baseball-Reference.com; Total Baseball; U.S. Federal Census; U.S. National Homes for Disabled Volunteer Soldiers, 1866–1938; Petermorrisbooks.com)*

Henry Luff played for six teams in four leagues in a major league career covering ten years. He began in the National Association with New Haven in 1875, hitting .271 in 38 games. After a three-game career with Detroit in the National League in 1883, he played for Cincinnati and Louisville of the American Association. In 1884, he hit .270 in 26 games for the Philadelphia Keystones of the Union Association before finishing with the Kansas City team of the same league. Overall, he hit .232 in 68 games. In the field he played every position except catcher at some point in his career, but at no position did his fielding statistics approach the league average. On the mound, Luff started seven games at New Haven, completing five, but ended with a 1–6 record. The *Philadelphia Inquirer* describes him as a rarity, a college graduate who played for the love of the game. Between major league stints, he played for Rochester and Pittsburgh of the International Alliance and for the Athletics and Atlantics of the Eastern Championship League. He may have played with the Expert club of Philadelphia as early as 1870. After leaving the majors, Luff was on the 1885 Albany roster. He is listed in the 1880 census and also in the 1890 Philadelphia city directory as a civil engineer. The 1870 and 1910 censuses show him as a clerk. Luff died in Philadelphia on October 11, 1916, at age 60. *(Total Baseball; Baseball-Reference.com; U.S. Federal Census; Philadelphia City Directory; Sporting Life; Philadelphia Inquirer)*

Denny Mack (Dennis McGee) was the first major league player from Villanova University, where he had studied for the priesthood. The regular first baseman for Rockford in 1871, the 20-year-old Mack hit .246. For the next three seasons, he played in Philadelphia—first for Athletic and then for Philadelphia, having his two best seasons of .288 and .293. Entering the National League in 1876, he became the regular shortstop for St. Louis, also playing with Buffalo (1880) in the NL. When the American Association opened in 1882, he played for Louisville, finishing with Pittsburgh in 1883. Overall, he hit .228 in eight seasons. In 173 games as a first baseman, he fielded more than 70

Denny Mack, from 1878 Buffalo team photograph (courtesy Mearsonlineauctions.com).

Fergy Malone (Wikimedia Commons).

points under the league average. In 169 games at shortstop he fielded more than 25 points above the average. Born in Easton, Pennsylvania, Mack appeared in the 1870 census under his real name. In the 1880 census for New Orleans Mack was listed as a "Professional B.B." According to the *New York Times*, the 37-year-old Mack died of a "sudden fit" on April 10, 1888. He was managing Wilkes Barre at that time. *(Baseball-Reference.com; New York Times; U.S. Federal Census; Sporting Life)*

Fergy Malone, an Irish-born catcher, spent five seasons in the NA with Philadelphia and Chicago teams. Playing for champion Athletic, he hit .343 in the inaugural season and led NA catchers in fielding in 1872. Malone also played with Philadelphia (1873 and 1875) and the Chicago White Stockings (1874). Malone was already well traveled when the NA opened, as he had played with Athletic in 1864 and 1870, Keystone in 1865, Quaker City in 1867, and Olympic in 1868–69. The 34-year-old Malone played in only 22 games for Athletic in the first National League season before injuring his arm. Eight years later he managed the Philadelphia Keystones in the Union Association, getting a hit in the only game he played. In all, Malone hit .274; the left-handed catcher fielded .845, nineteen points higher than the league average. In the 1880 census for Philadelphia he was listed as a grocer. The 1900 census showed him working for the government in customs. Bill Lee says that Malone became a special agent for the Treasury Department, stationed at Puget Sound, Washington. Born in 1842, Malone had served in the 196th Pennsylvania Regiment during the Civil War. He died in Seattle on New Year's Day, 1905, at age 62. *(Baseball-Reference.com; U.S. Federal Census; Baseball Necrology; Civil War Veterans Who Played Major League Baseball Research Project; New York Times; Civil War Pension Index)*

Martin Malone hit .375 in five games for Eckford in 1872, driving in three runs. He also made two pitching starts, going 0–2 with a 10.50 ERA. Among right field, second base and the pitcher's box, he committed eight errors in 13 fielding chances before finishing his major league career on

September 13. Malone only recently acquired a first name. Presumably the same Malone pitched and played outfield and second base for Eckford in 1867–68 and 1870–71. That Malone also played for Oriental in 1870 and for Atlantic in 1871. In 1867 the *New York Herald* noted that he was less successful as a pitcher because of the "swift balls" he threw. The Brooklyn city directory shows both Irish-born and New York–born Martin Malones of appproximately the right age. *(Baseball-Reference.com; National Association of Base Ball Players, 1857–1870; New York Herald; Lain's Brooklyn City Directory)*

Jack Manning entered the majors with the Red Stockings in 1873 when he was nineteen years old (seventeen, he said). In 1876 he moved with Boston into the National League. In all, Manning had three seasons in the NA and nine in the NL/American Association, hitting .257. Career stops include Lord Baltimore and Hartford in the NA, Cincinnati, Boston, Buffalo and Philadelphia of the NL, and Baltimore of the AA. Career highlights include a .346 average in 1874, a .317 average in 1878, and three homers in one game in 1884. Primarily one of the "greatest right fielders that ever caught a ball," he also pitched, going 18–5 with Boston in 1876 and leading the league with five saves. In 1887, when he had finished playing in the majors, he claimed to be 33 years old, but the *National Police Gazette* doubted this figure, asserting that by his grey hair he had to be fifty. *Boston Daily Globe* identified him as "superintendent of Congress st. grounds," but Bill Lee says that Manning was a "theatrical mechanic in the performing arts business." This is confirmed by the 1910 census. In 1900 he was listed as a clerk and in 1920 as a janitor. Born in Braintree, Massachusetts, to Irish parents, Manning died in Boston on August 15, 1929, at age 75. *(Total Baseball; Boston Daily Globe; National Police Gazette; U.S. Federal Census; Baseball Necrology)*

Albert D. Martin (Albert May) played four games at second base for Eckford at the beginning of 1872, hitting .278. He also played briefly with Atlantic in both 1874 and 1875, leaving the majors with a .164 average for 17 games. He had 23 errors in ten games as a second baseman but was a better outfielder. His records prior to the formation of the league are combined with those of Alphonse Martin (see below). SABR believes that Al Martin is the second baseman who played for Union of Morrisania, beginning in 1866. The SABR Biographical Research Committee has discovered that this Al Martin worked as a proofreader for the *New York Times*. He was from New Jersey but lived in Brooklyn. He died in Brooklyn on April 1, 1926. *(Baseball-Reference.com; SABR Biographical Research Committee Newsletter; U.S. Federal Census; National Association of Base Ball Players, 1857–1870)*

Alphonse "Phonney" Martin, credited with being "the first pitcher to hurl the slow curve

Jack Manning (courtesy Nigel Ayres).

Phonney Martin (Wikimedia Commons).

ball," pitched and played the outfield for teams in the New York City area, beginning in 1864. These teams included Empire, Mutual, and Eckford. In 1872 he became a member of Troy, and when the Haymakers disbanded, he joined Eckford. In 1873 he finished his major league career with Mutual. A regular for both seasons, Martin did not enjoy significant success on the field. Hitting .303 when Troy disbanded, he ended up batting .248 for the season and .221 for his career. As a pitcher, "Old Slow Ball" went 3–10 with a 4.03 ERA. Born in New York City in 1845, Martin served in the Civil War with the Ninth Regiment of Hawkins' Zouaves and was wounded at Antietam. He appeared in the 1880, 1900 and 1930 censuses. The 1880 census listed him as a bartender; the 1889 Brooklyn city directory listed him as a clerk. Martin died at Hollis, New York, on May 24, 1933, at age 87. *(Baseball-Reference.com; New York Times; National Association of Base Ball Players, 1857–1870; Civil War Veterans Who Played Major League Baseball Research Project; U.S. Federal Census; Lain's Brooklyn City Directory)*

Charles Mason played outfield for Centennial in 1875. In 12 games he hit .234. When Centennial folded, Mason played in eight games for Washington. Eight years later he played a game with the American Association champion Athletics, a club of which he

Charlie Mason (courtesy T. Scott Brandon).

was manager and part-owner. In 21 major league games, he hit .183. In 19 games in the outfield, he committed 11 errors but had range factors 39 points above the league average. Mason was from New Orleans and, according to Bullpen, played baseball at Williams College before joining Centennial. Continuing in baseball, Mason played for an independent team in Philadelphia, for Lynn and Rochester of the International Association, for Davenport of the Northwestern League, and for Philadelphia of the Eastern Championship Association. Listed as a clerk in the 1900 census, Mason returned to baseball as an operator of an independent baseball club according to the 1910 census and the family tree posted on Ancestry.com. The 1930 census listed him as a cashier at a ball park. *Sporting News* notes that Mason was one of the founders of the American Association. He died at Philadelphia on October 21, 1936. *(Baseball-Reference.com; U.S. Federal Census; Sporting News; Charles E. Mason Family Tree; New York Times; SABR Encyclopedia)*

Bobby Mathews, a 5′5″, 140-pounder, is credited with throwing the first spitball and the first outcurve. With Fort Wayne in 1871, the 19-year-old posted the first six of his 131 NA victories, which was followed with 25 victories for Lord Baltimore and 29-, 42- and 29-win seasons for Mutual. In 1875 he threw 69 complete games and 625 innings. Moving with Mutual into the National League in 1876, he had a 21–34 record for a second-division club that was expelled from the league. Over the next six seasons he sat out two while winning a combined 39 games among stints with Cincinnati, Providence and Boston. In 1883 he joined the Philadelphia Athletics and enjoyed a renaissance in the American Association, winning 90 games in three seasons and finishing in 1887 with 166 NL/AA victories. His combined 297 victories are the most for any pitcher not inducted in the Baseball Hall of Fame. He umpired in the AA as a substitute in 1888 and as a regular in 1891. Born to Irish parents, Mathews was a Baltimore native and began in Organized Ball with the Maryland club in 1869. He died in Baltimore on April 1, 1898, of diseases associated with syphilis. He was 46 years old. *(Total Baseball; Baseball Reference.com; David Zingler; Baseball Necrology; SABR BioProject; Early Baltimore Baseball)*

Michael "Bub" McAtee was known as "the butcher" when he played shortstop for Union of Lansingburgh in 1866. In 1870 he was one of three Union players to sign with Chicago and entered the NA with the White Stockings in 1871. A very good first baseman—a .945 fielding percentage—he was a less impressive batter, averaging just .249 for two seasons. When the White Stockings disbanded as a result of the Great Chicago Fire, McAtee returned to Union (now known as the Troy Haymakers) for 1872. By the end of that season, the tuberculosis that would kill him had begun, and he never played again. McAtee appeared in the 1860 census for Lansingburgh. The son of Irish immigrants, the 15-year-old was working as an apprentice brush maker. He died on October 18, 1876, at age 31. *(Baseball-Reference.com; U.S. Federal Census;*

Bobby Mathews (Wikimedia Commons).

Bub McAtee (courtesy T. Scott Brandon).

DeadballEra.com; Sporting Life; National Association of Base Ball Players, 1857–1870)

James Dickson "Dick" McBride pitched for and managed the first NA champion Athletic club. Born in Philadelphia, McBride served in the Civil War in the 189th Pennsylvania Infantry and, as a teenager, played Organized Baseball in Philadelphia before the war had ended. He joined Athletic in 1863; in 1866 he led the old NA in runs per game and finished runner-up in 1867. In 1870 he was the only listed pitcher on a team that played 77 games. In the years 1871–75 he won 149 league games for Athletic, working more than two thousand innings. He led the league in winning percentage in 1871 and in ERA in 1874. In 1875 he won 44 games and had two other seasons with 30 or more victories. After a brief appearance with the National League Boston club in 1876, he left the majors and went to work for the post office. *Sporting Life* called McBride "the first really great pitcher," saying he had "speed, control, and a change of pace that was most deceptive." McBride died in Philadelphia on January 20, 1916. *(Baseball-Reference.com; Baseball-Fever.com; SABR Biographical Research Committee Newsletter; National Association of Base Ball Players, 1857–1870; Civil War Veterans Who Played in the Major Leagues Research Project; Sporting Life)*

Frank McCarton, "the celebrated center fielder of their last year's nine," became the regular center fielder for the Mansfield club in 1872 at age 18. A .305 hitter, he was less impressive in the field with a percentage and range factors below the league average. When Mansfield disbanded in August, McCarton was through as a major leaguer. Born in the Bronx, he remained in Middletown, appearing in the 1880 census there as a worker in a silver plate shop. He later returned to the Bronx where, in 1883, he became a patrolman on the police force. In the 1900 census he was listed as a sergeant. His obituary says that he had reached the rank of lieutenant. The 52-year-old McCarton died of gangrene of the stomach on June 17, 1907. *(Baseball-Reference.com; U.S. Federal Census; Middletown [Connecticut] Constitution; New York Times)*

McCloskey caught 11 games for Washington in 1875, splitting duties with Andrew Thompson, but hit only .175. In the field he committed 17 errors for a .673 percentage, well below the league average of .856. Nothing further is known of McCloskey's life, though SABR believes he was a Brooklyn product. Bullpen suggests that he may be the same person as the Bill McCloskey who caught five games for the 1884 Wilmington Quicksteps. Bill McCloskey was born in Philadelphia to Irish parents; both the 1900 and 1910 censuses showed him as a Philadelphia resident working as a cigar maker. He died in Philadelphia on July 9, 1924, at age 70. *(Total Baseball; Baseball-Reference.com; U.S. Federal Census; Sporting Life; SABR Encyclopedia of Baseball)*

Joe McDermott played center field on Opening Day for Kekionga. In the second inning his single drove in Bill Lennon, the first RBI in major league history. In two games he hit .250 but had an error on one of his two fielding opportunities and was no longer with the team by the end of May. McDermott had been the main pitcher for Eckford in 1870 and returned to the NA as a pitcher for Eckford in 1872. His seven starts that season resulted in a 0–7 record and an 8.14 ERA as he gave up 143 hits and allowed 144 runs. Nothing further is known of his life at this time. *(Baseball-Reference.com; New York Herald; SABR Encyclopedia of Baseball)*

Daniel "Jack" McDonald, a local Brooklyn athlete, played for Atlantic from 1866 into

1872. In 1872 he was the team's regular right fielder. After 15 games he was hitting .258, but he had committed seven errors in 25 fielding chances before leaving the team. He then played one game as a shortstop for Eckford. That hitless day dropped his average to .242. Born in 1844, McDonald may have served in the Civil War; two different Daniel McDonalds from Brooklyn are listed on the military rolls. He died in Brooklyn on November 23, 1880, at age 36. *(Baseball-Reference.com; U.S. Federal Census; U.S. Civil War Soldier Records and Profiles; National Association of Base Ball Players, 1857–1870)*

McDoolan pitched the opening game for Maryland on April 14, 1873. In a 24–3 loss to Washington, he gave up 18 hits and 24 runs, only three of which were earned. The name McDoolan does not appear in any census for Baltimore nor is it indexed by Genealogy Bank anywhere in 1873. Peter Morris believes the name is a typo, possibly for McDonald. *(Baseball-Reference.com; U.S. Federal Census; petermorrisbooks.com)*

Mike McGeary was the regular catcher for Union of Lansingburgh in 1870 when he was 19 years old. He remained with the club in 1871, leading NA catchers in fielding and the league in stolen bases. He had his best seasons at the plate from 1872 to 1874 with Athletic, hitting .360, .302 and .323. After finishing in the NA with Philadelphia, he moved to St. Louis at the onset of the National League, also playing for Providence and Cleveland before concluding with Detroit in 1882. Overall, he hit .274. Weighing only 138 pounds, he soon moved from behind the plate to the infield, playing in 196 games at second base, 147 at shortstop, 117 at third base and 96 at catcher. He was a superior fielder in all positions. Born to Irish parents in Philadelphia, McGeary appeared in the 1880 census for Providence as a baseball player. But he is one of Peter Morris's

Mike McGeary, from 1876 St. Louis team photograph (courtesy T. Scott Brandon).

"Cold Cases of the Diamond." Morris says that McGeary pursued a career in gambling after leaving baseball, and that he was still alive in 1935. *Sporting Life* says that as a player, McGeary worked with gamblers. *(Baseball-Reference.com; U.S. Federal Census; Sporting Life; petermorrisbooks.com)*

Pat McGee was a good defensive outfielder for the Atlantic and Mutual clubs. He debuted with Atlantic in late September 1874, coming from the amateur Flyaway club, but hit only .169 in 16 games. He split 1875 between Atlantic and Mutual, hitting .174 in 43 games. In 53 games in the outfield, most as a center fielder, he fielded .849, 45 points above the league average. He may be the McGee who played outfield for the independent New Haven club in 1876 and worked as a substitute National League umpire. In 1889 the *New York Herald* reported that McGee had been bitten on the forehead by a spider and that the infection led to erysipelas. McGee died in Bellevue Hospital on June 20, 1889, at about the age of 36. At the time of his death, he was a New York City policeman. He was unmarried but left a sister and her six children in a destitute state. *(Baseball-Reference.com; U.S. Federal Census; New York Herald; Hartford Daily Courant)*

Tim McGinley was the regular catcher for Centennial for the first part of 1875; when that club folded, he became the regular catcher for Elm City. A year later he played in nine games for Boston, scoring the first run in National League history. Overall, McGinley hit .262 in 54 major league games. In 47 games as a catcher, he fielded .753, well under the league average of .836. The McGinleyClan.org website says that because of his good looks, he was one of the first players to develop a fan base and that he was a very popular after-dinner speaker. The same site speaks of his forced retirement from baseball, the result of an eye injury. The 1880 census for Philadelphia listed him as an unmarried clerk, still living at home with his Irish parents. *Sporting Life* says that McGinley became a United States shipping commissioner for Philadelphia. He later moved to California where he held positions in the sheriff's office and as a private secretary to the warden of San Quentin Penitentiary. The 1898 California voter registration lists his occupation as stenographer. McGinley died of consumption at Oakland on November 2, 1899, at about the age of 45. *(Baseball-Reference.com; U.S. Federal Census; McGinleyClan.org; Sporting Life; California Voter Registers, 1866–1898)*

Tim McGinley from 1876 St. Louis team photograph (courtesy T. Scott Brandon).

John McKelvey played right field for Elm City in 1875. The 27-year-old Rochester native hit .229 in 43 games. Thirty-nine of his games were in the outfield, where he had 21 errors, resulting in a .656 percentage, far below the league average of .854. He likely is the McKelvey who played for the Alert club of Rochester in 1869 and the Flour City club, also of Rochester, in 1870. His obituary says that he played shortstop for Rochester Pacific. McKelvey returned to Rochester, where both the 1880 census and the 1890 city directory show that he had become a clerk in the post office. By 1910 he had become an assistant superintendent of mails and was superintendent when he retired in 1928. Before his death in Rochester on May 31, 1944, the 96-year-old McKelvey was the last surviving NA player. He claimed to have learned to throw the curveball from Candy Cummings and took it back to Rochester. *(Baseball-Reference.com; National Association of Base Ball Players, 1857–1870; U.S. Federal Census; Rochester City Directory; Major League Baseball in Gilded Age Connecticut; New York Times)*

Ed McKenna had three major league trials that occurred eleven years apart. He played first base for Philadelphia on July 29, 1874, going hitless but performing flawlessly in the field. Three years later he played center field for the St. Louis Brown Stockings in the National League, getting a hit and fielding his position without an error. In the game against Boston, he hit a line drive that resulted in a triple play. In 1884 he played in 32 games for the Washington Unions and hit .188. Tried as a catcher, he suffered 47 passed balls and committed 22 errors in 23 games. Most sources give him a St. Louis birthplace. The censuses of 1880 and 1910 showed a brick mason named Edward McKenna, born to Irish parents, living in St. Louis. However, Peter Morris believes that the Ed McKenna records may have been the work of three different players, including a Philadelphian named F. McKenna and a St. Louis policeman named Patrick McKenna. *(Baseball-Reference.com; Retrosheet; petermorrisbooks.com; U.S. Federal Census)*

John "Lefty" McMullin is credited with throwing ten wild pitches in the ninth inning of a non-league game on August 17, 1871, allowing Eckford to defeat Troy, 15–13. However, he threw 249 of the Haymakers' 250 innings that season, winning 12 games. For the rest of his career (1872 with Mutual, 1873–74 with Athletic, and 1875 with Philadelphia), he played primarily in the outfield, hitting .284. In 1874 he hit .346 but led the NA by striking out 13 times. His .827 fielding percentage was well above the league average. The Philadelphia native began his career with his hometown Keystone club in 1867, moving on to Buckeye of Cincinnati (1868), Athletic (1869) and Union of Lansingburgh (1870) before entering the NA with Union. According to his death certificate, McMullin was married, and he operated a hat and cap store in Philadelphia. He died of pneumonia on April 11, 1881, at age 32. *(Baseball-Reference.com; U.S. Federal Census; National Association of Base Ball Players, 1857–1870; BaseballLibrary.com; Return of a Death in the City of Philadelphia)*

John "Trick" McSorley, a tiny infielder who stood only 5' 4", played with his hometown St. Louis Red Stockings in the NA in 1875 when he was 23 years old. According to Baseball-Fever.com, McSorley was "removed from the team for crooked play." He finished 1875 with the Covington Stars, and went to Indianapolis in 1876 when the Stars

Trick McSorley from 1878 Buffalo team photograph (courtesy Mearsonlineauctions.com).

disbanded, also playing with Buffalo and Peoria. In 1884 he returned to the majors for twenty-one games with Toledo of the American Association. He also played two games for the St. Louis Maroons in 1885 and five games with the St. Louis Browns in 1886. Counting his year in the NA, he had a major league career of 43 games over twelve years, in which he hit .233. McSorley played and umpired in the minors into the 1890s. The census of 1900 showed him living with his mother in St. Louis and working as a plumber. The 1920 census listed him as a police officer. According to Bill Lee, McSorley joined the St. Louis police force in 1903, retiring in 1931. He died on February 9, 1936, at age 83. According to Alfred Henry Spink, his nickname came from the fact that he was "so tricky." *(Total Baseball; Baseball Reference.com; Baseball-Fever.com; Baseball Necrology; U.S. Federal Census; Sporting Life; National Game)*

Cal McVey joined the Red Stockings as a 19-year-old in 1869 and moved with Harry

Cal McVey, from "First Nine of the Cincinnati (Red Stockings) Baseball Club" (LC-USZC4-1291 Library of Congress Prints and Photographs Division).

Wright to Boston. After helping the Red Stockings to a pennant in 1872, he went to Lord Baltimore as playing manager in 1873 and then returned to Boston for two more pennants, in 1874–75. He helped the White Stockings to a pennant in the inaugural National League season and then served as playing manager in Cincinnati in 1878–79. For nine seasons, he hit .346, with a high of .431 in 1871. He led the NA twice in hits and in total bases and once each in runs and slugging. Both as a first baseman and catcher, he had fielding marks well above the league average. He also played frequently in the outfield and at third base. He even compiled a 10–12 mark as a pitcher. Born in Montrose, Iowa, to parents from California, McVey appeared in the 1870 census for Indianapolis as a "baseballist." By 1900 he had moved to San Francisco and was working as a policeman. The 1906 earthquake destroyed his home and cigar store. A later venture into mining in Nevada was ended by a serious accident; therefore, he became one of the first players to be assisted by the Baseball Brotherhood. The 1920 census showed the 70-year-old McVey working as a watchman at a lumberyard. He died in San Francisco on August 20, 1926, just a few days shy of his 77th birthday. *(Baseball-Reference.com; U.S. Federal Census; Sporting Life; Baseball Necrology)*

Alfred Metcalfe (Metcalf) played for Mutual in May and June of 1875. In eight games he hit .219. Five of his games were at third base, where he committed 10 errors for a .667 fielding percentage. He had previously played for the Chelsea club of Brooklyn in 1873–74, and he moved to the Louisville Eagles after leaving Mutual. Born in Brooklyn to English parents, Metcalfe worked

Al Metcalf (courtesy Susan Metcalfe LaRock).

there as a clerk in the health department, according to the 1890 Brooklyn city directory and the 1900 and 1910 censuses. He died in Brooklyn on September 2, 1914. *(Baseball-Reference.com; U.S. Federal Census; Brooklyn City Directory; SABR Baseball Encyclopedia; New York Herald)*

Levi Meyerle began his career in 1867–68 with Geary, also playing with Athletic

(1869) and Chicago (1870) before the formation of the league. He was an NA regular for five years—two with Athletic, two with Philadelphia and one with Chicago—hitting NA pitching at a .365 clip. He led the league twice in hitting and once in homers. In the inaugural 1871 season he hit .491 for Athletic. In 1874, playing for the Chicago White Stockings, he batted .394. His strong hitting continued for the first two years of the NL as he hit .340 for the Athletics and .327 for the Cincinnati Red Stocking before an ankle injury ended his NL career. Meyerle continued to play for Springfield, Massachusetts, in 1878, for Washington (1879–80), Rochester (1880) and for independent teams around Philadelphia. In 1884 the 38-year-old Meyerle played in three games for the Union Association Keystones, managing one hit. In his eight-year career, he played every position except catcher but was used mostly at third base. Labeled "not a star defensively," he fielded .796 for his entire career, seventeen points below the league average. Born in Philadelphia, Meyerle was listed as a plasterer in the 1870 census. In 1890 the Philadelphia city directory gave his profession as lather. Meyerle died in Philadelphia on November 4, 1921, at age 76. Because he stood 6'1", he was nicknamed "Long Levi." *(Total Baseball; Baseball-Reference.com; U.S. Federal Census; Philadelphia City Directory; Sporting Life; National Association of Base Ball Players, 1857–1870; Springfield Republican)*

Joe Miller, at age 22, managed the 1872 Washington National club to an 0–11 record. He played first base for one game, collecting a hit. In 1875 he returned to the majors as a second baseman with Keokuk but hit only .120 in 13 games before the club disbanded. Shifting to the White Stockings, Miller played in 15 games, hitting at a .148 clip. He was, however, a solid fielder, with numbers at the league average. In 1877 he played for the St. Paul Red Caps of the League Alliance, and he may be the Miller who played second base for Indianapolis in 1876, coming from the disbanded Covington Stars. Born in Germany, Miller settled in Minnesota and was listed in the White Bear census for 1880 as a confectioner. An 1891 note in *Sporting Life* says that Miller was the proprietor of a saloon in White Bear, by which he had "accumulated a fair share of this world's goods." He died at White Bear on August 28, 1891, at age 41. *(Baseball-Reference.com; U.S. Federal Census; Sporting Life; Indianapolis Sentinel)*

Thomas "Reddy" Miller caught four games for his hometown Athletic club in 1874, after being a member of the amateur Easton team, a club with nine past or future major league players in the lineup. A year later he was the regular catcher for the Brown Stockings but hit only .164. These two seasons constituted his major league career. In 60 games, he hit .187, but in 57 games as a catcher, he fielded four points above the league average. When sportswriters looked for league catchers

Levi Meyerle (courtesy T. Scott Brandon).

against whom to compare the black catcher Louis Browne, Miller along with Deacon White and John Clapp headed the list. The 1870 census showed that the 19-year-old Miller, the son of Irish parents, was working as a basket maker in Philadelphia. He died of "obstruction of the bowels" in Philadelphia on May 29, 1876, at age 24. According to a report, the dying Miller thought he was talking to George Bradley, his pitcher, and his last words were, "Two out, Brad. Steady, now, he wants a high ball." *(Baseball-Reference.com; U.S. Federal Census; Sporting Life; Materials supplied by his great-grand nephew Frank Hannigan; The Early Image of Black Baseball; Jackson [Michigan] Citizen Patriot)*

Charlie Mills, a Brooklyn product, played with Eckford as early as 1865. After three seasons with Atlantic, he began playing for Mutual in 1869, moving with the club into the NA in 1871. While he hit only .247, the tall, lanky Mills had an .866 fielding percentage, third among league catchers. He again played with Mutual for six games in 1872, leaving the majors with a .226 batting average and an .854 fielding percentage. Mills is listed as a regular National Association umpire in both 1872 and 1873. A severe cold, contracted in the fall of 1873, turned into consumption, which carried him away on April 10, 1874. He was only thirty years of age. In the 1870 census, 24-year-old Charles F. Mills was listed as the engineer on a steamboat owned by his father. *(Baseball-Reference.com; U.S. Federal Census; New York Times; National Association of Base Ball Players, 1857–1870)*

Everett Mills played six seasons as a regular first baseman for Olympic (1871), Lord Baltimore (1872–73) and Hartford (1875–76). He hit a solid .284 against NA and National League pitching, reaching .332 with Lord Baltimore in 1873, when he hit a league-leading nine triples. In 336 games as a first baseman, he fielded .941, eight points above the league average with slightly below-average range factors. He led the league with a .949 fielding percentage in 1873. Mills, a Newark, New Jersey, product, began with the Eureka of Newark in 1864, later moving to Mutual, Irvington, and then to Olympic in 1870. After finishing his major league career with Hartford, he played with Milwaukee of the League Alliance in 1877. The 1880 census for Newark listed him as a currier, a leather finisher. In 1896 he was appointed sergeant at arms of the Essex County Criminal Court, a position he held for the

Charlie Mills, from 1870 Mutual team photograph (Wikimedia Commons).

Everett Mills, from 1870 Mutual team photograph (Wikimedia Commons).

remainder of his life. He died of heart disease at Newark on June 22, 1908, at age 63. *(Baseball-Reference.com; U.S. Federal Census; Sporting Life; National Association of Base Ball Players, 1857–1870)*

Ed Mincher, a 20-year-old Baltimore native, played in nine games for Kekionga at the beginning of 1871, hitting .222. He began his baseball career in 1868 with the Enterprise and Maryland clubs in his hometown, continuing with Maryland through 1870. Returning to Baltimore in mid-1871, he was signed by the Pastime club. A year later he played in all 11 games for National before that club folded. An above-average outfielder, he played in 20 games—all as a left fielder—with a range and percentage that exceeded the league average. Brian McKenna notes that Mincher played baseball around Baltimore until the late 1870s and that he played with Wilmington in 1877. Mincher appeared in the 1880 census for Philadelphia and the 1881 Philadelphia city directory as a street and railroad contractor. Mincher died in Brooklyn on December 8, 1918, at age 68. He was a brother-in-law of Kekionga and National teammate Bill Lennon. *(Baseball-Reference.com; U.S. Federal Census; National Association of Base Ball Players, 1857–1870; Philadelphia City Directory; SABR BioProject; Early Baltimore Baseball)*

Maurice "Mollie" or "Molly" Moore played in 21 games for Atlantic in 1875, hitting .221. Fourteen of his games were at shortstop, where he made 21 errors for a .747 fielding percentage. The *New York Times* singled him out as contributing to an Atlantic loss to the Brown Stockings by making "several very bad errors" that led to St. Louis runs. In 1878 the *New York Herald* reported that a Maurice "Mollie" Moore, one of the "denizens of the Bowery," was part of a drunken brawl in a bar that also involved a woman. Moore was shot in the chest by the bartender but later recovered. Peter Morris, citing the *New York Clipper*, says that Moore died in New York City on February 24, 1881. *(New York Times; Baseball-Reference.com; New York Herald; SABR Encyclopedia; petermorrisbooks.com)*

Daniel "Pidge" Morgan played in all 19 games for his hometown St. Louis Red Stockings in 1875, hitting .261, second highest on the team. He played in eight games as an outfielder, seven as a pitcher, and six as a third baseman. As a pitcher with "a very pretty delivery" (also described as a "legitimate delivery"), he went 1–3 with a 3.43 ERA for a team that had a 4–15 record. He pitched for the Red Stockings in 1874 prior to their entry into the league and continued with the team in 1876. In 1878 he played 14 games with the Milwaukee Cream Citys of the National League but hit only .196. He apparently played for an independent St. Louis team called the Standards in 1882; in 1886, "looking like the old Dan," he played in a benefit game for Tom Sullivan. Daniel Morgan has recently had his records separated from those of Bill Morgan. Daniel Morgan, the son of Irish parents, appeared in the census of 1880 as a married house painter with two children. In 1895 the *Milwaukee Journal* described him as "a successful businessman in St. Louis." In 1900 he was listed as a widowed laborer in the census. Morgan died in St. Louis on January 31, 1910. *(Baseball-Reference.com; U.S. Federal Census; Cincinnati Daily Gazette; Daily Inter Ocean [Chicago]; This Game of Games)*

Martin Mullen was an accidental major league player. A 19-year-old Cleveland amateur, he was pressed into service on August 17, 1872, when Forest City outfielder Rynie Wolters became ill after swallowing his chew of tobacco. In an 18–7 loss to the champion Red Stockings, Mullen went hitless in four at-bats but scored a run and com-

Martin Mullen (*Amateur Billiard Championship of America*, 1899).

mitted three errors in the field. Mullen's obituary states that he was much sought by professional teams but "refused to ally himself with any professional organization." In 1903 Mullen won the world's amateur billiards championship and held the title for eight years. Born in Cleveland, Mullen is described as a "pioneer coal man," being the "first to buy and sell coal at steamboat landings." Before his death, he was a partner in a number of coal companies. The 1910 census listed him as a capitalist. He was a lifelong resident of Cleveland and died suddenly of heart disease in his bachelor apartment on October 27, 1915. He was 63 years of age. (*Baseball-Reference.com; U.S. Federal Census; Cleveland Plain Dealer*)

Horatio Munn played second base for Atlantic on September 4, 1875. In a 13–4 loss to Mutual, Munn was hitless in four at-bats but handled five of six fielding chances successfully. The 23-year-old Munn was born in Newark but appeared in the 1860 census as a resident of Brooklyn. The ootpdevelopments.com says that Munn retired in 1882 and that he "never got into a game in 8 seasons." The Brooklyn city directory listed him as a clerk until 1889, when he becomes a bookkeeper. The census of 1900 showed him as an insurance agent. Munn died in Brooklyn on February 17, 1910, at age 45. (*Baseball-Reference.com; Lain's Brooklyn Directory; U.S. Federal Census; New York Times; ootpdevelopments.com*)

Tim Murnane began his major league career as a 20-year-old first baseman with Mansfield in 1872, hitting .359 in 24 games. After playing for Athletic (1873–74) and Philadelphia (1875), he entered the National League with Boston in 1876, moving on to Providence in 1878. By 1879 he was playing part time for the powerful Hop Bitters, an independent team from Rochester with nine past or future major leaguers in its lineup. By 1881 he was out of baseball to operate a saloon and billiards parlor. Murnane came

Tim Murnane (LC-DIG-bbc-0666f Library of Congress Prints and Photographs Division).

back in 1884 as playing manager of the Boston Reds, directing them to a fifth-place finish in the Union Association. In eight seasons in three leagues, he hit .261 and once led the NA in stolen bases. Murnane later served as president of the New England League, the Eastern League, and the National Board of Professional Baseball Clubs. For the last 30 years of his life, he was baseball editor for the *Boston Daily Globe*. Born in Naugatuck, Connecticut, to Irish parents, Murnane died in Boston on February 7, 1917, at age 64. In 1939 he was one of the twelve writers honored by the Baseball Hall of Fame. *(Total Baseball; Baseball-Reference.com; New York Times; Rich Eldred; Springfield (Massachusetts) Republican)*

John "Candy" Nelson began his baseball career with Eckford in 1867. Except for the 1870 season, he spent with Mutual, Nelson remained with Eckford until he debuted in the NA with Troy in 1872. When Troy disbanded in midseason, he returned to Eckford, also playing with Mutual from 1873 to 1875. He had National League trials with Indianapolis, Troy and Worcester before joining the New York Mets in 1882. When the Mets entered the American Association in 1883, Nelson hit a career-high .305 as the regular shortstop, and led the AA in walks in 1884, helping the Mets win the championship. After playing one game with the NL Giants in 1887, he played in the minors for Albany, Buffalo and Wilmington, before finishing with the AA Brooklyn Gladiators in 1890. In 13 seasons—seven as a regular—he hit .254, and as a shortstop, he fielded .872, nine points above the league average. When he retired in 1890, he was 41 years old ("the oldest player in active and continuous service"). Both *Sporting Life* (1893) and the *Washington Post* (1895) reported that Nelson "owns a milk route in Brooklyn." But in the 1900 census, he still listed his occupation as "ball player." In that census he gave his birthplace as Maine; he died in Brooklyn on September 4, 1910, at age 61. *(Baseball-Reference.com; Total Baseball; Washington Post; U.S. Federal Census; Sporting Life; Complete New York Clipper Baseball Biographies)*

Candy Nelson, from "Metropolitan baseball nine 1882" (LC-DIG-ppmsca-18773 Library of Congress Prints and Photographs Division).

Alex Nevin played third base for Resolute in 1873, directly from Yale. In 13 games he managed 11 hits for a .200 batting average. In the field he had 25 errors for a .561 percentage—against a league average of .802. The son of a bank president from Allegheny, Pennsylvania, Nevin attended Phillips Academy and appeared in the 1870 census as a resident there. According to the family tree, he played baseball for four years at Yale and captained the team in 1873, "making no errors in any Harvard or Princeton game." The 1880 census and the 1882–83 city directory both showed him back in Allegheny, working as a bank clerk. Around 1892 Nevin

Alex Nevin (*Biographical Record of the Class of 1874 in Yale College*).

disappeared. He was located 22 years later in 1914, managing an estate in Florida. He died in Pensacola on October 10, 1921. His family tree cites his volunteer service in the Spanish-American War in 1898. *(Baseball-Reference.com; U.S. Federal Census; Alexander B Nevin Family Tree; J.F. Diffenbacher's Directory of Pittsburgh and Allegheny Citys; Rockford Republic)*

Al Nichols was a light-hitting third baseman with Atlantic (1875) and with New York (1876) and Louisville (1877) of the National League. In 95 major league games, he hit only .171 and led the NL in errors in 1876. However, his .785 fielding average was just under the league average, and he led both the NA and NL in range factors for third basemen. Implicated in the 1877 scandal of Louisville players to fix games, he, along with Jim Devlin, George Hall, and Bill Craver, was banned from baseball after that season. In 1887 *Sporting Life* noted that Nichols had suffered enough and had repented of wrong-doings, but his appeal for reinstatement was denied. Born in England as Alfred Williams, Nichols came to the United States in 1861 and lived most of his life in New York City. The 1880 census showed the 28-year-old Williams living in Manhattan, working as a shipping clerk. He married Mary Anna Luther, a daughter of the family with whom he lived. Censuses of 1900, 1910 and 1920 showed English-born Alfred H. Williams and his wife Mary living in Brooklyn and later Queens, with Williams working as an inspector and later as a collector for a gas company. He died in Richmond Hill, New York, on June 18, 1936. *(Baseball-Reference.com; U.S. Federal Census; Sporting Life; Ancestry.com; petermorrisbooks.com)*

Frederick "Tricky" Nichols, a Bridgeport, Connecticut, product, pitched for six teams in three leagues in a six-year major league career. He began with the in-state Elm City club in 1875. Despite a 3.03 ERA, Nichols went 4–29 for 7–40 Elm City. After making one start for Boston in 1876, he pitched 350

Tricky Nichols (Wikimedia Commons).

innings for the St. Louis Brown Stockings in 1877, going 18–23 with a 2.60 ERA. Pitching behind Monte Ward at Providence in 1878, he had a 4–7 record. With the minor league Worcester team in 1879, Nichols pitched two losing NL games for the Ruby Legs in 1880. In 1882, he finished in the new American Association with Baltimore, going 1–12. Overall, he compiled a major league mark of 28–73 with a 3.04 ERA. He later pitched around New England through 1886. When he signed with Brockton in 1886, his manager predicted that the New England League was "as good as won." Nichols was released before the end of that season. His nickname came from his ability to change speeds on pitches. Nichols appeared in the 1890 city directory for Bridgeport as a partner in a firm dealing in hats, caps and furs. The 47-year-old Nichols died of pulmonary tuberculosis at Bridgeport on August 22, 1897. *(Baseball-Reference.com; U.S. Federal Census; Bridgeport City Directory; Sporting Life)*

Frank Norton (courtesy T. Scott Brandon).

Frank Norton struck out in his only at-bat and committed an error on the only ball hit to him on Opening Day of the 1871 season with Olympic. Substituting in right field after an injury to Art Allison, Norton threw low to first base, allowing two runs to score. Nevertheless, the Port Jefferson, New York, product had played Organized Baseball for seven seasons previous. Beginning with the Star of Brooklyn in 1863–65, Norton had played with Excelsior (1866–67), National (1868) and Olympic (1869–70). Like many Washington players, Norton held a government job, and was listed as a clerk in the Interior Department in 1870. The *Chicago Inter Ocean* reported in 1875 that Norton and his wife had inherited $500,000. Later censuses list Norton as an insurance agent (1880), a landlord (1900) and a real estate agent (1910). Norton died at Greenwich, Connecticut, on August 1, 1920. He was 75 years old. *(Baseball-Reference.com; National Association of Base Ball Players, 1857–1870; U.S. Federal Census; Chicago Inter Ocean; Cincinnati Commercial Tribune)*

Hugh O'Neil was previously listed as J O'Neill. He started four games for Atlantic in 1875—one of four starting pitchers tried by the Brooklyn club—going 0–4 with a 5.03 ERA. As a batter he had two hits in 26 at-bats for an .077 average. A competent first baseman in his one game there, he had two errors in six fielding chances as an outfielder. At O'Neil's debut on August 20, the *New York Times* noted that he was "formerly pitcher of the Keystone club." Most sources give him a Brooklyn birth. Even if this is true, tracing him would be difficult, since no fewer than seven Hugh O'Neils are listed in the Brooklyn 1888–89 city directory, men that include a coal dealer, a coffee roaster, a liquor dealer, a tailor, a watchman, a locksmith and a clerk. *(Baseball-Reference.com;*

Lain's Brooklyn City Directory; SABR Baseball Encyclopedia; New York Times)

Michael "Fancy" O'Neil played right field for Hartford in a game on October 23, 1874. In a 13–1 home loss to Boston, O'Neil went hitless in three at-bats and committed one error in three fielding chances. The *Hartford Courant* referred to him as being "of the Amateurs." Until recently O'Neil had no first name, and his last name was generally spelled "O'Neal." SABR now lists a Hartford birth for the player. If this is the case, a likely candidate is a Michael O'Neil, born in Hartford in September 1849. He was listed in the censuses of 1900 and 1910 as a Hartford city policeman. However, Peter Morris believes that O'Neil was born in Ireland in 1853, that his nickname "Fancy" came from a boxing career, and that he had "trouble with the law." David Arcidiacono cites an 1895 *Hartford Courant* article on an "old time boxer and ball player" named Michael "Fancy" O'Neil who had attacked his employer with a knife and as a result was taken to the Connecticut Hospital for the Insane. The common Irish name makes research difficult. *(Baseball-Reference.com; U.S. Federal Census; SABR Baseball Encyclopedia; petermorrisbooks.com; Hartford Courant; Major League Baseball in Gilded Age Connecticut)*

Tom Oran played right field for the St. Louis Red Stockings in their brief foray into the National Association in 1875. In 19 games he hit only .185 with four extra-base hits and 10 RBIs. With 11 errors (.633 fielding percentage), he also ranked low defensively. Born in California in 1847, Oran is the first from that state to play in the majors. He was also the first Native American to play. Peter Morris noted that Oran had played amateur baseball in St. Louis for the Union and Empire clubs before joining the Red Stockings. The 1870 census showed Oran living in St. Louis with his 18-year-old wife and infant son, working as a fireman. According to Jeffrey Kittel, the relationship between the Empire club and the St. Louis Fire Department provided employment for a number of players, including Oran. The Missouri death record shows that he died on September 22, 1886, of phthisis pulmonaris. In that document, his occupation is listed as "cattle driver." *Sporting News* says that he died from the effects of "fire water." *(Baseball-Reference.com; U.S. Federal Census; Missouri Death Records, 1834–1912; SABR BioProject; Sporting News; This Game of Games)*

O'Rourke pitched for Eckford in a game at Troy on July 9, 1872. In a complete-game loss, O'Rourke gave up 16 hits and 15 runs—eight earned. The *New York Times* referred to him as one of the new players who "appear to be an improvement over the recent incumbents." He did not play in the majors again. *(Baseball-Reference.com; New York Times)*

James "Orator" O'Rourke joined Mansfield as a 21-year-old shortstop and catcher in 1872. He went to Boston the following season, playing five different positions, and moved with that club into the National League in 1876. After helping the Providence Grays win a NL championship in 1879, he became a playing manager for Buffalo in 1881. From 1885 through 1892 he played in New York with the NL or Players League Giants, before finishing with Washington in 1893. In 23 seasons—18 as a regular—he hit .310, leading the NL three times in homers; he led in hits and average in 1884 and in walks and runs in 1877 (when he hit a career-high .362). The son of illiterate Irish immigrants, O'Rourke graduated from Yale Law School. His nickname came from his verbal skills. One obituary noted, "Words of great length and thunderous sound simply

Jim O'Rourke (LC-DIG-bbc-0276f Library of Congress Prints and Photographs Division).

1870. He was the main pitcher on the 25–3, 21–8, and 37–6 teams of 1866–68. In Pabor's obituary, the *New York Times* called him "the first great left-handed pitcher." In 1871 he joined the Forest City club of Cleveland as an outfielder. In the NA he also played with Atlantic (1873 and 1875), Philadelphia (1874) and New Haven (1875). Overall, he hit .285—but reached .360 in 1873—and fielded .789, about 30 points under the league average. He also compiled a 1–4 record as a pitcher. Pabor managed Cleveland in 1871, Atlantic (to a 2–40 record) in 1873 and New Haven. Overall, his teams registered a 13–64 record. In the minors he managed Columbus, and he is credited with the development of Fred Goldsmith and King Kelly. Having lost his savings in bad investments, Pabor became a policeman in New Haven after leaving baseball. He died of pneumonia in New Haven on April 23, 1916. *(Baseball-Reference.com; National Association of Base Ball Players, 1857–1870; New Haven City Directory; Sporting Life; New York Times)*

flowed out of his mouth." O'Rourke later was an NL umpire and playing manager and club owner in the Connecticut League, playing until he was 58 years old. In 1904, at age 52, he caught a nine-inning game for the Giants, going one-for-four at the plate. O'Rourke died at Bridgeport, Connecticut, his native city, on January 8, 1919, at age 68 and was elected to the Baseball Hall of Fame in 1945. *(Total Baseball; Baseball-Reference.com; New York Times; Encyclopedia of Minor League Baseball)*

Charlie Pabor was a fast but wild left-handed pitcher for Union of Morrisania in the late 1860s. The Brooklyn native began with Union in 1865, continuing through

Charlie Pabor (Wikimedia Commons).

Bill Parks pitched and played left field for Washington and Philadelphia in 1875 and for Boston in the National League in 1876. He had a 4–8 record and a 3.54 ERA as a pitcher, with all of his decisions coming with Washington. In 30 games he hit only .174 but was a solid .829 fielder. In 1875 he managed Washington for the last eight games, going 1–7. In 1874 he played on the semi-pro Easton team that contained nine past and future major league players. Parks, a native of Easton, served in the 196th Pennsylvania Regiment during the Civil War on a 100-day enlistment in 1864. He later served as senior vice commander of the state encampment of the Grand Army of the Republic. As early as 1870, the census listed Parks as a barber and continued to list him as such through 1910. *Sporting Life* notes that Parks had been an Eastern League umpire. He died in Easton on October 10, 1911, at age 62. *(Baseball-Reference.com; U.S. Federal Census; Sporting Life; Civil War Veterans Who Played Major League Baseball Research Project; Wilkes-Barre Times)*

Tom Patterson has been awarded the playing record formerly assigned to Dan Patterson. In 2006 researcher Peter Morris found that Dan Patterson finished his career with Mutual in 1866 and that the league records, therefore, should go to Tom Patterson, who played until 1875. Tom Patterson hit .205 as an outfield regular for Mutual in 1871. Thereafter, he played lesser roles for Eckford (1872), Mutual (1874), and Atlantic (1875). Overall, he hit .210 in 59 games and was an average outfielder. Tom Patterson was born in New York City around 1845. Beginning in 1866, he played for Enterprise and Eckford before joining Mutual in 1870. Records from 1869 list him as a compositor. In the 1870 census he is listed as a painter or a printer. Tom Patterson died on May 31, 1900, in New York City. He was approximately 55 years of age. *(Baseball-Reference.*

Tom Patterson, from 1870 Mutual team photograph (Wikimedia Commons).

com; SABR Biographical Research Committee Newsletter; U.S. Federal Census; National Association of Base Ball Players, 1857–1870)

Dickey Pearce revolutionized the shortstop position during his years with Brooklyn Atlantic (1856–70), by bringing himself into the infield instead of playing a rover position between the infield and outfield. *Sporting Life* also credits him with introducing the

Dickie Pearce, from St. Louis team photograph (courtesy T. Scott Brandon).

bunt. Already 35 years old in 1871, he continued as a regular for the next five seasons with Mutual (1871–72), Atlantic (1873–74) and the Brown Stockings (1875). When the National League opened, he continued in a lesser role with St. Louis through 1877, when he was past 40. He hit as high as .292 in 1874 and as low as .189 in 1872, finishing with a .251 mark. Not surprisingly, his .828 fielding percentage was 38 points above the league average, and he led NA shortstops in fielding twice. Pearce umpired for a couple of years and later worked as a groundskeeper. Born in Brooklyn to English parents, Pearce was listed as a laborer in the 1880 census for St. Louis; the 1900 census for New York City showed him as an "engineman." Apparently he fell upon hard times because *Sporting Life* reports that a benefit game was played for him in 1899. After his death, former manager Jack Chapman hoped that "something would be done for the family." Pearce died at Wareham, Massachusetts, on October 18, 1909, at age 75. *(Baseball-Reference.com; Sporting Life; U.S. Federal Census; National Association of Base Ball Players, 1857–1870; New York Times)*

John Peters, from *Chicago Champions* (LC-DIG-pga-18390 Library of Congress Prints and Photographs Division).

John Peters hit .351 to help the Chicago White Stockings win the first National League championship in 1876. He was in his third season with Chicago, being a veteran of the National Association White Stockings. In eleven seasons—eight as a regular shortstop or second baseman—he led the league twice in fielding, double plays, putouts, and chances; his .874 percentage was seventeen points higher than the league average for shortstops. Batting higher than .300 three times, Peters settled for a career .278 batting average. In addition to the White Stockings, he saw service with Milwaukee, Providence and Buffalo, before finishing with the American Association Pittsburgh Alleghenys in 1884. *Sporting Life* reported that Peters was "without an engagement" in 1885 and was looking to "re-enter the diamond" in 1886. Born to German parents in New Orleans, Peters appeared in the 1870 census for St. Louis, working as a bartender and living with the Oberbeck family, whose son, Henry, played in the American Association in 1883 and the Union Association in 1884. The 1880 census listed Peters as a ball player; the 1900 census reported him as a laborer in a brickyard. *Sporting News* says that he was an employee of the St. Louis Park Department; this is verified by the censuses of 1910 and 1920. Peters died in St. Louis on January 4, 1924, at age 73. *(Baseball Encyclopedia; Baseball-Reference.com; Retrosheet; New York Times; U.S. Federal Census; Sporting News)*

Nealy Phelps does not appear on any of the NA rosters through 1870. However, the 30-year-old played right field for Fort Wayne on July 1, 1871, in a game at Philadelphia. The New York City product later made nine appearances with Mutual between 1873 and 1875 and played one game with the club in the National League in 1876. His final appearance was as a loaner, when the Athletics had only eight men for a game with Mutual. Phelps, working as a ticket taker, was drafted as a catcher for the day. Overall, Phelps hit only .109 in 12 games. Ten of his games were as a right fielder, where he fielded above the league average. This may be the Phelps who played for the Dauntless club of New York City in 1871. Described as "a desirable player for any club to possess," that Phelps was rumored to be headed for Atlantic. Born to a German father, Phelps appeared in the 1870 census for New York City as a fish monger and in the 1880 census as the keeper of an oyster saloon. He may also be the Cornelius Phelps who served as a drummer in the Twelfth New York State Militia for three months in 1861. The death notice for the ball player says that he was a member of the Knights of Honor of the Grand Army of the Republic. Phelps died from pneumonia in New York City on February 12, 1885, at age 44. *(Baseball-Reference.com; U.S. Federal Census; New York Times; New York Herald; U.S. Civil War Soldiers, 1861–1865)*

Lip Pike, from 1876 St. Louis team photograph (courtesy T. Scott Brandon).

Lip Pike led the NA in homers four times in five seasons. A career .322 hitter, he batted higher than .300 six times, with a high of .377 in 1871. He also led the NA once in doubles, once in slugging, and once in RBIs. The New York City product began playing Organized Baseball in Philadelphia with Athletic in 1866; among the claimants to be the first professional player, he drew a regular salary of $20 per week from the club. Pike later played with Mutual and Atlantic before the league was organized. In the NA he played with Troy (1871), Lord Baltimore (1872–73), Hartford (1874), and the Brown Stocking club of St. Louis (1875). In the National League he played for the Brown Stockings (1876), Cincinnati (1877–78), Providence (1878), and Worcester (1881). He also played one American Association game with the Metropolitans in 1887. As an outfielder, Pike fielded above the league average in percentage but with lower range factors. The son a Jewish diamond broker, Pike was listed as a cigar maker in the 1870 census. In 1880 he was living in Albany and listed as a ball player. The 1890 Brooklyn city directory showed him to be a clerk. In 1892 *Sporting Life* reported that he was operating a "gents' furnishing goods store" in Brooklyn. Pike died of heart disease on October 10, 1893, at age 48. *(Baseball-Reference.com; U.S. Federal Census; Lain's Brooklyn City Directory; Sporting Life; International Jewish Sports Hall of Fame)*

Ed Pinkham was one of the Brooklyn players who went west to play for the new Chicago club in 1870, serving as the main pitcher. The White Stockings went 65–8, with Pinkham throwing 350 innings. He was the winning pitcher in what Chicago papers considered the game for the championship in those pre-league days, defeating Cincinnati, 16–13, on October 13. Previously he had played for Eckford (1865 and 1869), Enterprise (1866), and Oriental

Ed Pinkham, from Chicago composite photograph (courtesy Robert Edward Auctions).

(1867–68). In 24 games for the 1871 White Stockings—16 as a third baseman—he hit only .263 but drew a league-leading 18 walks, for a .381 on-base percentage. A very good fielder, he had a percentage of .754, 76 points above the league average. However, he left the club before the last road trip and never played in the majors again. Born in Brooklyn, Pinkham appeared in both the 1850 and 1860 censuses as the son of an English leather dealer. The 1882–84 Brooklyn city directories listed him as a salesman; later directories showed him as an agent. He died in Brooklyn on December 19, 1906, at age 60. *(Baseball-Reference.com; U.S. Federal Census; Lain's Brooklyn City Directory; National Association of Base Ball Players, 1857–1870; Duluth News-Tribune)*

George Popplein played in one game for Maryland in 1873. On July 11 he went hitless in four at-bats. Playing part of the game in center field and part at third base, he had one error as a third baseman. Brian McKenna notes that Popplein had been part of the Pastime club as early as 1861 and had made the first team in 1863, continuing through 1871. Born to a German father in Baltimore in 1840, Popplein was listed as a paint manufacturer as early as 1870 and as late as 1900. In 1880 he was manufacturing fertilizer; the 1890 city directory showed Popplein owning the Popplein Silicated Phosphate Company. McKenna says that he was a chemist for the plant. Popplein died of kidney disease at Baltimore on March 31, 1901, at age 61. Peter Morris says that George Popplein was one of "several ballplaying Popplein brothers," and that his record with Maryland should probably be credited to his younger brother, Joseph. *(Baseball-Reference.com; U.S. Federal Census; Baltimore City Directory; Early Baltimore Baseball; petermorrisbooks.com)*

Albert "Uncle Al" Pratt led the NA in strikeouts as well as losses in 1871 when he compiled a 10–17 record with 34 strikeouts for Forest City of Cleveland. A native of Pittsburgh, he had begun his career with Riverside of Portsmouth in 1868, moving on to Forest City the following year. After a 2–9 record in 1872, Pratt left the majors. However, his involvement with major league baseball continued. He signed with but did not play for Western in 1875; he umpired in the National League (1879) and the American Association (1883), and managed his hometown Alleghenys in 1882–83. *Sporting Life* says that Pratt "served with the colors" and that after Appomattox he "began to pur-

Al Pratt, from Cleveland team photograph (courtesy T. Scott Brandon).

sue base ball with a keen interest." Specifically, he served as a volunteer in both the 193rd Pennsylvania Infantry Regiment and the Sixty-first Pennsylvania Infantry Regiment from 1864 through the end of the Civil War. The censuses of 1900, 1910 and 1920 showed him employed in sporting goods as a salesman or merchant. *Sporting Life* notes in 1916 that Pratt was "representing Spalding interest." Pratt died in Pittsburgh on November 21, 1937, at age 90. *(Baseball-Reference.com; Sporting Life; U.S. Federal Census; National Association of Base Ball Players, 1857–1870; Civil War Veterans Who Played Major League Baseball Research Project)*

Tom Pratt was a star pitcher for Brooklyn Atlantic, beginning in 1863, and he pitched for the champion teams of 1864–65. According to his obituary, he was among the first to throw a curveball. His first Philadelphia engagement was with Quaker City in 1867; he joined Athletic in 1869. When the NA opened in 1871, his playing days were largely behind him. However, on October 18, 1871, he played first base for Athletic in a home game against Mutual. He had two hits and drove in a run in a 21–7 victory. In the field he committed three errors in 14 chances for a .786 percentage. Pratt is listed as a substitute umpire in the NA from 1871 to 1873 but "failed to give satisfaction" as a National League umpire in 1886. *Sporting Life* notes that Pratt was a "magnate," financially involved in Philadelphia baseball in three leagues. He lost heavily in his investment with the Union Association Keystones, but *Sporting Life* says that he was doing "exceedingly well" in a skating rink and was recovering his losses. Born in Chelsea, Massachusetts, Pratt grew up and spent his life in Philadelphia. In the 1880 census he was listed as a "whiting man." The 1900 census showed him to be a foreman in a whiting factory. Pratt died in Philadelphia on September 28, 1908, at age 64. Any service in the Civil War cannot be confirmed at this time. *(Baseball-Reference.com; U.S. Federal Census; Sporting Life; National Association of Base Ball Players, 1857–1870; Civil War Veterans Who Played Major League Baseball Research Project)*

Joe Quest entered the NA as an 18-year-old with the Forest City club of Cleveland in 1871. After hitting .231 in three games, he was away from the majors until 1878, playing for the Alleghenys and Indianapolis. When Indianapolis entered the National League, Quest returned as a regular second baseman, going from there to Chicago the following season. With the White Stockings he twice led NL second basemen in fielding and also posted the highest batting average of his career (.246) in 1881. Quest played with Detroit in both 1883 and 1885; in the American Association he played with the Browns and Pittsburgh before finishing with the Athletics in 1886. Over his nine-year career he batted .217, but his fielding percentage and range were above the league average. After

Joe Quest (courtesy Nigel Ayres).

umpiring in 1887, Quest was to be the Los Angeles captain in 1888. Claimed instead by St. Paul, he was promptly cut from the team. He played in the minors as late as 1892, but his career as a minor league umpire was shortened by the onset of consumption. For a number of years the New Castle, Pennsylvania, native lived on a plantation in Alabama to recover and was reported near death in 1912. Quest died in San Diego on November 14, 1924, two days short of his seventy-second birthday. *(Total Baseball; Chicago Daily Tribune; National Police Gazette; Los Angeles Times; Washington Post; Baseball-Reference.com; Cincinnati Daily Gazette)*

Quinlan played shortstop for Philadelphia in a game at Chicago on September 7, 1874. He had a single and drove in a run. In the field he handled three chances without an error. This was his only major league experience. It is possible that Quinlan was a Chicago area amateur, borrowed for the day. However, in October of 1874 the *Harrisburg Patriot* reported that a player named Quinlan was one of the new players on the Expert club of that city. *(SABR Encyclopedia; Harrisburg Patriot)*

Quinn played in two games for Atlantic on September 9 and 17, 1875 — home losses to Boston and Athletic. In eight at-bats he had a single and scored two runs. As a right fielder, he had four putouts and an error in five chances; tried at shortstop against Athletic, he had errors in both fielding chances. This is not the Paddy Quinn who played for Keokuk, Hartford and Chicago in 1875. However, a man named Quinn had played shortstop for the Pavonia club of Jersey City a week earlier. His play drew raves from the *Jersey Journal,* as he had made "one of the best one-handed fly catches ever made on the ground, thereby making doubly." *(SABR Encyclopedia; New York Times; Jersey Journal)*

Patrick "Paddy" Quinn joined Kekionga on July 26, 1871, catching the final five games before the team disbanded. He, along with shortstop Jimmy Hallinan, came from the amateur Aetna club of Chicago as replacements when Bill Lennon and Frank Selman were discharged from Kekionga. Quinn and Hallinan returned to the Aetnas when Kekionga disbanded. In 1875 Quinn again played major league baseball, splitting 33 games among Keokuk, Hartford and his hometown White Stockings, hitting .265, including .326 in 11 games with Keokuk. After the formation of the National League, he played in four games, with the White Stockings. Overall, he hit .243 in 42 NA and NL games. As a catcher, he fielded .849, 27 points over the league average. As an outfielder, he committed 17 errors in 35 fielding chances. It was said that his hands were so tough that a knife would not cut the calluses. Born to Irish parents, Quinn was listed in the 1900 census for Chicago as a coal dealer. The *Quinn Family History* says that he "made a small fortune as a 'plunger' (gambler) as the ponies became his passion." He died in Chicago on January 2, 1909, at age 59. *(Baseball-Reference.com; U.S. Federal Census; National Association of Base Ball Players, 1857–1870; Cincinnati Times-Star; Appendix H, Quinn Family History)*

John Radcliff (Radcliffe) hit .303 as the regular shortstop for NA champion Athletic in 1871. A year later he led the NA in games and at-bats as the regular shortstop for Lord Baltimore. Thereafter his hitting fell off, and he lost his regular status with Lord Baltimore, the Philadelphia White Stockings, and Centennial, ending with a .282 average for 157 games. Most of his games were at shortstop, where he fielded slightly below the league average, and at third base, where he fielded slightly above the norm. In 1874 he was expelled from the NA for attempting to bribe an umpire but was reinstated in

1875. Born in Philadelphia, Radcliff grew up in Camden, New Jersey, where he began playing Organized Ball with the Camden team. He played with Athletic in 1867–68 and 1870 and with Keystone in 1869. In 1868 he led the association in runs scored. Radcliff was listed in the Camden censuses for 1850, 1860 and 1870, the last time as a produce dealer. After his baseball career, he was listed in the 1900 and 1910 censuses as a poultry dealer. He died at Ocean City, New Jersey, on July 26, 1911, at age 63. *(Baseball-Reference.com; U.S. Federal Census; National Association of Base Ball Players, 1857–1870; Sporting Life; Philadelphia Inquirer)*

Al Reach, an English-born cricket player, learned baseball well enough to become a regular with the Athletic club of Philadelphia. He had played with Eckford (1861–64) before joining Athletic in 1865. He was second in runs scored in 1867 and first in 1868. The 31-year-old Reach was the regular second baseman for the championship A's in 1871, hitting .353. He continued with the A's until 1875. His hitting fell off after the first season, leaving him with a .247 mark for five seasons. Whether as an outfielder or a second baseman, he fielded above the league average. In 1874 he opened a store to sell baseball equipment. For a while the A.J. Reach Company was the largest sporting goods company in the United States. Reach's obituary says that he "made millions as sporting goods manufacturer." In 1883 when the Worcester team moved to Philadelphia, Reach became part-owner and club president. In the 1890 season he managed the club. In 1899 he stepped down as club president; in the same year he sold his sporting goods company to Al Spalding. Reach died at Atlantic City, New Jersey, on January 14, 1928, at age 87. His brother, Bob, played for Olympic and Washington, and his son, George, invented the cork-center baseball. *(Baseball-Reference.com; Sporting Life; U.S. Federal Census; National Association of Base Ball Players, 1857–1870; New York Times)*

Bob Reach, the younger brother of Al Reach, made a much smaller impact on baseball. Born in Brooklyn, he served with the New York Fifth Heavy Artillery Regiment from March 22, 1864, to July 19, 1865. His first recorded baseball engagement was with Philadelphia Keystone in 1868; he then played for Olympic in 1869–70. The 1870 census showed him living in Washington, D.C., working as a clerk in the post office. In 1872 he played shortstop in two games for Olympic; a year later he played in one game for Washington. In the three games he had three hits for a .231 average along with seven errors in 19 fielding chances. Reach was shown in both the 1880 census and the 1882 Washington city directory as a plumber with his own business. However, in 1887 he was able to patent an improved catcher's mask as well as the inflated punching bag to train boxers and some modern pieces of gymnastics equipment. The 66-year-old Reach then appeared in the 1910 census for

Bob Reach (*Springfield Republican*, May 1922).

Philadelphia, listed as a manufacturer. He was also responsible for a fad by inventing the "chestnut bell," a small bell people rang whenever someone tried to tell a stale joke. Reach died at Springfield, Massachusetts, on May 19, 1922, at age 78. *(Baseball-Reference.com; U.S. Federal Census; Washington City Directory; Sporting Life; Civil War Veterans Who Played Major League Baseball Research Project; Springfield Republican)*

Billy Redmon(d) was the regular shortstop for the St. Louis Red Stockings (1875) and the Milwaukee Cream Citys (1878) even though he was left-handed. He also played in three games for the Cincinnati Red Stockings in 1877. An .810 fielder, he was well below the league average, and in 70 games he hit only .221. Redmon(d) played independent ball for the Red Stockings in 1876, for Memphis and Milwaukee of the League Alliance in 1877, and for Rockford of the Northwestern League in 1879. Born in St. Louis, he appeared in the 1860 census as the son of an Irish-born river man. He had two entries in the 1880 census: William Readmond (working as a brick layer) and William Redmond (working as a wire puller); he had the same wife and two daughters under each name. The ball player died in St. Louis on April 3, 1894, at age 41. Deadball Era lists his occupation as brick layer. *(Baseball-Reference.com; U.S. Federal Census; SABR Biographical Research Committee Newsletter; Indianapolis Sentinel; DeadballEra.com)*

Hugh Reid (Reed) played right field for Lord Baltimore in a road game at Chicago on August 26, 1874. In the 6–2 loss, Reid went hitless in four at-bats but handled his only fielding chance cleanly. The pitcher for the amateur Aetna club of Chicago, Reid likely was borrowed for the game. Born in Cleveland to Irish parents, Reid became a resident of Chicago, working for the newspaper. He was married to Margaret Quinn, the sister of Paddy Quinn, his battery mate on the Aetnas. In 1900 Reid is listed as a stereotyper for the newspaper, and in 1920, by then a widower, he is simply listed as a newspaper man. Reid died in Chicago on December 22, 1928, at age 76. *(Baseball-Reference.com; SABR Encyclopedia; Hugh Alex Reid Family Tree; Cook County, Illinois Death Records, 1908–1988; Appendix H, Quinn Family History)*

Jack Remsen played with the Chicago White Stockings in 1878–79 while wearing a full beard. The Brooklyn native began his professional career in 1872 with Atlantic, also playing with Mutual and Hartford, moving with the Dark Blues into the National League in 1876. With St. Louis in 1877, Remsen moved on to Chicago, Cleveland (1881) and Philadelphia (1884) before finishing in the American Association with Brooklyn (1884). A big, speedy player, he led NL outfielders in fielding in 1878, but his career .233 batting average prompted the *Chicago Daily Tribune* to note that "but for his inability in bat [he] would be one of the most desirable ball-players in the country."

Jack Remsen (Wikimedia Commons).

He continued to play in the minors with Hartford; Ottawa, Illinois; and Lewiston, Maine. A John J. Remsen who seems to fit the ballplayer's age and background appeared in the 1900 Brooklyn census, working as a conductor. The same person is listed in the 1920 census as a building superintendent for a real estate company in Manhattan. *(Total Baseball; Baseball-Reference.com; Chicago Daily Tribune; Boston Daily Globe; U.S. Federal Census; petermorrisbooks.com)*

Larry Ressler was the first French-born player in the majors, having arrived in the United States in 1857 at age nine. Ressler was the regular left fielder for Washington in 1875, hitting .194 in 27 games. A very good outfielder, he fielded .831, 16 points above the league average and with greater range factors. Ressler had played with Reading clubs as early as 1870 and was the team captain of the Reading Actives before going to Washington. He played for and managed the Actives in 1876. Bullpen reports that he played at Erie in 1877. Ressler was a molder by trade and worked at the Reading Foundry. He also worked as a county detective, but for the most part he managed or was the proprietor of three different hotels in Reading. His obituary notes that he was a Civil War veteran, though he was only 14 when he enlisted. He is not included in SABR's list of veterans. Ressler died of gastritis at Reading on June 12, 1918, at age 70. *(Baseball-Reference.com; U.S. Federal Census; Sporting Life; Philadelphia Inquirer; Civil War Veterans Who Played Major League Baseball Research Project; Reading Eagle)*

Henry Reville played right field for Lord Baltimore on October 14, 1874. In a home 15–2 loss to Boston, Reville was hitless in four at-bats and had an assist in his only fielding chance. The *Cleveland Plain Dealer* lists a new Baltimore nine for 1879. On it, a player named Reville, a Baltimorean who had played with National of Washington in 1878, is listed as the third baseman. The 1890 Baltimore city directory showed two men named Henry Reville: Henry E. (no occupation listed) and Henry G. (a cooper). Henry E. was born in Baltimore in 1857 to Irish parents. The 1900 census showed Henry E. Reville living with his mother and working at a livery stable. He would have been 17 in 1874. *(Baseball-Reference.com; U.S. Federal Census; Baltimore City Directory; Cleveland Plain Dealer; SABR Biographical Committee Newsletter)*

William Rexter played right field for Atlantic on September 25, 1875. Hitless in four at-bats, he had a putout on his only fielding chance. The *New York Times* noted that Rexter had been added from the Greenpoint club. In 1877 the *New York Herald* reported that Rexter had been victorious in single sculls and finished second in two-oar and four-oar races at the Arlington Regatta. Born in Brooklyn, Rexter was listed variously as a pilot, an engineer, a seaman and a boatman in the 1880 census and Brooklyn city directories between 1879 and 1886. He was associated with the Williamsburg Yacht Club in Brooklyn, which his father helped found. A 1888 note in the *Brooklyn Eagle* shows that he had been removed and then reinstated in a custodial position with the club. Richard Malatsky found that Rexter had died at Staten Island, New York, on June 23, 1898, at age 48. *(Baseball-Reference.com; U.S. Federal Census; New York Times; New York Herald; Lain's Brooklyn City Directory; SABR Biographical Research Committee Newsletter; New York City Deaths, 1898–1902)*

John Richmond began with Athletic in his hometown in 1875, hitting .200 in 29 games. He returned to the majors with Syracuse in 1879. In that season the *Chicago Daily Tribune* included him in a list of former major leaguers "dropped because of inefficiency." After playing at Baltimore and Rochester, Richmond had trials with Boston (1880–81) and Cleveland (1882) in the National League and with the Athletics (1882) in the AA before landing with Columbus in 1883–84. In 1883 he hit .283 and led American Association shortstops in fielding. He finished with Pittsburgh in 1885. In all, Richmond hit .238 in eight seasons, three spent as a regular. His .866 fielding percentage was ten points higher than the league average. Richmond later played with Charleston of the Southern Association and Waterbury of the Eastern League. He died of heart disease in Philadelphia on October 5, 1898, at age 42. The occupation line on his death certificate is blank. *(Baseball-Reference.com; Chicago Daily Tribune; Washington Post; National Police Gazette; Baseball Almanac; Return of Death in the City of Philadelphia)*

William "Pigtail Billy" Riley was the regular left fielder for Keokuk in 1875 and for the Cleveland Blues in 1879. In neither place did he hit well—.144 in 51 games. A mediocre fielder in Keokuk, he became one of the National League's best at Cleveland, where his .850 percentage and 2.12 range factors were well above the league average. Between major league engagements, Riley played for Quincy, for Indianapolis of the League Alliance, and for the independent Forest City club of Cleveland. Riley was an American Association umpire in 1882; he may also be the William J. Riley listed as playing for Augusta in 1886. Born in Cincinnati to an English father, Riley died of peritonitis at Cincinnati on November 9, 1887. He was 32 years old. According to David Nemec, his nickname came from his Asian appearance. *(Baseball-Reference.com; U.S. Federal Census; DeadballEra.com; Cleveland Plain Dealer; Keokuk.net; Beer and Whiskey League)*

Val Robinson played for the Jefferson club in his hometown of Washington, D.C., in 1866 when he was 17. He played with the Olympic (1866–70) and Washington (1870) clubs before the formation of the NA. In 1872 he played in seven games as the regular right fielder of Olympic, hitting .200 with two errors in eight fielding chances. When Olympic disbanded after nine games, Robinson was out of the majors. Born in 1849, he was the son of a carpenter, appearing in the census of 1860 with the name Alfred V. Robinson. Otherwise, there are no Alfred V. Robinsons or Valentine Robinsons in the census or Washington city directory; the only Alfred Robinson is listed as a laborer. The ballplayer died in Washington, D.C., on August 2, 1898, at age 49. *(Baseball-Reference.com; U.S. Federal Census; National Association of Base Ball Players, 1857–1870; Boyd's Washington City Directory)*

Adam Rocap, a Philadelphia native, played with Athletic during most of 1875. Appearing in 16 games, he managed a .174 batting average. He performed capably in the outfield; both his percentage and range factors exceeded the league average. However, in

Adam Rocap (Wikimedia Commons).

four games at third base, he had 10 errors in 30 fielding chances. Rocap played for Pittsburgh (1876) and Indianapolis (1877) of the League Alliance and for Albany (1878–79) of the International League; he was still listed as a professional baseball player in the 1880 Philadelphia census. He and Lou Say both appeared in the 1880 Albany census, living in a boarding house and working as store clerks. Both the 1881 and 1889 city directories for Philadelphia listed him as a clerk. His death certificate calls him a shipping clerk. The 38-year-old Rocap died in Philadelphia on March 29, 1892, from obstruction of the intestine. *(Return of Death in the City of Philadelphia; Baseball-Reference.com; U.S. Federal Census; Philadelphia City Directory; Indianapolis Sentinel; Springfield (Massachusetts) Republican)*

Fraley Rogers played with the Resolute club of Brooklyn in 1865 when he was 15 years old. He then played with the powerful Star of Brooklyn club (with Candy Cummings) through 1871. In 1872 Harry Wright acquired him to replace Dave Birdsall in the Boston lineup. Rogers hit .275 for the NA champion Red Stockings, but his outfield play was mediocre. When he threatened to quit baseball in 1873, Wright signed future Hall of Fame player Jim O'Rourke to replace him. Rogers did play in two games in 1873 before leaving baseball at age 23. Born in Brooklyn, he became managing clerk for a fruit dealer. He shot himself on May 10, 1881. According to the *New York Herald-Tribune*, the 31-year-old Rogers had financial trouble. He left behind a wife and "several children." *(Baseball-Reference.com; National Association of Base Ball Players, 1857–1870; DeadballEra.com; Great Encyclopedia of Nineteenth Century Baseball; New York Herald-Tribune)*

Johnny Ryan, a 19-year-old local, made his debut with Philadelphia in October 1873.

Johnny Ryan (Wikimedia Commons).

He became a regular outfielder with Lord Baltimore in 1874 and with New Haven in 1875. He had his best season in the National League with Louisville in 1876, hitting .253, before finishing with Cincinnati in 1877. Outside the league, Ryan played with both Pittsburgh of the International League and Athletic of the League Alliance. Only a .208 career hitter, he twice led a league in striking out. However, he was one of the best outfielders of the time, leading the NA in putouts in 1874 and fielding .860, nearly 30 points over the league average. He also made six starts as a pitcher in 1875, leading to a 1–5 record and a 3.19 ERA. Ryan was out of baseball by age 23 and later became a city policeman in Philadelphia. While trying to make an arrest in a barroom brawl, he was killed on March 22, 1902. His death certificate lists the cause of death as "valvular heart disease"; however, the *Philadelphia Inquirer* says that Ryan was kicked in the abdomen and the arrested man was charged with his murder. Ryan was 50 years old. *(Baseball-Reference.com; Philadelphia Inquirer; Return of Death in the City of Philadelphia)*

Samuel "Pony" Sager played in eight games for Rockford in May of 1871. He hit well— a .282 average with five RBIs—but he did

Pony Sager (courtesy T. Scott Brandon).

not field well. In four games in left field, he had two errors for a .667 percentage; he fielded even worse as a shortstop, committing ten errors in four games. In introducing the 1871 Forest City club, Rockford newspapers said that Sager was from Marshalltown, Iowa, and had played for the Holmesburg club of Philadelphia. The June 2010 *SABR Biographical Research Committee Newsletter* reverses this, giving Sager a Pennsylvania birth. Bullpen says that Sager actually had played at Marshalltown with Cap Anson before both joined Rockford. In 1873 Sager returned to Rockford, playing shortstop for the independent Chicago White Stockings in a game with Forest City. In the 1870 census for Charlestown, New Hampshire, Sager was listed as a painter. He resurfaced in the 1920 census for Wakefield, Massachusetts, listed as a "helper," employed by the United States Government. Sager died at Newport, New Hampshire, on October 15, 1928, at age 80. *(Baseball-Reference.com; SABR Encyclopedia; SABR Biographical Committee Newsletter; U.S. Federal Census; Rockford Weekly Register-Gazette)*

Lou Say, allegedly the inventor of the hidden ball trick, played in three games for his hometown Maryland club as a 19-year-old shortstop in 1873. He also played with Lord Baltimore and Washington of the NA. After playing with the National League Cincinnati Red Stockings in 1880, Say played with Philadelphia and Baltimore of the American Association before finishing with Baltimore and Kansas City of the Union Association in 1884, making him a four-league player. In seven seasons—two as a regular—Say hit .232 and fielded .812, twenty-four points below the league average for shortstops. Between major league stops, he played for Manchester (1877) and Albany (1879–80); he later played for Omaha/Keokuk, Bridgeport, Charleston, and Haverhill. In the 1880 census for Baltimore he was listed as a "base ballist." However, the federal census for the same year listed Say and Adam Rocap as living in the same boarding house in Albany; Say was listed as a dry goods clerk. He was still listed as a ball player in the 1890 Baltimore city directory. *Sporting Life* reported in 1893 that Say would "confine his abilities to

Lou Say (Wikimedia Commons).

the management hereafter." The 1900 census showed him boarding in Baltimore, where he worked as a blacksmith. Say died on June 6, 1930, at Fallston, Maryland. He was 76 years old. His younger brother, Jimmy, was also a major league shortstop. *(Total Baseball; Baseball-Reference.com; U.S. Federal Census; Bill James' Historical Register; Baltimore City Directory; Sporting Life)*

Harry Schafer was the regular third baseman for the Red Stockings in all five seasons in the NA, coming from Athletic, for whom he had played in 1868–70. He began playing organized ball in 1867 with Arctic in his hometown of Philadelphia. In 1876 he continued as the regular third baseman for the National League Boston club before moving to part-time duty in 1877–78. In both 1872 and 1875 he reached a .288 average at the plate, settling for a .271 career mark for eight seasons. In the field he was a solid third baseman who exceeded the league average in both percentage and range. In later years he became critical of modern players who had to wear gloves in the field. In 1879 the *Cleveland Plain Dealer* reported that Schafer "is now the manager of a Boston club room." The 1930 census showed the 83-year-old Schafer living back in Philadelphia with his daughter. He died of a lingering illness on February 28, 1935, at age 88. Bill Lee states that the illness was the result of an earlier accident. *(Baseball-Reference.com; Sporting Life; Baseball Necrology; U.S. Federal Census; National Association of Base Ball Players, 1857–1870; Cleveland Plain Dealer)*

Frank Sellman (Selman), the regular third baseman for Kekionga in 1871, was another of the Baltimore players from the Maryland club that found their way to Fort Wayne. After playing 14 games for Kekionga, Sellman, along with manager Bill Lennon, was released for excessive drinking and returned to the Baltimore area. He finished his major league career with Olympic (1872), Maryland (1873), Lord Baltimore (1874) and Washington (1875). In all he played in 37 games, hitting .257, with a high of .296 in 1874. Statistically, he was a mediocre fielder as a third baseman or as a catcher. His one attempt at pitching resulted in 21 hits and 26 runs (eight earned) in a complete-game loss in 1873. According to William J. Ryczek, Sellman was also released in 1874 for "overindulgence in the flowing bowl." Outside the majors he played with Keokuk in 1874, Lowell in 1876 and Rhode Island in 1877. Born Charles Francis Sellman to a Baltimore merchant, Sellman played under the name Frank C. Williams. He last appeared in the 1880 census, living at home with five brothers and sisters, none of whom had a listed occupation. Sellman died in Baltimore on May 6, 1907. *(Baseball-Reference.com; SABR BioProject; U.S. Federal Census; National Association of Base Ball Players, 1857–1873; Chicago Daily Inter Ocean; Lowell Daily Citizen and News; Blackguards and Red Stockings)*

John "Count" Sensenderfer played for Athletic as early as 1866, and in 1868 he finished third in the NA in runs scored. The regular center fielder for the 1871 NA champions, he hit .323. He missed the final game of the season due to injury and played only sporadically over the next three seasons. His league career covered only 51 games in which he hit .299. An .807 fielder, he had above-average range. In 1874 he was part of the Boston/Athletic European touring party, even though he played only five regular-season games. Sensenderfer was a Philadelphia native, the son of a well-to-do carpenter. He studied law but did not practice. By the 1880 census, Sensenderfer, like his father, was listed as a "gentleman." Bullpen and *Sporting Life* both note that Sensenderfer was involved in politics, serving three terms as county commissioner and as a member of

Count Sensenderfer (courtesy T. Scott Brandon).

the Democratic City Committee. He died of a ruptured gastric ulcer in Philadelphia on May 3, 1903, at age 55. *(Baseball-Reference.com; U.S. Federal Census; Sporting Life; National Association of Base Ball Players, 1857–1870; City of Philadelphia Return of Death)*

George Seward played with three teams in three leagues over an eight-year period. The New York City product played in 25 games with the Brown Stockings in 1875, hitting .250. He played in one National League game with Mutual in 1876; when the American Association opened, he played in 38 games with the Brown Stockings. In 64 games he hit .226. Neither as an outfielder nor as a catcher did he have fielding statistics at the league average. In 1877 he played for Indianapolis of the League Alliance. Seward umpired in three major leagues between 1876 and 1884. He appeared in the 1870 census for New York City as a mason; in the 1880 census for St. Louis he was listed as a foreman at a gas works. In 1892 *Sporting Life* said that he was "a bricklayer in St. Louis." Seward died in St. Louis on March 24, 1904, following injuries incurred in an accident. He was 53 years old. His 1904 Missouri death certificate lists his occupation as a bricklayer. *(Baseball-Reference.com; U.S. Federal Census; Missouri Certificate of Death; Sporting Life)*

Shaffer played right field for Atlantic on September 15, 1875. In a 10–4 home loss to Mutual, he was hitless in four at-bats and committed an error on one of two fielding chances. *(Baseball-Reference.com)*

George "Orator" Shaffer (Shafer) spent 13 seasons as a major league outfielder, including ten as a regular. In 1879 he recorded 50 outfield assists, a still-standing major league

Orator Shaffer (Wikimedia Commons).

record. Over his career he hit .282, with a high of .360 with the Union Association St. Louis Maroons in 1884. He also hit .338 and .304 in 1878–79 but dropped to .214 in 1882 and .195 in 1885. A much-traveled player—some suggest because of his nickname—he began with Hartford in 1874. Along the way, he played with 10 clubs, finishing with his hometown Athletics of the American Association in 1890, making him one of the four-league players. Stops include Philadelphia and Mutual of the NA and Louisville, Indianapolis, Chicago, Cleveland, St. Louis and Buffalo of the National League. After his release from the Athletics, Shaffer had plans to open a tavern, but the *Detroit Free Press* reported that he "talks too much to be a bartender and should open a barber shop." His younger brother, Taylor, played shortstop with the Philadelphia A's in Shaffer's last season. Born in Philadelphia, Shaffer died there on January 21, 1922, at age 71. *(Total Baseball; Baseball-Reference.com; BaseballLibrary.com; SABR Baseball Encyclopedia; Detroit Free Press)*

John Sheppard played in three games—two in the outfield and one as a catcher—for Maryland in 1873. He had difficulty both in the field and at the plate, going 0-for-11 and committing five errors in 11 fielding chances. A player named Sheppard had played with Brandywine of West Chester in 1867–68 and had averaged 7.7 runs per game in 1867. One Baltimore John Sheppard, the son of a commission merchant from Virginia, moved to St. Louis after 1890 to work for Mercantile Trust; another, a liquor merchant, was cited several times in the 1870s for selling liquor on Sundays. *(Baseball-Reference.com; National Association of Base Ball Players, 1857–1870; U.S. Federal Census; Baltimore Sun)*

Sheridan played left field for Atlantic on the last day of the 1875 season. In a 20–7 home loss to Hartford on October 9, he was hitless in four at-bats and handled no chances in the field. *(New York Times; Baseball-Reference.com)*

Joe Simmons (Joseph Chabriel) came to the White Stockings in 1871 from Rockford. The New York City product began in 1865 with Gotham before moving to Empire. In 1868 he averaged six runs per game while playing for Excelsior of Chicago. At Rockford in 1870 he led the team in runs. Simmons became the regular right fielder for the White Stockings and was a better-than-average one but hit only .217. In 1872 he moved to the Forest City club of Cleveland, for whom he played an excellent first base and hit .256. He finished as playing manager with Keokuk in 1875. For his career, he hit .221 in 58 games. In the 1870 census he was listed as a resident of Rockford, Illinois, and a baseball player. *Sporting Life* and the *Encyclopedia of Minor League Baseball* show him remaining in baseball as a minor league umpire (Tri-State League) and manager at

Joe Simmons, from Chicago composite photograph (courtesy Robert Edward Auctions).

Wilmington (1884), Richmond (1885), Waterbury (1886), and Syracuse (1887). He managed the Quicksteps in their Union Association attempt in 1884. In the 1890s Simmons moved to Syracuse. He died at Jersey City, New Jersey, on July 24, 1901, at age 56. (*Baseball-Reference.com; Sporting Life; Encyclopedia of Minor League Baseball; U.S. Federal Census; SABR Biographical Research Committee Newsletter*)

Marty Simpson played second base and caught for the Maryland club of Baltimore during its short tenure in the NA in 1873. In four games he had four hits for a .133 average. In three games at second base he fielded .792, 46 points below the league average. He may have been a teenager. A young man named Martin Simpson, born in Baltimore in 1855, appeared in the 1860 census. Martin Simpson, a clerk, is listed in the 1890 Baltimore city directory. Maryland left the league in July, ending Simpson's major league career. (*Baseball-Reference.com; U.S. Federal Census; Baltimore City Directory*)

Bill Smiley played two games as a third baseman for Lord Baltimore at the end of 1874. The 18-year-old did not record a hit. Smiley played for Ludlow in 1876, for Albany in 1878, for Albany and Rochester in 1879, for Baltimore and Rochester in 1880, and for Albany and Atlantic in 1881. In 1882 when the American Association was founded, Smiley played second base for the St. Louis Brown Stockings and Baltimore Orioles. In 77 total games Smiley hit .195, but he was a competent second baseman, finishing second in assists. His .874 percentage and range factors were close to the league average. He played for Wilmington in 1883 and was a member of the Richmond Virginians at the time of his death. Suffering from "rheumatism in the region of the heart," the 28-year-old Smiley died in Baltimore on July 11, 1884. A baseball game featuring Hugh "One-Arm" Daley was played in October to benefit Smiley's widowed mother. (*Baseball-Reference.com; Baltimore Sun; Rochester Hop-Bitters, 1879–1880; Trenton State Gazette*)

Bill Smith played in all six games for Maryland in 1873: three as a center fielder, two as a catcher, and one as a second baseman. He was a decent catcher (.800 fielding percentage) and mediocre in the other positions (overall .667). Offensively, he had four hits for a .174 average. Smith also managed the team to an 0–6 record. According to Bullpen, Smith umpired a game in the Union Association. Not surprisingly, William J. Smith is a common name in the Baltimore census. (*Baseball-Reference.com*)

Charlie Smith played third base on the great Atlantic teams of the 1860s, including the 1864–65 national champions. Born in 1840, Smith began with Atlantic in 1858. In 1864 he became the first player to score 100 runs in a season, needing just 19 games to reach that mark. *Sporting Life* remembered him as a player who "never struck out or missed a ball that came in his direction." Already 30 years old when the NA formed, he was selected by Mutual because of his past accomplishments. In 14 league games before leaving the team in August, he hit .256 and fielded 18 points below the league average. Bullpen asserts that he suffered a nervous breakdown. *Sporting Life* says that Smith spent the last years of his life in a "neat cottage" at Great Neck, New York, on Long Island. G. Smith Stanton described Smith as an "unassuming gentleman" with crooked fingers from his years of playing third base without a glove. Smith died at Great Neck on November 15, 1897, at age 56. (*Baseball-Reference.com; Sporting Life; National Association of Base Ball Players, 1857–1870; New York Times; petermorrisbooks.com*)

John Smith played for three NA clubs, from 1873 to 1875. He seems to have been a Baltimore native, for he began as a shortstop and left fielder with Maryland in 1873, hitting .105 in five games. He shifted to Lord Baltimore in 1874, playing in six games and raising his average to .190. He ended his major league career by playing in one game for New Haven in 1875, finishing with a .722 fielding percentage and a .140 batting average for 43 at-bats. (*Baseball-Reference.com; SABR Encyclopedia*)

Tom Smith played three games at second base for Atlantic between September 15 and October 9, 1875. In these games he managed one hit for an .077 average. In the field he had five errors for a .783 percentage. The *New York Times* noted that Smith was one of three amateur players added to the reorganized Atlantics. He was described as being "of the Nassaus." Born at Guelph, Ontario, in 1851, Smith was the first Canadian to play in the majors. He died in Detroit on March 28, 1889, at age 38. Citing the *New York Clipper*, Peter Morris argues that the player is actually A. Smith of the Concord club. The common name makes this search difficult. (*Baseball-Reference.com; SABR Encyclopedia; New York Times; petermorrisbooks.com*)

Charlie Snow caught in one game for Atlantic on October 1, 1874. That day made the 25-year-old Snow unique in baseball history. In a 29–0 loss at Boston, Snow had a single in his only plate appearance for a 1.000 batting average. In the field he had three errors in as many fielding chances for an .000 percentage. Born in Lowell, Massachusetts, Snow lived in Brooklyn most of his life. In the 1910 census he was listed as manager of a stationery store. In 1920, he described himself as a stationery salesman. He died in Brooklyn on August 27, 1929, at age 80. (*Baseball-Reference.com; U.S. Federal Census*)

Charles "Pop" Snyder, a Washington, D.C., product, began his professional career while still a teenager with Washington in 1873, also playing with Lord Baltimore and Philadelphia. After leading NA catchers in fielding in 1875, he joined the Louisville Grays of the National League in 1876–77. He played with Boston (1878–81) before becoming a playing manager of the Cincinnati Red Stockings in 1882, leading them to a league championship. Remaining with the Red Stockings through 1886, he then played with three Cleveland entries—the American Association Blues (1887–88), the NL Spiders (1889) and the Players League Infants (1890), finishing back with Washington in 1891. In eighteen seasons he caught at least 50 games twelve times, hitting .236. He hit .291 with the 1882 AA champions. An .893 fielder, he was a dozen points higher than the league average for catchers. After leaving the playing ranks, he umpired in both the AA (1891) and the NL (1892–93 and 1898–1901). He also umpired in the Eastern League. Born to a German father, Snyder appeared in both the 1910 and 1920 censuses for D.C., living with his brother-in-law and having his own income. Snyder died at Washington, D.C., on October 29, 1924, at age 70. (*Total Baseball; Baseball-Reference.com; Washington Post; Chicago Daily Tribune; U.S. Federal Census*)

Jim Snyder was the regular shortstop for Eckford in 1872, hitting .291 in 24 games. While his fielding percentage was 25 points under the league average, his range statistics were the average of the league. Born in Brooklyn, Snyder caught for Eckford in 1870 but managed only 20 hits in 19 games. He is also listed as a team member of the "reorganized" Eckford team for 1871. When Eckford disbanded at the end of 1872, Snyder was out of baseball. The son of an undertaker, Snyder was listed as an undertaker in the 1870 census. He is so listed in the 1881 city directory for Brooklyn and in censuses through 1920, when he had moved out to Rockaway Beach. He died at Rockaway Beach on December 1, 1922, at age 75. *(Baseball-Reference.com; U.S. Federal Census; Brooklyn City Directory; National Association of Base Ball Players, 1857–1870)*

Josh Snyder began playing for Eckford in 1860 when he was 16 years old. He appeared on the roster periodically through 1871. When Eckford entered the NA in 1872, Snyder played left field for nine of the club's 29 games. He contributed only a .162 batting average and played his last game in July. His father was a Brooklyn undertaker, and Snyder inherited that profession. He was so listed in the 1880 census and in Brooklyn city directories prior to 1880. Snyder died in Brooklyn on April 21, 1881, at age 37. Despite the fact that both are sons of Brooklyn undertakers, and the *Herald-Tribune* refers to the "Snyder brothers," Josh Snyder apparently was not a brother of Eckford teammate Jim Snyder. *(Baseball-Reference.com; U.S. Federal Census; Brooklyn City Directory; National Association of Base Ball Players, 1857–1870; New York Herald-Tribune)*

Ed Somerville entered the majors as the regular second baseman for his hometown Centennial club in 1875. After Centennial disbanded, he joined Elm City, continuing as the regular second baseman. When the National League formed, he was the regular second baseman for Louisville in 1876 but hit only .188 and was not a part of the 1877 team. In 111 games with three clubs, he hit .200. However, he earned his keep defensively. His percentage of .838 was slightly below the league average, but his range far exceeded that of his contemporaries. Fielding statistics for 1876 show that Somerville was almost in a league of his own. While leading NL second basemen in errors, he also led in assists and was second in putouts,

Ed Somerville, from Tecumseh team photograph (courtesy T. Scott Brandon).

one behind Jack Burdock. He handled 510 chances—eighty more than runner-up Burdock. Somerville first appeared in the census of 1870. One of nine children born to an Irish carpenter, the 16-year-old Edward was apprenticed to a printer. At the time of his death, he was an active player with Tecumseh of London, Ontario. He died in London on October 1, 1877. He was only 24 years old. *(Baseball-Reference.com; U.S. Federal Census)*

Al Spalding led the NA in wins in each of the five years of its existence. As a sixteen-year-old in 1867, Spalding pitched the Rockford Forest City club to a 29–23 victory over the touring Washington Nationals. In 1870, he had a win and a tie against the Cincinnati Red Stockings. As a result, Spalding entered the NA pitching for the Red Stockings in Boston. After posting won-lost records of 19–10, 38–8, 41–14, 52–16, and 54–5 for the Red Stockings, he entered the National League with the White Stockings, leading the NL with a 47–12 record in 1876. In all as a pitcher, he compiled a 253–65 record

Al Spalding, from "Chicago Champions" (LC-DIG-pga-18390 Library of Congress Prints and Photographs Division).

and a 2.14 ERA in seven seasons. His .795 winning percentage remains the all-time record. A career .313 hitter, Spalding shifted to first base in 1877, his last season as a regular. After playing in one final game in 1878, he then became owner of the White Stockings. Born in Byron, Illinois, Spalding grew up in Rockford. In 1876 he and his brother opened a sporting goods company in Chicago, manufacturing baseball equipment. This led to a chain of sporting goods stores across the United States. In 1888 he acquired the competing sporting goods company owned by Al Reach. Spalding died in San Diego on September 9, 1915, at age 65. He was elected to the Baseball Hall of Fame in 1939. *(Baseball-Reference.com; Sporting Life; National Association of Base Ball Players, 1857–1870; "Al Spalding")*

Spencer played shortstop for National on June 3, 1872, in a 13–2 loss to Athletic. Spencer went hitless in four at-bats but scored a run. In the field he had errors on four of seven chances. Because the game was played in Philadelphia, Spencer may have been a Philadelphia amateur recruited for the day. Peter Morris suggests that the name, listed with quotation marks in the box score, is an alias for an established player recruited for the game. *(Baseball-Reference.com; SABR Encyclopedia; petermorrisbooks.com)*

Joe "Old Reliable" Start had a career that spanned three manifestations of professional baseball. Born in New York City in 1842, Start played for Enterprise of Brooklyn (1860–61) before joining the powerful Atlantic club (1863–70). He led the amateur association in runs in 1861, finishing second in 1865 and third in 1867. He was also second in hits in 1865. Already 29 years old when the league was formed, Start hit .360 for Mutual in the inaugural season. When the National League formed, he played with the Mutuals (1876), Hartford (1877), Chicago (1878), and Providence (1879–85), before finishing with Washington (1886) at age 43. From 1878 on, he was the oldest player in the league. A .300 hitter for the eleven NL seasons (.299 for 16 seasons overall), he hit .351 and led the NL in runs in 1878 and batted .329 as late as 1882. Start led the NA or NL first basemen in fielding six times, finishing with a .963 percentage, eleven points above the league average. He was captain at both Hartford and Providence, helping Providence to its World Series championship in 1884. When Start left baseball, he "went into the hotel business [and] amassed a small fortune" and became a "retired capitalist." He died in Providence, Rhode Island, on March 27, 1927, at age 84. *(Total Baseball; Baseball-Reference.com; Boston Daily Globe; New York Times; National Association of Base Ball Players, 1857–1870)*

Bill Stearns was the youngest player in the NA in 1871. The 18-year-old right-hander started two games for Olympic, winning both. A year later he lost all 11 decisions while National folded without a team win. Subsequent seasons were hardly better, as he went 7–25 with Washington in 1873, 3–14 with Hartford in 1874, and 1–14 with Washington in 1875. He left the majors with a 13–64 record and a 4.28 ERA. Despite a .191 batting average and a .700 fielding percentage, he also played in 26 games as an outfielder. Suspended in 1874 for drawing a salary advance and skipping out on Hartford, he was reinstated for the 1875 reason. Born in Washington, D.C., Stearns was listed in the 1880 census (as William Stern) and in the 1890 Washington city directory as a clerk in the U.S. Pension Office. His obituary in the *Washington Post* says that he was a Spanish-American War veteran who died in Washington, D.C., on December 30, 1898, from malaria contracted while serving in Puerto Rico with the Eighty-sixth D.C. Infantry. It also states that he was a member of the Grand Army of the Republic and was "a soldier of two wars." His widow, Kate, applied for a Civil War pension in 1899, giving the Eighty-sixth D.C. Infantry as his unit. But the SABR Committee points out that Stearns would have been only 11 years old at the end of the Civil War. *(Baseball-Reference.com; U.S. Federal Census; Washington City Directory; Washington Post; Civil War Veterans Who Played Major League Baseball Research Project; Civil War Pension Index)*

Robert Stevens played right field for Washington on May 4, 1875. In a 21–3 loss to Athletic, he had a hit in four at-bats but committed an error in his only fielding chance. That the game was in Washington suggests that Stevens was a local player, pressed into service for the day. One candidate is Robert W. Stevens, born in D.C. in August 1852. The son of an insurance agent, he was listed in the 1870 Washington census. By 1900 he was living in Chicago, working as a day laborer. He was a nursing home resident in the 1920 census. Another possibility is Robert E. Stevens, son of a House of Representatives clerk from California. Born around 1855, Robert E. Stevens was listed as a page in the House of Representatives in 1870 and as a student in 1880. Either Robert Stevens would have been around 22 or 23 in 1875. *(Baseball-Reference.com; U.S. Federal Census)*

Garret C. "Gat" Stires, who began playing with Rockford in 1868, was the regular right fielder in 1871. In 25 games the 21-year-old New Jersey product hit .273—second highest on the team behind Cap Anson—with 12 extra-base hits and a team-leading 24 RBIs. In the field he had an .837 percentage, seven points better than the league average. Not surprisingly, Stires, along with Scott Hastings, was the highest-paid player on the team, earning $100 per month between April 15 and October 15. (Cap Anson earned $66.66 per month.) Despite these

Gat Stires, from Rockford composite photograph (courtesy T. Scott Brandon).

figures, Stires did not play in the majors after the 1871 season. He first appeared in the 1860 census as a resident of Byron Village in Illinois, where his father was a farmer. He also appears in censuses for 1870, 1900, 1910 and 1930 as a resident of Byron Village. After leaving baseball, Stires mined in Colorado and worked as a government surveyor in the Northwest before farming in Iowa. In 1887 he was appointed postmaster for Byron. In 1896 *Sporting Life* said that Stires was living in Hot Springs, Arkansas. He died on June 13, 1933, at age 84. *(Baseball-Reference.com; U.S. Federal Census; Sporting Life; National Association of Base Ball Players, 1857–1870; Rockford Weekly Gazette)*

Stoddard played in the final two games for Atlantic in 1875—a 10–7 loss at Mutual and a 20–7 home loss to Hartford. In nine at-bats, Stoddard had one hit. In one game in center field and one in left field, he had an error in five fielding chances. Atlantic did not enter the National League, and Stoddard's major league career ended. More than 30 men named Stoddard appeared in the 1889 Brooklyn city directory. *(Baseball-Reference.com; Brooklyn City Directory)*

Ed Stratton pitched three games for Maryland in 1873. In three complete games, he pitched 27 innings without recording either a strikeout or a base on balls. He did, however, give up 75 hits and 75 runs—25 of which were earned. He also played one game in right field without handling a fielding chance. At the plate he had two hits for a .125 average. Baseball-Reference.com says that he later played in the Eastern League for Richmond (1884) and Norfolk (1885). Stratton appeared in the 1870 census as a fifteen-year-old student. He also appeared in the 1879–80 Baltimore city directory, still living at home, with "base ball" as his occupation. Peter Morris says that Stratton was living in Richmond, but there is no trace of him after 1892. *(Baseball-Reference.com; U.S. Federal Census; Woods' Baltimore City Directory; SABR Encyclopedia; Petermorrisbooks.com; Cleveland Plain Dealer)*

Seymour "Sy" or "Seem" or "Warhorse" Studley began playing for National in 1866 when the Comptroller of the Currency brought him from Rochester and gave him a place in the Redemption Division. In 1872 the 31-year-old Studley played center field for five games before National disbanded. In these games he hit .095 and committed nine errors in 21 fielding chances. Newspaper articles in 1907 credit Studley with being the first person to slide headfirst into a base, this occurring in 1867. Born in New York State in 1841, Studley served in the Fifty-fourth New York Infantry in 1864, suffering a severe sunstroke. Originally declared dead in 1874, he moved to Nebraska in 1883, where he applied for a military pension as an invalid in 1890. The Omaha city directory listed him first as a machinist for the Union Pacific Railroad and later as a solicitor. He died at the Soldiers and Sailors Home in Grand Island, Nebraska, on July 9, 1901, at age 60. *(Baseball-Reference.com; National Association of Base Ball Players, 1857–1870; SABR Biographical Research Committee Newsletter; Civil War Veterans Who Played Major League Baseball Research Project; Baseball Magazine; Omaha City Directory; Salt Lake Telegram)*

Sullivan played in two games as a right fielder for New Haven on May 15 and May 17, 1875. Described as an amateur, he replaced an injured Henry Luff in the Elm City lineup. In home losses to Washington, Sullivan had three hits, scoring three runs and driving in two. He handled his only fielding chance cleanly. Despite this promising start, Sullivan never played again in the majors, and his first name has not been recorded. *(Baseball-Reference.com; Major*

League Baseball in Gilded Age Connecticut; Hartford Courant)

Ezra Sutton hit the first home run in major league history and led NA third basemen in fielding as a 21-year-old in 1871. Beginning with the Alert club of Rochester, New York, in 1869, Sutton transferred to the Forest City club of Cleveland in 1870 and played two NA seasons with them. He moved to Athletic in 1873 and continued with them into the National League in 1876. When that club folded at the end of 1876, he transferred to Boston, where he finished his major league career in 1888. The career .288 hitter batted better than .300 four times in NL play, topped by a .346 mark in 1884, when he led the league in hits. His fielding percentage of .849 is twenty-eight points higher than the league average for third basemen. In 1888 he was released to Rochester of the International League and later played for Hartford and Milwaukee. After Sutton left baseball, his story is not a happy one. His business venture into an ice plant failed in 1890. At this time Sutton came down with the crippling locomotor ataxia disease. A product of Palmyra, New York, he died at Braintree, Massachusetts, on June 20, 1907, at age 56. Harold Seymour says that Sutton died destitute. *(Total Baseball; Baseball-Reference.com; Baseball: The Golden Age; U.S. Federal Census; National Association of Base Ball Players, 1857–1870)*

Marty Swandell (Schwandel), a German-born player, was an outfielder on the undefeated Eckford team in 1863. That year he led the NA by averaging four hits per game. Continuing with Eckford through 1867, he shifted to Mutual in 1968. He returned to Eckford in 1871 and entered the NA with them in 1872, playing in 14 games and hitting .231. In 1873 he played in two games for Resolute, leaving the majors with a .211 average for 16 games. He had below-average fielding percentages both as a third baseman (six games) and as a center fielder (five

Ezra Sutton (LC-DIG-bbc-0095f Library of Congress Prints and Photographs Division).

Marty Swandell, from 1870 Mutual team photograph (Wikimedia Commons).

games). In the 1880 census, Swandell lived in Brooklyn and "keeps a bakery." A note in *Sporting Life* in 1888 says that he still lived in Brooklyn. The 1888–90 Brooklyn city directories listed him under his birth name, also as a baker. He died in Brooklyn on October 25, 1906, at age 65. *(Baseball-Reference.com; National Association of Base Ball Players, 1857–1870; Sporting Life; U.S. Federal Census; Lain's Brooklyn City Directory)*

Charlie Sweasy (Swasey) played second base for the 1869–70 Cincinnati Red Stockings, drawing an annual salary of $800. He began with Irvington (1866–67) and the Buckeye club of Cincinnati (1868) before joining the Red Stockings. When the NA opened, he played five games for Olympic, continuing in a reserve role with the Forest City club of Cleveland, the Boston Red Stockings, Atlantic, and Lord Baltimore before again becoming a regular with the St. Louis Red Stockings (1875) and the National League Cincinnati Red Stockings (1876) and Providence Grays (1878). While he was a statistically average second baseman, he was only a .194 hitter over his career. Continuing in the minors, he played for Manchester and Attleboro before rheumatism forced him to give up the game. In 1898 *Sporting Life* described him as a "full-fledged New Jersey farmer." The 1900 census showed him as a resident of Irvington, New Jersey, working as a watchman at the town hall. He died from a "complication of diseases" on March 30, 1908, at age 60. *(Baseball-Reference.com; National Association of Base Ball Players, 1857–1870; U.S. Federal Census; Sporting Life)*

Z.H. Taylor played first base for Lord Baltimore in September and October of 1874. In 13 games he hit .250 and was a competent first baseman. His .914 fielding average was just under the league average, but his range factors were well above. The Lords disbanded at the end of 1874, ending Taylor's major league career. There is a Zachery H. Taylor, born in Baltimore in 1850. The son of a Scottish-born butter merchant, Taylor was listed as being three months old at the time of the 1850 census. In the 1870 census he was still living at home with no occupation given. The 1910 census showed him living in Baltimore with his sisters and brothers, working as a clerk. Peter Morris says that Taylor died in Baltimore on November 21, 1917. *(Baseball-Reference.com; U.S. Federal Census; petermorrisbooks.com)*

Walter "Wallace" Terry played in six games for Washington in 1875. At the plate he had four hits for a .182 average. He had eight errors in four games as a first baseman and three errors in four chances as an outfielder. The 5–23 Washingtons finished on July 4, and Terry was out of the majors. He apparently finished that season with the Trenton club. In 2010 researcher Peter Morris found

Charlie Sweasy, from "First Nine of the Cincinnati (Red Stockings) Baseball Club" (LC-USZC4-1291 Library of Congress Prints and Photographs Division).

Wallace Terry (from *Nine Thousand Miles on a Pullman Train* by Milton M. Shaw, 1898).

a positive identification of Terry. An 1899 article in the *Reading Eagle* noted that Walter Terry, a Philadelphia native and Pennsylvania railroad conductor, was visiting his old 1875 Washington teammate Larry Ressler. Terry could be traced through his residence and occupation. The 1880 census for Philadelphia showed him to be married and employed by the railroad. On February 20, 1908, Terry died from a fractured skull at Colonia, New Jersey, the result of an accident when his head apparently struck a post while he was leaning from the cab to check the side of the train. He was 57 years old. *(Baseball-Reference.com; SABR Biographical Research Committee Newsletter; Nine Thousand Miles on a Pullman Train; Philadelphia Inquirer; Trenton State Gazette)*

Al Thake, an English-born outfielder, hit .295 for Atlantic in 1872, his only year in the league. The 22-year-old drove in 15 runs in 18 games and had an .808 fielding percentage. On September 1, 1872, while on a fishing expedition with teammates in New York Harbor, he fell from the boat and drowned. The *New York Post* noted that Thake "was a good swimmer, but it is thought he got entangled in the fish lines." However, the *New York Times* reported that the tide immediately carried him beyond assistance. The *Brooklyn Eagle* noted that Thake had played with the Star club in Brooklyn before joining Atlantic. Arriving in the United States in 1857, he grew up in Cleveland, Ohio. *(Baseball-Reference.com; DeadballEra.com; Hartford Daily Courant; Brooklyn Eagle; New York Times; New York Post; U.S. Federal Census)*

Andrew Thompson shared catching duties for the 1875 Washington club. In 11 games he hit .098. In ten games as a catcher he committed 32 errors for a .624 percentage. In addition, he allowed 25 passed balls. Peter Morris believes that Thompson's first name was not Andrew, but that he did later play for the T.B.F.U.S. club of Bridgeport. On May 21, the Hartford newspaper reported that Thompson was shifting to the Bridgeport club. Thompson is not the Andrew Thompson who managed St. Paul in 1884, but see the entry for Frank Thompson below. *(Baseball-Reference.com; petermorrisbooks.com; Hartford Daily Courant)*

Frank Thompson played right field for Atlantic on September 11, 1875. In a 13–6 loss to Elm City, Thompson had two hits, scored a run and drove in a run. However, he had errors on both of his fielding chances. He and Andrew Thompson (above) may be the same person. Both SABR and Baseball-Reference.com say that Thompson played for Erie of the League Alliance in 1877. When giving background information on members of the Erie team, the *Wheeling Register* notes that Thompson, the right fielder, had caught for Bridgeport the previous season. *(Baseball-Reference.com; SABR Encyclopedia; Wheeling Register)*

Jim Tipper played left field and third base for his hometown Mansfield club as early as 1869. When Mansfield joined the NA in 1872, Tipper hit .264 in 24 games before the club disbanded. In 1874 he became the regular left fielder for the Dark Blue club of Hartford, hitting .305. However, in 1875 Tipper's average fell to .157 as the regular left fielder for Elm City, and he left the majors with a .245 average for 110 games. His .798 fielding percentage was average for left fielders at the time, though *Sporting Life* reported that his one-hand catches of line drives had no equals in those bare-hand days. *Sporting Life* also says that Tipper played for Live Oak of Lynn and the Syracuse Stars in 1876. His obituary says that he played for Rochester in 1877–78. His playing career ended when an infection caused him to lose the middle finger of his left hand. Born to Irish parents in Middletown, he was listed in the 1870 census as an iron moulder. He died of alcoholism at New Haven on April 21, 1895, at age 44. His obituary notes that he died penniless, leaving his family in needy circumstances. *(Baseball-Reference.com; Sporting Life; U.S. Federal Census; Middletown City Directory; National Association of Base Ball Players, 1857–1870; New Haven Register)*

Fred Treacey led NA hitters with four homers and outfielders with a .918 fielding percentage in the inaugural 1871 season with Chicago. The Brooklyn-born Treacey had played earlier for Eckford before jumping to the White Stockings in 1870. He later played with Athletic (1872), Philadelphia (1873 and 1875), the Chicago White Stockings (1874), and Centennial (1875) and in the National League with the Mutuals (1876). After the first season his hitting fell

Fred Treacey, from Chicago composite photograph (courtesy Robert Edward Auctions).

off drastically, to a low of .189 in 1874, and he finished with a .244 average for six seasons, though his fielding percentage and range continued to be far above the league average. He is mentioned in *Sporting Life* in 1887 as one who had played with Excelsior. In that publication his name is spelled "Treacy." Peter Morris believes that the Frederick B. Treacy who appears as a clerk in the Brooklyn city directory between 1879 and 1891 may be the player. Morris believes the player died in 1891. Morris further calls into question the assertion that the Pete Treacey who played alongside of Fred on the 1876 Mutuals is Fred's brother. *(Baseball-Reference.com; Sporting Life; National Association of Base Ball Players, 1857–1870; Petermorrisbooks.com)*

George Trenwith broke in with his hometown Centennial club in 1875. The 24-year-old played third base in ten of the club's 14 games. After Centennial disbanded, he finished the season with Elm City. In 16 games between the two clubs, he hit .200. In the field, he struggled with a .629 percentage when league third basemen were fielding .805. Trenwith appeared in the census for 1870, the 19-year-old living at home with his Irish mother. The 1881 Philadelphia city directory showed the unemployed Trenwith still living at home with his mother, a dressmaker. He died in Philadelphia of chronic pulmonary phthisis on February 1, 1890. His death certificate lists his occupation as moulder. *(Baseball-Reference.com; U.S. Federal Census; Gopsill's Philadelphia City Directory; Return of Death in the City of Philadelphia)*

Charlie Waitt is alleged to be the first baseball player—other than the catcher—to wear a glove. To the ridicule of fans and fellow players, he donned a flesh-colored glove in 1875, and thus changed baseball. He had four major league trials with four different teams in four years. He played in 30 games with the Brown Stockings in 1875, 10 games with the White Stockings in 1877, 72 games with the Orioles in 1882, and one game with the Quakers in 1883. Perhaps helped by the glove, he was a better-than-average defensive outfielder, but he hit only .165. Born in Hallowell, Maine, Waitt was still listed as living at home in the 1880 census. In 1886 *Sporting Life* stated that Waitt was employed by the Pennsylvania Railroad, and after his family moved to California, Waitt worked for the railroad as a fireman or brakeman. In the 1910 census the 59-year-old Waitt was working as a janitor. He died at San Francisco on October 21, 1912, at age 59. *DeadballEra.com* says that he held a job as a window washer and died as a result of injuries sustained from falling from a ladder. *(Baseball-Reference.com; U.S. Federal Census; San Francisco City Directory; DeadballEra.com; Sporting Life)*

Oscar Walker, a left-handed outfielder/first baseman, played in one game for his hometown Brooklyn Atlantics in 1875. In 1877 he signed with St. Paul but jumped to Manchester and was banned for contract jumping. In 1879 he returned to the majors with Buffalo, hitting .275 as the regular first baseman, but became the first player to strike out five times in a nine-inning game. In 1882 Walker joined the St. Louis Browns of the American Association and became a regular outfielder, leading the AA with seven homers. In 1884, back with Brooklyn, he hit .270 as an outfield regular with the Trolley Dodgers, before finishing with Baltimore in 1885. For his career he hit .254 in 281 games. Born to German parents, Walker was listed as a painter in the 1880 census. He died in Brooklyn on May 20, 1889, at age 35. His obituary noted that he was a "big-hearted man and had many friends." His widow left destitute after his long illness, a benefit game was played for her relief. *(Total Baseball; Baseball-Reference.com; U.S. Federal Census; Wikipedia; Major League Baseball's "Permanently ineligible list"; Sporting Life; St. Louis Republic)*

Charlie Waitt from "Chicago Champions" (LC-DIG-pga-18390 Library of Congress Prints and Photographs Division).

Howard Wall played shortstop for Washington on September 13, 1873. In a 7–4 home loss to Boston, Wall had an error in his only fielding chance but stroked a hit and scored a run in three at-bats. He was a local Washington, D.C., player, 18 years old on the day. In the 1880 census, he was still living at home, working as a bookkeeper. The 1900 Washington city directory and the 1900 census showed him as a coal merchant, a single man living with his mother. His obituary in the *Washington Post* describes him as a well-known coal dealer. He died on March 15, 1909, at age 55. *(Baseball-Reference.com; U.S. Federal Census; Washington City Directory; Washington Post)*

Fred Warner began his major league career with his hometown Centennial club in 1875 and played in one game with the A's in the inaugural National League season. He played for Indianapolis in the League Alliance in 1877 before becoming the regular shortstop for that club in the NL in 1878 and the regular third baseman for Cleveland in 1879. After playing in the minors with Washington, Newark, and the Camden Merrits, he returned to Philadelphia to play for the Quakers in 1883; he finished as the regular third baseman for Brooklyn in 1884. In six major league seasons, Warner hit as high as .248 in 1878, settling for a .234 average. A good-fielding shortstop—thirty points above the league average—Warner was well below the league average for third basemen in both percentage and range. The son of a druggist, Warner was still living at home with no listed occupation in 1880. In 1885 he was jailed in Philadelphia for refusing to support his wife and two children. His death notice in *Sporting Life* says that he worked as a railway conductor. Only 31 years old, Warner died of pulmonary phthisis in Philadelphia on February 13, 1886, following a four-month illness. *(Total Baseball; Baseball-Reference.com; U.S. Federal Census; Sporting Life; DeadballEra.com)*

Fred Waterman began as third baseman for the Empire Club of New York City in 1865, moving on to Mutual a year later. In 1868 he joined Cincinnati and became a part of the Red Stockings in 1869–70. When the NA opened, he joined Olympic as the regular third baseman, hitting .316. He played bit roles for Olympic in 1872 and Washington in 1873, finishing with the White Stockings in 1875. In 61 games in the NA he hit .333 and fielded .707—just under the league average. He was listed as being in insurance in 1869, when he commanded a $1,000 salary from the Red Stockings. However, after leaving baseball, he fell upon hard times. When he died of pneumonia in Cincinnati on December 16, 1899, *Sporting Life* described him as "a wreck and friendless." Only donations from friends kept him from being buried in Potter's Field. He was 54 years old. *(Baseball Reference.com; Sporting Life; National Association of Base Ball Players 1857–1870; Sporting Life; New York Clipper Baseball Biographies)*

Fred Waterman, from "First Nine of the Cincinnati (Red Stockings) Baseball Club" (LC-USZC4-1291 Library Congress Prints and Photographs Division).

Sam Weaver, a Philadelphia native, began as an amateur with the Expert club in his hometown in 1872. He made one successful start for Philadelphia in 1876, before turning up at Milwaukee in 1877. He returned to the majors in 1878 as a 31-game loser (despite a 1.95 ERA) for the National League Cream Citys. When the American Association was formed in 1882, Weaver won 26 games for the Athletics, completing all 41 of his starts. After going 24–22 for the Louisville Eclipse in 1883, he seized the chance to return to Philadelphia to pitch for the Union Association Keystones. His ERA ballooned to 5.76 and his win total dropped to five; in addition he was blacklisted for jumping clubs. Two years later he made two starts for the Athletics again, leaving the majors with a 67–80 record and a 3.22 ERA. Weaver also played in 25 games as an outfielder/first baseman, hitting .207. Bill Lee asserts that from 1887 until 1908 Weaver was a patrolman for the Philadelphia police force, retiring after a serious injury. The 1900 census listed him as a "special police officer." Weaver died of angina pectoris in Philadelphia on February 1, 1914. He was 59 years of age. *(Total Baseball; Baseball-Reference.com; Baseball Necrology; U.S. Federal Census; Sporting Life; DeadballEra.com; Chicago Daily Inter Ocean)*

Billy West was one of thirteen players tried at second base by Atlantic over the course of the 1874 season. Coming from the amateur Chelsea club of Brooklyn, West hit .229 in nine games. Two years later he had a one-game trial with the New York Mutuals in the National League. Between the clubs, he hit .205, and in ten games as a second baseman he had 22 errors for a .722 percentage. In 1877 he played in the International League with Manchester and Pittsburgh. Born in Williamsburg, New York, to English parents, West is listed in both the 1890 Brooklyn city directory and the 1900 census as a hatter. He died in Richmond Hill, New York, on October 27, 1928, at age 75. *(Baseball-Reference.com; U.S. Federal Census; Brooklyn City Directory; New York Times)*

Elmer White, "nearly as well known as his cousin James," was from Caton, New York,

Sam Weaver (Wikimedia Commons).

Elmer White, from Cleveland team photograph (courtesy T. Scott Brandon).

and he joined the Forest City club of Cleveland in 1870 to play with his cousin. After 15 games as an outfielder in 1871, Elmer White broke his arm and was finished for the season. The *Plain Dealer* determined that he needed "rigid practice" in batting. White had hit .257, and his fielding percentage and range were both below the league average. Elmer White died on March 17, 1872, in his hometown. He was 23 years of age and suffered from a lung disease. He was also a cousin of the bespectacled Cincinnati pitcher Will White. *(Baseball-Reference.com; U.S. Federal Census; Corning (New York) Democrat; National Association of Base Ball Players, 1857–1870)*

James "Deacon" White, whose nickname came from his clean living habits, began his career as a catcher with Forest City in 1871. In five NA seasons with Cleveland and Boston, he hit .347 and won a batting title in 1875, hitting .367. When the National League was formed, he helped the White Stockings win the 1876 championship. A year later he hit a league-leading .387 for the NL champion Boston, before moving on to Cincinnati, Buffalo, Detroit and Pittsburgh. The 42-year-old White finished his career as a regular with the Buffalo Players League club in 1890. In fifteen seasons in the National/Players leagues, he hit .303. Dan Brouthers, Hardy Richardson, Jack Rowe and White comprised the "Big Four" that helped the Detroit Wolverines win the 1887 championship. White played every position but spent most of his NL career as a third baseman. However, in 1879, he caught 75 games that his brother, Will, pitched in Cincinnati. After leaving baseball, White worked for his brother as an optician and later operated a livery stable and garage in Buffalo. He died at Aurora, Illinois, on July 7, 1939, at age 91. He remains one of the players mentioned for inclusion in the Baseball Hall of Fame. *(Total Baseball; Sporting News; Baseball-Reference.com; SABR Baseball Encyclopedia; Dictionary of Biography—Baseball)*

Deacon White, from Cleveland team photograph (courtesy T. Scott Brandon).

Warren White (William Warren), born in 1844, was a Civil War veteran who had served with the Fourteenth Heavy Artillery regiment of New York. The Milton, New York, native played with and managed National Association teams in Washington—Olympic (1871), National (1872) and Washington (1873). He was playing manager for Lord Baltimore in 1874 and played for the

Chicago White Stockings in 1875. In all, he hit .260 and fielded much above the league average for third basemen. In 1884 the forty-year-old White, who was serving as secretary for the Union Association, donned a uniform again for four games as an infielder with the Washington club. He had one hit and two RBIs, but also had seven errors in 23 fielding chances. White was a resident of Washington, D.C., where, according to the 1880 census, he worked as a Treasury Department clerk. He was described as a "Special Examiner of Pensions" when he became ill with malaria in Arkansas. White died at Little Rock on June 12, 1890, at age 46. *(Total Baseball; Baseball-Reference.com; Wikipedia; U.S. Federal Census; Arkansas Gazette; Civil War Veterans Who Played Major League Baseball Research Project)*

Rynie Wolters, from 1870 Mutual team photograph (Wikimedia Commons).

Charles Witherow was the starting pitcher for Washington on July 1, 1875, in a game at St. Louis. In a 14–2 loss to the Brown Stockings, Witherow lasted one inning, giving up four hits and five runs—two earned. Bullpen says that Witherow pitched in St. Paul in 1877. Born in Washington, D.C. in 1852, Witherow appears regularly in D.C. censuses from 1860. Like many Washington ball players, he worked as a clerk in the U.S. Treasury Department, and is so listed in 1880; thereafter, he was listed as a janitor and ultimately as a sexton. Witherow was the final known survivor of the National Association, dying at D.C. on July 3, 1948, at age 96. *(Baseball-Reference.com; U.S. Federal Census; Sporting News; Boyd's Washington City Directory)*

Reinder Albertus "Rynie" Wolters threw the first no-hitter in baseball history, according to *Sporting Life*, when he pitched Mutual to a 9–0 victory over the Chicago White Stockings on July 23, 1870. In 1871, he compiled a 16–16 record for Mutual, leading the NA in complete games and innings. He also hit .370 and led the NA with 44 RBIs. Wolters later played for Cleveland (1872) and Elizabeth City (1873), leaving the majors with a 19–23 record and a 3.90 ERA and a .318 batting average for 49 games. According to William Ryczek, throughout his career Wolters had a reputation for going AWOL, leaving his team in a lurch. Born in the Netherlands, Wolters came to the United States at age four. He began pitching with Irvington (1865–66) before moving on to Mutual; he was 28 years old when the NA opened. The 1891 Newark city directory listed him as a salesman. The 1900 federal census showed him living in Newark, working as a produce salesman. He died in Newark on January 3, 1917, at age 74. *(Baseball-Reference.com; Sporting Life; U.S. Federal Census; Newark City Directory; Philadelphia Inquirer; Blackguards and Red Stockings)*

Wood played second base for Lord Baltimore on September 30, 1874, in a game at Hartford. He replaced an injured Asa Brainard in the second inning. In a 9–4 loss, Wood was hitless in five at-bats, and in the field he had an error in his only fielding chance. It is possible that he was a Hartford-area sandlot player recruited for the day. *(Baseball-Reference.com; Hartford Courant)*

Jimmy Wood was perhaps the premier second baseman in the beginning years of the NA. He had begun playing with Eckford as a 16-year-old in 1860. He was second in the league in runs scored in 1862 and third in 1863. In 1870 he went west to join Chicago. In three seasons as playing manager of the White Stockings, Troy, Eckford, and Philadelphia, he hit .332 and fielded .871— 53 points above the league average. In 1871 he hit .378 and led the White Stockings to a second-place tie. In 1874 he tried to operate on his leg with a pocket knife, leading to an infection and subsequent amputation of the leg on July 13. (Other sources say the wound was accidental.) He returned as manager of the White Stocking through 1875. After leaving baseball, Wood moved to Florida and was involved in citrus farming. In the 1890s he and Chicago star Ned Williamson operated a sports "emporium" in Chicago. After that Wood moved around. Peter Morris of SABR's Biographical Research Committee was able to find a record that Wood had died in San Francisco on November 30, 1927, at age 83. He is buried in New Orleans. *(Baseball-Reference.com; SABR Biographical Committee Newsletter; Sporting Life; National Association of Base Ball Players, 1857–1870)*

James "Red" Woodhead went hitless in one game as a shortstop for Maryland on April 15, 1873, coming from Chelsea. He later played for a semi-pro team in Lowell in 1875–76 and for Manchester in 1877–78, before returning to the majors with the National League Syracuse Stars in 1879. As a third baseman for the Stars he hit .160 in 34 games and fielded .792—46 points under the league average. He was projected as a player for a new Boston team in 1881. The son of an English-born tailor, Woodhead appeared in the 1870 Boston census as a laborer and in the 1880 census as a baseball player. He died in Boston on September 7, 1881, at age 30. *(Baseball-Reference.com; U.S. Federal Census; New York Herald; Lowell Daily Citizen and News)*

Favel Wordsworth was the shortstop for the Resolute club in 1873. In 12 games he hit .250. In the field, he committed 23 errors for a .662 fielding percentage—150 points under the league average. In November of 1872, the *Philadelphia Inquirer* reported that Wordsworth, described as an "excellent player," was under contract to Philadelphia for 1873, but he played for Resolute instead. Bullpen says that Wordsworth played for Easton after Resolute disbanded in early August. Born in New York City in 1850, the son of an English-born lawyer, he died there on August 12, 1888, at age 37. *(Baseball-Reference.com; U.S. Federal Census; New York Herald; Philadelphia Inquirer)*

Herb Worth played right field for Atlantic on July 29, 1872. In a home loss to Boston, he had a single in five at-bats and handled

Jimmy Wood, from 1870 Chicago team photograph (courtesy Robert Edward Auctions).

his only fielding chance. While this is his only line in the record books, Marshall Wright shows a Herb Worth or a "Worth" playing for the Star club of Brooklyn each year between 1863 and 1870. Newspaper accounts show him active with Star in 1871, so he was likely a pick-up for the Atlantic game. The census of 1870 showed Herbert Worth living in Brooklyn, married to a slightly older Irish wife, and working as a bookkeeper. Brooklyn city directories through the 1890s and federal censuses through 1910 all showed him working in some capacity—bookkeeper, cashier, agent—for a sugar refinery. Worth died in Brooklyn on April 27, 1914, at age 66. *(Baseball-Reference.com; U.S. Federal Census; Lain's Brooklyn City Directory; National Association of Base Ball Players, 1857–1870; New York Herald)*

George Wright, a world-class cricket player, took up baseball in 1863 when he was 16 years of age. By 1869 he was the shortstop for the powerful Cincinnati Red Stockings and the highest-paid player in baseball at $1,400. That season he had 304 hits and scored 339 runs in 57 games. In 1870 he averaged 4.27 hits per game. One of four Red Stockings to make the move to Boston, Wright helped Boston to four straight NA championships (1872–75) before the club moved into the National League. He later played with the NL Bostons (1876–78 and 1880–81) and with Providence (1879 and 1882). A career .301 hitter, he had five seasons hitting above .300 and one above .400, leading the NL in triples in 1874. An outstanding shortstop, he was a career .870 fielder—more than 50 points over the league average—with above-average range. Also a top golfer, he was called "the father of American Golf." Born in New York City to an English father and an Irish mother, Wright lived most of his life in Boston. After leaving the playing ranks, he opened a sporting goods store and is so listed in the censuses of 1900, 1920 and 1930, when he was 82 years of age. Wright died in Boston on August 21, 1937, at age 90. In 1937 the Centennial Commission named him to the Baseball Hall of Fame. *(Baseball-Reference.com; Sporting Life; U.S. Federal Census; National Association of Base Ball Players, 1857–1870)*

George Wright from "First Nine of the Cincinnati (Red Stockings) Baseball Club" (LC-USZC4-1291 Library of Congress Prints and Photographs Division).

William Henry "Harry" Wright, an English-born cricket player, began playing baseball with the Knickerbocker Club of New York in 1858, moving on to Gotham in 1963 and to Cincinnati in 1867. In 1869 he formed the first professional club in history, the Cincinnati Red Stockings, for whom he played center field and managed. Taking his brother, George, Cal McVey, and Charlie Gould with him, he reformed the Red Stockings in Boston as an NA entry in 1871. The regular center fielder through 1874, he managed the club to four consecutive NA championships before moving them into the National League in 1876. In seven years as an NA/NL player, he hit .276 but reached .315 in 40 games at age 39. As a center fielder, he fielded .839—well above the

Harry Wright (LC-DIG-bbc-0336f Library of Congress Prints and Photographs Division).

Sam Wright (Wikimedia Commons).

league average. In addition to his five seasons with the Red Stockings, Wright also managed Boston in the NL (1876–81), Providence (1882–83) and Philadelphia (1884–93). In 22 seasons he had six championship teams. When Wright left the managerial ranks, he became chief of NL umpires. In 1953 he was named to the Baseball Hall of Fame as an executive/pioneer. Wright died in Atlantic City New Jersey, of lung disease on October 3, 1895, at age 60. *Sporting Life* termed him "the Father of Professional Baseball." *(Baseball-Reference.com; Sporting Life; National Association of Base Ball Players, 1857–1870)*

Sam Wright was a substitute on the Boston Red Stocking team for its 1874 tour of England with Athletic. The *New York Clipper* determined that Wright would "undoubtedly become as famous as his two brothers." In 1875 he played shortstop for Elm City, hitting .189 in 33 games. A year later he played two games for Boston, joining his brothers there. After playing for Lowell and New Bedford, he returned to the majors for brief trials with Cincinnati and Boston in 1880–81, adding ten games to his totals. In a major league career of 45 games, he hit just .168. However, he led NA shortstops in range factors in 1875, and overall as a shortstop he fielded just under the league average. Born in New York City, he was 27 when he debuted. He appeared in the 1920 census for Boston, still working at age 72, stringing tennis rackets in a sporting goods store — likely that of his brother, George. Wright died in Boston on May 6, 1928. *(Baseball-Reference.com; U.S. Federal Census; SABR Baseball Encyclopedia; New York Clipper; Blackguards and Red Stockings)*

Bill Yeatman played right field for National on Opening Day of 1872. In a 1–0 loss to Lord Baltimore, the 33-year-old Yeatman went hitless in four at-bats with a strikeout;

in the field he had an error on the only ball hit to him. That game ended his major league career. Marshall Wright lists a Sam Yeatman playing for National (1865–66), Jefferson (1966–68) and Olympic (1869)—all Washington clubs. This is possibly the same player. Born in Alexandria, Virginia, Yeatman was a resident of Washington, D.C. He appeared in the censuses of 1850, 1860, 1870 and 1880 and the 1890 city directory as a disbursing clerk in the War Department. Although there is no record of military service, his death notice refers to him as Colonel William S. Yeatman. He died of congestion of the lungs and heart failure in a York, Pennsylvania, hotel on April 20, 1901. The *Wilkes-Barre Times* reported that Yeatman was registered under an assumed name and was in the company of an unidentified younger woman, who then left town on an early train. Peter Morris believes that Sam Yeatman and Bill Yeatman are different persons and that the major league record should go to Sam Yeatman. (*Baseball-Reference.com; U.S. Federal Census; Washington City Directory; National Association of Base Ball Players, 1857–1870; Wilkes-Barre Times; petermorrisbooks.com*)

Tom York made his major league debut with the Haymakers as a 20-year-old in 1871. He also played with Lord Baltimore, Philadelphia, and Hartford, moving with the Dark Blues into the National League in 1876. In 15 seasons—five in the NA—he was a regular outfielder for 13 seasons, leading the NA in fielding in 1873 and the NL in 1880. His career .877 fielding percentage was more than 40 points above the league average. A career .273 hitter, York batted better than .300 four times with a high of .310 in 1879, a year after he had led the NL with ten triples and 125 total bases. As playing manager at Providence, he led the Grays to a third-place finish in 1878 and a second-place finish in 1881. He played with Cleveland (1883)

Tom York (courtesy T. Scott Brandon).

before finishing his major league career in the American Association with Baltimore in 1884–85. York umpired in both the NL and AA. In later years the Brooklyn native was placed "in charge of the press box gate" at the Polo Grounds. He died in New York City on February 17, 1936, at age 84. (*Total Baseball; Baseball-Reference.com; Boston Daily Globe; U.S. Federal Census; Sporting Life*)

George Zettlein is remembered as the pitcher who ended the 89-game winning streak of the Cincinnati Red Stockings in 1870, a game in which he also drove in the winning run. He posted the lowest ERA in the NA in its inaugural season, going 18–9 with a 2.73 ERA for Chicago. Zettlein began his baseball career with Eckford in 1865, after serving in the U.S. Navy under Admiral Farragut in the Civil War. He then began a six-year stint with Atlantic as its top pitcher in 1866. Zettlein went west in 1871, but after the Great Chicago Fire ended professional baseball in Chicago, he went to Troy in 1872 and then back to Eckford after Troy disbanded. One of the "revolvers," he won 36 games for the Philadelphia White Stockings in 1873 and 27 games for the Chicago White Stockings in 1874. Splitting

George Zettlein, from 1870 Chicago team photograph (courtesy Robert Edward Auctions).

1875 between Chicago and Philadelphia, he led the NA with seven shutouts. Entering the National League with the depleted Philadelphia Athletics, he finished his major league career there with a 4–20 record. Overall, in six seasons he compiled a 129–112 record and a 2.55 ERA. Born in Brooklyn to German parents, Zettlein is listed as a liquor dealer in the 1889 Brooklyn city directory. The 1900 census showed him as a special policeman in Brooklyn. He died of Bright's disease in Brooklyn on May 23, 1905. Daniel Ginsberg notes that Zettlein was "quite a personable man," hence his nickname, "the Charmer." *(Baseball-Reference.com; U.S. Federal Census; Lain's Brooklyn City Directory; Sporting Life; Civil War Veterans Who Played Major League Baseball Research Project; The Fix Is In)*

Club Dictionary

ATHLETIC BASE BALL CLUB
Philadelphia, Pennsylvania
1860–1876

History

While 1860 is the listed founding of Athletic by James Kerns, the club first appeared in National Association standings in 1863. Athletic and Keystone were the first clubs from Philadelphia to appear in the standings. Dick McBride and Nate Berkenstock were members of that 1863 club, which won seven of 12 games, including victories over the Excelsior and Star clubs of Brooklyn. Fergy Malone joined Athletic in 1864, Al Reach in 1865, and Wes Fisler, Lip Pike and Count Sensenderfer in 1866. Victory totals continued to mount—from eight in 1864, to 15 in 1865, to 23 in 1866. The addition of Ned Cuthbert and John Radcliff in 1867 helped Athletic to an NA-leading 44–3 record; in 1868 they were awarded the championship with a 47–3 record.

Among the hitting stars of the early years of Athletic history were McBride and Reach, who finished first and third, respectively, in scoring in 1866; Isaac Wilkins, who led in hits, and Reach in runs in 1867; and Radcliff, who led in runs, and Fisler in total bases in 1868.

Athletic fell to third and fourth places in the next two seasons but remained among the elite of the NA, going 45–8 (15–7) in 1869 (when the Red Stockings were undefeated) and 65–11–1 (26–11–1) in 1870.

After winning the inaugural National Association pennant in 1871 with a win over Chicago on the last day, Athletic contended for every pennant thereafter but lost the battle for league supremacy to Harry Wright's Boston Red Stockings; for a season they even lost the battle for Philadelphia to the upstart Philadelphia Base Ball Club.

Athletic won the right to represent Philadelphia in the new National League but fell on hard times. Locked in seventh place and strapped for cash, the club refused to make the final road trip to play western teams. At season's end, the league dismissed both Athletic and Mutual; Athletic then passed into history. An independent team took the name, which has been associated with American Association and American League baseball in Philadelphia, Kansas City and Oakland to the present day.

A bird's-eye view of Jefferson Street Grounds, home to both Athletic and Philadelphia. An almost square lot, Jefferson Street Grounds contrast markedly with Columbia Park, only three blocks away (*Philadelphia in 1886, H.S.P. del*, Library of Congress Maps and Geography Division).

Grounds

Jefferson Street Grounds opened in 1871 in north Philadelphia near Girard College, the first enclosed grounds in Pennsylvania. It was home to both Athletic and the Philadelphia Base Ball Club. The center field fence was 500 feet from home plate. Listed capacity was 3,000, but *Charlton's Baseball Chronology* says that a June 11, 1873, game between Athletic and Philadelphia drew 10,000. At any rate, the grounds allowed Athletic to be profitable enough to pay shareholders a $25 dividend in 1873.

Management

Hicks Hayhurst, a member of Athletic from 1864, is listed as manager in 1871, though other sources list pitcher Dick McBride. McBride managed until the last six games of 1875, when he turned the reins over to Cap Anson. A non-playing manager named Al Wright took the team into the National League.

Uniforms and Logos

Newspapers occasionally referred to the team as the Blue Stockings, especially after

Al Reach shows off the traditional Athletic uniform. Note the long trousers (National Baseball Hall of Fame Library, Cooperstown, New York).

the Philadelphia Baseball Club began wearing white stockings. The basic blue color was confirmed by a report in the *Hartford Constitution* in 1875, noting that Hartford, New Haven, Western and Athletic all wore "nearly alike" white uniforms with blue stockings and trimmings.

Earliest photographs of Athletic players show they wore the traditional fireman's breastplate with the now-familiar Old English A, which was later adopted by Connie Mack and is worn on Oakland uniforms today. But by the mid-1870s, Athletic had begun putting the name "Athletic" on the front, as shown in the photograph of John McMullin on page 143.

Athletic in the League

1871

From the 1870 club that won 65 games, six starters returned for 1871: first baseman Wes Fisler, second baseman Al Reach, shortstop John Radcliff, center fielder Count Sensenderfer, catcher Fergy Malone and pitcher Dick McBride. This was a veteran group. McBride had been with the club since its inception; Reach was a six-year starter; Fisler and Sensenderfer were five-year men; and Radcliff had been with the club for four years.

To help with the 1871 campaign, three starters from 1869 returned to the fold. Outfielder Ned Cuthbert and third baseman Levi Meyerle returned from Chicago and outfielder George Heubel from Cleveland. In addition, a strong reserve player, George Bechtel, returned from the 1870 team, as did veterans Tom Pratt and Tom Berry. The result was that Athletic entered the NA race with a pat hand.

Eight players started at least 25 of the club's 28 games. Only Heubel, the 22-year-old right fielder, missed more than three games; as a result, Bechtel played in more games. Bechtel also started three games as pitcher in place of McBride. Pratt, Berry and Nate Birkenstock each played in one game.

After losing the opening game at Boston, Athletic won 11 of the next 12 games, moving into first place on June 29. However, on August 2, they slid into second place with a 16–5 record. They returned to first place on September 18 and won their final four games to remain in first over Boston.

The veteran Athletic club swung big bats to win the pennant. Seven regulars hit above .300, headed by Meyerle's monster .492. Reach (.353), Bechtel (.351), Malone (.343), Sensenderfer (.323), Heubel (.307), and Radcliff (.303) helped Athletic to a .320 average, best in the league. This led to 376 runs scored in 28 games, a 13.42 runs-per-game average. Such hitting and fielding—a team .845 fielding average with three position leaders in McBride, Malone and Radcliff—helped Athletic overcome a horrid 4.95 ERA by the pitchers. The defense allowed only 129 unearned runs, third best in the league.

1872

From the 1971 champions, Athletic lost three key players—shortstop John Radcliff (to Lord Baltimore), outfielder George Heubel (to Olympic) and utility player George Bechtel (to Mutual). But Athletic brought back seven regulars in first baseman Wes Fisler, second baseman Al Reach, third baseman Levi Meyerle, outfielders Ned Cuthbert and Count Sensenderfer, catcher Fergy Malone and pitcher Dick McBride. Meyerle had led the league with a .492 batting average in 1871; Reach (.353), Malone (.343), and Sensenderfer (.323) were among the top twenty hitters.

The club quickly went about replacing lost players. Cap Anson and Denny Mack came from the defunct Rockford club, and Fred Treacey arrived from the defunct White

Stockings. Athletic also helped deplete Troy's ranks by adding Mike McGeary and Dickie Flowers from that club. Treacey (.338), Anson (.325) and Flowers (.314) added more punch to an already-potent offense.

These additions gave the 1872 Athletic club a new look. Fisler replaced Reach at second base, McGeary became the shortstop. The Rockford additions, Mack and Anson, took over first and third bases, pushing Meyerle to the outfield, where he joined Cuthbert and Treacey. Sensenderfer, plagued by an injury from the end of the 1871 season, played in only one game. From the NA pennant-winners, only the battery of McBride and Malone, along with Cuthbert, held their 1871 positions.

Athletic hit well again. Anson batted .415, second only to Boston's Barnes. McGeary (.360), Fisler (.348), Cuthbert (.338) and Meyerle (.329) helped the team to a .317 mark, the same as champion Boston. They were even more prolific in scoring, averaging 11.47 runs per game.

McBride threw every inning of every game for Athletic. His 2.85 ERA was third best in the league, behind future Hall of Fame members Spalding and Cummings. However, Athletic was less impressive on defense, fielding .858, only fourth best in the NA and well below Boston's .875. Shaky defense led to Athletic giving up 4.60 unearned runs per game, far behind Boston's 3.06.

Athletic finished with a 30–14 record (three ties), good for fourth place, though the winning percentage of .682 would have given them second place. Three issues kept the team from repeating as NA champions. First, its road record (9–11) was under .500. Second, its record against the top-of-the-table teams (12–14) was also under .500 (as compared to an 18–0 record against lower teams). Finally, the team did not close well, going 8–7 in the months of September and October.

1873

Despite being raided by the new Philadelphia Base Ball Club, Athletic was far from toothless entering 1873. Four key players returned to form the nucleus of the team—pitcher/manager Dick McBride, along with infielders Wes Fisler, Mike McGeary and Cap Anson. To restock, Athletic plucked three players from defunct clubs, getting Ezra Sutton from Cleveland and Tim Murnane and John Clapp from Mansfield. The team also added Cherokee Fisher from Lord Baltimore and John McMullin from Mutual.

Sutton took over at third base, allowing Anson to move to first base, a position he held for the next 25 seasons. Fisler and McGeary remained in the middle. Newcomers McMullin, Fisher and Murnane took over outfield spots and Clapp became the catcher. McBride pitched most games, with Fisher as the change pitcher. Veteran Count Sensenderfer was still available as a reserve.

Athletic hitters scorched the ball for a .301 average. Anson led the way with a .398 average, followed by Fisler (.344), Sutton (.333), Clapp (.304) and McGeary (.302). Still, the 474 runs scored ranked only fourth in the league

Unfortunately, Athletic leaked runs. McBride and Fisher combined for a 3.05 ERA, and the club fielded at a .840 rate, which was third best. But Athletic gave up 403 runs total, fifth-highest in the league. The practice of shifting players around the field could not have helped the defense. Five different players worked at both first base and second base. Athletic also used three catchers, third basemen and shortstops and seven outfielders—from a roster of twelve players.

Athletic began the season reasonably well. A nine-game winning streak—its longest—gave Athletic a 10–3 record on June 9. However, by the halfway mark, the team had dropped to fourth place with a 16–10 record. In the second half, Athletic lost more than it won. By today's calculation, Athletic was 10 games behind on September 8 and 12.5 games behind in October. A modest three-game winning streak allowed the team to finish in fifth place at 28–23.

1874

Unlike the decimated 1873 club, the 1874 Athletic team began the campaign with a pat hand. Only outfielder Cherokee Fisher was missing, replaced by Count Gedney from Mutual and newcomer Joe Battin, who had played in only one game in 1873. But while Cap Anson, Dick McBride, Ezra Sutton and John McMullin played in all 55 games, only McBride, Gedney and McMullin played as many as 50 games in a position. Wes Fisler, Battin, Mike McGeary, Anson, Sutton, John Clapp, Al Reach and Tim Murnane filled in as circumstances demanded.

Athletic was the second-most productive team in the league. With four hitters above .300—McMullin (.346), Anson (.335), Fisler (.328) and McGeary (.321)—Athletic hit .286 as a team, second behind Boston. This helped them score 441 runs, just over eight runs per game.

McBride pitched every inning and led the NA with a 1.64 ERA. However, Athletic gave up 344 runs—6.25 per game, third lowest. They finished third in the NA in fielding with an .839 percentage, allowing 4.64 unearned runs per game, also third lowest.

In the first half of the 1874 season, Athletic enjoyed five- and nine-game winning streaks but slogged along in second place. On July 15, when they and Boston headed off for England, Athletic had a 23–10 record, 4.5 games behind Boston. Once back in the league race, Athletic lost to Boston on September 10 and fell into third place. In the second half of the season, they never put together a significant winning streak, and in fact lost more games (12) than they won (10). As Boston closed the season with a championship surge, Athletic fell further behind. Anchored in third place, they finished 11.5 games behind Boston.

1875

Athletic lost some of the big bats from the third-place team of 1874. John McMullin (.346) and Mike McGeary (.321) took their averages across town to Philadelphia, joined by utility player Tim Murnane. Infielder Joe Battin went to the Brown Stockings and Outfielder Count Gedney to Mutual. Cap Anson (.335) and Wes Fisler (.328) returned, along with third baseman Ezra Sutton, catcher John Clapp, and pitcher-manager

This woodcut of John McMullin features the 1874 Athletic uniform (*Harper's Weekly*, July 1874).

Shortstop and manager Bill Craver led Centennial to a 2–12 record before being Traded to Athletic in May (Wikimedia Commons).

Dick McBride. Davy Force (.313) came from Chicago, Dave Eggler (.318) from Philadelphia, and George Hall from Boston. McBride (33–22, with a league-leading 1.64 ERA) would again do the bulk of the pitching. Veteran Al Reach was still available, as was promising newcomer John Richmond.

The *New York Herald-Tribune* projected a "nine" of Clapp and McBride; Anson, Fisler, Sutton and Force; Hall, Eggler and Richmond.

In the first player purchase in history, Athletic acquired Bill Craver and George Bechtel from Centennial in May just before that club disbanded. Both claimed regular positions with Athletic—Craver at second base and Bechtel in the outfield. Anson hit .324 in 69 games, without regular status at any position. Athletic had seven players appear in at least 60 games; the club used 16 players over the season, with Richmond, Adam Rocap and Lon Knight also appearing in more than ten games.

Athletic again swung big bats in 1875, finishing just behind Boston in important offensive categories. Anson (.325), Sutton (.324), Craver (.319), Force (.311), Eggler (.302) and Hall (.299) led the team to a .290 average. This led to 699 runs, just over nine per game.

McBride (44–14, 2.33 ERA) led Athletic to a team 2.40 ERA, seventh-best in the league. Also with four position leaders—McBride, Force, Hall, and Eggler—Athletic was the second-best fielding team in the league. This allowed them to limit unearned runs to 2.84 per game, third-best in the league. The measure of their success was that they outscored opponents by 3.84 runs per game.

In almost any other season, people would have said that Athletic had a very successful campaign by finishing with a .726 winning percentage. They had winning records in both halves of the pennant race; they had winning records both at home and on the road; they had winning records in every month except September, when they were 3–3. They had winning records against every team in the league except Boston (2–8) and Hartford (3–4). Yet after May 5, they steadily dropped in the race.

ATLANTIC BASE BALL CLUB
Brooklyn, New York
1855–1875

History

Founded in 1855, Atlantic was the oldest club in Brooklyn and one of the founding clubs of the National Association of Base Ball Players. With a 7–1–1 record, Atlantic had the best record in the inaugural 1857 season. They were undefeated in 1858 but played only seven games and finished behind Mutual. Their 11–1 record in 1859 was second to Excelsior, and their 12–2–2 record in 1860 placed them third. The 1864 team compiled a 20–0–1 record and was considered to be NA champions. The 1865 team also was an undefeated league champion. Despite an embarrassing loss to Irvington, New Jersey, early in the season, the 1866 team finished 17–3, winning its third pennant in a row. A 17–1 road trip helped the 1868 team to a 47–7 record, but late-season losses to Mutual cost Atlantic the pennant. The 1869 and 1870 teams slid to fourth and fifth places. However, on June 14, 1870, Atlantic ended the 57-game winning streak of the Cincinnati Red Stockings with an 8–7 victory in 11 innings at the Capitoline Grounds.

Early on, players that would impact National Association and National League teams began appearing in the Atlantic lineup. Dickie Pearce was the shortstop on the 1857 champions, beginning a career that lasted into the National League. Joe Start, Charles Smith and Fred Crane became regulars in 1862; they were the top three hitters in the league in 1865. Third baseman Bob Ferguson, catcher Charlie Mills and pitcher George Zettlein arrived in 1866.

The 1865 "Champions of America" Atlantic team: unidentified player, Sid Smith, Dickie Pearce, Joe Start, Pete O'Brien, Charlie Smith, John Chapman, Fred Cone, John Galvin, and Tom Pratt (LC-DIG-ppm-sca-09310 Library of Congress, Prints and Photographs Division).

The 1868 Atlantic Base Ball team: Everett Mills, George Zettlein, Dickie Pearce, Joe Start, Charlie Smith, Bob Ferguson, Fred Crane, Tom Pratt, and Jack Chapman (courtesy Robert Edward Auctions).

Lip Pike was added in 1869 and George Hall in 1870.

Atlantic decided to forego league play in 1871, operating instead as an independent. As a result, their top players scattered to league teams—Start, Pearce, Mills and Ferguson to Mutual; Pike to Troy; Hall to Olympic; and Zettlein to Chicago. A change of heart in

1872 brought Atlantic into the league; however, by this time the club was only a shadow of its glorious past. After a last-place finish in 1875, the club disbanded.

Home Grounds

Atlantic's home in 1872 was Capitoline Grounds in Brooklyn, named for the Capitoline Hill in Rome. Part of a farm, Capitoline Grounds had opened in 1862 as a skating pond. Baseball was first played there in 1865.

Bounded by Putnam Avenue, Nostrand Avenue, Halsey Street and Mercy Avenue, Capitoline Grounds were located in what is today the Bedford-Stuyvesant section of Brooklyn. There was a double-decked stand with a capacity of 5,000 persons. There was a large brick building in right field. Players received a bottle of champagne for hitting a ball over the building. After each baseball season, the grounds were flooded and used as a skating pond.

In 1873 Atlantic moved to Union Grounds (see Eckford). Capitoline Grounds were razed in 1880. Today a housing development occupies the site.

Management

In 1872 Ferguson returned from Mutual to manage Atlantic and play third base, roles he continued in 1873 and 1874. When Ferguson departed for Hartford in 1875, outfielder Charlie Pabor became the manager. When the Atlantic's record reached 2–40, second baseman Bill Boyd took the reins for the last two games, neither of which Atlantic won.

Uniform and Logo

Marshall Wright describes Atlantic as being "resplendent in light blue pants with

The crest worn by the vintage Brooklyn Atlantic team today is based on that worn by the 1866 Atlantics (courtesy Vintage Brooklyn Atlantic team).

white flannel shirts emblazoned with an old English 'A'" (94). The accompanying team photograph shows that uniform. However, the picture of the 1865 "Champions of America" Atlantic team (on page 145) shows players wearing dark trousers and white shirts with the scripted letters *ABBC* for Atlantic Base Ball Club. Below the letters was a design of crossed bats and a ball. The Brooklyn Atlantic vintage team wears that uniform today. The trousers are blue; the trim and lettering are dark red; the crossed bats and ball are gold. Today's team wears a white cap with dark red bands.

Atlantic in the League

1872

Since Atlantic had played an independent schedule in 1871, when they anted up the $10 membership dues in 1872 the team was made up almost entirely of players without league experience. The exception was manager and third baseman Bob Ferguson, who came over from Mutual. Another veteran player, outfielder Jack McDonald, had been with the club since 1866. Among the rookies tried by Atlantic were 22-year-old English-born outfielder Al Thake, 21-year-old outfielder Jack Remsen, 20-year-old catcher Tom Barlow, 20-year-old infielders Dutch Dehlman and Jack Burdock, and 16-year-old pitcher Jim Britt.

Atlantic operated as a cooperative in 1872, paying salaries and expenses strictly from gate receipts.

Four wins in September and October allowed Atlantic to finish with nine wins against 28 losses. Tom Barlow hit .316 on a team that batted .259, an average aided by Jim Hall (.316) and Eddie Booth (.306) in part-time service. Thake hit .295 before his tragic drowning death in September. Atlantic averaged only 6.41 runs per game—ninth-best in the league. While Jim Britt had a 4.53 ERA, sixth-best in the league, Atlantic allowed 8.22 unearned runs. Part of Atlantic's problem was the disparity between what their offense generated and what they gave up. However, Atlantic tried nine different players at second base, eight in right field and six in left field. They used 22 different players in the course of the season, with half playing in fewer than 10 games. Among the short-term players used were Charlie Lowe (seven games), John Kenney (five), Oliver Brown (four), Denny Clare (two), Herb Worth (one), John Galvin (one) and Higby (one). In each case these games constituted a major league career for the player.

1873

The good news for Atlantic was that six starters returned from 1872. The bad news was these players had been part of a terrible 9–28 club. Infielders Dutch Dehlman, Jack Burdock, and Bob Ferguson, outfielder Jack Remsen, catcher Tom Barlow and pitcher Jim Britt were back for another trial. Light-hitting shortstop Dickie Pearce and third baseman Bill Boyd came from Mutual and veteran pitcher and outfielder Charlie Pabor arrived from the defunct Forest City club of Cleveland.

The result was a much more stable team than the 1872 squad. Pearce was installed at shortstop, where he played every inning of every game. The same was true for Burdock at second base, Pabor in the outfield and Barlow at catcher. Dehlman missed one game at first base; Britt started 54 games; Remsen in the outfield and Ferguson at third base played 50 games in their respective positions. Only Boyd played fewer than 45 games at his position.

Atlantic was a poor-hitting club. Only Pabor topped .300 among the regulars, and the team settled for a .266 average, giving them 366 runs—6.65 per game. In contrast, opponents scored 549 runs, one run shy of a 10-runs-per-game average. Britt, still only 17 years old, had a 4.08 ERA. The team ERA was 4.14. Unfortunately, Atlantic was also a poor defensive team with an .817 team fielding average, also good for sixth place.

Atlantic finished 20 games under .500 with a 17–37 record. After winning three of their first four, they dropped eight in a row. In September and early October, Atlantic endured a 12-game losing streak, dropping their record to 15–35. Losing two of the next three, they fell 21 games under .500 and 24 games behind Boston. It is hard to find many highlights in a season in which Atlantic won only three road games and had winning records against only Resolute and Washington.

1874

Four key players returned from the sixth-place team of 1873 in first baseman Dutch

Dehlman, shortstop Dickie Pearce, third baseman Bob Ferguson, and outfielder Eddie Booth, who was acquired in mid-season from Elizabeth. The top returning hitter, Pearce had hit .275 in 1873. Charlie Pabor took his .360 bat to Philadelphia, and 18-year-old Jim Britt returned to the semi-pro ranks.

Athletic again had difficulty recruiting veteran players, which meant replacements came from the minors and amateur ranks. John Farrow arrived from Resolute to play second base. Outfielders Bobby Clack and Jack Chapman, catcher Jake Knowdell and 18-year-old pitcher Tommy Bond had no previous league experience. In all, Atlantic tried 21 players before the end of the season.

Atlantic was far and away the weakest offensive team in 1874, carrying only a .230 batting average. The 38-year-old Pearce was the only Atlantic who approached the .300 mark, with a .294 average. And while Atlantic scored 301 runs—just under 5.5 per game—they gave up 440 runs, eight per game.

Bond had a 2.03 ERA, but Atlantic gave up 334 unearned runs. The team fielded .822, good for fifth in the NA. Only Dutch Dehlman was among the league leaders at his position.

In May Atlantic split four games with Boston and twice hammered hapless Baltimore, 24–3 and 8–3, to enter June with a 4–4 record. But a 1–8 record in June brought the club back to reality as four of the losses were by ten or more runs. Through the heat of July and August Atlantic played poorly, and entered September with a 9–27 record. Over the final two months, Atlantic went 13–6 with a modest five-game winning streak in October.

1875

Atlantic had gone 22–33 in 1874, good for another sixth-place finish. From that team first baseman Dutch Dehlman, shortstop Dickie Pearce and outfielder Jack Chapman headed west to St. Louis; pitcher Tommy Bond and third baseman Bob Ferguson went to Hartford; outfielder Eddie Booth went to Mutual; and utility man Charlie Sweasy joined the St. Louis Red Stockings. Second baseman Jack Farrow sat out the season. Neither of the returning regulars—outfielder Bobby Clack (.170) and catcher Jake Knowdell (.140)—hit well.

The projected lineup for the 1875 Atlantics showed the club lacked the resources to replace lost players with those of equal skill, much less to attract those who could make them a contender. First baseman Fred Crane, a 34-year-old veteran of pre-league baseball in Brooklyn, had played one game for Resolute in 1873. Projected second baseman Tom Patterson had been an outfielder for various New York City and Brooklyn teams since 1866; a regular in 1871, he had played in only one game for Mutual in 1874. Third baseman Al Nichols was a rookie. Shortstop Henry Kessler had hit .304 in 14 games as a utility player in 1874. Clack was projected as one outfield regular. Charlie Pabor, once a big bat for Atlantic, had hit only .221 in 17 games at Philadelphia, and Bill Boyd had hit .350 in 26 games for Hartford. Tom Barlow, who had played shortstop for Hartford in 1874, hitting .297 and leading the league in stolen bases, was projected as the catcher, and a rookie named Roseman from Bridgeport T.B.'s was the projected pitcher.

While seven of these projections were considered to be regulars, Atlantic used 35 players in 1875. Only eight played in as many as half of the team's 44 games. Knowdell played in 43 games, Pabor in 42, 18-year-old pitcher John Cassidy in 41, Boyd in 36, Nichols in 32, infielder Frank Fleet in 26, Kessler in 25, and infielder Molly Moore in 22. Fourteen players were limited to a single appearance, including four Philadelphia amateurs signed when Atlantic had only five players in uniform for the day.

Not surprisingly, the result was one of the worst teams in major league history. Only Boyd and Kessler hit above .250, and the team as a whole batted .195 and averaged only three runs per game. Cassidy (1–21, 3.03 ERA) won half of the victories; Jim Clinton (1–14, 2.41 ERA) won the other.

The team won its last game on May 26, losing its last 31 games. The much-patched Atlantic defense fielded .801, 11th-best in the league, and the team gave up 6.8 unearned runs per game, more than twice what Atlantic scored. All in all, this was a sad end for a storied franchise.

BOSTON RED STOCKINGS BASE BALL CLUB
Boston, Massachusetts
1871–present

History

The Boston club was formed in Cincinnati in 1866, and after Harry Wright was hired as "captain" in 1868, the club enjoyed a 36–7 season. Allowed to compensate players and armed with a $9,300 budget, Wright brought to Cincinnati the best players from throughout the country. Outfitted in knickers with long red stockings, the Cincinnati team became known as the Red Stockings. They went undefeated in 1869, winning 57 games. After a 67–6–1 record in 1870, Wright lost his financial backing in Cincinnati, and the club disbanded. Wright promptly took four of his best players—himself, his brother George, Harry Schafer, and Cal McVey—and the Red Stocking name and set up shop in Boston. There he stocked the club with the best talent available, including Ross Barnes and Al Spalding during the first year and Jim O'Rourke and Deacon White in subsequent seasons. That year Wright entered his club in the new professional league and became one of three clubs to contest all five NA pennants. In addition, Wright took the club to England in 1873 on a tour with Athletic to create a European taste for baseball.

After winning four straight NA pennants, Wright took the Red Stockings into the new National League. Before the move, the Chicago club did to him as he had done to other clubs by stripping him of his stars. Barnes, White, and Spalding helped the White Stockings to the initial NL pennant. Under various names—Beaneaters, Doves, Rustlers, Bees, and Braves—the Red Stockings continued in Boston until 1953. After a move to Milwaukee, the club moved on to Atlanta in 1966, where it still plays. Throughout its NL history the club has won 17 pennants— 1877, 1878, 1883, 1891, 1892, 1893, 1897, 1898, 1914, 1948, 1957, 1958, 1991, 1992, 1995, 1996, and 1999. The club has been world champions in 1914, 1957 and 1995.

English-born Harry Wright organized, managed, and played for the Red Stockings. From "First Nine of the Cincinnati (Red Stockings) Baseball Club" (LC-USZC4-1291 Library Congress Prints and Photographs Division).

Bird's-eye view of Southend Grounds in Boston. From *Boston bird's-eye view from The north. J. Bachman, del. and lith* (Library of Congress Geography and Maps Division).

Grounds

South End Grounds opened in 1871, the first of three baseball parks of that name. According to projectballpark.org, its shape was roughly a square: 250 to left, 440 to center and 255 to right. Its listed capacity was 3,000, but the attendance for a game with Athletic on June 12, 1872, was twice that.

The Grounds were located in the Roxbury section of Boston, at the intersection of Columbus Avenue and Walpole Street. The first South End Grounds were razed in 1887 to make way for a new South End Grounds, built for 1888. That ballpark burned in 1894 and was rebuilt as the home of the Boston Braves until 1915. Today, the area of South End Grounds is home to the Ruggles MBTA station and parking facilities.

Management

Harry Wright managed the Red Stockings throughout their time in the NA, and continued as manager into the NL.

Uniforms

The knee-length trousers and red stockings were the distinctive parts of the Boston uniform, as they had been in Cincinnati. In Cincinnati the team had worn the old English C on a breastplate. In Boston, the uniforms carried the name of the city. The sketch of the 1874 team shows the uniform with "Boston" arched on the front.

Boston in the League

To a nucleus of first baseman Charlie Gould, shortstop George Wright, outfielder Cal McVey and himself—a group that had gone 124–6–1 over the past two years—Harry Wright added a trio of stars from Rockford in pitcher Al Spalding, second baseman Ross Barnes, and outfielder Fred Cone. Third baseman Harry Schafer came from Athletic, outfielder Dave Birdsall from Union of Morrisania and infielder Frank Barrows from Tri Mountain. The *Cincinnati Daily Gazette* believed that this group "would undoubtedly win for themselves ... high renown during the approaching season."

As a team, Boston hit almost as well as Athletic, .310 to .320. Three Red Stockings—Cal McVey (.431), George Wright (.413) and Ross Barnes (.401)—batted better than .400, with Dave Birdsall at .303. This offense created a league-leading 402 runs, with 66 by Barnes and 51 by Birdsall. Led by Al Spalding's 3.36 ERA, Boston was second in team ERA but gave up 194 unearned runs. The loss of shortstop George Wright for part of the season unsettled the defense, making it only fifth best in the league. Third baseman Harry Schafer was a position leader in fielding.

The Red Stockings remained solid throughout the season, using only 11 players. When George Wright suffered a broken leg after 16 games, Barnes moved to shortstop while Sam Jackson, called up from the amateur ranks, filled in at second. Cone hit only .260 and split playing time with Barrows. Otherwise, seven players started in at least 29 games, and five started every contest.

1872

The runner-up Red Stockings used the offseason to strengthen a contending team. Three light bats—infielders Sam Jackson and Frank Barrows and outfielder Fred Cone—left the team. As replacements, Harry Wright added outfielders Andy Leonard, a .291 hitter from Olympic, and Fraley Rogers from the amateur Star of Brooklyn team. These two joined Wright in the Boston outfield. Shortstop George Wright (.412) returned from a broken leg that cost him half of the 1871 season to rejoin Charlie Gould (.285), Ross Barnes (.401), and Harry Schafer (.282) in a star-quality infield. Al Spalding (19 wins) and Cal McVey, a .431 hitter, formed the battery. Despite a .303 batting average in 1871, Dave Birdsall found himself as Boston's only reserve player in 1872.

Unlike 1871, when George Wright missed part of the season and Fred Cone and Frank Barrows shared a position, the 1872 Red Stockings presented a solid front. Nine players played at least 45 games each, starting in the same position for at least 37 games.

After three road wins, the Red Stockings lost at Philadelphia 10–7 on May 4. They did not lose again until July 20, reeling off 19 straight wins. Boston scored ten or more runs 22 times in 48 games while shutting out opponents on four occasions.

Led by Barnes (.430), the Red Stockings had five hitters bat higher than .300, leading to a .317 team average, tops in the league, and a scoring average of 10.85 runs per game. The Red Stockings were also the top fielding team in the NA with a composite .875 average. Barnes and Spalding were position leaders in fielding. The Red Stockings swept performance honors by compiling the lowest ERA in the league. Spalding had a 1.85 ERA for 405 innings pitched and Boston allowed only 3.06 unearned runs per game, lowest in the league.

A frightening outlook for opponents was that seven of Boston's starters were 25 years of age or younger. Only Harry Wright, at age 37, was older than 30. Leonard, the next oldest, was 26.

1873

The defending champions lost three players. Charlie Gould decided to retire; right fielder Fraley Rogers was also reluctant to commit to another season; and catcher Cal McVey went to Lord Baltimore as manager. Once again, Harry Wright was forced to reload. Future Hall of Fame outfielder/first baseman Jim "Orator" O'Rourke came from the defunct Mansfield club; catcher James "Deacon" White arrived from the defunct Forest City club of Cleveland to replace McVey; and rookie Jack Manning from the Boston Juniors was projected as the new first baseman. When the season began, the lineup was Manning at first base, Ross Barnes at second, George Wright at shortstop and Harry Schafer at third, with Andy Leonard, Harry Wright and Dave Birdsall in the outfield and White catching Al Spalding.

Ten games into the season, Bob Addy, no longer necessary in Philadelphia when Jimmy Wood arrived on the scene, took over an outfield spot vacated by Rogers. The result was an awesome offensive team. Seven regulars hit above .320—Barnes .431, White .392, George Wright .387, Addy .355, O'Rourke .350, Spalding .328 and Leonard .320. The team as a whole hit .340 and led the league in every offensive category, averaging more than 12 runs per game.

Defensively, the Red Stockings were more ordinary, as they committed the second-highest number of errors, and their fielding percentage placed fourth at .836. Part of the problem may have stemmed from a number of gifted athletes shifting positions. Boston used nine different outfielders, four different first basemen and three different second basemen.

Spalding also was less intimidating in 1873. He led the league in wins and winning percentage but his ERA slipped to 2.99. That combined with the 4.12 ERA of Harry Wright gave Boston a 3.07 ERA, good for fourth place.

For much of 1873 Boston ran in the pack. On July 26, the Red Stockings sat in fourth place with a 17–11 record, nine games behind Philadelphia. However, a 12–1 record in September allowed the Red Stockings to move into a tie for first on October 1. They never looked back, going 11–3 in October to finish 43–16–1, good enough for a 3.5-game lead over second-place Philadelphia.

1874

Once again, Harry Wright was able to retain key players, so making the 1874 Red Stockings a reloaded version of 1873. Only outfielder Bob Addy, a .355 hitter, was miss-

Harper's woodcut of the 1874 Boston Red Stockings. Standing: Cal McVey, Al Spalding, Deacon White, Ross Barnes; seated: Jim O'Rourke, Andy Leonard, George Wright, Harry Wright, George Hall, Harry Schafer, Tommy Beals (*Harper's Weekly*, July 1874).

ing. Once again Wright presented a lineup that included Jim O'Rourke, Ross Barnes, George Wright, Harry Schafer, Andy Leonard, Deacon White and Al Spalding in addition to himself. Cal McVey returned from a year with Lord Baltimore and brought with him George Hall. Tommy Beals came from Washington.

For the most part, McVey, Leonard and Hall manned the outfield, sending Harry Wright into a reserve role. With both McVey and White on hand to catch, one was always available for duty elsewhere. Barnes missed 20 games and George Wright 11, which made Beals a valuable acquisition.

As usual, Boston hit well, leading the NA with a .314 team batting average. McVey hit .359, Barnes .340, Spalding and George Wright .329, O'Rourke .314, Leonard .313, and White .301. Harry Wright batted .315 in 40 games. Such hitting led to a league-leading 735 runs scored in 71 games, an average of more than 10 per game. Spalding started all 71 games; he and Harry Wright combined for a 1.93 ERA, third in the league. As a team the Red Stockings yielded 415 runs, a 5.85 average. Led by O'Rourke's .943 fielding average, Boston led the league in fielding with an .850 percentage.

In contrast to 1873, when the Red Stockings had to produce a strong second half to catch the runaway Philadelphia White Stockings, the 1874 season saw Boston lead from wire to wire. After winning the first 13 games, Boston lead by 6.5 games on May 22. At the mid-season point, Boston's record was 30–8, with a 4.5-game lead over Mutual. Boston did not play another league game until September 10, using the midseason to tour Europe for a series of games with the Athletics. For the remainder of September, Boston played poorly and saw its lead shrink to a single game on September 30. A final surge saw the Red Stockings win 17 of the final 21 games to finish 7.5 games ahead of Mutual.

1875

Harry Wright fielded another loaded team for 1875. Only outfielder George Hall was missing from the 1874 champions, his place more than filled by Jack Manning, who hit .346 at Baltimore and Hartford. This meant that Cal McVey (.359), Ross Barnes (.340), Al Spalding (.329), George Wright (.329), Harry Wright (.315), Jim O'Rourke (.314), Andy Leonard (.313) and Deacon White (.301) returned along with top fielding third baseman Harry Schafer. Spalding (52–16, 1.92 ERA) and Manning (4–16, 2.09 ERA at Baltimore) would handle the pitching. Also returning was utility player Tommy Beals.

On March 16, the *New York Herald-Tribune* projected lineups for all the league teams. For Boston the nine included White and Spalding; O'Rourke, Barnes, George Wright and Schafer; Leonard, Harry Wright, and McVey.

The 40-year-old Harry Wright played in only one game, his lineup spot going to Manning. When Schafer missed 30 games, O'Rourke moved over to third base, and Beals filled out the lineup. In addition to outfield duties, Manning started 17 games as pitcher, spelling Spalding. Over the course of the season, Boston used 13 players, with Juice Latham and Frank Heifer filling in.

Boston was an awesome offensive machine again. With six regulars hitting higher than .300, the team batted .321. White hit .367, Barnes .364, McVey .355, George Wright .333, Leonard .321 and Spalding .312. O'Rourke was just outside the circle with a .296 norm. That kind of hitting led to 831 runs scored, slightly more than 10 per game.

To support this offense, Spalding (1.52 ERA) helped the pitchers to a 1.87 ERA, fourth-best in the league. And while its fielding was only third best, Boston gave up the fewest unearned runs—2.33 per game—in the league.

As one can imagine, Boston dominated the 1875 championship race. Undefeated at home (37–0), the Red Stockings won their first 26 games. On June 23, their record had swelled to 35–2, and on August 19 the record was 50–4. Following a 6–3 loss to Athletic on September 4, their record was 55–7. They did not lose their eighth game until October 29, a 9–8 loss at Hartford, and their lead was 14.5 games over the Dark Blues. In the course of the season, only the Brown Stockings, Athletics and Chicago were able to win more than one game against Boston. Seven teams were unable to win a single game. Boston had a 34–0 record against Atlantic, Centennial, Mutual, Philadelphia, the St. Louis Red Stockings, Washington and Keokuk.

CENTENNIAL BASE BALL CLUB
Philadelphia, Pennsylvania
1875

History

Long-time player and manager Elias "Hicks" Hayhurst determined to leave Athletic and form his own club in Philadelphia. The financial success of both Athletic and the Philadelphia BBC led him to believe that a third club also could operate profitably there. He also apparently thought that in 1875 the Centennial name would help sell the club as a part of the upcoming U.S. Centennial celebration.

As with all the new clubs of 1875, Centennial had trouble signing a team. Hayhurst was able to acquire only four veteran players. Unfortunately, at least three of the four brought baggage with them. John Radcliff had been suspended in 1874 for attempting to bribe an umpire. Bill Craver had a "sullied reputation," dating to 1870 (Ryczek 212). Fred Treacey had signed with Chicago while still under contract with Philadelphia in 1873. The fourth, George Bechtel, would ultimately be—like Craver—blacklisted from baseball for throwing games. All four made the *Brooklyn Eagle*'s "All Star" team of "Rogues."

Centennial lost the first four games of the season before defeating Elm City, 12–5, on May Day; after three more losses, they found the high point of their existence—an 11–2 win over Athletic on May 8. Centennial played its final league game on May 24, 1875, finishing a five-game losing streak.

However, on May 26, before officially withdrawing from the league, Centennial made baseball history by selling Craver and Bechtel to the crippled Athletic club for $1,500, the first such transaction in baseball history.

Grounds

Since the Jefferson Street Grounds were used by both Athletic and Philadelphia BBC, Hayhurst acquired a disused baseball ground called Columbia Park for his club. Columbia Park had been used for baseball as early as 1860 and was reportedly the site of the first baseball game ever played in Philadelphia. It had been a Union Army camp during the Civil War. The grounds occupied a lot bounded by Columbia Avenue, Ridge Road, and 24th and 25th streets. Since Ridge Road "meandered," the park configurations were unusual: 300 feet down the left field line, 331 feet to dead center, and 247

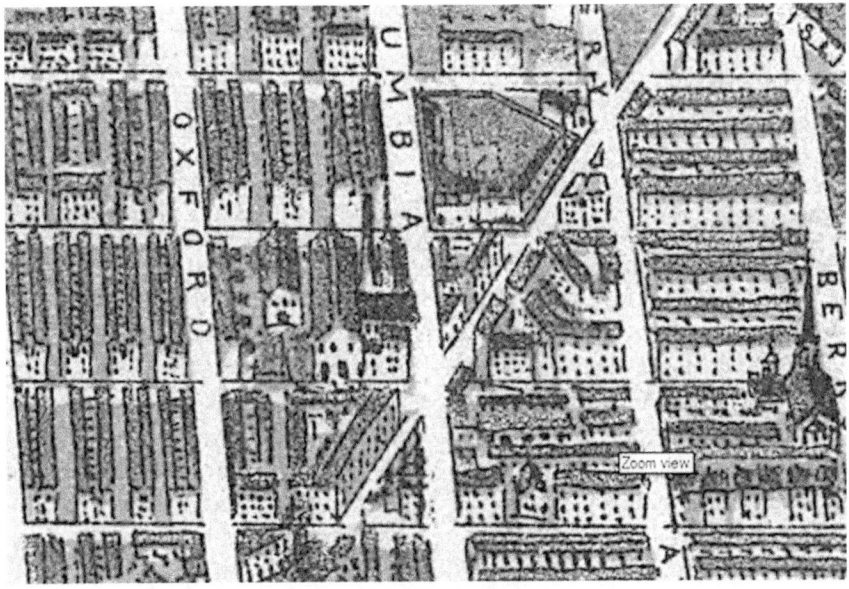

Bird's-eye view of Columbia Park in Philadelphia, home to Centennial. Note the strange configuration of the diamond and fences (*Philadelphia in 1886, H.S.P. del*, Library of Congress Maps and Geography Division).

feet down the right field line. Additionally, since first base was on a rise, all fielders had to throw uphill to that base. Philadelphia clubs, including Athletic, had used Columbia Park prior to the opening of the league. The field was poorly maintained, and Athletic moved into the new Jefferson Street Grounds in 1871. Hayhurst had the Columbia Park re-sodded and built a new ten-foot fence, a grandstand, and a clubhouse in time for the 1875 season. According to Jerrold Casway, "the most distinctive feature of the park was a mammoth sign advertising the *Sunday Item* newspaper," a sign that "could be seen from throughout the city." Hayhurst had the park renamed Centennial Park. However, Centennial had only seven home games. Their top game drew 1,500 fans against Athletic; two other games drew crowds of around 1,000, but at least three home games drew fewer than 500.

After Centennial disbanded, the park again fell into disrepair but was renovated in 1883 by Al Reach for his National League club. When Baker Bowl was completed, the Quakers relocated in 1886; Centennial Park was razed around 1890. Today the area is an industrial area.

Management

Craver served as captain and field manager under Hayhurst.

Uniforms and Logo

William J. Ryczek cites a *New York Clipper* article describing the Centennial uniform as white flannel trousers and shirts with chocolate brown stockings.

Players

Centennial used 12 players in its 14 games. Including Irish-born George Trenwith and Len Lovett, a native of Lancaster County, nine of the 12 were Philadelphia residents.

Except for the four veterans, the team consisted of, in Shiffert's terms, "local amateurs and semi-pros." Seven had no previous league experience. The eighth, Len Lovett, had played in one league game with Resolute in 1873. Seven of the 12 were short-term players: Trenwith and John Abadie had one-year careers; Lovett, Sam Field, Charlie Mason, Tim McGinley and Ed Somerville played in at least parts of two seasons. Radcliff, Bechtel, and Treacey played for four years. Fred Warner was in and out of the majors six times through 1884; only Craver exceeded that, his seven-year career ending with his expulsion from baseball following the 1877 season.

Team performance reflected the amateur/semi-pro status of most of the players. As a team Centennial hit .236, with only Bechtel (.279) and Craver (.277) reaching respectability. The team averaged five runs per game while allowing almost twice that (9.86). While Bechtel's 2.71 ERA was respectable, Centennial was the poorest fielding team in the NA, allowing more than seven unearned runs per game.

Surprisingly, when Centennial disbanded, most of the players were able to catch on—however briefly—with another club: Trenwith, McGinley and Somerville went to New Haven; Mason and Field to Washington; Abadie to Atlantic; and Treacey to Philadelphia. Radcliff and Lovett ended their careers with Centennial.

CHICAGO BASE BALL CLUB
Chicago, Illinois
1870–1871, 1874–present

History

The Chicago Base Ball Club was organized in 1870 in response to the success of the Cincinnati Red Stockings. Following the pattern established by Harry Wright, Chicago resolved to field a team of the best players money could hire. The 1870 team was composed entirely of Eastern players—five came from Brooklyn (Eckford); three came from Lansingburgh (Union); and three came from Philadelphia (Athletic).

The 1870 team was very successful, posting a 65–8 record. The White Stockings, as they came to be known, entered the new league in 1871. In October of that season their home grounds were burned in the Great Chicago Fire, during which they lost not only their home park but also all their uniforms and equipment. They finished the season as a road team in borrowed uniforms, losing a playoff game with Athletic for the championship.

White Stocking president Norman Gassette rebuilt the club and park after the Great Fire (courtesy *Baseball History Blog*).

The demands on people and money to rebuild Chicago were such that the White Stockings were not a part of the league for 1872, though the Chicago Baseball Associ-

White Stocking Grounds (marked 3) before the Great Fire. Note the relative distances to the right and left field fences. From *The City of Chicago as it was before the great conflagration of October 8th, 9th, & 10th, 1871* (Library of Congress Maps and Geography Division).

ation remained intact under the leadership of Norman T. Gassette. During 1872 and 1873 Chicago rebuilt an enclosed baseball ground and hosted league games for others. By 1874 they were ready to put together a team to re-enter the league. Neither the 1874 nor the 1875 team was successful. However, Chicago became a charter member of the new National League and once again raided the East for players to compete successfully, winning the initial NL championship with a team made up of former Red Stocking and Athletics.

Under various names, including White Stockings (1876–89), Colts (1890–97), Orphans (1898–1902), and Cubs (1903–present), the Chicago franchise has been a part of the National League. They have won 16 NL pennants—1876, 1880, 1881, 1882, 1885, 1886, 1906, 1907, 1908, 1910, 1918, 1929, 1932, 1935, 1938, and 1945. They recorded world championships in 1907 and 1908.

Grounds

White Stocking Grounds were located in downtown Chicago on a narrow strip of land between the Illinois Central Railroad tracks and Michigan Avenue. The new property was in poor shape, with piles of debris and trash littering it. At a cost of $5,000, a 7,500-seat facility was erected—the first enclosed baseball-dedicated park in Chicago—known as White Stocking Grounds. The limited space created quirky dimensions, which in 1871 included a short right field wall. These can be seen in the accompanying map.

A crowd of around 10,000 saw the White Stockings defeat Mutual on July 28. After the Great Fire, the ground became part of Lakeside Park in 1878.

A new facility, built in 1872, was called 23rd Street Grounds. This served as home for the White Stockings when they returned to the league in 1874–75. It was located in a block between what is today Cermak Road, Clark Street, Dearborn Street and Federal Street. It had a large pavilion that seated 2,000 behind home plate and seating along the side for another 5,000 fans. It closed in 1877. The club moved to White Stocking Park in 1878.

Management

Second baseman Jimmy Wood managed the team in 1871. Fergy Malone managed the new White Stockings in 1874, but in August with an 18–18 record, he was replaced by Wood, for whom the team went 10–13. Wood remained as manager in 1875.

Uniform and Logo

In 1871 Chicago wore the white stockings that gave them their name. These were worn with blue pants, white shirts and blue caps.

Chicago second baseman and captain Jimmy Wood displays the trademark white stockings (Wikimedia Commons).

When the club returned to the league in 1874, the new uniform consisted of a white cap, a white shirt with a broad blue collar and blue wristbands, and white corduroy knee britches with blue cord on the side seams.

Chicago in the League

1871

With Cincinnati disbanded, Chicago (22–7 against professional teams) led the remaining teams into the new professional league. The White Stockings—termed by the *Cincinnati Daily Gazette* as an "expensive and poorly harmonized machine"—lost three big bats from their 1870 lineup when Levi Meyerle and Ned Cuthbert returned to Philadelphia and Clipper Flynn went to Troy. But Chicago retained a solid core of players with pitcher Ed Pinkham, first baseman Bub McAtee, second baseman and manager Jimmy Wood, shortstop Ed Duffy, outfielder Fred Treacey and catcher Charlie Hodes. To fill holes in the lineup, Chicago grabbed third baseman Tom Foley and outfielder Joe Simmons from Rockford and hard-throwing pitcher George Zettlein—called "The Charmer"—from Atlantic. Signing Zettlein allowed Chicago to move Pinkham to third base.

Before the end of October, the league determined that the winner of a game between Athletic and Chicago on October 30 would claim the whip pennant. The rationale consisted of several factors. Chicago had won six series (two shortened) with the Troy series tied. Athletic had won five series (one shortened) with a loss to Boston. Chicago and Athletic had split four previous games: Athletic winning 15–11 in June and 11–6 in September; the White Stockings winning 11–9 in July and 6–3 in August. If Chicago won the October 30 game, the White Stockings would take the series three games to two and finish with a 7-0-1 record compared to Athletic's 6-2 record. If Athletic won, they would win the series three games to two and finish with a 7-1 record to Chicago's 6-1-1 mark. With the pennant riding on the outcome, Dick McBride outdueled Zettlein, 4-1, at Union Ground in Brooklyn. After all protests and appeals had been settled at the December meeting, the league awarded the pennant to Athletic.

Chicago's success centered on pitching. Working 241 of the club's 251 innings, Zettlein posted a league-leading 2.73 ERA, and the White Stockings allowed only 241 runs—25 fewer than Athletic and 62 fewer than Boston. But White Stocking batters hit fifty points under Athletic. With only two hitters batting higher than .300—Wood .378 and Treacey .339—the club hit .270 overall. Run production was also lower at 302 runs, fifth best in the league. Chicago fielding was even more mediocre, ranking sixth best in the league, though Treacey led NA outfielders.

1874

After an absence of two years, Chicago returned to the NA in 1874, building a team with the same tactics that the Philadelphia White Stockings had used to build the 1873 team. In fact, Chicago signed six of the Philadelphia players to form the nucleus of the club. Levi Meyerle, Ned Cuthbert, Fred Treacey, Fergy Malone, George Zettlein and Jim Devlin changed uniforms. John Glenn and Paul Hines came from Washington and Davy Force jumped from Lord Baltimore. Only Treacey and Zettlein had played with the 1871 Chicago team.

As was often the case with NA teams, a group of solid players could not produce a stable lineup. In the team's 59 games, only Zettlein as pitcher and Cuthbert in the outfield played as many as 50 games at a position. With 13 players—nine of whom played at least 40 games—the White Stockings used seven outfielders, five shortstops and third basemen, four catchers, three second basemen and pitchers, and two first basemen. Meyerle and Force each played four positions.

The White Stockings were the third-best hitting team in the NA in 1874 with a .278 average. Meyerle hit .394 and Force reached .313. However, they scored only 418 runs, just over seven per game. When the other team batted, Chicago was only the seventh-best team. Led by Zettlein, Chicago pitchers had a 2.65 ERA. That average and the 480 runs allowed were seventh. Since opponents scored more than eight runs on average, perhaps the overall record is surprisingly good. Though the team fielded .829, good for fourth, no individual fielder stood out at a position.

Chicago flirted with the .500 mark all season. The team never won more than five games in a row and never lost more than seven. On July 5 the White Stockings were six games under .500 at 9-16. On August 31, they were four games over at 22-18. In the first half of the season they had a 17-16 record; in the second half an 11-15 record. Under Malone's management, they had an 18-18 record; under Jimmy Wood, a 10-13 mark. Against teams above them in the standings, they had an 11-26 record; against teams below them, they were 17-5. At home they were 18-10; on the road, 10-21. In essence, they were a mediocre team.

1875

Five White Stockings from the disappointing fifth-place team of 1874 took their talents to other clubs. Batting champ Levi Meyerle and infielder Fergy Malone went to Philadelphia; Fred Treacey joined Centennial, while shortstop Davy Force went to Athletic and outfielder Ned Cuthburt to St.

Louis. The defection of Meyerle and Force took away the team's best hitters.

Back for another trial were first baseman John Glenn, infielder John Peters, outfielder Paul Hines, pitcher George Zettlein (27–30, 2.43 ERA) and utility player Jim Devlin. Both Hines (.295) and Peters (.289) were solid hitters.

Catcher Scott Hastings (.324 at Hartford) and Dick Higham (.261 in a down year with Mutual) were promising replacements for Force and Meyerle. From the defunct Lord Baltimore club came outfielder Oscar Bielaski and infielder Warren White.

The *New York Herald-Tribune* projected the following lineup: Hastings and Zettlein; Glenn, Peters, White and George Keerl; Hines, Higham and Devlin.

Disregarding position shifts, the newspaper projected eight regulars. Keerl played very little (six games); Bielaski became a regular outfielder. Neither Higham nor Zettlein finished the season with the club, with Zettlein going to Philadelphia and Higham returning to Mutual. Devlin and Mike Golden, acquired along with Joe Miller and Paddy Quinn from the defunct Western club, took over the pitching. The White Stockings, managed by Jimmy Wood, used 17 players, five of whom played in fewer than ten games.

Paul Hines hit .328, sixth-best in the league; he received some support from Jim Devlin (.289) and John Peters (.286) in helping Chicago to a team .260 average, good for third-best in the league. But Chicago was not productive, averaging fewer than five and a half runs per outing. Headed by George Zettlein (17–14, 1.28 ERA), the pitching staff allowed only 1.63 earned runs per game. Glenn was an outfield leader in fielding percentage, but Chicago as a team fielded .853, sixth best. They allowed a whopping 4.39 unearned runs per game, which meant that overall Chicago had a negative half a run per game.

ECKFORD BASEBALL CLUB
Brooklyn, New York
1855–1872

History

Eckford Baseball Club, founded in Brooklyn in 1855, was named for Scottish-born shipbuilder Henry Eckford. This was one of the first blue-collar clubs in the city, as many of the players worked at the Eckford shipyard. One of the great teams of the 1850s and 1860s, Eckford was declared champion of the NABBP in 1862 with a 15–2 record and of the 1863 season with a 10–0 mark. Earlier, the team had had second-place finishes in 1860 and 1861 and a third-place

Scottish-born shipbuilder Henry Eckford. Employees at his Brooklyn shipyard formed the first baseball club made up primarily of blue-collar workers (Wikimedia Commons).

showing in 1859. Names such as Al Reach, Jimmy Wood, Josh Snyder, Ed Duffy and Marty Swandell appeared in the Eckford box scores during this period. Wood finished second in runs scored in 1862 and first in 1863. However, the Eckford club fell on hard times after the war; it rebounded with a 47–8 record in 1869, second only to the undefeated Cincinnati Red Stockings. First baseman Andy Allison was the hitting star of that team.

Eckford was one of founding members of the professional league in 1871 but did not join initially. Later, following the withdrawal of Kekionga, some sources assert that Eckford joined unofficially by playing out the Kekionga schedule. Preston Orem asserts that Eckford played 60 games overall, more than most of the league teams.

In 1872, they determined to participate in the league, but their day had passed. Without strong financial backing, they operated as a cooperative, paying salaries and expenses from gate receipts. As a result, they were not able to compete with the well-funded stock teams. Consequently, 1872 was a sad ending to a storied franchise.

Grounds

Union Grounds in the Williamsburg section of Brooklyn were the first enclosed grounds in baseball. In 1862 William Cammeyer built a six-foot fence around Union Grounds so that he would be able to charge spectators to watch baseball. The Eckford club was among the first tenants, which means Union Grounds witnessed the greatest period of Eckford history. Other top clubs that made Union Grounds their home were Mutual (1868–76), Atlantic (1873–75) and the Hartford Dark Blues (1877). The last major league game played there was on July 26, 1878, when Providence defeated Milwaukee. Baseball games were played through 1882; the grounds were razed in 1883.

Union Grounds were very large with fences 500 feet away (350 to right). The seating capacity was listed as 1,500. During the winter, the grounds were flooded and used for ice skating. The pagoda, a warming house for the skaters, had lights in the windows for evening skating. For baseball games, the pagoda was in play.

Management

Pitcher Jim Clinton managed the first 11 games of 1872, none of which Eckford won. After Troy disbanded, its manager and second baseman, Jimmy Wood, returned to Eckford and managed the remainder of the season; under Wood the team posted a 3–15 record, to go 3–26 overall.

Union Grounds in Brooklyn. The pagoda in center field, a warming house during skating season, was in play in baseball games. Union Grounds was home to Atlantic, Mutual, Eckford and later Hartford (courtesy www.19cbaseball.com).

Uniform and Logo

According to Orem, the 1871 uniform of Eckford consisted of "white flannel trimmed with orange, stockings and belt of a 'rich orange color,' an orange 'E' on the shirt bosom and small round hats instead of caps."

Eckford in the League

While Eckford was able to pick up outfielder Tom Patterson from Mutual, most of the players were veterans of the independent 1871 Eckford team. These included Andy Allison, Jim Snyder, Josh Snyder, Frank Fleet, Dick Hunt, Marty Swandell and Jim Clinton. The projected "nine" included a battery of George Bunting and R. J. Fitzsimmons from the Riverside club of Portsmouth, Ohio; W. Gallagher from Rose Hill College; and Ed Shelley from the 1871 Eckfords—none of whom played in 1872.

On July 9, the Eckford record was 0–11 under Clinton. Ten of those losses were by at least 10 runs. Before Eckford resumed league play in August, Troy disbanded. From the Haymakers, Eckford was able to add Candy Nelson, Count Gedney, Doug Allison, Phonney Martin, George Zettlein and Jim Wood, with Wood assuming the managerial reins. Eckford also added Jim Holdsworth from the defunct Forest City club of Cleveland, but the new players performed much as the old players had, losing 15 of 18 games.

Eleven additional players appeared in the Eckford lineup over the course of the season. Some (Joe McDermott, Martin Malone, Bill Allison and Nat Jewett) had played with Eckford in the past. Others (James Cavanagh, Al Martin, William Bestick, David Lenz, George Fletcher and a pitcher named O'Rourke) were local amateurs picked up for a game or two. Jack McDonald came from Atlantic.

Using 26 players created instability that did not help Eckford's performance. Andy Allison was the regular first baseman, but four others also played there. Nelson played the most games (eight) at second base, one of nine players who tried his hand at the position; Fleet was the busiest of four third basemen. Jim Snyder was the regular shortstop, but four others also filled in. Doug Allison caught the last 18 games, preceded by five men. Phonney Martin and George Zettlein did most of the pitching, but four others tried. Among 15 outfielders, Patterson, Gedney and Josh Snyder got the most work.

Overall, Eckford scored just over five runs per game while allowing more than 14. They were ninth in team defense, allowing 8.72 unearned runs per game. Doug Allison hit .337 and Hunt .325 on a team that batted just .232. Martin won two of the three games with a 3.92 ERA for a staff that allowed 5.55 runs per game.

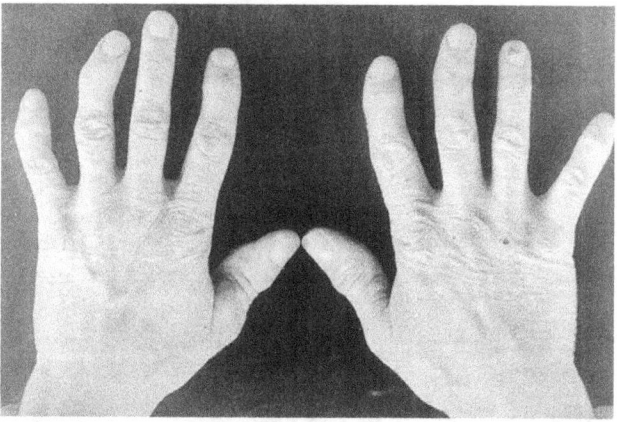

The hands of Doug Allison (Hands of former professional baseball player, Douglas Allison, showing results of baseball playing, Dorsal surface (Feb 12, 1889. [NS31]. OHA 78: New Series Photographs. Otis Historical Archives. National Museum of Health and Medicine).

ELM CITY BASE BALL CLUB
New Haven, Connecticut
1875–1876

History

The Elm City Base Ball Club was formed in 1875, organized by a 24-year-old former Mansfield player named Willis Arnold. New Haven, with a population of 51,000 and a famous college, was experiencing strong economic growth. With a league club now operating in Hartford, New Haven seemed to be a sound choice to host a second club located between Boston and New York City. Arnold argued that for $3,100 a first-class club could be created and that it would be supported by the city. The money was pledged, a lot on Howard Avenue was secured, and former Cincinnati Red Stockings star Charlie Gould was hired as captain.

Elm City was a club without antecedents or supporting structure. David Arcidiacono reports that given the bloated league—13 clubs scrambling for players—and the late start, Elm City had difficulty signing players and getting those signed to report to New Haven. They began the season with only nine players and were forced to improvise a lineup as they went along by picking up fill-in players, such as gymnastics instructor Lester Dole and Yale medical student George Knight, and shifting positions to accommodate injured players. Not surprisingly, the club experienced little success on the field.

It also experienced little financial success. Even before the grounds were ready, Elm City had run through the initial $3,100 and had raised another $5,000 in an attempt to be ready to open the season. Even so, their grounds were not completed on time, and they later had to cancel a scheduled trip to the West for league games in Chicago and St. Louis because of a lack of funds. The club structure also failed. Arnold left the club before the season began, likely over a dispute with Gould about scheduling. However, Gould was relieved of his field management duties in June.

When the new National League was formed in 1876, Elm City was not invited to become a member. Their appeal for membership was denied, and they played through that season as an independent club while facing many of the league clubs. Apparently they disbanded at the close of 1876, as they do not appear in newspapers accounts for 1877.

Grounds

Howard Avenue Grounds, a rough trapezoid measuring 549 feet by 530 feet by 305 feet by 597 feet, were located on the west side of Harbor Fort. They were bounded by Howard Avenue, Spring and Cedar streets, and the New York–New Haven–Hartford Railroad tracks. The grounds were enclosed and were perhaps the first grounds to sell advertising on the fences. Since the grounds were not ready by Opening Day, Elm City opened by playing Boston at Hamilton Park, home grounds for Yale University. Elm City then moved into Howard Avenue Grounds on April 26, 1875. At that time neither the grandstand nor the bleachers had been constructed. Against Hartford on both June 11 and October 4, they drew 1,500 fans to the grounds. During that season, Howard Avenue Grounds hosted 26 games, the last against Boston on October 28.

Today, the area of the grounds is occupied by residential housing.

A bird's-eye view of Howard Avenue Grounds in New Haven. From *The city of New Haven, Conn. 1879. Drawn & pub. by O. H. Bailey & J. C. Hazen* (Library of Congress Maps and Geography Division).

Management

In 47 games, Elm City went through three managers. When the record reached 2–21 on June 14, Charlie Gould was replaced by George Latham, who had just arrived from Boston. Improvement under his guidance was marginal, as the record stood at 6–35 on September 11. At that point Charlie Pabor joined the club from Atlantic and managed Elm City to a 1–5 record over the final six games.

Uniform and Logo

The research of David Arcidiacono showed that Elm City wore white flannels with the name "New Haven" stitched in blue across the front. They wore white and blue checkered socks. Unfortunately, we have no photo of this uniform.

Elm City in the League

1875

For the most part Elm City was able to attract players with some league experience but few that had enjoyed regular status. Outfielder Jim Tipper had hit .305 down the road at Hartford in 1874; first baseman Charlie Gould managed only .224 as a regular for Lord Baltimore; outfielder Johnny Ryan hit even lower (.193) on the same club.

Projected catcher John Radcliff hit .243 as a reserve in Philadelphia; battery mate Tricky Nichols had no league experience. Joining Gould on a projected infield was shortstop Sam Wright, younger brother of Harry and George Wright, second baseman Billy Geer (two games for Mutual in 1874), and third baseman Herm Doscher (out of the league in 1874, seven games of league experience with Atlantic). Tipper and Ryan

Charlie Gould played first base and managed Elm City during the first part of 1875. from "First Nine of the Cincinnati (Red Stockings) Baseball Club" (LC-USZC4-1291 Library Congress Prints and Photographs Division).

were accompanied in the outfield by newcomer Henry Luff from Philadelphia.

Many of Elm City's on-field problems can be seen from the breakdown of positions. Gould was the regular first baseman but shared the position with four others: Studs Bancker, John Cassidy (from Atlantic), Geer, and Ed Somerville (from Centennial). Somerville became the regular second baseman but shared that position with three others: Geer, Bancker and Fred Goldsmith, who later would make his name as a curveball pitcher. Sam Wright was the regular shortstop, but no fewer than 10 others tried the position: Bancker, Tom Barlow, Geer, Rit Harrison, George Latham (from Boston), Luff, Ryan, Somerville, John Smith (from Lord Baltimore), and an amateur named Booth borrowed from Bridgeport for a day. Third base was almost as crowded. Luff played the most games, but eight others also received playing time there: Bancker, Geer, a local amateur named Jim Keenan, Latham, John McKelvey (from Rochester Pacific), Tim McKinley (from Centennial), Somerville, and George Trenwith (also from Centennial). In the outfield, Tipper, McKelvey and Ryan played most often but had help from Geer, Luff, Gould, Nichols, former pitching great Charlie Pabor, and amateurs Lester Dole, Sullivan and a Washington, D.C., pickup named Evans. McKinley caught, as did Bancker, Gould, Harrison, Keenan, and Ryan. Nichols started 33 games in the box, Luff and Ryan started 10 each, and Yale student George Knight started one. Neither Radcliff nor Doscher, both projected starters, found his way to New Haven.

Elm City opened at Boston on April 19, losing, 6–0. After dropping their first 15 games, Elm City won their first game on May 31—a 9–2 victory at Washington. By mid–June, when Charlie Gould was replaced as manager, the record stood at 2–21. William Ryczek believes the team play improved after the addition of Centennial players. Still, Elm City lost 40 games, 13 by ten or more runs. In addition to the opening 15-game losing streak, they had losing streaks of seven and five games and no back-to-back wins. They also had losing records against all of the teams against whom they played.

Luff hit .279 and McGinley batted .277, but as a team, Elm City hit only .218 and scored only 3.62 runs per game, good for tenth in the league. Tricky Nichols (4–29, 2.38 ERA) headed a staff that had a 2.65 ERA. However, a leaky Elm City defense (.814 percentage) yielded another 5.79 unearned runs. Part of the Elm City problem can be seen in the 3.62 runs scored versus 8.44 runs against.

FOREST CITY BASE BALL CLUB
Cleveland, Ohio
1868–1872

History

The *Encyclopedia of Cleveland History* gives 1865 as the founding date for the Forest City Base Ball Club. However, Forest City does not appear in the National Association standings until 1868, when it compiled an 11-11-1 record. That club played mostly Ohio and midwestern opponents but ventured outside to receive an 85-11 drubbing by Athletic and a 25-7 defeat administered by Union of Morrisania, New York. Twenty-year-old Deacon White, who was working in Cleveland at the time, played shortstop.

In 1869 Forest City fielded a professional club. This allowed them to attract pitcher Al Pratt and first baseman Art Allison in addition to White. The professional club went 19-6 for the season, with all six losses coming at the hands of professional nines, such as the Cincinnati Red Stockings, Union of Lansingburg, Olympic of Washington and Alert of Rochester.

By 1870 the Forest City lineup included a number of players who would make a mark in professional baseball. In addition to Allison, Pratt and White, these included Ezra Sutton, Chick Fulmer, George Heubel, Jim Charlton and Elmer White. However, this team enjoyed only moderate success against professional opponents, losing 15 of 24 games.

A charter member of the National Association of Professional Base Ball Players, Forest City played the first game in major league history, losing to Kekionga and Bobby Mathews, 2–0, on May 4, 1871. Despite adding Charlie Pabor and John Bass from Union of Morrisania, the 1871 Forest City club continued to struggle against professional competition, dropping 19 of 29 league games to finish seventh in the nine-

Deacon White began a career with Forest City that may yet award him Hall of Fame Honors. From *National League Galaxy* (Library of Congress Prints and Photographs Division).

Bobby Mathews shut out Cleveland in the first major league game ever played. From Philadelphia Athletics 1887 team photograph (LC-DIG-ppmsca-09630 Library of Congress Prints and Photographs Division).

Forest City (Cleveland)

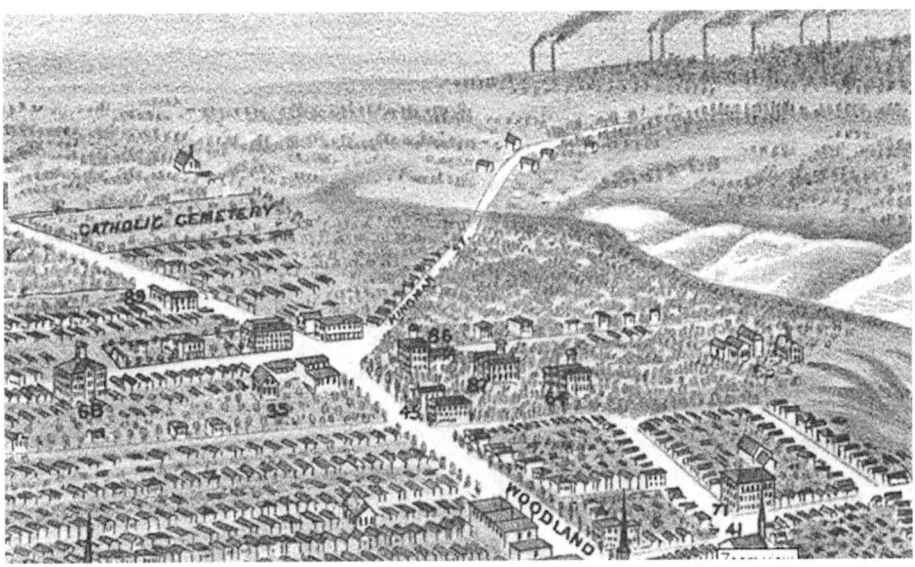

Approximate location of National Association Grounds. Catholic Cemetery (now St. Joseph's) is beyond the baseball grounds, which were located at the intersection of Woodland Avenue with Kinsman Road. From *Birds eye view of Cleveland, Ohio 1877. A. Ruger artist. Lith. by Shober & Carqueville* (Library of Congress Maps and Geography Division).

team league. The 1872 edition of Forest City was even less successful. The club withdrew from the league in August

Grounds

National Association Grounds was the home of Forest City for both of its seasons in the league. The grounds were located in the Central Neighborhood section of Cleveland, between what are known today as E 55th Street and Kinsman Road and between Ensign Avenue and Grand Avenue. On May 29, 1872, a crowd of 4,000 witnessed the 5–2 loss to Lord Baltimore.

The *Cleveland Indians Encyclopedia* says there were no seats. Spectators could stand, sit on the ground, or sit in their carriages surrounding the field. Fans were given the opportunity to buy season tickets for $6 for a single admission or $10 if they wished to bring a lady.

The area today appears to be occupied by two warehouses.

Management

Pabor managed the 1871 team to a 10–19 record. Scott Hastings, who had come from Rockford, managed the team to a 6–14 record in 1872; in August he was replaced by Deacon White. After two games—both losses—Forest City disbanded following an August 19 contest.

Uniform and Logo

According to the Fort Wayne newspaper, Forest City wore white uniforms with blue stockings and belts. The logo on the breastplate was a stylized FC, also in blue. See the photo of Deacon White on page 131.

Forest City in the League

1871

Forest City had gone 25–16 overall in 1870, but only nine of those wins were against professional clubs. Seven Forest City veterans, augmented by shortstop John Bass and pitcher Charlie Pabor from Union of Morrisania, were available for the club's venture into the league. Pabor, who managed the team, went to the outfield, leaving the pitching to "Uncle Al" Pratt. Three holdovers from 1870—Jim Carleton, Gene Kimball, and Ezra Sutton—joined Bass on the infield. Art Allison and Elmer White joined Pabor in the outfield. The catcher, whom the Cincinnati newspaper termed the "most valuable man in that position in America," was a 20-year-old amateur named James "Deacon" White. That newspaper stated that Forest City "will worthily represent our state next season."

Forest City got off to a rocky start in 1871 by being shut out by Bobby Mathews on Opening Day, 2–0, and later losing to Chicago, 14–12, despite Sutton's grand-slam homer. Matters improved little thereafter as the club gave up at least ten runs 20 times in 29 games. Season highlights would include series wins over the other Forest City from Rockford (3–1) and Mutual (3–2).

Sutton (.352), White (.322) and Bass (.303) helped Forest City post a .277 batting average, but the team was seventh in runs scored. Pratt had a 3.77 ERA, but the defense allowed 6.69 unearned runs per game. Forest City was outscored 288–249 during the season.

1872

For 1872 Forest City brought back seven regulars from the 1871 team. Losses included twenty-three-year-old outfielder Elmer White, who died in March, and shortstop John Bass (.303 with a league-leading 10 triples), who went to Atlantic. Back to the fold were third baseman Ezra Sutton (.352), catcher Deacon White (.322), outfielders Charlie Pabor (.296) and Art Allison (.292), first baseman Jim Carleton (.252) and pitcher Al Pratt (10–17). From the defunct White Stockings came outfielder Joe Simmons; from the defunct Rockford club arrived catcher Scott Hastings. Forest City also acquired Rynie Wolters (.370 with 16 wins) from Mutual and utility player Charlie Sweasy from Olympic.

In the 1872 lineup, Simmons replaced Carleton at first base, joining Sweasy, Sutton and rookie Jim Holdsworth in the infield. Allison and Pabor were joined by Wolters in the outfield. White was the catcher. Pratt, Wolters and Pabor shared the pitching duties. Hastings, who managed the club, filled in as needed.

Cleveland opened with two road wins against National and Olympic but dropped six of the next seven. Among the few high points were back-to-back wins over Baltimore and Mutual in June and a 24–5 shellacking of Eckford in July. Low points included two five-game losing streaks, a 17–0 loss at Boston, and a 20–1 loss at Mutual.

Led by Hastings (.391), Deacon White (.339), and Holdsworth (.300), Cleveland hit .288, fifth-best in the league. But like many lower-echelon teams, Cleveland leaked runs. The three-man staff of Al Pratt, Rynie Wolters, and Charlie Pabor gave up 5.7 earned runs per game and the defense—sixth-best in the league—allowed another 5.82 unearned runs. Cleveland was outscored on average 11.55–7.91.

When the team played its last game on August 19, the record was 6–16.

FOREST CITY BASEBALL CLUB
Rockford, Illinois
1867–1871

History

In those early years of Organized Baseball, it was Rockford and not Chicago that emerged as the hotbed of baseball in the West. We first hear of Forest City in 1867 when the National Club of Washington, D.C., included Rockford in its western tour. Headed by 16-year-old pitcher Al Spalding, Forest City defeated the powerful National club, 28–23, in Chicago.

The 1868 club went 11–4 and the 1869 team went 20–4. In addition to Spalding, Rockford was able to attract such future league stars as Ross Barnes, Bob Addy and Scott Hastings. Joe Simmons was added in 1870. Despite the presence of an expensive Chicago club next door, Forest City won 42 games against 13 losses and a tie.

When the league opened in 1871, Rockford quickly became educated in high-level sports competition. First, Forest City did not have the financial base to compete for top players. Future Hall of Fame member Cap Anson received $66.67 per month—about $400 total for the 1871 season. Harry Wright enticed Forest City's two greatest stars, Al Spalding and Ross Barnes, to come east to play for his Red Stockings. According to rumor, Spalding was paid $2,000 in Boston. Second, as a small-town club, Forest City was not able to afford travel expenses. To increase the problem, few eastern clubs were interested in visiting Rockford, demanding instead that Forest City meet them in Chicago.

Forest City completed the initial league season but did not enter a team for 1872 and thus passed into major league history.

Eighteen-year-old Cap Anson played the first of his 27 major league seasons for Forest City. From *Chicago Champions* (LC-DIG-pga-18390 Library of Congress Prints and Photographs Division).

Grounds

Forest City played home games at Agricultural Society Fair Grounds, located within easy walking distance of downtown Rockford. A description of the grounds, appearing in 1939, indicated that this was the worst possible venue for baseball. The grounds were surrounded by large trees, whose limbs encroached on the field, especially behind home plate. Foul space was almost nonexistent, and many pop-ups were lost in the trees. The highest point on the infield was third base, while home plate was in a depression, forcing base runners to make a downhill sprint to score. The outfield contained a "warning track," a deep gutter used to drain the adjacent horseracing track. "Only providence" protected outfielders

Forest City (Rockford)

A bird's-eye view of the racetrack at Agricultural Society Fair Grounds in Rockford. Jim Nitz says that the baseball grounds may have been inside the track or beyond it (*Bird's eye view of the city of Rockford, Ill. 1880. Beck & Pauli Lith*. Library of Congress Maps and Geography Division).

from serious injury caused by running into the ditch.

Jim Nitz notes that while a small stand seated a few hundred fans, crowds of 2,000 or more were frequent.

Today the grounds are part of Fairground Park.

Management

Catcher Scott Hastings managed the 1871 team.

Uniform and Logo

According to newspaper accounts, the Forest City colors were green. The breastplate has an interlinked FC, much less elaborate than that worn by Cleveland. The photo of the 1870 team is shown.

Forest City in the League

When the 1871 season began, five key players that had helped Forest City to a 43–10–1 record in 1870 were wearing enemy colors. Harry Wright snatched Fred Cone as well as Barnes and Spalding for his new Boston team, while Chicago seized Tom Foley and Joe Simmons. As replacements, Cap Anson came from the amateur ranks at Marshaltown, Iowa, to play third base, and Denny Mack arrived from Villanova University to play first. George Bird and Ralph Ham held two outfield positions. Chick Ful-

Members of the Forest City club of Rockford around 1870 display the uniform (*Rockford Republic*, June 21, 1922).

mer, a reserve player in 1870, played shortstop. Bob Addy (second base), Gat Stires (outfield) and Scott Hastings (catcher) were holdover starters. Cherokee Fisher from Union of Lansingburgh became the pitcher.

An opening 12–4 loss to the other Forest City of Cleveland started Rockford on a 16-game losing streak. The club would not win its first league game until July 31. Included in this streak were four games in which Forest City was leading or had won on the field and were forced to forfeit.

After defeating Mutual, 18–5, on July 31, Forest City embarked on a three-game winning streak, topped by Fisher's 4–0 shutout of Kekionga on August 3. The club would win one more game, closing on September 15 with a 4–21 record.

Forest City used 11 players, with Pony Sager (eight games) and Al Barker (one game) as the only reserves. The team hit .264 (eighth-best of nine), and fielded .821 (seventh-best). Anson hit .325 as the most effective offensive player.

HARTFORD BASEBALL CLUB
Hartford Connecticut
1874–1877

History

Hartford was the largest city in Connecticut, and its location made a convenient stopping place for teams traveling between Boston and New York City. Ben Douglas, Jr., whose attempt to place a successful team in Middletown, Connecticut, in 1872 ended in failure, was able to convince Hartford businessmen to put up $5,000 to finance a team in 1874.

Unlike his earlier effort in Middletown, Douglas was able to attract a team of talented professional players to Hartford. No fewer than seven had started for one of the established teams in 1873. But this team never fulfilled its potential. It was neither successful on the field nor disciplined off it. David Arcidiacono notes that the players tended to "cling to their love for strong drink." As a result, Hartford finished in seventh place, ahead of only the hapless Lord Baltimores.

Morgan Bulkeley, president of the Hartford Base Ball Club, in 1876 led the team into the new National League, of which he was also president (LC-DIG-hec-15814 Library of Congress Prints and Photographs Division).

The 1875 team reorganized from the top down. Morgan Bulkeley became the new president. He brought in tough disciplinarian Bob Ferguson to manage the team and almost an entirely new team, featuring pitching and defense. These factors allowed the Dark Blues to finish in second place behind run-away champion Boston.

Bulkeley then took Hartford into the new National League, of which he was also president. The smallest city in the NL, Hartford finished in third place in the inaugural season but was unsuccessful at the gate. At the end of that season, Bulkeley took the club to Brooklyn for the 1877 campaign. Playing as Hartford of Brooklyn, the Dark Blues finished third in the six-team league and then passed into history.

Grounds

The club selected a lot south of downtown Hartford, known as the Colt property, on which to build a ballpark. While the property was not on a streetcar line, the club felt that transportation could be handled by running special trains on game days. The grounds were located on the corner of Wyllys Street and Hendricxsen Avenue. Adjacent was the Church of the Good Shepherd built by Mrs. Samuel Colt in honor of her husband and children, who had died in infancy. An eight-foot fence surrounded the grounds, which measured 400 feet by 500 feet.

When Morgan Bulkeley became club president, he had the grounds upgraded so that they were among the best in the league. A pavilion seating more than 500 was located behind home plate. On its roof was the section for sportswriters and the scorers. Under the pavilion were club rooms for both the Hartford team and the visitors. Seating sections were added along both the first and third base lines. Overall, the grounds seated between 8,000 to 10,000 spectators.

Today, only the church remains.

Management

Lip Pike managed—or perhaps mismanaged—the 1874 team. Running a loose ship, he exerted little control over the lives of players, whose behavior scandalized the citizens of Hartford. The result was a 16–37 record. In 1875 Bob Ferguson brought a tough, nononsense approach to managing the club. Despite conflicts with his players, he was able to steer the club into second place with a 54–28 record. He continued to manage the club in the National League until it disbanded.

Uniform and Logo

Hartford adopted dark blue as a club color, hence the popular name for the team.

Photos show white shirts and knee pants with the dark blue stockings and lettering on the shirts. Like Boston, Hartford chose to have the city name on its shirts. The caps appear to be white.

Hartford in the League

1874

For a start-up organization Hartford was able to recruit more veteran players than had been the case with Mansfield and would be the case with Elm City. From Lord Baltimore came first baseman Everett Mills (.331), outfielder Lip Pike (.314), and catcher Scott Hastings (.281). From Atlantic came outfielder Bill Boyd (.276) and catcher Tom Barlow (.273). Second baseman Bob Addy had hit .355 in helping Boston win the 1873 pennant; Cherokee Fisher batted .261 as an outfield regular for Athletic while compiling a 3–4 record as a pitcher. In addition, outfielder Jim Tipper had hit .292 for Mansfield in 1872.

Candy Cummings posted a 35–12, 1.61 ERA record for Hartford in 1875 (Wikimedia Commons).

The *Hartford Courant* projected a battery of Fisher and Hasting, an infield of Mills, Addy, Barlow and Boyd, and an outfield of Tipper, Pike, and rookie William Stearns. These projections proved correct. Another rookie, Billy Barnie, earned regular status as a catcher/outfielder; Stearns shared pitching with Fisher.

Hartford hit reasonably well. Headed by Pike (.355), Boyd (.350), Hastings (.324) and Tipper (.305), the team hit .276, fifth-best in the league, leading to 371 runs, sixth-best. Fisher (2.32 ERA) and Stearns (2.95 ERA) held enemy batters in reasonable check. However, the team gave up 336 unearned runs, and Hartford was outscored 471 to 371. It did not help that at .797 Hartford was the poorest fielding team in the league. Among regulars, Barnie fielded only .702, and Boyd an even-worse .669.

Hartford used 15 players in 1873. Reserve Steve Brady hit .314 in 27 games but fielded only .650. Orator Shaffer (nine games after coming from Boston), Jack Farrell (three games), Jack Manning (one game after coming from Lord Baltimore) and a local amateur named Fancy O'Neil (one game) also made appearances.

1875

Hartford used a broom to sweep away the unsuccessful and undisciplined remnants of 1874. Bob Addy, Cherokee Fisher and Orator Shaffer took their wares to Philadelphia. Lip Pike took his big bat to St. Louis; Scott Hastings went to Chicago, Jim Tipper to Elm City and Bill Stearns back to Washington. When new manager Bob Ferguson came from Atlantic, he brought along pitcher Tommy Bond. Hartford raided Mutual for second baseman Jack Burdock, shortstop Tom Carey, catcher Doug Allison and outfielder Jack Remsen. Pitcher Candy Cummings and outfielder Tom York came from Philadelphia.

Members of the 1875 Hartford Dark Blues team. Standing: Doug Allison, Tom York, Candy Cummings, Tommy Bond, Bill Harbidge; Seated: Jack Burdock, Everett Mills, Bob Ferguson, Tom Carey and Jack Remsen (courtesy Robert Edward Auctions).

The projected lineup was Doug Allison and Bond; Mills, Burdock, Carey and Ferguson; York, Remsen and Cummings. As it turned out, Bond, a good-hitting pitcher, played 29 games as an outfielder. Cummings started 47 games as pitcher but played little otherwise. Art Allison, who started the season with Washington, took over as an outfield regular when Washington disbanded in July.

The loss of Pike, Hastings, Boyd and Tipper cut into the Hartford firepower. In 1875 no Dark Blue hit .300, with York (.296) and Burdock (.294) the only heavy hitters. The team settled for a .260 average, but this was good enough for third place, as were the 557 runs scored. It helped that Bond (1.41 ERA) and Cummings (1.60 ERA) combined for a league-leading 1.57 ERA. This team excelled on defense, with a league-leading .881 fielding percentage. The bottom line for the team success was that Hartford outscored opponents, 557–343.

The Dark Blues won their first 12 games and never experienced a serious losing streak during the season. They never rose above second place and never fell below fourth; on August 10 the team settled into third place for the remainder of the season. They split with Philadelphia and the Brown Stockings and had winning records against every club except Boston, against whom they lost nine of ten. In the end, their 54–27 record was 18.5 games behind Boston.

HAYMAKER BASEBALL CLUB
Troy, New York
1860–1872

History

Union Baseball Club of Lansingburgh, New York, dates from 1866, though earlier editions of the club existed prior to the Civil War. In 1861 National of Lansingburgh merged with Priam of Troy to form the Union club of Rensselaer County. By 1867, when the Union club first appeared in National Association standings with a 14–6 record, it included Bub McAtee, Clipper Flynn and Bill Craver. That same year, the term "Haymakers" was first used by New York Mutual players and supporters, who were upset over losing to a small-town club. A year later Union went 15–5 with two victories over Mutual. By 1869 they had declared themselves a professional club and had acquired hard-throwing Cherokee Fisher, moves that helped the club to a 24–9–1 record. The 1870 team added pitcher Lefty McMullin, outfielder Tom York, and catcher Mike McGeary, who captained the team.

The 1871 team was described as a joint-stock corporation, one that could compete in the new professional league. It officially adopted the derogatory Haymakers as the club name and changed the club address from Lansingburgh to Troy. As charter members of the league, the Haymakers finished in the middle of the pack along with big-city rivals Mutual and Olympic. But after a 15–10 start in 1872, the board of directors disbanded the club "on account of an empty treasury."

The Haymakers in 1870 armed with pitchforks but still wearing the Union uniform. Standing: Mart King, Michael McAtee, Thomas Abrams, Bill Craver, Steve King; seated: Jimmy Wood, Peter McCune, Sonny Leavenworth, Cal Penfield (*Baseball [1845–1881]: From the Newspaper Accounts by* Preston Orem).

Grounds

Haymakers' Grounds—called Rensselaer Park—were located on Central Island in Lansingburgh, near where the Hudson and Mohawk rivers meet. The map shows a field surrounded by what appears to be a race track. The playing area featured a short left field and very deep right and right-center fields. The grounds were still in use when the Troy Trojans played in the National League in 1880–81. The Haymakers drew 5,000 fans for a July 4, 1872, game with Lord Baltimore, ironically their final home game before disbanding. Today the park region lies between 103rd and 104th streets and between Second and Fifth avenues. It is now

Haymaker

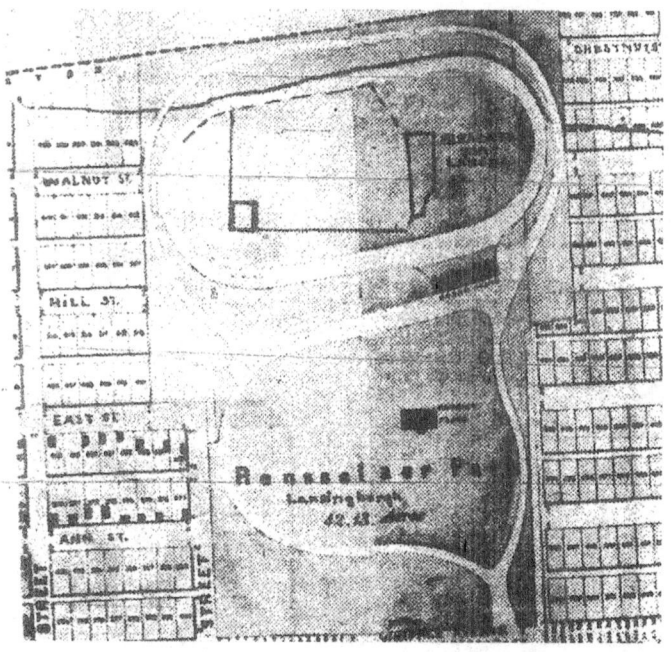

Part of a Lansingburgh city map from the 1860s showing the layout of Haymakers' Grounds (courtesy Troy Public Library).

a residential area not far from Knickerbocker Park and Knickerbocker Arena.

Management

In 1871, Lip Pike managed the team's first four games. With the record at 1–3, Bill Craver took over as manager, helping the team to a 12–12 record. Both Pike and Craver were gone in 1872, but Jimmy Wood, who had managed Chicago in 1871, became the manager until the team disbanded.

Uniform and Logo

In the poster of Haymaker B.B.C. the team seems to be wearing the old Union uniforms with the black letter U on the breastplate. Another photo (above) shows the team wearing long, dark trousers and a white shirt with the Old English U, surrounded by stars. Earlier photos show a dark shirt with a shield-shaped flag. (See photo of Bub McAtee) In the team photo, two members carry pitchforks. The Troy Public Library provided a type of a logo with the haystack, scythe, pitchforks and what appears to be a water jug.

Haymakers in the League

1871

Union of Lansingburgh had compiled an 11–13–1 record (30–15–1 overall) in 1870. The 1871 Troy Haymakers promised to be better. Clipper Flynn returned from Chicago to play first base, and Lip Pike was recruited from Atlantic to play outfield. The rest of the lineup consisted of veteran players from the 1870 Union team. Bill Craver, Dickie Flowers, and Cuban star Steve Bellan from Fordham University joined Flynn on the infield. Tom York and Steve King joined Pike in the outfield. Mike McGeary caught Lefty

Haymakers' logo. Note that the address is still Lansingburgh (courtesy Troy Public Library).

McMullin. The *Cincinnati Daily Gazette* noted that the club was now a joint-stock organization and that it would "take a higher rank among first-class clubs this year than formerly."

With five hitters—Steve King, Pike, Craver, Flowers and Flynn—batting better than .300, Troy hit .308 as a team, just behind Boston. King (.396) and Pike (.377) finished fourth and sixth in hitting. The team's 351 runs were third best in the league and its .845 fielding average was second. However, McMullin gave up a league-leading 362 runs. He had a 5.51 ERA, and Troy also allowed 209 unearned runs. While the Haymakers scored more than 12 runs per game, they yielded almost 12 and a half to finish with a 13–15 record. They hovered around the .500 mark most of the season, enjoying a five-game winning streak in July and August but suffering a four-game losing streak in September and October. By the standings at the time, the Haymakers finished sixth in the nine-team league. They won series from Mutual and Rockford, lost series to Athletic, Boston and Olympic, and tied series with Chicago and Cleveland.

1872

The Haymakers appeared to begin 1872 well off financially, with a reported $30,000 of capital stock—even more than Boston. However, of the five top players who contributed to the .308 team batting average in 1871, four were gone, snapped up by teams willing to pay more. Bill Craver and Lip Pike had gone to Lord Baltimore along with Tom York; Clipper Flynn was now with Olympic; Mike McGeary and Dickie Flowers were with Athletic; in addition, Mutual took John McMullin. Only Steve King and Steve Bellan remained among the starters.

The failure of the White Stockings to field a team in 1872 helped the Troy cause to a great extent. That event brought second baseman Jimmy Wood back; with him came veteran Union first baseman Bub McAtee and pitcher George Zettlein (18-9, 2.73 ERA), along with Charley Hodes and Mart King. The Haymakers also were able to raid Olympic for infielder Davy Force and catcher Doug Allison.

As a result, the new lineup for 1872 included McAtee at first base, Wood at second, Force at third, with Bellan at shortstop. Rookies Phonney Martin and Count Gedney joined Steve King in the outfield. Zettlein and Allison formed the battery. King (.396) and Wood (.389) were the top returning hitters.

After winning their first seven games, the Haymakers were leading the league on May 9. On May 24 their record was 11–3, when they led the league for the final time. By July 9 their record had fallen to 12–10, and they were trailing Boston by nine games. The Haymakers rebounded to win three games in a row before being dismissed by their stockholders on July 23 and having their salaries withheld.

Led by Gedney (.412), Force (.398), Wood (.328), and Steve King (.310), the Haymakers hit an even .300, third in the league. Such hitting led to an average of almost 11 runs per game (10.92). George Zettlein was third in ERA at 2.57, and the team was third in fielding at .861, with two position leaders in Force and Gedney.

The Haymakers present the strangest case in the 1872 season. Even with a strong and successful team, a seemingly strong financial base, and strong fan support, they passed into history.

KEKIONGA BASE BALL CLUB
Fort Wayne, Indiana
1866–1871

History

According to Patrick Mondout, the Kekionga club was founded in 1866, one of a group of amateur Fort Wayne clubs organized after the Civil War. The team first appeared in the National Association lists of clubs in 1868. The 1869 club lost twice to the Cincinnati Red Stockings—86–8 and 41–7. Chad Gramling says that the 1870 club was the champion of Indiana. Mondout reports that Kekionga was "a bit of a joke" because of frequent losses and reports of "re-organization." However, the listed record for the club against other NA teams was 6–6, and one of those losses was a disputed game with the Chicago White Stockings, 16–13. After that game Chicago fans pelted Kekionga players with rocks.

During that 1870 season, the Maryland club of Baltimore disbanded in Fort Wayne, and Kekionga was able to acquire seven of the Maryland players to form the basis of a stronger club. The *Chicago Tribune* reported that Kekionga "now feel confident of holding their position among the first clubs of the country during the upcoming season."

Kekionga defeated Forest City of Cleveland 2–0 in the first-ever major league game; however, the club had difficulty making the leap from the amateur ranks into the NA. Several issues worked against their success. First, Kekionga was one of the cooperatives in which players were paid from gate receipts. The Maryland and Pennsylvania players who filled the Kekionga roster soon began to look for better pay. Two—Pete Donnelly and Ed Mincher—asked for pay advances and then skipped town. The team then dismissed manager and catcher Bill Lennon and third baseman Frank Sellman for public drunkenness and insubordination. After an August 29 game, Bobby Mathews returned to Baltimore to pitch for the Pastimes. On September 6, the board of directors disbanded Kekionga.

Grounds

Kekionga Base Ball Grounds were located in the Nebraska neighborhood of Fort Wayne, west of the downtown area. The six-acre grounds were tucked in among a railroad track, the St. Mary's River, Cherry Street, and West Main Street and were surrounded by a "high, tight board fence." Previously the land had been Camp Allen, a Civil War camp. The stands and later the grounds acquired the nickname "Grand Duchess" because of the elaborately ornamental grandstand. This was the site of the first major league baseball game ever played, on May 4, 1871. Attendance for that rainy season opener is listed at 200. The largest listed crowd was 1,500 for a game with Chicago on May 13.

The stands burned in November of 1871. Today, among other structures, the former Kekionga Base Ball Grounds contain a riverfront park and a Catholic school, but much is residential.

Management

Bill Lennon caught for and managed Kekionga to a 5–9 record. When he was dismissed from the club, Harry Deane, a utility player, managed the final five games, going 2–3.

Camp Allen in Fort Wayne was the site of the Grand Duchess. The Main Street bridge over the St. Mary's River was part of the right field boundary (from *Bird's eye view of the city of Fort Wayne, Indiana 1868. Drawn by A. Ruger*, Library of Congress Maps and Geography Division).

Uniforms and Logo

Like many clubs, Kekionga wore the fireman's breastplate on their uniforms. The breastplate carried the old English letter K. Note the picture of Kekionga players Wally Goldsmith, Bill Lennon and Tom Carey.

The Kekionga uniform featured an elaborate old English K on the breastplate (from Kekionga composite photograph, courtesy Robert Edward Auctions).

Kekionga in the League

The 1871 Kekionga club was made up almost entirely of players from outside Fort Wayne. Like professional hockey teams in the Sun Belt cities, Kekionga lacked a local base of players to attract community support. Second baseman Tom Carey, shortstop Wally Goldsmith, third baseman Frank Sellman, outfielders Bob Armstrong and Ed Mincher, catcher Bill Lennon, and pitcher Bobby Mathews had played with the Maryland club of Baltimore. Outfielder Bill Kelly may have played with Maryland. First baseman Jim Foran came from Union of Lansingburgh. Lennon managed the team.

Kekionga had the highest player turnover in the league. Nine other players appeared in at least one game during the season. Henry Kohler (three games), Bill Barrett (one), and Charley Bierman (one) had Baltimore connections; catcher Paddy Quinn (five) and shortstop Jimmy Hallinan (five) were drafted from the Aetna club of Chicago as replacements for Lennon and Sellman.

Other players came from the East: Pete Donnelly (nine) was from Champion of New Jersey; Joe McDermott (two) came from Eckford; Nealy Phelps (one) came from New York City. The closest thing to a local player on the club was outfielder Harry Deane (six), who was from Indianapolis.

After that 2–0 opening day win over Cleveland, Kekionga played reasonably well. When they defeated Mutual, 5–3, on June 26, they stood in fourth place with a 5–3 record. They did not win again until August 11, losing nine straight and dropping into eighth place. After closing with home wins over Cleveland and Troy, Kekionga disbanded with a 7–12 record.

Kekionga was a poor offensive team. Foran batted .348 but the team hit .239, worst in the league. Only Foran and Mathews (.270) among the regulars hit above .230. The team fielded .803, also worst in the league. Mathews had a 5.17 ERA—only Troy's Lefty McMullin was worse—and the team allowed 146 unearned runs in 19 games. As a result, Kekionga was outscored on average 13–7 per game.

LORD BALTIMORE BASEBALL CLUB
Baltimore, Maryland
1872–1874

History

The Pastime club was one of the early Baltimore clubs, organized around the beginning of the Civil War. Brian McKenna lists them as an organized club in 1861, with a base in northwest Baltimore, playing at Madison Avenue Grounds. Pastime remained an amateur club and fell behind rival Maryland when Maryland became the city's first professional club in 1869. In 1870 the Maryland club disbanded while on tour, and their key players—including pitcher Bobby Mathews—signed with Kekionga of Fort Wayne for 1871. But before the end of the season, the Kekiongas disbanded and many of the players returned to Baltimore. In the meantime, the Pastime club had reorganized, and some of the returning players finished the season with that club.

McKenna says the Pastime club adopted the name Lord Baltimore for an entry into the league for 1872. But it is also true that with the exception of Mathews and shortstop Tom Carey, the 1872 Lord Baltimore club had little relationship with any previous Baltimore baseball history. With Mathews as the key component, Lord Baltimore was able to go into the market and recruit an all-star team to surround him for a run at the whip pennant.

Lord Baltimore remained a strong league team through 1873. However, by 1874 the funding for the club had dried up. When the veteran players sought new homes with more money, the team that called itself Lord Baltimore in 1874 was an embarrassment to the name.

With the closure of the Lords, Baltimore was without major league baseball until the American Association was formed in 1882.

Grounds

Newington Park was completed in 1872 in time for Lord Baltimore's entry into the league. *Baseball in Baltimore* believes that after Madison Avenue Grounds, Newington Park was built with the idea that anyone would actually want to watch a game of baseball. However, there are no pictures or drawings remaining to testify to its features. James Bready says that it was located only

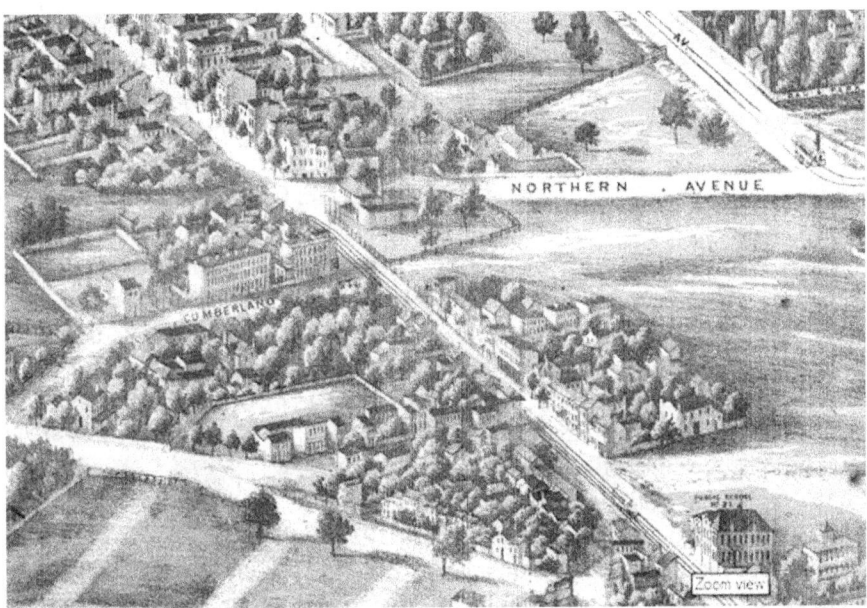

Bird's-eye view of the site for Newington Park. It will likely be built in the fenced ground surrounded by trees and buildings in the lower left of the map. Farther out Pennsylvania Avenue (center of the map) is Madison Avenue Grounds. From *E. Sachse, & Co.'s bird's eye view of the city of Baltimore, 1869* (Library of Congress Maps and Geography Division).

three blocks from Madison Avenue Grounds, the venue it replaced. Lord Baltimore's game with Philadelphia on May 20, 1872, drew 4,000 fans. Newington Park became a major league ground again in 1882 when the Orioles entered the American Association. After the Orioles moved to Oriole Park I in 1883, Newington Park was used for circuses and semi-pro games until it was razed.

Management

Bill Craver, who had managed Troy to a 12–12 record in 1871, started 1872 as manager. After a 27–13 start, he was replaced by Everett Mills, who led the team to an 8–6 record. Cal McVey was hired from Boston to manage the Lords for 1873. With the record 20–13, he was replaced by shortstop Tom Carey, under whom the team had a 14–9 mark. Warren White was appointed manager of the rag-tag 1874 team. He somehow survived the 9–38 season.

Uniform and Logo

Lord Baltimore wore the most striking uniforms in the league. The shirts were

Coat of Arms of Lord Baltimore which formed the crest on the Lord Baltimore uniforms (*Narrative and Critical History of America: English Explorations and Settlements in North America 1497–1689*, by **Justin Winsor,** *1884*).

heavy silk, white with the Lord Baltimore crest on the front. The trousers were black with black and gold checkered stockings. This led to the nickname Canaries.

Lord Baltimore in the League

1872

Like the Cincinnati Red Stockings and Chicago White Stockings before them, Lord Baltimore recruited an all-star team to be able to compete instantly. Baltimore native Bobby Mathews and infielder Tom Carey came from the defunct Fort Wayne team. Another pitcher, hard-throwing Cherokee Fisher, came from the defunct Rockford club. Lord Baltimore stripped Troy of the services of Tom York, Lip Pike and Bill Craver. George Hall and Everett Mills came from Olympic. Lord Baltimore plucked John Radcliff from the champion Athletic club and Dick Higham from Mutual.

The resulting lineup included Mills at first base, Carey at second, Fisher at third, Radcliff at shortstop, Pike, York and Hall in the outfield, Craver catching and Mathews pitching, with Higham filling in wherever needed. Davy Force came from Troy when the Haymakers disbanded, replacing Fisher at third base.

Led by Pike's seven home runs, Lord Baltimore had a league-leading 14 homers, but otherwise their offensive numbers were more ordinary. Force hit .432 in 19 games; Higham hit .343 and Hall .336, but as a team Lord Baltimore hit .293, fourth-best in the NA. They scored 10.64 runs per game, also fourth-best. Perhaps because of numerous lineup combinations, Baltimore committed a league-leading 432 errors, giving them a team fielding percentage of .830—good for fifth place. York and Force were position leaders. And while both Mathews (25–18) and Fisher (10–1) had winning seasons, their combined ERA of 2.90 was no better than fourth, and Baltimore gave up an additional 4.62 unearned runs per game.

Lord Baltimore won their first three games and four of the first five—all pitched by Fisher. At this point they led the league by a game and a half. But despite seven straight May wins—all pitched by Mathews—they fell behind the Red Stockings and never took the lead.

Twenty-six of Lord Baltimore's 36 wins

John Radcliff displays the Lord Baltimore uniform. Note the stockings. From 1872 Lord Baltimore team photograph (*The Home Team* by James H. Bready).

came against the bottom of the league, as they went 26–3 against Atlantic, Eckford, Cleveland, Troy, Olympic and National. Conversely, they barely broke even against Mutual and Athletic and lost all seven decisions to Boston.

1873

Lord Baltimore opened the 1873 campaign with nearly a pat hand. First baseman Everett Mills, second baseman Tom Carey, shortstop John Radcliff, third baseman Davy Force, outfielders Lip Pike, Tom York and George Hall and catcher Bill Craver returned intact from a runner-up finish in 1872. Key reserve Scott Hastings also returned.

Pitcher Bobby Mathews was the only missing Lord of note. He essentially changed places with Mutual's curveballer Candy Cummings—Mathews going to New York. Another key addition was catcher Cal McVey, who arrived from the champion Red Stockings as a playing manager. Veteran pitcher Asa Brainard also joined the team.

Lord Baltimore was an awesome offensive team, finishing just behind the Red Stockings in most categories. With seven regulars—McVey (.380), Force (.365), Hall (.345), Carey (.337), Mills (.332), Pike (.316) and York (.302)—hitting higher than .300, the team finished with a .316 average, scoring 644 runs for an average of 11.5 per game.

But despite a league-leading fielding percentage of .862, Lord Baltimore leaked runs. They gave up 451 runs—sixth-most in the league—and had a team ERA of 3.08, fifth-best.

A promising season never quite materialized for the Lords. Following a four-game winning streak, they were tied for first on May 16, and then began to fall behind as the Philadelphia White Stockings surged. By July 11 they were 8.5 games off the pace with a 20–13 record. At that point Carey replaced McVey as manager. Lord Baltimore twice got within 2.5 games of first before finally settling for a 34–22 record, 7.5 games behind the Red Stockings. As in 1872, Lord Baltimore was finally done in by an inability to beat the top teams, going 5–13 against the Red Stockings and White Stockings.

1874

The swagger of Lord Baltimore was gone by 1874. Not a single member of the team that had run away with the first half of the 1872 race was still wearing the Canary uniform. In fact, only veteran pitcher Asa Brainard returned from the 1873 team, and he had been the change pitcher for Candy Cummings. The *New York Times* noted that this edition of Lord Baltimore had "nine pretty good players," players that would "annoy the other clubs in about the same way that a mosquito annoys a jackass."

Charlie Gould, the former Boston first baseman who sat out the 1873 season, played first; Jack Manning, another former Boston first baseman, played second; a local player, Lou Say from the Marylands, played shortstop; and Civil War veteran Warren White managed the club and played third. Johnny Ryan (two games for Philadelphia in 1873), Oscar Bielaski from Washington and former Kekionga Harry Deane (out of baseball since 1871) manned the outfield; Pop Snyder (also from Washington) caught Brainard. Four regulars—Say, Ryan, Snyder and Manning—were twenty years old or younger; back-up catcher Joe Gerhardt was 19. Brainard (34) and White (30) were graybeards.

Ryan and Deane played in every game for Lord Baltimore, with Brainard, White, Manning, Snyder, Gould and Bielaski considered regulars. Brainard and Manning shared both pitching and second base duties. Z.H. Taylor took over for Gould at first base late in the season. Say and Gerhardt divided time at shortstop, supported by three others who played at least five games there. Lord Baltimore used a league-high 23 players, 11 of whom played in fewer than ten games, including five one-game pickups.

As reflected by their standing in the league, Lord Baltimore finished near the bottom in every key offensive and defensive category. Before departing for Hartford, Jack Manning hit .346 on a club that batted .245.

Such hitting led to a mere 4.83 runs per game. On the other hand, Manning's solid 2.09 ERA was more than offset by Brainard's 3.91, leading to a team 3.13 ERA. The leaky defense led to another 7.63 unearned runs. All told, the Lord were outscored by almost six runs per outing. Their 9–38 record secured the cellar position, 31.5 games behind Boston.

MANSFIELD BASEBALL CLUB
Middletown, Connecticut
1866–1872

History

Mansfield had been formed in 1866 in the town of Middletown, Connecticut. The club came out of the Douglas Pump Company, a large factory that produced hydraulic pumps. Ben Douglas, Jr., the owner's 16-year-old son, formed the club and named it for a Middletown hero, Civil War general Joseph Mansfield. The club began ignominiously by losing, 50–1, to New Britain, but won a return match. Making steady improvement, Mansfield first appeared on the National Association lists as an amateur club in 1869. David Arcidiacono notes that in 1870 the club first had an enclosed field in order to charge admission. Thus, they were able to upgrade their schedule by splitting gate receipts with visiting clubs. After making an extended trip to Boston to play area clubs, Mansfield hosted Athletic of Philadelphia, the first professional club to play in Connecticut, losing, 32–5. Later in that season Mutual visited Middletown and won, 50–20. At the end of the season, Mansfield, with a 21–13 record, was voted the amateur champion of Connecticut.

In 1871 Mansfield was still an amateur club, but that season they built a new ballpark and played seven games against professional clubs, including Troy, Boston, Atlantic and Eckford. While the result was a worse record (19–19), Mansfield showed improvement in scheduling, player personnel, and grounds.

In 1872 Mansfield paid the $10 entry fee for the league and began to upgrade the roster to compete. They added catcher John Clapp of the Clipper club of Ixion, New York, and pitcher Frank Buttery and catcher Jim O'Rourke from the Osceola club of Stratford. Mansfield entered NA play with a team whose average age was 20.

Mansfield lasted into August. Organized as a co-op club, Mansfield had only gate receipts from which to pay salaries. Since Middletown's population was only 11,000, Mansfield lacked the fan base from which to pay players and was unable to compete with clubs from Boston, New York and Philadelphia. The team played its last game on August 13

Grounds

Mansfield Club Grounds were built on lands granted by the Middletown Brick Factory in 1870. They were located between Silver Street and the River Road with the railroad running beside. Built on a hillside, the 350 by 450 grounds were enclosed by an

Bird's-eye view of the hillside site of Mansfield Club Grounds between River Street and Silver Street with the railroad beside. The Asylum—right edge of the map—later took over the grounds (*Middletown Conn, 1877* Library of Congress Maps and Geography Division).

eight-foot fence. The seating capacity was 800, but 1,200 were on hand for a game with Troy on July 23, 1872.

The grounds were not completed until June 9, 1872, when Mansfield played Atlantic. Because of the high ground, spectators had a good view of the Connecticut River and the town of Middletown.

The last major league game played at Mansfield Club Grounds was on August 9, 1872. The grounds later became part of the next-door Connecticut Home for the Insane; today the grounds are part of the Maplewood Terrace public housing project.

Management

Though a rookie, catcher John Clapp was a self-appointed manager of Mansfield in 1872. He arrived in Middleton wearing a belt with the word "captain" on it, and so he became.

Uniform

The 1872 uniform consisted of a white shirt and knee britches with blue trim, blue stockings, a blue belt, and a white cap with a blue band. An earlier uniform had been a blue checkered shirt and cap, blue stockings, and red piping.

The only photo of the Mansfields—probably the 1873 amateur club—shows them in a parade. The logo appears to be a Old English M—likely blue—on the breastplate.

Mansfield in the League

Mansfield remained an amateur club through 1871 and enjoyed some success against mid-level professional clubs. Harry Wright reportedly told the club that if it really wanted to play professional teams, it should join the league, which Mansfield did for 1872. In the process, Mansfield became a professional club.

Jim O'Rourke began a Hall of Fame career as a teenage shortstop for Mansfield in 1872 (LC-DIG-bbc-0276f Library of Congress Prints and Photographs Division).

Of the 12 men who played for Mansfield in 1872, only pitcher Asa Brainard (12–15 with Olympic) had played in the NA in 1871. Six of the 12 had played only as amateurs with Mansfield. Twenty-year-old John Clapp caught for and managed a team composed of 21-year-old Jim O'Rourke, 21-year-old Tim Murnane, 19-year-old Frank McCarton and 18-year-old George Fields. Twenty-two-year-old Cy Bentley started 17 games at pitcher. Brainard, at age 31, was the club's ancient. Mansfield also was a cooperative club, paying salaries from gate receipts.

Murnane (.360), Eddie Booth (.319) and McCarton (.305) hit well for Mansfield. But the team was seventh in hitting (.271) and sixth in scoring (9.17 runs per game). In 24 games, opponents scored at least 15 runs on eleven occasions. Mansfield pitchers allowed 5.55 earned runs per game and the defense yielded another 9.05 unearned tallies. They closed their league run with seven straight losses before disbanding on August 14.

MARYLAND BASEBALL CLUB
Baltimore, Maryland
1861–1873

History

The Maryland club, which entered the league in 1873, had its roots much earlier in Baltimore history. Brian McKenna lists Maryland as one of the clubs in existence in Baltimore in 1861, its home territory being northwest Baltimore. Maryland, along with the Pastime club, was the most prominent team in Baltimore throughout the 1860s. Maryland won the state championship in 1866 and continued in 1867. At the end of 1866, Maryland became one of five Baltimore clubs to join the National Association. In 1867 they had a 4–4 record against league teams. In 1868 they won the state championship for the third year; by defeating National of Washington, they became the unofficial champions of the South. That year they also made a northern tour into metropolitan New York City, losing to Atlantic, Mutual, and Eckford. In 1869 Maryland became a professional club and began bringing outside players to Baltimore. Bobby Mathews arrived that year, joined by Frank Sellman and Bill Lennon. That 14–13 club had wins over Mutual, Athletic, and Eckford. The 1870 club was only 2–14 against league opponents and saw many of their best players, including Lennon, Sellman and Mathews, leave the team in Fort Wayne in August.

The 1873 Maryland team was a reorganized club, described as a combination of the best players of the earlier Maryland and Pastime clubs, with the addition of talented amateurs. The new club played sporadically in the league before disbanding in July, leaving the Lord Baltimore club as the area's only league representative.

Grounds

Maryland had one home game in 1873, a season opener against Washington on April 14. Most sources say that game was played at Newington Park. (See Lord Baltimore). However, James H. Bready believes the game was played at Madison Avenue Grounds. These grounds were built by the Waverly Club before the Civil War and became the first enclosed grounds in Baltimore in 1866. The grounds were used by the Pastime, Maryland, and Excelsior clubs through the 1860s. They were the site of the inter-city game between Excelsior of Baltimore and Excelsior of Brooklyn in 1860 and of a visit from the Cincinnati Red Stockings in 1869.

Admission was 25 cents, with ladies admitted free.

Bready was able to locate the grounds precisely on the northwest edge of Baltimore. The E. Sachse panoramic map picturing the ballpark is shown.

Management

Center fielder Bill Smith managed Maryland to an 0–6 record, his only major league experience.

Uniform and Logo

Like many National Association clubs, Maryland had blue as a base uniform color.

Bird's-eye view of Madison Avenue Grounds, home for the Maryland club. From *E. Sachse, & Co.'s bird's eye view of the city of Baltimore, 1869* (Library of Congress Maps and Geography Division).

In 1866 the *Baltimore Sun* reported that "Maryland players wore blue caps with white visors, blue pants, white shirts and red belts." In 1869 the *New York Times* noted that the Maryland uniforms consisted of "blue pantaloons and check shirts and caps." Another source noted that the Maryland uniform was "composed of white caps, white shirts, with a letter M inscribed on their bosoms, white knee breeches and blue stockings."

Maryland in the League

The Maryland club was composed of local Baltimore players. Among the regulars only Bill Lennon and Henry Kohler had previous league experience: Lennon had caught for the winless National team in 1872, and both he and Kohler had played for the defunct Kekionga team of 1871. Two other former Kekiongas, Wally Goldsmith and Frank Sellman, played briefly for Maryland. Bill Smith, who managed the team while playing shortstop and left field, was one of fourteen Maryland players with no previous NA experience.

Maryland had difficulty acquiring or maintaining a stable team. While playing only six games, the team went through 19 players. Only Kohler and Bill Smith played in every game; Lennon, Bill French, and John Smith each played in five; Marty Simpson and Ed Stratton played in four; Mike Hooper, John Sheppard and Lou Say played in three; Joe Kernan played in two; eight players—including Goldsmith and Sellman—appeared once. Maryland tried at least three men at each position, with six catching and 13 playing the outfield. Four different pitchers started games, with Stratton starting three. No starter was relieved regardless of scores, which were 3–24, 7–27, 5–26, 0–20, 1–35 and 10–20. Of the 19 players, 12 never played in the majors again.

By virtue of odd scheduling, Maryland played twice in April, once in May, twice in June and once in July. Their only home game was an Opening Day loss to Washington, whom they played in Washington the following day. All other games were against inter-city foe Lord Baltimore at Newington Park.

French, Bill Smith and Lennon led the team with four hits each. French led the regulars with a .222 batting average. The team as a whole hit only .156 and scored 26 runs, just over four per game. As the scores above show, opponents scored 152 runs, an average of more than 25 per game. Only Lennon, splitting time among first base, third base and catching, fielded above .900 on a team that fielded .761 and allowed 104 unearned runs.

The team disbanded after the July 11 loss to Lord Baltimore.

MUTUAL BASE BALL CLUB
New York City
1857–1876

History

Mutual Baseball Club was named for the Mutual Hook and Ladder Company, a local fire department. Formed in 1857, Mutual began play in 1858 and laid claim to the championship that season with an 11–1 record. This was one of four times Mutual led NA teams in victories. During the Civil War, the 1863 and 1864 teams posted 10–4 and 20–3 records, respectively. By 1870 Mutual had become a professional team, attracting such later stars as Dave Eggler, John Hatfield, Dick Higham, Tom Patterson,

Charlie Mills and Rynie Wolters. The 1870 team won 68 games, but its 17 losses placed them behind Cincinnati, Chicago, and Athletic in the standings.

Mutual became a charter member of the professional NA in 1871, and were one of three clubs to contest all five NA championships. However, they were not a particularly successful NA club. Their highest finish was second place in 1874 when Bobby Mathews started all 65 games, winning 42.

Despite dropping to sixth in 1875, Mutual was one of eight clubs invited to become a charter member of the National League. Mutual struggled against NL competition, winning just 21 of 56 games for a sixth-place finish. The cash-strapped Mutuals were unable to make the final road trip to the West. They were dismissed from the NL at the end of the season, thus ending the existence of one of the great teams of the 1860s.

Grounds

Home grounds for Mutual during its NA years were Union Grounds in Brooklyn. (See Eckford) But until 1868, the club played at the legendary Elysian Fields in Hoboken, New Jersey. For one game in 1872, they returned to Elysian Fields to play Mansfield.

Described as "a grassy picnic grove overlooking the [Hudson] River" (Ward 4), Elysian Fields had been the site of the first organized game ever played between the Knickerbocker and the New York Base Ball clubs in 1846. As the Currier and Ives print shows, it was an unenclosed ground without stands. Ward goes on to describe the grounds as "a beautiful place filled with trees and flowers and conveniently edged with taverns."

Elysian Fields in Hoboken, NJ was the site of the first baseball game ever played in 1845. It was home for Mutual until 1868. From *The American national game of base ball. Grand match for the championship at the Elysian Fields, Hoboken, N.J.* (Library of Congress Prints and Photographs Division).

Management

The principal financial backer of Mutual was Tammany Hall boss William Tweed, which meant Mutual—like today's New York clubs—had a larger operating budget than many NA competitors.

In each of five seasons in the NA, Mutual began with a different manager. Third baseman Bob Ferguson managed the 1871 team. When Ferguson went to Atlantic, shortstop Dickey Pearce began 1872 as skipper; with the team at 10–6, second baseman John Hatfield replaced Pearce. Under Hatfield the team did marginally better, going 24–14. When the 1873 team began 11–17, Hatfield relinquished management to first baseman Joe Start, under whom Mutual went 18–7. Shortstop Tom Carey began 1874, but with a 13–12 mark, Mutual replaced him with catcher Dick Higham, who managed the team to a 29–11 record. New catcher Nat Hicks managed the 1875 club during a losing season, going 30–38.

William M. "Boss" Tweed of Tammany Hall was a chief financial backer of Mutual (LC-USZ62-22467 Library of Congress Prints and Photographs Division).

Uniform and Logo

Mutual was sometimes called the Green Stockings because of their uniforms. The breastplate had the letter M in green. The unidentified Mutual player below displays the full uniform. The same uniform is worn by the Vintage New York Mutual clubs today.

Mutual in the League

1871

Mutual (29–15–3 against professional teams in 1870) opened the 1871 season with six key players from the 1870 team: second baseman John Hatfield, outfielders Dave Eggler and Tom Patterson, catcher Charlie Mills, pitcher Rynie Wolters and utility

Studio photograph of an unidentified Mutual player in the traditional "Green Stockings" uniform (Wikimedia Commons).

player Dick Higham. The only big loss was first baseman Everett Mills. Having the "private wealth of William M. Tweed ... to draw on," Mutual was able to outbid Chicago for the services of a trio of Atlantic players in first baseman Joe Start, shortstop Dickey Pearce and third baseman Bob Ferguson. Start, in particular, had a big bat. Former Atlantic great Charlie Smith and rookie Frank Fleet also played bit roles for Mutual. The *Cincinnati Daily Gazette* believed that Mutual's 1871 team would be "stronger by far than they have ever yet placed in the field." This, of course, was not the case. Mutual (16–17) struggled along as a middle-of-the-pack team along with Olympic (15–15) and the Haymakers (12–15).

Mutual hit ten points higher than Olympic but scored eight fewer runs. Rynie Wolters (.370), Dick Higham (.362), Joe Start (.360) and Dave Eggler (.320) all hit above .300 on a team that batted .287 and scored .302 runs—fifth in the league. The relatively low offensive production was somewhat offset by superior pitching. Wolters had a 3.43 ERA, third-lowest in the league, behind George Zettlein and Al Spalding. Led by Start at first base, Mutual fielded .840, fourth-best in the league, but yielded 192 unearned runs. Mutual scored 9.15 runs per game and allowed 9.48, leading to the 16–17 record.

1872

Mutual sustained heavy off-season losses. Second baseman Dick Higham went to Lord Baltimore; manager and third baseman Bob Ferguson returned to Atlantic in the same role; pitcher Rynie Wolters, who won all 16 of Mutual's victories in 1871, went to Cleveland; and light-hitting outfielder Tom Patterson went to Eckford.

But Mutual returned five players from the 1871 team that finished fifth in first baseman Joe Start, shortstop Dickie Pierce, outfielders Dave Eggler and John Hatfield, and catcher Charlie Mills. Start (.360) and Eggler (.320) were the top returning hitters.

In addition, Mutual acquired heavy-hitting George Bechtel (.351) from Athletic, pitcher John McMullin (12–15) from Troy, and infielder Chick Fulmer from the defunct Rockford club. The most important acquisition was the battery from Star of Brooklyn—pioneer curveballer Candy Cummings and his catcher, Nat Hicks. These, along with rookie Bill Boyd, formed the 11-man Mutual entry.

The new Mutual lineup included Start at first base, Hatfield at second, and Boyd at third, with Pierce at shortstop. Bechtel joined Eggler and McMullin in the outfield. Cummings and Hicks formed the battery.

Among the contending teams of 1872, Mutual carried the lightest bats, hitting just .276 as a team (sixth among all NA teams). Eggler (.334), Hatfield (.323), Hicks (.307) and Bechtel (.300) were the only regulars above .300. Start fell to .271 while Pearce hit only .189. Nevertheless, Mutual was third in the league in scoring, averaging just a hair over nine and a half runs per game.

Mutual was also strong in the field. Seven players played more than 50 games; only at third base, which was shared by Boyd and Fulmer, did a starter play fewer than 42 games. The result was a .868 fielding percentage, good for second place. Start and Pearce were position leaders.

Cummings started 55 games and completed 53. His 2.52 ERA was second behind Boston's Spalding, and the team ERA of 2.55 ranked second behind Boston. Mutual gave up only 3.39 unearned runs per game, just behind Boston. Mutual finished 14 games above .500, thanks in part to scoring almost three runs per game more than the opposition.

1873

From the third-place finisher of 1872, Mutual retained a solid core of players—first baseman Joe Start, third baseman John Hatfield, outfielder Dave Eggler and catcher Nat Hicks. From the defunct Eckford club, Mutual acquired second baseman Candy Nelson, shortstop Jim Holdsworth, and outfielders Count Gedney and Phonney Martin. From Lord Baltimore came pitcher Bobby Mathews and catcher Dick Higham, offsetting the loss of pitcher Candy Cummings and outfielder George Bechtel.

Overall, Mutual used 13 players in 1873. In addition to the above ten, Doug Allison came from Resolute to spell Hicks; Cuban star Steve Bellan and Nealy Phelps played bit parts.

Mutual posted only average offensive numbers for 1873. Holdovers Eggler and Hatfield hit .338 and .306, respectively; among newcomers Nelson hit .327, Holdsworth .323 and Higham .316. Overall the club hit .281—right at the league average of .280. They scored 424 runs, fifth-best.

Defensively they were somewhat better. The pitching staff had a 2.64 ERA, best in the league. Opponents scored 385 runs, 7.26 per game, lowest in the league. The team fielded only .819, placing them in the lower half among league teams.

Mutual began the season atrociously. Under the management of Hatfield, Mutual did not win its third game until June 13. On July 12, the team had an 8–17 league record and were 16.5 games behind the Philadelphia White Stockings. With the record at 11–17, Start replaced Hatfield, but it was September 13 before Mutual finally reached the .500 mark at 20–20. They then won nine of their last 13 games to finish at 29–24, 11 games behind Boston.

Even with the terrible start, Mutual was far from a contending team. Against teams with winning records, Mutual had a 14–21 record, giving them a 15–3 mark against bottom-tier teams. They also lost 15 of 22 road games.

1874

Mutual's off-season losses were heavy: catcher Nat Hicks, shortstop Jim Holdsworth and the entire outfield of Dave Eggler, Count Gedney and Phonney Martin. Still, the well-heeled New Yorkers were able to offset losses with strong pickups. They plucked Jack Burdock and Jack Remsen from Atlantic and Tom Carey from Lord Baltimore to go with holdovers Bobby Mathews, Joe Start, Candy Nelson, John Hatfield, and Dick Higham. In addition, they would have the services of Doug Allison for the entire season.

What the *New York Times* called "a nine strong in every respect" was projected to be a battery of Mathews and Allison; Start, Nelson, Carey and Burdock on the infield; Hatfield, Remsen and Higham in the outfield.

Mutual in 1874 was as solid as projected. Higham and Allison split time between catching and the outfield; Higham caught more often while Allison played outfield more. Carey and Nelson had roughly the same arrangement at second base and shortstop. Of the four reserves—Nealy Phelps, Billy Geer, Tom Patterson, and Orator Shaffer—none played in more than six games.

On June 25, Mutual was in fourth place with a 13–12 record, 8.5 games behind Boston. At that point Higham replaced Carey as manager. Shortly thereafter, Boston and Philadelphia, the top teams in the league, left for an extended trip to England to promote the sport of baseball there. In their absence Mutual feasted on second-division clubs, enjoying a 16-game winning streak. Two road wins in Boston on September 22 and 24 allowed Mutual to reduce Boston's lead to one game. However, Mutual won only 11 of the last 21 games and steadily lost ground to Boston, finishing with a 42–23 record, 7.5 games behind.

Only Joe Start (.314) hit higher than .300 on runner-up Mutual. As a team Mutual hit only .271—sixth-best in the league—but averaged 7.71 runs per game, fourth-best. Mutual's success came from pitching—Bobby Mathews, who started every game, posted a 1.90 ERA—and defense. Joe Start and Jack Remsen were position leaders, helping Mutual to an .847 fielding percentage and a league-low 3.89 unearned runs per game.

1875

Four members of second-place Mutual fled eastward to Hartford for the 1875 season, leaving the team to rebuild its infield and outfield. Shortstop Tom Carey, third baseman Jack Burdock, and outfielders Jack Remsen and Doug Allison departed; in addition, versatile Dick Higham went to Chicago. Mutual retained fielding leader Joe Start and second baseman Candy Nelson to anchor the infield. John Hatfield returned to the outfield. Pitcher Bobby Mathews (42–22, 1.90 ERA) was arguably the league's best at his position.

A key acquisition for Mutual was Nat Hicks, returning from Philadelphia. Hicks, who had caught Mathews in 1873, managed the team. New players included outfielder Count Gedney from Athletic, infielder Jim Holdsworth from Philadelphia, Eddie Booth and Pat McGee from Atlantic, and Joe Gerhardt from the defunct Lord Baltimores. Only Holdsworth (.340) and Gerhardt (.328 in 16 games) looked to improve the light-hitting Mutuals.

The projected Mutual nine for 1875 listed Hicks and Mathews as the battery; Start, Nelson, Hatfield and Gerhardt as infielders; Gedney, McGee and Booth as outfielders.

While Hatfield played in only two games, Holdsworth became the regular shortstop. After Western folded, Jim Hallinan came over, replacing Holdsworth, who moved to the outfield. Late in the season Higham returned from Chicago, and Western catcher Billy Barnie joined the team. All told, Mutual used 15 players, including Al Metcalf and Nealy Phelps.

Offensively, the 1875 Mutuals resembled the anemic 1874 Mutuals. With only three hitters over .250—Hallinan, Start, and Holdsworth—Mutual hit .236 as a team. This average translated to 4.62 runs per game, eighth-best. Without a position leader on defense, Mutual fielded just .838.

Mathews (29–38, 2.49 ERA) started 70 of 71 games and was not as effective as some contemporaries. Additionally, Mutual allowed 3.54 unearned runs per game, meaning that opponents scored six runs per game, nearly a run and a half more than Mutual was able to plate.

Despite the losing record (30–38), Mutual was one of the eight teams invited to contest the 1876 pennant in the National League.

NATIONAL BASE BALL CLUB
Washington, D.C.
1859–1872

History

National Base Ball Club was founded in November of 1859 by a group of government clerks. The club practiced in a lot behind the White House before getting their own grounds. By 1865 they began to collect such players as Harry Berthrong and Sam Yeat-

The first baseball game played in Washington, DC, saw Potomac defeat National on the White Lot, located on the South Grounds of the White House. The White Lot was home to National until they built their own grounds and also the site of amateur games through World War II (from *The national capital, Washington, D.C. Sketched from nature by Adolph Sachse, 1883-1884* Library of Congress Maps and Geography Division).

man, who would figure in the league later, and were playing teams such as Athletic and Atlantic. The 1866 team went 10–5 with losses to Athletic, Excelsior, Gotham and Union of Morrisania. The 1867 team was the first Eastern club to travel west of the Alleghenys, embarking on a ten-game tour with stops at Columbus, Cincinnati, Louisville, Indianapolis, St. Louis, Rockford and Chicago. That team, which included George Wright, won nine of ten games on the tour, and 29 of 36 overall. As it turned out, the tour, which cost $5,000, was subsidized by the United States Treasury.

Later National teams did not fare so well, going 7–3 in 1868, 13–13 in 1869 (but only 4–12 against professional teams) and 5–12 in 1870 (2–9 versus professionals). Although National attended the 1871 meeting, they elected to play that year as an independent.

Their 1872 attempt to compete in the professional league was a disaster.

Grounds

National played in the first game ever on the White Lot on the South Grounds of the White House on May 5, 1860, losing to Washington rival Potomac, 35–15. Because of the Treasury Department location, National practiced on the northern corner of the Ellipse, which meant the clerks that comprised the team could walk out the door and begin practicing. Later, National had grounds a few blocks directly north, at the corner of 16th Street and R Street. The enclosed 400-foot-square ground was located only a block or so from Olympic Grounds. Listed attendance for games in 1872 was fewer than 300.

Management

The 22-year-old Joe Miller is listed as the National manager for all eleven games in 1872, none of which the team won.

Uniform and Logo

Orem describes the National uniform as blue trousers, white shirts with a blue shield and blue caps. (67) There are no photos of the team.

Paul Hines began a 20-year major league career with National in 1872. From "Chicago Champions" (LC-DIG-pga-18390 Library of Congress Prints and Photographs Division).

National in the League

1872

Like the Brooklyn clubs, National played independently in 1871 but determined to compete for the whip pennant in 1872. They were able to pick up four players with league experience. Catcher Bill Lennon and infielder Ed Mincher, two Baltimore players, had been members of the defunct Kekionga club. Infielder Warren White and pitcher Bill Stearns—local Washington men—had played for Olympic. The rest were newcomers to the league: Seem Studley (who had made the 1867 Western tour), Oscar Bielaski, Dennis Coughlin, and John Hollingshead were National veterans; shortstop Jacob Doyle was 16 years old; first baseman Paul Hines, the manager, was 20. John Glenn (after Olympic folded), Bill Yeatman, manager Joe Miller and a Philadelphia amateur named Spencer each played in a single game with National.

National was one of five cooperative clubs operating in the league in 1872.

National finished last in the important offensive and defensive categories. Hollingshead hit .318, but as a whole National batted .220, far below the .249 posted by Olympic. The team fielded a league-low of .774—12 points below Olympic. Bill Stearns, who pitched every inning, had a 6.18 ERA, the second-highest in the league.

National played their last game on June 26 before disbanding. The National name continued to be used by various National and American League teams, even to the present Washington team.

OLYMPIC BASE BALL CLUB
Washington, D.C.
1867–1872

History

Olympic first appeared in NA standings in 1867. The club was formed by Civil War veteran Nick Young, who played outfield, and included third baseman/shortstop Davy Force. That first year, Olympic won ten of 15 games against Washington, Philadelphia and Baltimore opponents, losing four times to National and Athletic. The 1868 team with Force and Fergy Malone finished 12–11–1. After going professional in 1869, Olympic improved to 22–14, but finished only 9–12 against fellow professionals. The 1870 club lost Malone to Athletic but added Harry Berthrong, John Glenn and Henry Burroughs—players that would survive into the professional league. However, the team still struggled, going 29–21 overall and 10–18 against professional clubs.

Prior to the 1871 season, Young made two moves that thrust Olympic into the forefront of baseball. First, when the Cincinnati Red Stockings ceased operations, Young swooped in and collared those players that escaped Harry Wright's move to Boston. The 1871 Olympics included Andy Leonard, Fred Waterman, Charlie Sweasy, Doug Allison and Asa Brainard. Second, Young was one of the organizers of the meeting that led to the creation of the National Association of Professional Base Ball Players.

Despite the influx of five players from a successful club, Olympic was only an average team in the inaugural NA season, winning 15 of 30 games and sharing the middle of the table with Mutual and Haymakers. Stripped of most of its star players, Olympic won only two games in 1872, withdrawing from the league before the end of May and passing into history.

Apparently, Olympic, like National, had government connections since many of the players held clerical positions in Washington.

Nick Young organized the Olympic Club, for which he played and managed (courtesy T. Scott Brandon).

Grounds

Olympic Grounds, built in 1870, were located thirteen blocks north of the White House. The grounds were located in a rectangular block bounded by 17th Street NW on the west and 16th Street NW on the East, with S Street NW to the south. The stands had a listed capacity of only 500. However, on Opening Day of 1871, a crowd of 5,000 witnessed the game with Boston.

Olympic Grounds continued to be used by Washington clubs in the National Association.

Management

Nick Young managed Olympic in both 1871 and 1872. He had retired as a player and was the only non-playing manager in the league.

Uniform and Logo

In describing an 1871 game between Olympic and Forest City of Cleveland, played at Fort Wayne, the Fort Wayne newspaper noted that both clubs wore "substantially the same uniform—white knee-clouts and shirts, with blue stockings and belts—the difference being that the Eastern players had 'O' embroidered in blue on their breast, and wore blue-trimmed hats." Sportswriters frequently referred to Olympic as the "Blue Stockings."

There seems to be no picture of the Olympic team in uniform.

Olympic in the League

1871

The 1870 Olympic club had the ninth-best record among the 15 top professional clubs, winning 29 of 50 overall but only ten of 28 against professionals. The 1871 club benefited greatly from the breakup of the Red Stockings. Olympic manager Nick Young was able to acquire infielder Charlie Sweasy, second baseman Andy Leonard, third baseman Fred Waterman, catcher Doug Allison and pitcher Asa Brainard to strengthen his lineup. In addition, he picked up first baseman Everett Mills from Mutual and outfielder George Hall from Atlantic. These players joined shortstop Davy Force and outfielders John Glenn and Harry Berthrong in a revamped lineup. The *Cincinnati Daily Gazette* pointed out that Washington baseball benefited greatly from a "judicious use of government patronage," which took the form of "official sinecures" for top players. In addition to the ten, Olympic used four local players—Henry Burroughs, William Stearns, Warren White and Frank Norton—and Tommy Beals from Union of Morrisania.

Olympic won four series, defeating Haymakers, Forest City of Cleveland, Forest City of Rockford, and Kekionga. Their 4–4 series record allowed them to finish ahead of Mutual and Haymakers in the battle for fourth place

Olympic earned that fourth place on the basis of fielding. The Olympic team was mediocre with a bat in the hand; only Waterman (.316) and Glenn (.308) reached the .300 mark, and the team hit .277. Yet from this average Olympic coaxed 310 runs, fourth-best in the league. Star pitcher

Doug Allison began his league career with Olympic in 1871. From "First Nine of the Cincinnati (Red Stockings) Baseball Club" (LC-USZC4-1291 Library Congress Prints and Photographs Division).

Brainard, not the pitcher he once was, sported a 4.50 ERA, leading to a team ERA of 4.37, seventh in the league. But Olympic was the best defensive team at .850, and the team allowed only 166 unearned runs, which ranked third.

1872

From a respectable 1871 club that finished either fourth (by series) or fifth (by overall record), Olympic lost six regulars. Everett Mills and George Hall went to Lord Baltimore, Davy Force and Doug Allison joined Haymakers, and Andy Leonard went to Boston. Harry Berthrong retired.

Olympic retained its two best hitters in third baseman Fred Waterman (.316) and outfielder John Glenn (.308). Pitcher Asa Brainerd (12–15) and utility player Tommy Beals also returned. Manager Nick Young was able to acquire Wally Goldsmith and Frank Sellman from the defunct Kekionga club, Clipper Flynn from Troy and George Heubel from Athletic. Flynn (.338) and Heubel (.307) gave Olympic four .300 hitters.

The new configuration featured Flynn, Beals, Goldsmith and Waterman on the infield; Glenn, Heubel and newcomer Val Robinson patrolled the outfield. Sellman caught Brainard.

This Olympic lineup was not up to NA competition. Waterman hit .378, Brainard .372 and Beals .306, but the team as a whole batted only .249, 10th in the NA. Opposing teams scored 140 runs in nine games, a 15.5-per-game average. Brainard's 6.38 ERA was highest in the league. In addition, Olympic fielded just .786, tenth-best in the NA.

Olympic lost the first six games—five at home—all blowout losses. The team had victories only over winless National to show for its first nine games. In no outing did the recorded attendance top 500. Following an 11–7 victory over National on May 24, Olympic played no more league games, finishing with a 2–7 record.

PHILADELPHIA BASEBALL CLUB
Philadelphia, Pennsylvania
1873–1875

History

Philadelphia Baseball Club—called the White Stockings in 1873 and Pearls thereafter—was a new club formed in 1873. The club began by raiding Philadelphia rival Athletic, stealing no fewer than five starting players and completing their lineup by taking two players each from Mutual and Eckford.

After a 27–3 start, the club suffered a meltdown in the second half of the season, finishing a distant second to Boston. William J. Ryczek asserts that the team "tanked" in the second half, though that assertion has never been proved. However, John Shiffert notes that well before the end of the season, seven members of the team had already signed with Chicago for 1874.

Philadelphia, which had taken six of seven games from Athletic in 1873, finished behind its rivals in 1874. Reloading with "revolvers," the Pearls played only .500 ball that season, beating out their old teammates from Chicago for fourth place. An almost entirely new team finished fifth in 1875. Their major league history concluded at the end of that season as the new National League awarded the Philadelphia territorial rights to Athletic.

Grounds

Philadelphia shared Jefferson Street Grounds with Athletic.

Management

Fergy Malone was originally selected to manage the 1873 team. But after former Chicago and Troy skipper Jimmy Wood joined the club, he replaced Malone as manager. Some suggest that part of the late-season collapse of the team resulted from conflicts between the two. Philadelphia was 8–2 under Malone and 28–15 under Wood. In 1874 Bill Craver managed the club to a fourth-place finish. The new 1875 team was managed by Mike McGeary (34–27) and, in late season, by Bob Addy (3–4).

Uniforms and Logos

Oran cites accounts that describe the Philadelphia uniform as "drab" colored knee-trousers and hat with white shirts and stockings—"an appropriate Quaker garb." Another newspaper account says the uniform was "mouse-hued." Their pantaloons were tucked into white stockings. The tight-fitting shirt had no ornamentation but the belt carried the club name. They wore a light linen cap.

Philadelphia in the League

1873

The White Stocking began by raiding long-time Philadelphia club Athletic of Denny Mack, Levi Meyerle, Fred Treacey, Ned Cuthbert and Fergy Malone, who also managed the team. From Mutual came Chick Fulmer and George Bechtel, and from the defunct Eckford club came Jimmy Wood and pitcher George Zettlein. Initially, Bob Addy, who did not play in the NA in 1872, manned second base but left the club after Wood arrived. Mack, Wood, Fulmer and Meyerle formed the infield, with Treacey, Cuthbert and Bechtel in the outfield and Malone catching Zettlein.

The White Stockings ran away from the league in the first half. Posting a pair of ten-game winning streaks, they had a 27–3 record on July 10, to lead the league by eight games. After 20 days off from league games, they began the second half on a five-game losing streak, and saw the lead fall to 2.5 games. A five-game winning streak followed before they lost eight of their next ten to fall into second place, from which they never recovered. John Shiffert notes that the second half of the season was marked by strange decisions concerning lineups and pitching. Ten games into the season, with an 8–2 record, the club replaced Malone as manager with Wood. Late in the campaign, Wood began playing regulars out of position and using position players as pitchers. In addition, team play was marked with errors and a

Levi Meyerle played with Philadelphia in both 1873 and 1875, hitting .349 and .320 (courtesy T. Scott Brandon).

lackluster effort. The club had a 9–14 record in the second half and finished with a 36–17 mark, four games behind Boston.

Still, the White Stockings had nothing approaching the fire power of the Red Stockings. Only Meyerle (.349) and Wood (.321) hit over .300, giving the club a .277 average, fifth-best in the NA. They scored 526 runs, just under 10 per game.

Zettlein had a 2.86 ERA; the contributions of Bechtel and Fulmer raised that figure to 2.92, second-best in the league. The club gave up 396 runs, fourth-highest in the league. The White Stockings were a good defensive team; the .849 fielding percentage was second overall.

1874

The runner-up club put together by the White Stockings in 1873 had disintegrated by 1874. Second baseman and manager Jimmy Wood, third baseman Levi Meyerle, outfielders Fred Treacey and Ned Cuthbert, catcher Fergy Malone, pitcher George Zettlein and utility player Jim Devlin had signed with the new Chicago club even before the end of the 1873 season. Only first baseman Denny Mack, shortstop Chick Fulmer and outfielder George Bechtel remained. But Philadelphia—now called the Pearls—went into the market and signed a new group of players, many designated as "revolvers." From Lord Baltimore came Bill Craver, who managed the team, outfielder Tom York, John Radcliff, and pitcher Candy Cummings. From Mutual came Jim Holdsworth, Dave Eggler, and catcher Nat Hicks, who was reunited with his old New York battery mate, Cummings. Atlantic contributed Charlie Pabor.

The *New York Times* judged the players to be skillful, but the paper was highly critical of their placement. They thought that Radcliff at second base "is considered a failure," and "ditto for Holdsworth at third." The rest of the lineup—Hicks catching Cummings, Mack at first, Fulmer at shortstop, and the outfield of York, Eggler and Bechtel—was either the best or among the best. The *Times* recommended a lineup that included Craver instead of Radcliff and Fulmer and Holdsworth trading places.

The *Times* was partially correct. Craver put himself at second base for 53 of 58 games while Radcliff played a utility role. Fulmer and Holdsworth alternated almost equally between shortstop and third base. Bechtel played in only 32 games, spelled by Radcliff and Pabor. Philadelphia used 14 players in 1874, with three—Pete Donnelly, Ed McKenna, and a pick-up named Quinlan—playing six or fewer games.

By July 1, Philadelphia had settled into fourth place with an 11–10 record, 9.5 games behind Boston. An 11-game winning streak in August and September raised the record to 25–20, still 7.5 games behind. But a 4–9 record at the end, coupled with a Red Stocking surge, dropped the Pearls 17 games behind. One indicator of Philadelphia's problems was that in head-to-head meetings with their two key rivals—Boston and Athletic—the Pearls went 3–17.

Bill Craver (.343) and Dave Eggler (.318) led the team to a .278 batting average, good for a third-place tie. But they used their hits well to produce 8.21 runs per game, second behind Boston. Candy Cummings and George Bechtel combined for a 1.93 ERA; however, the leaky Philadelphia defense (only seventh-best in the league) helped opponents to 5.45 unearned runs per game, making the average victory margin under a run per game.

1875

The doors of the Philadelphia club revolved once more, bringing in an almost entirely new team for the 1875 campaign. Of fourteen players who wore the Philadelphia uniform in 1874, only shortstop Chick Fulmer remained. Leading hitter Bill Craver, along with George Bechtel and John Radcliff, went to the new Centennial team; pitcher Candy Cummings and outfielder Tom York went to Hartford; Nat Hicks and Jim Holdsworth joined Mutual; Dave Eggler took his .318 average across town to Athletic. Denny Mack sat out 1875.

To replace lost players, Philadelphia once again poached on neighbor Athletic. First baseman Tim Murnane, third baseman Mike McGeary (.321), and outfielder John McMullin (.346) traded in the blue stockings of Athletic for white. Outfielder Bob Addy and pitcher Cherokee Fisher came from Hartford. Batting champion Levi Meyerle and catcher Fergy Malone (whose $2,800 salary request was considered too rich) kept their white stockings but moved from Chicago back to Philadelphia. Catcher Pop Snyder came from the defunct Lord Baltimores, while outfielder Orator Shaffer arrived from Mutual.

The *Herald-Tribune* projected a lineup of Snyder and Fisher; Malone, McGeary, Meyerle and Fulmer; McMullin, Shaffer and Addy.

The newspaper got seven of the nine correct. Malone played in 29 games but lost his regular position to Murnane. When Centennial folded in late May, Fred Treacey became available to shore up the Philadelphia outfield, replacing Shaffer. Late in the season, George Zettlein arrived from Chicago, easing the pitching workload of Cherokee Fisher. Philadelphia used 16 players over the season, four of whom—Bill Crowley, Joe Borden, Bill Parks and Sam Weaver—played fewer than ten games. McGeary, who managed the club through the first 63 games, filled in at five positions. Addy managed the club to a 3–4 record over the last seven games.

Meyerle hit .316 and McGeary a respectable .290, helping Philadelphia to a .251 average, fifth-best in the league. The team scored 470 runs, 6.71 per game, good for third-best.

Fisher (22–19, 1.99 ERA) and George Zettlein (12–8, 1.59 ERA after joining the club from Chicago) helped lead Philadelphia to a 2.12 ERA, sixth-best. Philadelphia had one position leader in fielding—third baseman McGeary—but overall fielded .848, only sixth-best. As a result, they gave up 228 unearned runs—3.26 per game—fifth-best.

Not surprisingly, Philadelphia finished fifth with a 37–31 record. When the new National League allowed only one club per city, Philadelphia passed into history.

RESOLUTE BASE BALL CLUB
Elizabeth, New Jersey
1866–1873

History

The Resolute Base Ball Club first appeared in *National Association of Base Ball Players, 1857–1870* as having played Independent of Brooklyn in 1866. Included is a note that Resolute was not an association member. They first appear as a member in 1868. In 1870 Resolute absorbed Irvington, a very strong New Jersey club. The reorganized Resolute club won 14 games and was declared the amateur champions of New Jersey after defeating Amateur of Newark, 28–17, at Waverly. That club included Hugh and Mat Campbell and John Farrow, players that would later figure in Resolute's venture into the league.

Patrick Mondout believes the club went

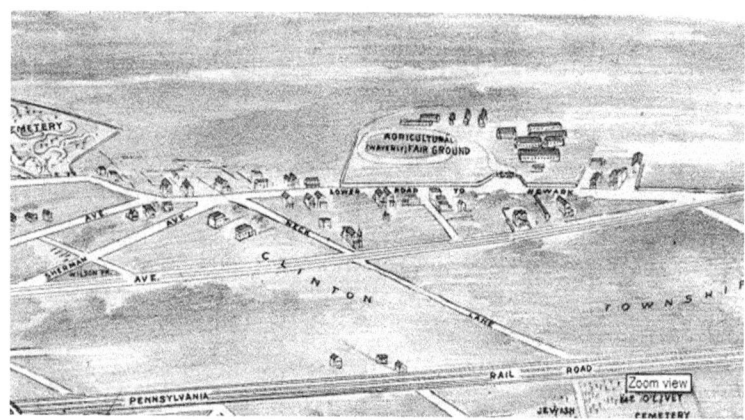

By 1898 all traces of the baseball ground are gone, but the rural Waverly Fairgrounds with race track still appear on the panoramic Elizabeth map (from *Elizabeth, NJ, 1898*, Library of Congress Maps and Geography Division).

professional in 1873, the same year they entered the league. The most significant of the five added professionals was Doug Allison from the defunct Eckford club.

After winning only two of 23 games, Resolute disbanded.

Grounds

Waverly Fairgrounds, located in what was then the independent town of Waverly, was the home for Resolute in 1873. Originally a farm owned by Otto Meeker, the grounds contained an oval for cycle and horse races, which attracted thousands of spectators. In 1856 it hosted its first state agricultural fair. The grounds were described as being "about a mile from town."

Today part of the fairgrounds is in the city of Newark and part is in the city of Elizabeth. The Newark part is Weequahic City Park; the Elizabeth part is B'nai Jeshuron Cemetery.

Management

Doug Allison managed the team to an eighth-place finish in 1873.

Uniforms and Logo

All we know of the Resolute uniform is found in a report in the *New York Times* to the effect that Resolute appeared in a game against Neptune in new "costumes," part of which were "pink stockings." It is, of course, possible that "pink" actually refers to the light red color. However, the term "pink" had the force of "stylish," suggesting that the Resolute uniform featured the knee pants and high stockings popularized by the Cincinnati Red Stockings two years earlier. Pink may also be the color associated with British fox hunting attire, i.e., scarlet.

The vintage Elizabeth Resolutes wear a traditional fireman's breastplate with the Old English E in navy blue (courtesy Elizabethresolutes.com).

Resolute in the League

1873

When Resolute determined to enter the league in 1873, they added five players with previous NA experience. In addition to manager Doug Allison, who came from the defunct Eckford club along with Frank Fleet, Resolute signed Art Allison and Rynie Wolters from the defunct Cleveland club and Eddie Booth from Atlantic. These five joined a group of veteran Resolute players. This created a projected nine of Doug Allison catching Wolters, Mat Campbell, Ben Laughlin, John Farrow, and Fleet on the infield, with Henry Austin, Art Allison and Hugh Campbell in the outfield.

This starting version did not work out. When Wolters found that no Resolute could catch his pitches, he left the team. Hugh Campbell started 18 games. Booth claimed an outfield position; Favel Wordsworth and Alex Nevin started on the infield.

Former Eckford players Jim Clinton (nine games) and Marty Swandell (two games) appeared in pickup-roles. Fred Crane—possibly another former Eckford great—and amateur Len Lovett each played in one game.

As Resolute discovered quickly, the league represented a considerably higher level of play than they had the talent for. After dropping the first six games, Resolute defeated Atlantic on June 5. Eight more losses followed before they defeated Boston 11–2 in the first game of a July 4 doubleheader. Then came seven more losses, so with a record of 2–21 on August 7, Resolute withdrew from the league. Their talent gap can be seen in the fact that eight of the 21 losses were by 10 or more runs. Of the 16 Resolutes who saw action in 1873, nine did not play again in the majors.

Only the two Allisons reached the .300 mark—Art hit .320 and Doug .300. The club batted .235 as a team, scoring only 98 runs, 4.26 per game. And while Hugh Campbell had a solid 2.95 ERA, the team gave up 299 runs, 13 per game. Among the poorer defensive teams, Resolute managed only a .789 team fielding percentage.

ST. LOUIS BASE BALL CLUB
St. Louis, Missouri
1875–1877

History

In *The National Game*, Alfred H. Spink wrote that the professional St. Louis club grew from two sources. The first was a desire to build on the enthusiasm generated by the amateur clubs in St. Louis in 1874, specifically the Reds, Empire, Unions and Stocks. The second was a desire to emulate the success of professional clubs in other cities, such as Cincinnati and Chicago. In 1874 a group of St. Louis gentlemen got together and put up the funds to recruit a professional team to represent the Mound City. As with Chicago, they went east to acquire the best players available.

The 1875 club was one of the more successful ones in the NA, finishing fourth, ahead of such established clubs as Philadelphia, Mutual and Chicago. In 1876 they became one of the eight charter members of the new National League, finishing second behind the powerful Chicago White Stockings. However, the 1877 club wound up in the second division with a losing record. After this showing, St. Louis did not field a club in 1878.

The Brown Stocking name by which they

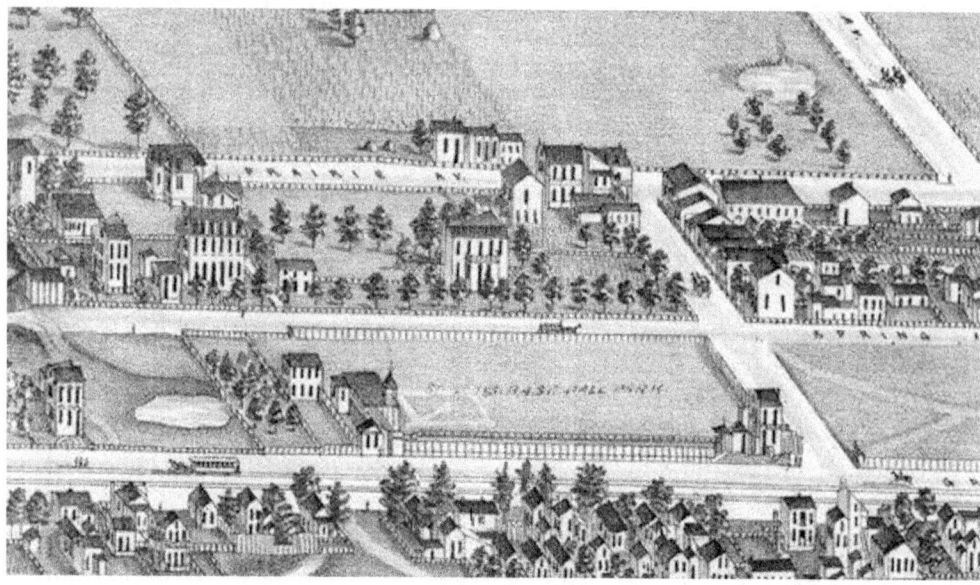

Grand Avenue Grounds were the home of the St. Louis Brown Stockings. Also called Sportsman's Park I, they were the site of three more editions of Sportsman's Park, used until 1966 (from *Pictorial St. Louis*, Library of Congress Maps and Geography Division).

were known passed on to an American Association club in 1882. In shortened form it was used by the St. Louis American League entry until 1954.

Grounds

The Brown Stockings played at Grand Avenue Grounds, also called the St. Louis Base Ball Park. The grounds were located in north St. Louis between North Grand Boulevard, Spring Street, Dodier Street and Sullivan Avenue. Originally farm land, the property was purchased in 1866 by August Solari, who built a park for the use of the Empire club, with twice-weekly leases to the Union club. The first game on the new grounds was played in 1868. According to Phillip Lowry, the capacity of the park had been 3,000 in 1875.

Following the disbanding of the original Brown Stockings in 1877, Grand Avenue Grounds fell into disrepair and were rebuilt in 1881, as the new Brown Stocking club prepared to move into the American Association. Major league baseball was played on these grounds under various structures until 1966, when August Busch built a new Busch Stadium at another location. Today, the Herbert Hoover Sports Club occupies part of the Grand Avenue Grounds.

Management

For their only entry into the NA, the Brown Stockings were managed by shortstop Dickie Pearce.

Uniform and Logo

If the photo of the 1876 team is to be believed, St. Louis was among the first to wear a short-sleeve jersey. Perhaps a summer in St. Louis breeds such uniform innovation. The uniform consisted of white knit jerseys and knickers with a classical trim around the neck in brown with brown stockings. Like

Boston and Hartford, St. Louis had the name of the city on the front.

St. Louis Base Ball Club in the League

1875

The Brown Stockings were by far the strongest of the six new clubs entering the league. Seven members of the club had previous league experience, including five as regulars. The Brown Stocking outfield included Lip Pike (.355 with a league-leading 22 doubles at Hartford), Ned Cuthburt (.268 at Chicago) and Jack Chapman (.264 at Atlantic). Also from Atlantic came first baseman Dutch Dehlman, shortstop Dickie Pearce and third baseman Frank Fleet. Catcher Thomas "Reddy" Miller had played briefly with Athletic but spent most of the season with the powerful Easton semi-pro team, where he caught George Bradley. Bradley and second baseman George Bathis were the only non-veterans on the team.

The second baseman turned out to be Joe Battin, a veteran of the 1871 Cleveland Forest City club who played at Easton with Miller and Bradley. The third baseman was Bill Hague, yet another Easton product. The Brown Stockings used four reserves in 1875 in outfielder Charlie Waitt with his flesh-colored fielder's glove, catcher George Seward, pitcher and outfielder Pud Galvin, and Fleet, who played in one game before returning to Atlantic.

Lip Pike hit .346, but no other Brown Stocking topped .250; so the team settled for a .240 batting average, sixth-best in the league. They parlayed this average into 5.51 runs per game, fifth-best.

Hall of Fame pitcher James "Pud" Galvin started seven games for the Brown Stockings as an 18-year-old in 1875, posting a 1.16 ERA (LC-DIG-bbc-0356f Library of Congress Prints and Photographs Division).

George Bradley (33–26, 2.13 ERA) led St. Louis to a team 2.10 ERA (fifth-best). The team finished fourth in fielding with an .869 percentage, but Dutch Dehlman led the league's first basemen in fielding. The team gave up 3.17 unearned runs per game, so the victory margin of 5.51–5.27 was very thin for a contending team.

ST. LOUIS RED STOCKING BASE BALL CLUB
St. Louis, Missouri
1862–1876

History

J. Taylor Spink noted that the Red Stockings (or Reds) were formed in the early 1860s, one of a group of amateur clubs in St. Louis; however, Marshall Wright does not list the club among NA members. In St. Louis, the Red Stockings were a top-level club in 1874, along with Empire, Union, Elephant, and Stocks. In fact, they claimed the championship of St. Louis that year by defeating Empire. That club included most of the core players of the 1875 team.

In 1875 when a group of businessmen created the professional Brown Stockings to enter the league, the Red Stockings determined to enter the league as well. Initially, St. Louis fans preferred the homegrown Red Stockings to the imported Brown Stockings, but the Red Stockings did not fare well in the league.

The *St. Louis Globe-Democrat* noted that the Red Stockings were victimized in a couple of ways. Even though the Red Stockings were reasonably competitive, rumors began that they would fold; other clubs were reluctant to schedule them, since under league rules, games against teams that had disbanded were erased from the record. Second, other clubs considered the Red Stockings to be a poor draw at the gate. The eastern clubs made one visit to St. Louis but showed no interest in having the Red Stockings come east. As a result, the Red Stockings played their final league game on July 4, losing to Washington. This also was Washington's final game.

While key players left the club for Covington, Kentucky, or Indianapolis, the Red Stockings continued to operate through 1876, and helped to form a new organization called the International Alliance, which soon folded in competition with the National League–sanctioned League Alliance.

Grounds

Red Stocking Base Ball Park was developed by the club in 1874 on six acres of land in central St. Louis beside the Missouri Pacific Railroad yards. The club erected a grandstand and enclosed the field with a stockade fence. In 1875 it was the site of the first professional baseball game in St. Louis, with the Brown Stockings defeating the Red Stockings, 15–9.

The Red Stockings, as well as amateur clubs, continued to use the park. The Black Stockings, a black club, also used the park. It was razed around 1898.

Today the grounds are used as a repair yard by the Bi-State Development Agency, the city transportation system. In 2008 a plaque was erected, marking the location of Compton Avenue Grounds.

Uniforms

In 1875 the *St. Louis Globe-Democrat* described the Red Stockings uniform as follows: "The uniform of the St. Louis Reds will consist of red stockings, gray pants, shirts, and caps trimmed with red. A small 'Red Stockings' will be worked on the shirts, and the word 'St. Louis' over it." No photo is known to exist.

St. Louis Red Stockings in the League

1875

Not surprisingly, Red Stockings players tended to be young local players with little or no league experience. The *New York*

Compton Avenue Base-Ball Park, home to the St. Louis Red Stockings, was the site of the first major league games played in St, Louis (from *Pictorial St. Louis*, Library of Congress Maps and Geography Division).

Herald-Tribune projected a lineup of Seward and McCall; Dillon, Mullhall, McSorley, and Redmond; A. Blong, T. Blong and Morgan. But this nine had little relationship to the team that actually took the field

The pitcher was Joe Blong, a teenage brother of Andrew and Thomas Blong—neither of whom played for the team in 1875. His catcher was Silver Flint, another local teenager who later had a distinguished career in the National League with the White Stockings. First baseman Charlie Hautz, shortstop Billy Redmond, third baseman Trick McSorley, and outfielders Art Croft and Pidge Morgan were all local players. Outfielder Tom Oran, the first Native American to play in the league, was a Californian living in St. Louis. Second baseman Charlie Sweasy was the veteran, having played with the Cincinnati Red Stockings in 1869. He may

Silver Flint hit only .179 as a teenage catcher for the Red Stockings in 1875 but later helped Chicago win four National League championships (LC-DIG-bbc-0123f Library of Congress Prints and Photographs Division).

have come to St. Louis to play for the Brown Stockings.

In 19 games, the Red Stockings used only 12 players, with three local players—Joe Ellick, Packy Dillon and John Dillon—filling in as needed. Flint missed two games, Blong missed three, and McSorley missed four; no other regular missed a game.

Most would consider the highlight of the Red Stockings' short league career to be the 1–0 loss to Chicago, a score unheard of at the time. The Red Stockings defeated Western twice in three early-season meetings and enjoyed back-to-back shutouts of Washington, including one pitched by Blong and one by Morgan. A loss to Washington on July 4 ended their season with a 4–15 record.

Hautz hit .301, but six regulars hit .200 or below, for a team .222 average and 60 runs scored. And while Blong and Morgan allowed only 50 earned runs, the defense surrendered 111 additional runs.

WASHINGTON BASE BALL CLUB
Washington, D.C.
1873

History

After the disastrous attempt to field two major league clubs in 1872, Washington determined to combine forces and enter one team in 1873. The combined Olympic and National team was officially named the Washington Club, and is so referred to by newspapers of the time. Since blue was the base color for both the National and Olympic clubs, the new team is now occasionally called the Blue Legs and sometimes the Nationals. Newspapers at the time also viewed the club as a "new aspirant," not a continuation of the 1872 clubs.

By whatever name the team was known, Washington in 1873 was only marginally more successful than Olympic and National in 1872. Unlike its predecessors, Washington finished the season, leaving the legacy of an 8–31 record.

Grounds

Washington played home games at Olympic Grounds (see under Olympic).

Management

Veteran Olympic player and manager Nick Young managed Washington throughout the 1873 season.

Uniforms and Logo

Other than the blue stockings that gave the team its name, we have no further information or photos.

Washington in the League

1873

A number of players from Olympic and National were available to organize a new team for the 1873 campaign. John Glenn, Tommy Beals, Fred Waterman, Bob Reach, and manager Nick Young were all ex-Olympics; Paul Hines, Warren White, Oscar Bielaski, John Hollingshead and Bill Stearns were ex-Nationals. Glenn also had played in one game for National in 1872.

The Washington nine included Glenn at first base, Beals at second, Joe Gerhardt or

Former Cincinnati Red Stockings star Fred Waterman hit .350 for Washington in 1873 (courtesy www.19cbaseball.com).

Pete Donnelly at shortstop, White at third, Bielaski, Hines and Hollingsworth in the outfield, Pop Snyder at catcher and Stearns at pitcher. Waterman was the key reserve. The *Boston Daily Advertiser* noted that except for Waterman, none of the players "has more than a local reputation." Gerhardt, Donnelly and Snyder were rookies. Another rookie, pitcher Jack Greason, started seven games; rookies Ed Adkinson (two games), and Howard Wall (one game) also played for Washington.

Washington opened with two blowout triumphs over Maryland and then went a month before winning its third decision and another month before gaining victory number four. They had a 4–14 record, 15.5 games behind the White Stockings at midseason. In the second half they experienced an eight-game losing streak, dropping into ninth place on September 13, and continued in ninth place, 26 games behind the Red Stockings. The club had winning records against Maryland (2–0) and Resolute (1–0) and was a combined 0–21 against Athletic, Baltimore and Boston.

Washington ultimately finished in seventh place, a spot they earned by almost every statistic. Despite Hines' .331 batting average (and Waterman's .350 in 15 games), the club as a whole hit .262. They scored 283 runs (7.25 per game) but gave up 485 (12.43 per game). Stearns had a 4.61 ERA, but the team ERA was 4.84 and the team gave up 299 unearned runs. Team fielding was .812 — not surprisingly, seventh place.

WASHINGTON BASEBALL CLUB
Washington, D.C.
1875

History

Without league representation in 1874, Washington organized a club for 1875. Some sources refer to the club as the Nationals, but newspaper accounts invariably refer to the club as "Washington." An advertisement in the *Washington Critic-Record* noted that in regard to major league baseball, Washington "should not be behind her sister cities in this respect." Fans were encouraged to "place her on a par with the rest." Preston Orem notes that the club was "made up of Washington and Baltimore men of no particular distinction." Of the projected "nine," only two — pitcher William Stearns (with Hartford) and shortstop Lou Say (with Lord Baltimore) — had been in the league in 1874. Outfielders Art Allison and John Hollingshead also had prior league experience, while five were newcomers.

Not surprisingly, Washington experienced

Washington (1875)

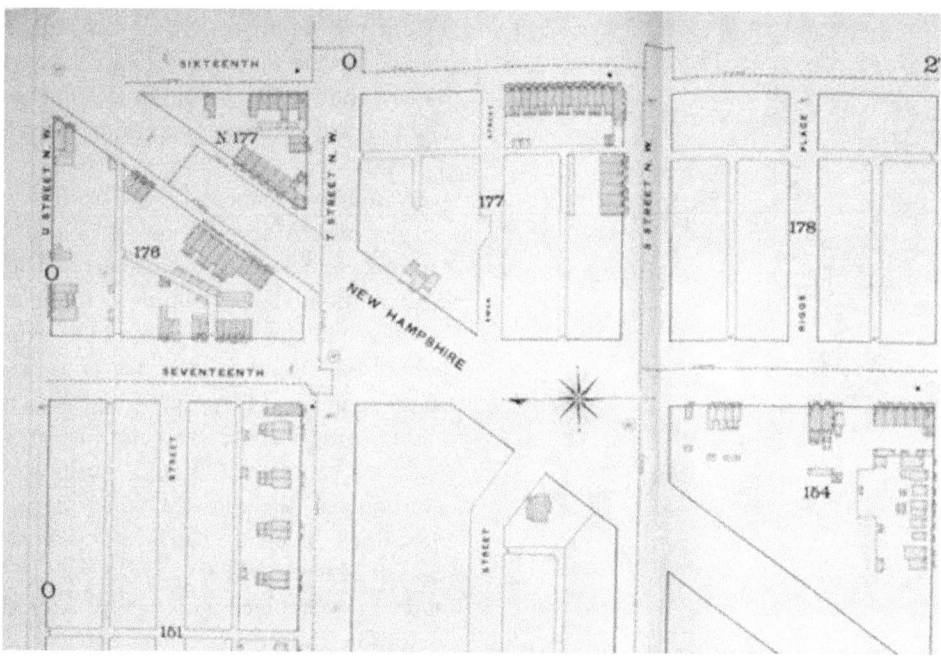

Olympic Grounds (Lot 177) were located between Sixteenth and Seventeenth Streets NW, with S Street to the south. The 1888 Sanborn Fire Protection Map shows brick buildings on the south and east sides of the lot (Library of Congress Maps and Geography Division).

little success. Shut out five times, Washington lost by at least ten runs on 11 occasions, including a 24–0 loss to Boston. In a game at Hartford, Washington committed 27 errors. Of its five victories, four came over equally challenged New Haven.

After drawing 4,000 in a season-opening loss to Boston, Washington played before crowds measured often in the hundreds. In late June they traveled to St. Louis for six games against the Brown Stockings and Red Stockings. They played for the last time on July 4, defeating the Red Stockings 12–5. The *National Aegis* reported on July 6 that the Washington business agent "had absconded ... with all the money of the club leaving them no means to get home." The newspaper reported that "a subscription is being raised ... for their benefit."

This was Washington's last experience with major league baseball until 1884, when both the American Association and Union Association placed teams in the city.

Grounds

Washington, like the Washington club of 1873, played home games at Olympic Grounds.

Management

Hollingshead, a veteran of the 1872 Nationals and the 1873 Washingtons, became the manager of Washington. After 20 games, in which the club won four, the management passed the baton to rookie outfielder and pitcher Bill Parks, under whom the club won one of eight.

Uniform and Logo

Washington teams had traditionally worn blue. However, this Washington team is not listed among the wearers of blue for 1875.

Washington in the League

1875

Of the six new clubs in the league, Washington had the greatest tradition. While the city had no representation in 1874, this new club would be the fifth Washington entry in the NA: Olympic in 1871, Olympic and National in 1872, and the combined club in 1873. Washington teams had compiled a lackluster 25–64 record in league play.

On March 16, *New York Herald-Tribune* projected a lineup of Studs Bancker and William Stearns for the battery; an infield of Wallace Terry, Larry Ressler, John Daily and Lou Say; and an outfield of Art Allison, Bill Parks, and Holly Hollingshead. Of these players, five—Bancker, Terry, Ressler, Daily, and Parks—had no league experience. Stearns, a Washington veteran since 1871, had gone 3–14 with a 2.95 ERA at Hartford in 1874 and had been suspended for leaving the club. Say had 21 games of league experience with Maryland and Lord Baltimore. Allison and Hollingshead, with previous league experience, had both been out of the league in 1874.

Allison, Dailey, Ressler, Hollingshead, Parks, and Stearns became regulars. Other regulars were second baseman Steve Brady from Hartford; third baseman Herm Doscher, who had played for Atlantic in 1872; and newcomer Andrew Thompson, who shared the catching duties with another newcomer named McCloskey. Washington used 19 players in 28 games.

With only two regulars hitting as high as .200 and none reaching .250, Washington lacked the offense necessary to win. Their .193 team batting average led to just 3.82 runs per game. Bill Parks (4–8, 3.54 ERA) and William Stearns (1–14, 4.02 ERA) had the league's two highest ERAs among regular pitchers. In addition, Washington was one of two clubs to field below .800. As a result, they allowed 8.32 unearned runs per game. By scoring under four runs per game and giving up more than 12, their won-lost record and lack of fan support were understandable.

WESTERN BASEBALL CLUB
Keokuk, Iowa
1872–1875

History

The Keokuk Westerns were formed as an amateur team and incorporated in 1872. They began competing for the Iowa championship during that season. By 1874 they had accomplished their goal by defeating Iowa City. Before the end of that season, they had also defeated a top Missouri team, St. Louis Empire, and a top eastern club from Staten Island. The Westerns posted a 23–9 record, with five losses coming against National Association clubs, including home losses to the Chicago White Stockings and New York Mutual.

Despite a population base of only 12,000 (perhaps considerably smaller), John Irwin, C.L. Williams, Robert McGuire and William Trimble, the four-member board of directors, determined to enter the team into the National Association in 1875. Ralph Christian argued that this action must be viewed against the regional pride that caused many to feel that the center of national life, including baseball, had shifted west, that consequently the national capital should be shifted to the Midwest, and that Keokuk would be an ideal location for that capitol. Fielding a major league baseball team would be a part of Keokuk's fulfilling its destiny.

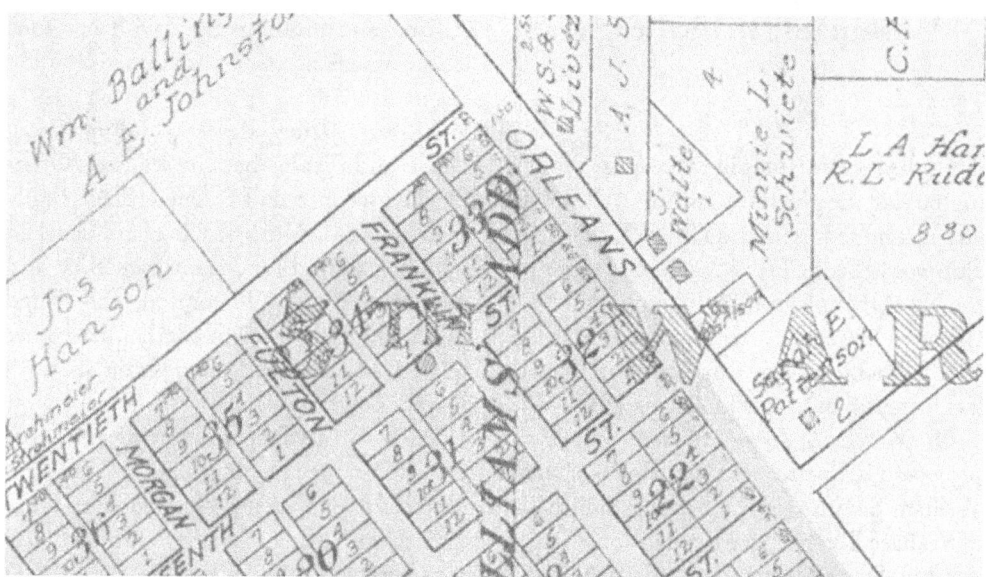

Michael Benson places Perry Park, home field of Western, in Lot 34 of the Reeves, Perry & Williams Addition in Keokuk. Note that a triangular property just to the right of the Addition is owned by a J. Walte. Another name for the ballpark was Walte's Pasture ("Map of the City of Keokuk," from: Alfred T. Andreas' 1875 *Illustrated Historical Atlas of the State of Iowa*. Chicago, 1875. Online images from the University of Iowa Libraries Map Collection/ Iowa Heritage Digital Collections http://digital.lib.uiowa.edu/maps/).

Therefore, the directors began raising funds to move from amateur to professional status and to upgrade Perry Park.

Western soon discovered they were out of their league. Two problems emerged. First, despite some close games, the team was not able to win. In thirteen games, they had only a 15–2 victory over the St. Louis Red Stockings to show for their efforts. Even worse, they were not a financial success. Plagued by cool and blustery weather during an initial homestand, they had few gate receipts to share with visiting teams. The White Stockings received only $68 for two games and vowed never to return to Keokuk. When Boston received $13 as its share of the gate for a June 10 game, the team forfeited the second game and left town. Mutual also left after one game. The team's lack of success made them a poor draw on the road, and their share of gate receipts in Chicago and St. Louis did not cover expenses.

On June 16, the directors disbanded Western. Keokuk was without a professional team until mid–1885, when the city inherited the Western League Omaha franchise. That club featured Bud Fowler, who in 1878 had been the first black player in previously all-white Organized Baseball.

Grounds

Walte's Pasture or Perry Park was the home ground of Western in 1875. The grounds were north of today's Rand Park, located beside the Mississippi River. In *Green Cathedrals*, Phillip J. Lowry wrote that the outfield had two lakes, causing outfielders to get wet on occasion. He says that today the area is a municipal swimming pool. *Two in the Field: A Novel* describes a game played at Walte's Pasture and includes the loss of an outfielder, who fell into a "cow hollow."

Management

Outfielder Joe Simmons managed the 1875 team.

Uniform and Logo

The *Daily Constitution* of Middletown, Connecticut, reported in March 1875, "The Uniform adopted by the Western club of Keokuk, Iowa, is white with blue stockings and trimmings with the letter K on the bosom of the shirt and on the cuff of each sleeve, making the appropriate trio of K's. A hat is to be worn instead of a cap."

Western in the League

From the 1874 Iowa state champions, Keokuk retained five starters: pitcher Mike Golden, shortstop Wally Goldsmith, second baseman Joe Miller and outfielders Charley Jones and Billy Riley. Of these Goldsmith had 29 games of NA experience with Kekionga, Olympic, and Maryland, while Miller had played a single game with National in 1872. To strengthen their hand, Western added five players, including first baseman Jack Carbine, shortstop Jim Hallinan, outfielder Joe Simmons and catcher/outfielders Paddy Quinn and Billy Barnie. Like Goldsmith, Hallinan and Quinn had played for Kekionga in 1871. Barnie, an outfield regular, had hit .181 for Hartford in 1874; Simmons had been a regular at both Chicago (1871) and Cleveland (1872).

Western rotated the above ten players, with only Riley playing in fewer than ten games. They also picked up former Atlantic Edwin Hall for one game in St. Louis.

Financially unable to travel south to train, Western made do with practice allowed by Keokuk weather in their own park and such preseason games as local opposition provided. They began the season with a six-game homestand against Chicago and St. Louis teams, games played in cool and blustery weather. With only a 15–2 victory over the Red Stockings to show for their early efforts, Western embarked on a five-game road trip, playing the same teams and losing all five games. With a 1–10 record, Western returned home to face eastern leaders Boston and Mutual, again losing both games to go 1–12, their final mark.

In the field Western was bedeviled by a host of problems. First, they generated little offense. While Quinn hit .326, and Jones, who was beginning a distinguished career, and Hallinan had respectable .277 and .275 averages, the team as a whole hit .180. In 13 games they scored only 45 runs—3.5 per game. Only twice did they score as many as five runs.

On the other hand, Ralph Christian pointed out that most of Western's problems stemmed from wildness on the part of Golden and a very bad defense. The team gave up 88 runs—6.76 per game. Sixty-five of these runs were unearned. Led by shortstop Hallinan (16 errors) and second base-

A utility outfielder and catcher for Western in 1875, Billy Barnie went on to a 55-year career in baseball (courtesy T. Scott Brandon).

man Miller (13 errors), Western committed 78 errors in 13 games. In truth, the hard-throwing Golden had a 1.83 ERA but undercut this with 12 wild pitches in 13 games. The other end of the battery—Quinn and Barnie—had 34 passed balls between them.

When the team disbanded, Miller and Golden caught on with the White Stockings; Barnie and Hallinan went to Mutual; Jones and Quinn were picked up by Hartford; Carbine and Riley returned to the majors with Louisville and Cleveland, respectively, in 1879. Simmons, Goldsmith and Hall saw their major league careers end in Keokuk.

Bibliography

Databases

Ancestry.com (http://www.Ancestry.com). This subscriber Internet service is the source for all of the U.S. Federal Censuses, city directories, family trees, voter registers, mortality schedules, naturalization records, and military records cited in the book.

Genealogy Bank.com (http://www.genealogybank.com). This subscriber Internet service is the source for many of the newspapers cited. These include: *Arkansas Gazette, Baltimore Sun, Boston Daily Advertiser, Boston Journal, Chicago Daily Inter Ocean, Cincinnati Commercial Tribune, Cincinnati Daily Enquirer, Cincinnati Daily Gazette, Cincinnati Times-Star, Cleveland Plain Dealer, Detroit Free Press, Duluth News-Tribune, Fort Worth Star-Telegram, Harrisburg Patriot, Hartford Courant, Indianapolis Sentinel, Jackson Citizen-Patriot, Jersey Journal, Lowell Daily Citizen and News, Middletown Daily Constitution, New Haven Register, New Orleans Times-Picayune, New York Herald-Tribune, New York Morning Telegraph, New York Post, Quincy Whig, Philadelphia Inquirer, Rockford Morning Star, Rockford Republic, Rockford Weekly Gazette, St. Louis Republic, Salt Lake Telegram, Seattle Daily Times, Springfield Republican, Trenton Evening News, Trenton Evening Times, Trenton State Gazette, Wheeling Register, Wilkes-Barre Times.*

LA84 Foundation-Sports Library (http://www.lafoundation.org). The digital library is the source for *Sporting Life* and *Baseball Magazine*.

Paper of Record (http://www.paperofrecord.com). This digital newspaper service is the source for *The Sporting News*.

ProQuest Historical Newspapers (http://www.umi.com/en-US/catalogs/databases/detail/pq-hist-news.shtml). Formerly provided for members of the Society for American Baseball Research, this University of Michigan service provides digital copies of nineteenth and early twentieth century *Boston Globe, Chicago Daily Tribune, Los Angeles Times, National Police Gazette, New York Times* and *Washington Post.*

Russo, Mark. *The Deadball Era: Where Every Player Is Safe at Home* (http://www.thedeadballera.com). This omnibus site is a storehouse for information on deceased players. It contains obituaries, death certificates, and photographs and lists of post-baseball occupations and causes of death for players who died young, including suicides, accidents, and murders.

Playing Records

Baseball Almanac: Where What Happened Yesterday Is Preserved Today (http://www.baseball-almanac.com).

Baseball Encyclopedia: The Complete and Official Record of Major League Baseball. 8th ed. New York: Macmillan, 1990.

Baseball-Reference.com. (http://www.baseball-reference.com).

Society for American Baseball Research. *SABR Encyclopedia of Baseball.* (http://sabrpedia.org).

Thorn, John, Pete Palmer, Michael Gershman, and David Pietrusza, with Matthew Silverman and Sean Lahman, eds. *Total Baseball: The Official Encyclopedia of Major League Baseball.* 6th ed. New York: Total Sports, 1999.

General Sources

Arcidiacono, David. "The Curious Case of Tommy Barlow." *Elysian Fields Quarterly,* 2004. (http://www.efqreview.com/NewFiles/v21n1/onhistoricalground.html).

_____. *Major League Baseball in Gilded Age Connecticut: The Rise and Fall of Middletown, New Haven and Hartford Clubs.* Jefferson, NC: McFarland, 2009.

Baseball: An Illustrated History. Narrative by Geoffrey Ward. Based on a documentary filmscript by Geoffrey C. Ward and Ken Burns. New York: Knopf, 1994.

Baseball Fever. (http://www.baseball-fever.com/content.php).

Baseball Historian: "Where Faded Memories Return." (http://www.baseballhistorian.com).

Baseball History Blog. (Baseballhistoryblog.com).

BaseballLibrary.com. (www.baseballlibrary.com).

Benson, Michael. *Ballparks of North America: A Comprehensive Historical Reference to Baseball Grounds, Yards, and Stadiums, 1845 to Present.* Jefferson, NC: McFarland, 1989.

Bready, James H. *The Home Team: A Full Century of Baseball in Baltimore, 1859–1959.* Baltimore: Self-published, 1958.

Brock, Darryl. *Two in the Field.* New York: Plume, 2002.

Brunson, James E., III. *Early Images of Black Baseball: Race and Representation in the Popular Press, 1871–1890.* Jefferson, NC: McFarland, 2009.

Bullpen. A Collaborative Encyclopedia Sponsored by Baseball-Reference.com.

Bundgaard, Axel. *Muscle and Manliness: The Rise of Sport in American Boarding Schools.* Syracuse, NY: Syracuse University Press, 2005.

Burke's American Families with British Ancestry. Ancestry.com.

Cagnon, Cappy. *Notre Dame Baseball Greats from Anson to Yaz.* Mount Pleasant, SC: Arcadia, 2004.

Caillault, Jean-Pierre. *Complete New York Clipper Baseball Biographies: More Than 800 Sketches of Players, Managers, Owners, Umpires, Reporters and Others, 1859–1903.* 2 vols. Jefferson, NC: McFarland, 2009.

Chadwick, Henry. "Old Battles on the Baseball Field." *Outing.* May, 1888: 117–120.

Charlton, James, and Others. *Charlton's Baseball Chronology.* (http://www.baseballlibrary.com/chronology).

Christian, Ralph. *"High Expectations, Small Market, Regionalism and a Short-lived Season."* Monograph provided by Keokuk Public Library.

Descendants of John Joseph Abercrombie and Sarah Denormandie. (http://www.facebook.com/pages/Descendants-of-JOHN-JOSEPH-ABERCROMBIE-and-SARAH-DENORMANDIE/347061701024).

Dressed to the Nines: A History of the Baseball Uniform. (http://exhibits.baseballhalloffame.org/dressed_to_the_nines/index.htm).

Eldred, Rich. "Timothy Hayes Murnane." *Baseball's First Stars.* Cleveland: Society for American Baseball Research, 1996.

Flynn, Tom, and Sean Welsh. *Baseball in Baltimore.* Mount Pleasant, SC: Arcadia, 2008.

Gerlach, Larry R., and Harold V. Higham. "Dick Higham: An Umpire at the Bar of History." *National Pastime: A Review of Baseball History.* 20 (2000): 20–32.

Ginsburg, Daniel E. *The Fix Is In: A History of Baseball Gambling and Game Fixing Scandals.* Jefferson, NC: McFarland, 1995.

Gmelch, George, ed. *Baseball Without Borders: The International Pastime.* Lincoln: University of Nebraska Press, 2006.

Gramling, Chad. "Baseball in Fort Wayne." (www.baseballinfortwayne.com).

Griswold, B.J., and Mrs. Samuel R. Taylor. *The Pictorial History of Fort Wayne, Indiana: A Review of Two Centuries of Occupation of the Region About the Head of the Maumee River.* 2 vols. Chicago: Robert O. Law, 1917.

"History of Keokuk, Iowa Baseball." (http://keokuk.net).

"Irish Americans." Answers.com. (http://www.answers.com/topic/irish-american).

James, Bill. *The New Bill James Historical Baseball Abstract.* New York: Free Press, 2001.

Johnson, Lloyd, and Miles Wolfe, eds. *The Encyclopedia of Minor League Baseball: The Official Record of Minor League Baseball.* 2nd ed. Durham, NC: Baseball America, 1997.

Kermisch, Al. "From a Researcher's Notebook." *Baseball Research Journal* 19 (1990): 93–94.

Kittel, Jeffrey. *This Game of Games: Blogging the History of 19th Century St. Louis Baseball.*

(http://thisgameofgames.blogspot.com). Most citations of St. Louis newspapers are from this site.
Lee, Bill. *The Baseball Necrology: The Post-Baseball Lives and Deaths of Over 7,600 Major League Players and Others*. Jefferson, NC: McFarland, 2003.
"Lipman 'Lip' Pike." *International Jewish Sports Hall of Fame*. (http://www.jewishsports.net).
Marlin, Brooks. "Major League Baseball's 'Permanently Ineligible' List." Everything2. (http://everything2.com).
McGinley Clan. (mcginleyclan.org).
McKenna, Brian. "Early Baltimore Baseball." (http://baseballhistoryblog.com).
Mondout, Patrick. "Baseball Chronology: The Game Since 1845." (http://www.Baseball Chronology.com).
Morris, Peter. *Baseball Fever: Early Baseball in Michigan*. Ann Arbor: University of Michigan Press, 2003.
_____. "Peter Morris, Baseball Historian." (http://www.petermorrisbooks.com. 2007–2009).
National Baseball Hall of Fame. "Albert Spalding." (http://baseballhal.org/hof/spalding-albert).
_____. "Cap Anson." (http://baseballhall.org/hof/anson-cap).
Nemec, David. *Beer & Whiskey League: Illustrated History of the American Association— Baseball's Renegade League*. Guilford, CT: Lyons, 2004.
_____. *Great Encyclopedia of Nineteenth Century Major League Baseball*. New York: D.I. Fine, 1997.
Nitz, Jim. "Fair Grounds (Rockford, IL)." SABR Bio-Project. (http://bioproj.sabr.org/bioproj).
Ooptdevelopments.com.
Orem, Preston D. *Baseball (1845–1881): From the Newspaper Accounts*. Altadena, CA: Self-published, 1961.
"Philadelphia Athletics History." Baseball Chronology. (http://www.baseballchronology.com).
Quinn Family History, Appendix H. (http://www.Constablequinn.com/AppendixHQuinnFamilyHistory.htm).
Retrosheet. (www.Retrosheet.org).
"Rochester Hop Bitters, 1879–1880." (http://baseballhistoryblog.com).
Roer, Mike. *Orator O'Rourke: The Life of a Baseball Radical*. Jefferson, NC: McFarland, 2005.
Ryczek, William J. *Blackguards and Red Stockings: A History of Baseball's National Association*. Wallingford, CT: Colebrook, 1992.
_____. *When Johnny Came Sliding Home: The Post–Civil War Baseball Boom, 1865–1870*. Jefferson, NC: McFarland, 2006.
"Salaries in the 1880s." *eHow Money*. (http://www.ehow.com/info_7792066_salaries-1880s.html).
Schaefer, Robert T. "The Lost Art of Fair-Foul Hitting." *National Pastime 20* (2000): 3–7.
Schneider, Russell. *Cleveland Indians Encyclopedia*. 3rd ed. Champaign, IL: Sports Publishing, 2004.
Seymour, Harold, and Dorothy Seymour Mills. *Baseball: The Golden Age*. New York: Oxford, 1989.
Shaw, W.W. "Nine Thousand Miles on a Pullman Train: An Account of a Tour of Railroad Conductors from Philadelphia to the Pacific Coast and Return." (http://www.thaddeuslowe.name/Nine_Thousand_Miles_on_a_Pullman_Train.pdf).
Shiffert, John. *Baseball in Philadelphia: A History of the Early Game, 1831–1900*. Jefferson, NC: McFarland, 2006.
Society for American Baseball Research. Civil War Veterans Who Played Major League Baseball Soldiers Research Project. (http://sabr.org/cmsFiles/Files/Civil%20War%20veterans.pdf).
Society for American Baseball Research. *SABR Biographical Research Committee Newsletter*. (http://sabr.org/research/biographical-research-committee).
_____. The Baseball Biography Project. (http://bioproj.sabr.org/). Among its 1,680 biographies to date, nine have been of National Association players. Some NA ballparks are also included.
Spink, Alfred Henry. *The National Game: A History of Baseball, America's Leading Out-Door Sport*. St. Louis: National Game Publishing, 1910.
Taylor, William Harrison. *Taylor's Legislative History and Souvenir of Connecticut, 190-: Portraits and Sketches of State Officials, Senators, Representatives, etc. List of Committees. Portraits and Roll of Delegates to Constitutional Convention of 1902. The Proposed Constitution and the Vote*. Putnam, CT: W.H. Taylor, 190-.
Van Tassel, David Dirck, John J. Grabowski, and Cleveland Bicentennial Commission.

Encyclopedia of Cleveland History. Bloomington: Indiana University of Press with Case Western Reserve University and Western Reserve Historical Society, 1996.

Wright, Marshall D. *National Association of Base Ball Players, 1857–1870*. Jefferson, NC: McFarland, 2000.

Zingler, David. "Bobby Mathews." Simply Baseball Notebook: Forgotten In Time. (http://z.lee28.tripod.com/sbnsforgottenintime/id26.html).

Index

Abadie, John 13, 156
Abercrombie, David 13
Abercrombie, Frank 8, 13–14
Abrams, Thomas 175
Active BBC (New York, NY) 69
Addy, Bob 6, 7, 14, 152, 169, 171, 173, 199, 201
Aetna BBC (Chicago, IL) 7, 67, 108, 110, 179
Agricultural Society Fair Grounds (Rockford, IL) 169–70
Aiguier *see* Geer, William H.
A.J. Reach Company 132
Albany BBC (Albany, NY) 17, 47, 72, 77, 84, 98, 113–14, 118
Alert BBC (Rochester, NY) 75, 79, 91, 124, 166
Allen, Frank E. "Ham" 14
Allen, Homer S. "Ham" 14
Allentown BBC (Allentown, PA) 48
Allison, Andy 14, 16, 162
Allison, Art 15, 16, 100, 166, 168, 174, 203, 209, 211
Allison, Bill 15, 162
Allison, Doug 7, 10, 15, 16, 162, 173–74, 177, 192–93, 196–98, 202–3
Alpha BBC (Brooklyn, NY) 44
Amateur BBC (Newark, NJ) 201
American Association 9, 16–17, 21–22, 33, 35–36, 39–40, 42, 45–47, 50, 53, 60–62, 70, 72, 74, 76–77, 80–82, 84, 86–88, 92, 98, 100, 104–7, 110, 112, 114, 116–19, 128, 130, 136, 139, 180–81, 204, 210
American Civil War 3, 5, 11, 14, 16, 18–19, 22, 26–28, 33–34, 38, 45, 54, 56, 60, 75–76, 85, 87, 89–90, 103, 107, 111, 122, 131, 136, 154, 175, 178, 180, 183–84, 187–88, 196; District of Columbia units 122; Illinois units 19, 69; Maryland units 38; Massachusetts units 4; New Jersey units 34; New York units 18, 20, 22, 26–28, 33, 38, 45, 56, 61, 75, 87, 105, 109, 123, 132; Pennsylvania units 14, 16, 25–26, 60, 76, 85, 89, 102, 107; United States Navy 56, 136
Amity BBC (Brooklyn, NY) 41
Anson, Cap 1, 7–9, 16, 114, 122, 140–44, 169–71
Arctic BBC (Philadelphia, PA) 114
Armstrong, Bob 17, 179
Armstrong, Sam *see* Armstrong, Bob
Arnold, Willis S. "Billy" 17, 163
Arundel, Harry 8, 17–18, 70
Astoria BBC (Washington, DC) 66
Athletic BBC (Brooklyn) 30
Athletic BBC (Chicago) 29
Athletic BBC (Philadelphia) 8–10, 12, 16–17, 22, 24–25, 27, 29, 36, 41, 44–45, 47, 51, 55, 57–58, 60–61, 64, 67–68, 70–71, 80, 84–85, 89, 92–94, 97, 105, 107–9, 111–12, 115, 121–22, 124, 127, 130, 135, 139, 144, 151, 154–56, 158–59, 166, 173, 177, 182–84, 186, 189, 191, 193–94, 196, 198–201, 205, 209
Atkinson, Ed 18
Atlanta Braves 3, 149
Atlantic BBC (Brooklyn) 3, 8, 12–13, 17, 19–20, 22, 24, 29–31, 34–36, 39–45, 47–48, 50–51, 53, 55, 60–61, 63, 67, 70–73, 75, 78, 81, 83, 84, 86, 89–90, 95–97, 99–100, 102–5, 107–8, 110–11, 116–119, 121, 123, 125–26, 128, 130, 133–34, 136, 144–49, 154, 156, 158, 161–62, 164–65, 168, 173, 176, 183, 185–86, 190–194, 197, 200, 203, 205, 211, 213
Atlantic BBC (Chicago) 29
Attleboro, MA (Meteor BBC) 125
Auburn BBC (Auburn, NY 13, 17, 77
Augusta BBC (Augusta, GA) 112
Austin, Henry 18–19, 203

Baker Bowl (Philadelphia, PA) 155
Baltimore, MD: American Association Orioles 16, 21, 42, 52, 65, 114, 118, 128, 136; Enterprise BBC 38, 65, 96; Excelsior BBC 30, 33, 46, 56, 61, 67, 82, 100, 127, 139, 145, 187, 194; Lord Baltimore BBC 7–10, 12, 21, 27, 29,

219

Index

33–34, 38, 45–46, 48, 55, 58, 62, 66–67, 69, 72, 77, 81, 86, 88, 93, 95, 105, 108, 110–11, 113–15, 118–19, 125, 131, 135–36, 141–42, 151, 153, 159–60, 64–65, 167, 171, 173, 175, 177, 180–84, 187–88, 191–93, 198, 200–1, 209, 211; Maryland BBC 1, 8, 12, 17, 27, 38, 52, 59, 65, 74, 76–78, 81–82, 88, 90, 96, 106, 114–15, 117–19, 123, 133, 178–80, 183, 186–88, 209, 211, 213; Pastime BBC 21, 77, 96, 106, 178, 180, 186, 187; Union Association Monumentals 23, 47, 52, 114; Waverly BBC 187
Bancker, John "Studs" 19, 165, 211
Barker, Al 7, 19, 171
Barlow, Tommy 19–20, 147–48, 165, 173
Barnes, Ross 7, 9, 11, 20–21, 75, 142, 149–53, 169
Barnie, Billy 7, 21, 173, 193, 213–14
Barrett, William 21–22, 179
Barrows, Frank 22, 150, 151
Bass, John 22, 166, 168
Battin, Joe 22–23, 28, 66, 143, 205
Bay City BBC (Bay City, MI) 81
Beacon BBC (Boston, MA) 82
Beadle's Dime Base Ball Player 5
Beals, Tommy 23, 152–53, 197–98, 208
Beavens, Edward (E.P. Bevens) 24
Bechtel, George 10, 24, 141, 144, 154, 156, 191–92, 199–201
Bellan, Steve 6, 24–25, 176–77, 192
Bentley, Clytus "Cy" 25, 186
Berkenstock, Nate 6, 25, 139
Berry, Tom 25–26, 141
Berthrong, Harry 2, 8, 26, 193, 196–98
Bestick, William 26, 162
Bielaski, Oscar 26–27, 160, 183, 208–9
Bierman, Charlie 27, 179
Binghamton BBC (Binghamton, NY) 17, 50
Bird, George 7, 8, 27–28, 170
Bird, Homer 28

Birdsall, Dave 9–28, 113, 150–51
Birmingham BBC (Birmingham, AL) 42
"black list" 24, 28, 46, 50, 76, 77, 130, 154
Blong, Andrew 29, 207
Blong, Joe 7, 10, 22, 28–29, 49, 70, 207–8
Blong, Thomas 207
Boardman, Fred 29
Boland 29
Bond, Tommy 6, 29–30, 34, 148, 173–74
Booth 30, 165
Booth, Eddie 30, 147–48, 186, 193, 203
Borden, Joe 30–31, 201
Bostick, William *see* Bestick, William
Boston, MA: Beacon BBC 82; Boston Red Stockings 1, 3, 9–12, 14, 20, 22, 28–30, 42, 55, 61, 66, 70, 75, 83, 86, 91, 93, 101, 108, 111, 113, 115, 119–20, 125, 129, 131, 133–35, 139, 141–44, 147–54, 158–59, 163–65, 168, 170, 172–74, 177, 181, 183–84, 191–93, 196, 198, 200, 203, 209–10, 212–13; National League BBC 20, 29–31, 35, 46, 72, 76, 83, 86, 88, 89, 91, 97, 99, 101, 103, 112, 115, 119, 124, 131, 134–35; Tri Mountain BBC 22, 150; Union Association Reds 30, 98
Boyd, Bill 31, 146–48, 173, 191
Bradley, George 31–32, 66, 95, 205
Brady, Michael "Spike" 32
Brady, Steve 32–33, 173, 211
Brainard, Asahel "Asa" 7, 33, 132, 183–84, 186, 196–98
Brandywine BBC (West Chester, PA) 117
Brannock, Mike 33–34
Bridgeport BBC (Bridgeport, CT) 53, 114, 127
Britt, Jim 34, 147–48
Brockton, MA (Brockton BBC) 100
Brooklyn, NY: Alpha BBC 44; American Association Dodgers 35–36, 39, 53, 61, 110, 128–29; American Association Gladiators 62, 98; Amity BBC 41; Athletic BBC 30; Atlantic BBC 3, 8,

12–13, 17, 19–20, 22, 24, 29–31, 34–36, 39–45, 47–48, 50–51, 53, 55, 60–61, 63, 67, 70–73, 75, 78, 81, 83, 84, 86, 89–90, 95–97, 99–100, 102–5, 107–8, 110–11, 116–119, 121, 123, 125–26, 128, 130, 133–34, 136, 144–49, 154, 156, 158, 161–62, 164–65, 168, 173, 176, 183, 185–86, 190–194, 197, 200, 203, 205, 211, 213; Burnsides BBC 40, 72; Chelsea BBC 40, 82, 93, 130, 133; Concord BBC 119; Eckford BBC 3, 5, 12, 14–15, 26, 40, 42–43, 51, 55–56, 61, 73–76, 83, 85–87, 89–90, 92, 95, 98, 101, 103, 105, 109, 119–20, 124, 127, 133, 136, 146, 156, 160–62, 168, 180, 183–84, 186, 189, 191–92, 198–99, 202–3; Enterprise BBC 40, 44, 53, 67, 103, 105, 121; Excelsior BBC 30, 33, 46, 56, 61, 67, 82, 100, 127, 139, 145, 187, 194; Exercise BBC 61; Harmonic BBC 71; Henry Eckford BBC 76; Nameless BBC 34; Nassau BBC 39, 50, 119; National League Bridegrooms 21, 35, 36, 51; Oriental BBC 86, 105–6; Peconic BBC 24; Powhatan BBC 24; Resolute BBC 113; Star BBC 24, 30, 46, 67, 71, 74, 100, 113, 126, 134, 139, 151, 191
Brown, Oliver 34, 147
Brown, Robert 34
Browne, Louis 95
Buckeye BBC (Cincinnati, OH) 7, 30, 55, 66, 75, 83, 92, 125
Buffalo, NY: Buffalo BBC 92, 98; National League Bisons 40, 41, 46, 52, 58–60, 77, 84, 86, 92, 101, 104, 117, 128, 131; Niagara BBC 11; Players League Bisons 131
Bulkeley, Morgan 172
Burdock, John "Black Jack" 9, 35, 120, 147, 173–74, 192–93
Burnsides BBC (Brooklyn) 40, 72
Burroughs, Henry 35, 36, 196
Bushong, Albert "Doc" 8–9, 36, 70
Buttery, Frank 36–37, 184

Index

California League 23
Camden, NJ (Merrit BBC) 109, 129
Camp Allen (Fort Wayne, IN) 178–79
Campbell, Hugh 6, 37, 201, 203
Campbell, Michael "Mat" 6, 37, 201, 203
Canmeyer, William 161
Capitol BBC (Washington DC) 27
Capitoline Grounds (Brooklyn, NY) 10, 145–46
Carbine, John 37–38, 213–14
Carey, Tom (J.J. Norton) 38, 173–74, 179–83, 190, 192–93
Carl, Lewis (Louis) 38–39
Carleton, Jim 8, 39, 168
Cassidy, John 39, 148–49, 165
Cavanagh, James 2, 6, 40, 162
Centennial BBC (Philadelphia, PA) 8, 12–13, 24, 30, 45, 54, 83, 87, 91, 108, 120, 127, 129, 144, 154–56, 159, 165
Centennial Park (Philadelphia, PA) 154–55
Champion BBC (Jersey City, NJ) 50
Champion City BBC (Springfield, MA) 33
Chapman, Jack 40, 104, 145, 148, 205
Charleston, SC (Charleston BBC) 112, 114
Chelsea BBC (Brooklyn) 40, 82, 93, 130, 133
Chester BBC (Greenville, NJ) 50
Chicago, IL: Aetna BBC 7, 67, 108, 110, 179; Athletic BBC 29; Atlantic BBC 29; Blue Stockings BBC 33; Colts 157; Cubs 157; Emmett BBC 32; Franklins BBC 37, 58; National Association White Stockings 3, 7, 9, 10, 12–14, 16, 20, 25, 27, 29, 32–33, 42–43, 45, 47–48, 51, 57, 64, 69, 72–73, 77, 79, 85, 88, 94, 104–5, 108, 110, 127, 132–33, 136–37, 139, 141, 144–45, 154, 156–60, 163, 168–70, 173, 176–78, 189, 191, 193, 198–201, 203, 205, 208, 211, 213; National League White Stockings 3, 14, 16, 20, 27, 32, 39, 50–53, 56, 64–65, 68, 72, 104, 110, 117, 121, 157; Orphans 157; Union Association Browns 52
Cincinnati, OH: American Association Red Stockings 42, 60, 76, 77, 84, 119, 131; Buckeye BBC 7, 30, 55, 66, 75, 83, 92, 125; Cincinnati BBC 69; National Association Red Stockings 7, 9, 11, 15, 28, 33, 48, 66, 69, 74–75, 83, 94, 105, 120, 125, 120, 125, 129, 134, 136, 145, 149, 156, 161, 163, 178, 182, 187, 196, 202, 207; National League Red Stockings 14, 20, 40, 47, 51, 54, 57, 61–62, 64, 66, 68–69, 71, 76–78, 83, 86, 88, 93–94, 105, 110, 113, 125, 131, 135; Union Association Outlaw Reds 32
Clack, Bobby 6, 40–41, 148
Clapp, John 41, 95, 142–44, 184–86
Clare, Denny 41–42, 147
Cleveland, OH: American Association Blues 119; Forest City BBC 7, 15, 22, 39, 59, 73, 76, 79, 96, 102, 106–7, 112, 117, 124–25, 131, 147, 151, 162, 166–68, 171, 178, 197, 205; National League Blues 32, 36, 38, 41, 46, 50, 63, 90, 110, 112, 117, 129, 136; National League Spiders 119; Players League Infants 119
Clinton, James "Big Jim" 42, 149, 161–62, 203
Clinton BBC (Clinton IA) 34, 63, 77
Collins, Dan 7, 42
Colt Property (Hartford, CT) 172
Columbia Park (Philadelphia, PA) *see* Centennial Park
Columbus, OH 11, 117, 194; American Association Buckeyes 112; Columbus Buckeyes 21, 56, 102
Compton Avenue Grounds (St. Louis, MO) 206–7
Concord BBC (Brooklyn, NY) 119
Cone, Fred 11, 22, 42–43, 145, 150–51, 170
Connecticut League 101
Connell, Terry 43
Connor, Ned 43
Coon, William 44
cooperative clubs 8, 147, 161, 178, 184, 186, 195
Corcoran, Larry 65
Coughlin, Dennis 44, 195
Covington Stars BBC (Covington, KY) 28, 49, 56, 92, 94, 206
Crane, Fred 44–45, 145, 148, 203
Craver, Bill 10, 24, 45, 67, 99, 144, 154–56, 175–77, 181–83, 199–201
Croft, Art 7, 45, 207
Crowley, Bill 46, 201
Cummings, William "Candy" 46–47, 65, 68, 71, 91, 113, 142, 173–74, 183, 191–92, 200–1
Cuthbert, Edgar "Ned" 9, 47, 139, 141, 142, 158–59, 199–200

Dailey (Daily), John 47, 211
Dailey, John J. 47
Daley, Hugh "One Arm" 118
Dauntless BBC (New York, NY) 105
Davenport BBC (Davenport, IA) 87
"Dean" 47
Deane, John Henry "Harry" 47–48, 178, 180, 183
Dehlman, Herman "Dutch" 47–48, 147–48, 205
Detroit, MI 11, 36; National League Wolverines 32, 40, 57, 62, 63, 72, 77, 80, 84, 90, 107, 131
Devlin, Jim 9, 10, 24, 48–49, 67, 99, 159–60, 200
Dillon, John 7, 49, 208
Dillon, Patrick "Packy" 7, 49, 207–8
Dole, Lester 4, 49–50, 163, 165
Donnelly, John 50
Donnelly, Pete 50, 178, 180, 200, 209
Doscher, John Henry "Herm" 50, 51, 164–65, 211
Douglas, Ben, Jr. 171, 184
Doyle, Jacob 8, 51, 195
Duffy, Ed 6, 51, 158, 161

Eagle BBC (New York City) 51, 56, 71
East Liberty BBC (East Liberty, PA) 17

Index

Eastern League 43, 48, 53, 98, 103, 112, 119, 123
Easton BBC (Easton, PA) 13, 15, 19, 32, 48, 66, 94, 103, 133, 205
Eckford, Henry 160
Eckford BBC (Brooklyn) 3, 5, 12, 14–15, 26, 40, 42–43, 51, 55–56, 61, 73–76, 83, 85–87, 89–90, 92, 95, 98, 101, 103, 105, 109, 119–20, 124, 127, 133, 136, 146, 156, 160–62, 168, 180, 183–84, 186, 189, 191–92, 198–99, 202–3
Edwards 51
Edwards, Charles 51
Eggler, Dave 51–52, 144, 188, 190–92, 200–1
Eland 52
Elephant BBC (St. Louis, MO) 206
Elizabeth, NJ 12, 18, 36, 82, 132, 148, 201–2; Resolute BBC 8, 12, 15, 18, 37, 42, 44–45, 53, 55, 82–83, 98, 113, 124, 133, 147–48, 156, 192, 201–3, 209
Ellick, Joe 7, 52, 208
Elm City BBC (New Haven, CT) 12, 17, 19–20, 34, 51–52, 65, 68, 81, 91, 99, 120, 123, 126–27, 135, 154, 163–65, 173
Elysian Fields (Hoboken, NJ) 188–89
Emmett BBC (Chicago) 32
Empire BBC (New York, NY) 72, 76, 129
Empire BBC (St. Louis, MO) 7, 42, 101, 203–4, 206, 211
Enterprise BBC (Baltimore, MD) 38, 65, 96
Enterprise BBC (Brooklyn, NY) 40, 44, 53, 67, 103, 105, 121
Erie BBC (Erie, PA) 111, 126
Eureka BBC (Newark, NJ) 35–36, 95
Eureka BBC (Philadelphia, PA) 64
European Tour 55, 60, 115, 149, 153
Evans 52–53, 165
Ewell, George 53
Excelsior BBC (Brooklyn, NY) 30, 33, 46, 56, 61, 67, 82, 100, 127, 139, 145, 187, 194
Excelsior BBC (Chicago, IL) 117

Excelsior BBC (Rochester, NY) 42
Exercise BBC (Brooklyn, NY) 61
Expert BBC (Philadelphia, PA) 84, 130

Fairmount BBC (Fairmount, MA) 14
Farrell, "Hartford Jack" 53, 173
Farrow, Jack 53, 148, 201, 203
Ferguson, Bob 53–54, 145–148, 172–74, 190–91
Field, Sam 54, 156
Fields, George 54–55, 186
Fiorito, Len 1
Fisher, William "Cherokee" 7, 10, 20, 54–55, 142–43, 171, 173, 175, 182, 201
Fisler, Wes 9, 55, 139, 141–44
Fleet, Frank 10, 55–56, 148, 162, 191, 203, 205
Fletcher, George 55, 162
Flint, Frank "Silver" 56, 70, 207–8
Flour City BBC (Rochester, NY) 75, 91
Flowers, Charles "Dickie" 56–57, 142, 176–77
Flyaway BBC (New York, NY) 26, 34, 56, 82, 90
Flynn, William "Clipper" 57, 79, 158, 175–77, 198
Foley, Tom 7, 8, 57, 58, 158, 170
Foley, Will 57–58
Foran, Jim 57–58
Force, David "Wee Davy" 10, 28, 58–59, 144, 159–60, 177, 182–83, 196–98
Fordham University 24–25, 176
Forest City BBC (Cleveland, OH) 7, 15, 22, 39, 59, 73, 76, 79, 96, 102, 106–7, 112, 117, 124–25, 131, 147, 151, 162, 166–68, 171, 178, 197, 205
Forest City BBC (Rockford, IL) 7, 11, 14, 20, 27, 43, 57, 68–69, 114, 120, 169–71, 197
Fort Wayne, IN 11, 38, 42, 47, 65, 67, 88, 104, 115, 178, 179, 180, 182, 187, 197; Kekionga BBC 7, 11, 17, 21, 42, 48, 50, 58, 67, 74, 78, 81–82, 89, 96, 108, 115, 161, 166, 171, 178–80, 183, 188, 195, 197–98, 213

Fowler, Bud 212
Franklin BBC (Chicago, IL) 37, 58
Franklin BBC (Franklin, PA) 17, 78
French, Bill 59, 108, 188
Friendly United Social BBC (Bridgeport, CT) 30, 126, 148, 165
Fulmer, Charles "Chuck" 8, 59–60, 166, 191, 199–201
Fulmer, Washington 8, 60, 70

Galvin, James "Pud" 7, 9, 60, 205
Galvin, John 61
gamblers 10, 22, 28, 67, 72, 90
Gassette, Norman 157
Gavern 61
Geary BBC (Philadelphia, PA) 15, 70, 93
Gedney, Alfred "Count" 61, 143, 162, 177, 192–93
Geer, George H. 62
Geer, William H. "Billy" 61–62, 164–65, 192
Gerhardt, Joe 62–63, 183, 193, 208
Gilligan, Barney 63
Gilmore, Jim 7, 63
Gilroy 64
Girard College 80, 140
Glenn, John 2, 64, 159–160, 195–98, 208
Golden, Mike 64, 160, 213–14
Goldsmith, Fred 65, 102, 165
Goldsmith, Warren "Wally" 65, 179, 188, 198, 213–14
Gotham BBC (New York, NY) 69, 117
Gould, Charlie 7, 17, 66, 134, 150–51, 163–65, 183
Grand Army of the Republic 103, 105, 122
Grand Avenue Grounds (St. Louis, MO) 204
Grand Duchess (Fort Wayne, IN) 11, 178–79
Grand Rapids BBC (Grand Rapids, MI) 17
Greason, Jack 66, 209
Great Chicago Fire 12, 88, 136, 156–57
Greenpoint BBC (Greenpoint, NY) 111
Guelph, Ontario: Guelph Stars BBC 34; Maple Leaf BBC 75

Index

Hackensack BBC (Hackensack, NJ) 61
Hague (Haug), William "Bill" 66–67, 205
Hall, George 6, 10, 67, 99, 144–45, 152–53, 182–83, 197–98
Hall, Jim (Edwin Hall) 67, 147, 213–14
Hallinan, Jimmy 6, 7, 67–68, 108, 179, 193, 213–214
Ham, Ralph 68, 170
Hamilton Park (New Haven, CT) 163
Harbidge, Bill (Harbridge) 68, 174
Harlem BBC (New York City) 28
Harmonic BBC (Brooklyn, NY) 71
Harrisburg, PA (Expert BBC) 53, 68, 81, 108
Harrison, Rit 68–69, 165
Hartford, CT 42, 53, 124; Hartford BBC (Dark Blues) 9–10, 14–15, 19, 21–22, 29–32, 35, 38–39, 46, 53–55, 68–69, 76, 86, 95, 101, 105, 108, 110, 117, 122, 127, 132, 136, 141, 144, 146, 148, 153–54, 160, 163–64, 171–74, 184, 193, 201, 205, 209–11, 213–14; National League Dark Blues 16, 22, 29–30, 35, 38–39, 46, 53, 68, 72, 74, 95, 110, 121, 136
Harvard University 30, 98
Hastings, Scott 7, 69, 122, 160, 167–71, 173–74, 183
Hatfield, John 9, 69, 188, 190–93
Hautz, Charlie 7, 70, 207–8
Havana, Cuba (Havana BBC) 24
Haverhill BBC (Haverhill, MA) 114
Hayhurst, Hicks 140, 154–55
Haymakers BBC (Troy, NY) 13, 24, 43, 45, 56–57, 87–88, 92, 136, 162, 175–77, 182, 195–98
Heifer, Frank 70, 153
Hellings 1, 8, 70
Henry Eckford BBC (Brooklyn, NY) 76
Heubel, George 6, 70–71, 141, 166, 198
Hicks, Nat 71, 190–93, 200–1
Higby 71, 147

Higham, Dick 6, 10, 72, 160, 182, 188, 190–93
Hines, Paul 9, 72–73, 159–60, 195, 208–9
"hippodroming" 10, 28
Hodes, Charlie 73, 158, 177
Holdsworth, James 9, 73–74, 168, 192–93, 200–1
Hollingshead, John "Holly" 74, 195, 208–11
Holy Cross, College of the 30
Hooper, Mike 74, 188
Hornell BBC (Hornell, NY) 77
Howard Avenue Grounds (New Haven, CT) 163–64
Hudson River BBC (Newburgh, NY) 83
Hunt, Charles 74
Hunt, Dick 74–75, 162
Hurley, William F. see Hurley, William H. "Dick"
Hurley, William H. "Dick" 75

Ilion BBC Clippers (Ilion, NY) 40
Indianapolis, IN 11, 117; American Association BBC "Hoosiers" 30, 74, 77; Indianapolis BBC 15, 56, 64, 70, 92, 94, 107, 112–13, 116, 206; National League BBC "Hoosiers" 41, 45, 56, 68, 72, 98, 107, 117
International Alliance 206
International Association 14, 42, 87
International League 20, 40, 113, 124, 130
Irvington BBC (Irvington, NJ) 36–37, 83, 95, 125, 132, 145, 201

Jackson, Sam 6, 75, 151
Janesville BBC (Janesville, WI) 17
Jefferson BBC (Washington, DC) 112, 136
Jefferson Street Grounds (Philadelphia) 140, 154–55, 199
Jersey City, NJ 33, 42; Pavonia BBC 108
Jewett, Nat 75–76, 162
Johns, Tommy 76
Johnson, Caleb 7, 76
Jones, Charley (Benjamin Rippy) 76, 213–14
Jones, Levin 77
Josephs see Borden, Joe

Kansas City 52; American Association Cowboys 77; Union Association Cowboys 52, 84, 114
Kavanagh (Kavanaugh) see Cavanagh, James
Keenan, Jim 9, 77, 165
Keerl, George 77–78, 160
Kekionga Base Ball Grounds (Fort Wayne, IN) 178–79; see also Grand Duchess
Kekionga BBC (Fort Wayne, IN) 7, 11, 17, 21, 42, 48, 50, 58, 67, 74, 78, 81–82, 89, 96, 108, 115, 161, 166, 171, 178–80, 183, 188, 195, 197–98, 213
Kelly, Bill 6, 78, 179
Kelly, King 56, 102
Kenney, John 78, 147
Keokuk, Iowa 12, 21, 49, 64–65, 67, 76, 94, 108, 112, 114, 115, 117, 154, 211–14; Western BBC 8, 12, 37, 64, 76, 106, 141, 160, 193, 208, 211–14
Kernan, Joe 78, 188
Kerns, James 139
Kessler, Henry 78, 148–49
Keystone BBC (New York, NY) 82, 100
Keystone BBC (Philadelphia, PA) 13, 24, 43, 47, 53, 57, 59, 85, 92, 109, 139
Kimball, Gene 8, 79, 168
King, Marshall "Mart" 79, 175, 177
King, Steve 79, 80, 175–77
Knickerbocker BBC (New York, NY) 3, 5, 134, 189
Knight, George 7, 80, 163, 165
Knight, Lon (Alonzo Letti) 80–81, 144
Knowdell, Jake 81, 148
Kohler, Henry 81, 179, 188

Lancaster BBC (Lancaster, PA) 43
Latham, George "Juice" 10, 81–82, 153, 164–65
Laughlin, Ben 6, 82, 203
Lawrie, John see Lowry, John
Leadville Blues BBC (Leadville, CO) 78, 82
League Alliance 13, 18, 33, 64, 70, 77, 94–95, 110, 112–13, 116, 126, 129, 206
Leavenworth, Sonny 175
Ledwith, Michael 82

Index

Lennon, Bill 48, 82, 89, 108, 115, 178–79, 186, 188, 195
Lenz, David 83, 162
Leonard, Andy 6, 7, 9, 83, 151–53, 196–98
Leutz *see* Lenz, David
Lewiston BBC (Lewiston, ME) 111
Liberty BBC (New Brunswick, NJ) 11
Liberty BBC (Norwalk, CT) 36
Live Oak BBC (Lynn, MA) 82, 87, 127
Locke *see* Brown, Robert
Locke, Marshall 35
Locke, William 34
Lord Baltimore BBC (Baltimore) 7–10, 12, 21, 27, 29, 33–34, 38, 45–46, 48, 55, 58, 62, 66–67, 69, 72, 77, 81, 86, 88, 93, 95, 105, 108, 110–11, 113–15, 118–19, 125, 131, 135–36, 141–42, 151, 153, 159–60, 64–65, 167, 171, 173, 175, 177, 180–84, 187–88, 191–93, 198, 200–1, 209, 211
Los Angeles, CA 108
Louisville, KY 11, 52, 93, 117; American Association Eclipse 61, 62, 81, 84, 130; National League Grays 10, 15, 21, 24, 37, 40, 42, 45–46, 48, 62, 66–67, 69, 81, 84, 99, 113, 117, 119–20, 214; National League Colonels 21, 40
Lovett, Len 83, 155–56, 203
Lowe, Charlie 84, 147
Lowell BBC (Lowell, MA) 115, 133, 135
Lowry, John 84
Ludlow BBC (Ludlow, KY) 13, 33, 118
Luff, Henry 84, 123, 165

Mack, Connie 141
Mack, Denny (Dennis McGee) 84–85, 141–42, 170, 199–201
Madison Avenue Grounds (Baltimore) 180–81, 187
Malatsky, Richard 40, 111
Malone, Fergie 6, 9, 43, 64, 85, 139, 141–42, 158–59, 196, 199, 200–1
Malone, Martin 85, 162
Manchester BBC (Manchester, NH) 42, 47, 114, 125, 130, 133

Manhattan College 62
Manning, Jack 86, 151–53, 173, 183–84
Mansfield, Joseph 184
Mansfield BBC 8, 11, 14, 17, 22, 25, 30, 33, 36–37, 54, 56, 89, 97, 101, 127, 142, 151, 163, 173, 184–86, 189
Mansfield Club Grounds 184–85
Marazzi, Richard 1
Marion BBC (Bushwick, NY) 14
Marshalltown BBC (Marshalltown, IA) 17, 114
Martin, Albert D (Albert May) 86, 162
Martin, Alphonse "Phonney" 86–87, 162, 177
Maryland BBC (Baltimore) 1, 8, 12, 17, 27, 38, 52, 59, 65, 74, 76–78, 81–82, 88, 90, 96, 106, 114–15, 117–19, 123, 133, 178–80, 183, 186–88, 209, 211, 213
Mason, Charles 7, 9, 87, 156
Mathews, Bobby 9, 53, 71, 74, 82, 88, 166, 168, 178–80, 182–83, 186, 189, 192–93
McAtee, Michael "Bub" 79, 88, 158, 175–77
McBride, James Dickson "Dick" 9, 89, 139–44, 159
McCarton, Frank 89, 186
McCloskey 89, 211
McCloskey, Bill 89
McClune, Peter 175
McDermott, Joe 89, 162, 180
McDonald, Daniel "Jack" 89–90, 147, 162
McDoolan 90
McFadden, Archie 19
McGeary, Mike 10, 28, 90, 142–43, 175, 177, 199, 201
McGee, Pat 6, 90, 193
McGinley, Tim 91, 156, 165
McGovern *see* Gavern
McKelvey, John 91, 165
McKenna, Ed 91–92
McKenna, F. *see* McKenna, Ed
McKenna, Patrick *see* McKenna, Ed
McMullin, John "Lefty" 7, 92, 142–43, 175, 177, 180, 191, 201
McSorley, John "Trick" 7, 70, 92, 207–8
McVey, Cal 7, 66, 92–93, 134, 149–53, 181, 183

Meeker, Otto 201
Memphis, TN 110
Metcalf (Metcalfe), Alfred 93, 193
Metropolitan BBC (New York) 28, 32
Meyerle, Levi 93–94, 141–42, 158–60, 199–201
Middletown, CT 11, 17, 171, 184–85; Mansfield BBC 8, 11, 14, 17, 22, 25, 30, 33, 36–37, 54, 56, 89, 97, 101, 127, 142, 151, 163, 173, 184–86, 189
Miller, Joe 6, 94, 160, 195, 213–14
Miller, Thomas "Reddy" 66, 94–95, 205
Mills, Charlie 95, 145, 189–91
Mills, Everett 95, 145, 173–74, 181–83, 191, 197–98
Milwaukee, WI 17, 21, 95, 110, 124, 130; National League Cream Citys or Grays) 40, 52, 57, 64, 81, 96, 104, 110, 130
Mincher, Ed 50, 96, 178–79, 195
Minneapolis, MN 34
Moore, Maurice "Mollie" 6, 96, 148
Morgan, Bill *see* Morgan, Daniel
Morgan, Daniel "Pidge" 7, 96, 207–8
Mullen, Martin 7, 8, 96–97
Munn, Horatio 97
Murnane, Tim 9, 97–98, 142–43, 186, 201
Mutual BBC (Jackson, MI) 37
Mutual BBC (New York City) 9, 10, 12, 15, 21, 24–25, 27, 29–31, 35, 38–39, 42, 46, 51, 53, 55, 59, 61–62, 68–69, 71–74, 76, 80, 87–88, 90, 92–93, 95, 97–98, 103–105, 107, 110, 116–18, 121, 123–24, 129, 132, 139, 141–43, 145–48, 153–54, 157, 160–62, 164, 168, 171, 173, 175, 177, 180, 182–84, 186, 188–93, 196–201, 203, 211–214
Mutual Hook and Ladder Company 188

Nameless BBC (Brooklyn) 34
Nashville, TN 42
Nassau BBC (Brooklyn) 39, 50, 119

National Association Grounds (Cleveland, OH) 167
National BBC (Lansingburgh, NY) 175
National BBC (Washington, DC) 8, 11, 12, 26, 28, 33, 44, 51, 56, 64, 71–72, 74, 82, 94, 96, 100, 120–23, 131, 135–36, 168–69, 183, 186, 188, 193–96, 100, 121–23, 131
National Board of Professional Baseball Clubs 98
Nedrob *see* Borden, Joe
Nelson, John "Candy" 98, 162, 192–93
Nevin, Alex 7, 98–99, 203
New Bedford BBC (New Bedford, MA) 135
New Haven, CT 10–12, 17, 30, 39, 49–50, 61, 66, 77, 80, 84, 90, 102, 113, 119, 123, 141, 156, 163–65, 210; Elm City BBC 12, 17, 19–20, 34, 51–52, 65, 68, 81, 91, 99, 120, 123, 126–27, 135, 154, 163–65, 173
New York City 3, 5, 11, 15, 18, 21, 23, 26, 28, 30–31, 41, 50, 55–56, 58, 61, 63, 73–77, 82, 86–87, 90, 96, 99, 103–5, 116–17, 121, 129, 133–36, 163, 171, 180, 186; Active BBC 69; Eagle BBC 51, 56, 71; Empire BBC 72, 76, 129; Flyaway BBC 26, 34, 56, 82, 90; Gotham BBC 69, 117; Harlem BBC 28; Keystone BBC 82, 100; Knickerbocker BBC 3, 5, 134, 189; Metropolitan BBC (Mets) 41, 81, 98, 105; Mutual BBC 9, 10, 12, 15, 21, 24–25, 27, 29–31, 35, 38–39, 42, 46, 51, 53, 55, 59, 61–62, 68–69, 71–74, 76, 80, 87–88, 90, 92–93, 95, 97–98, 103–105, 107, 110, 116–18, 121, 123–24, 129, 132, 139, 141–43, 145–48, 153–54, 157, 160–62, 164, 168, 171, 173, 175, 177, 180, 182–84, 186, 188–93, 196–201, 203, 211–214; National League Gothams/Giants 41, 54, 62, 98, 101; National League Mutuals 24, 30, 45, 58, 68–69, 71, 74, 76, 88, 99, 105, 121, 127, 189; New York Mutuals (NL) 24, 30, 45, 58, 68–69, 71, 74, 76, 88, 99, 105, 121, 127, 189; Players League Giants 101
New York State League 17, 47
Newark, NJ 33, 37, 53, 82, 129; Amateur BBC 201; Eureka BBC 36, 95
Newington Park (Baltimore, MD) 180–81
Niagara BBC (Buffalo, NY) 11
Nichols, Al 6, 10, 67, 99, 148
Nichols, Frederick "Tricky" 49, 99–100, 164–65
Norfolk BBC (Norfolk, VA) 123
Norton, Frank 8, 100, 197
Notre Dame University 16–17, 28, 34, 49

Oakland, CA 23, 58
Oberbeck, Henry 104
O'Brien, Pete 145
Olympic BBC (Philadelphia, PA) 83, 85
Olympic BBC (Washington, DC) 10, 12, 15–16, 21, 23, 26, 33, 35, 53, 57–58, 64–65, 67, 71, 74–75, 83, 95, 100, 109, 112, 115, 12, 125, 129, 131, 136, 141, 145, 151, 166, 168, 175, 177, 182–83, 186, 191, 195, 196–98, 208, 211, 213
Olympic Grounds (Washington DC 196–97, 208, 210
Omaha BBC (Omaha, NE) 58, 114, 212
O'Neil, Hugh 100
O'Neil, Michael "Fancy" 6, 101, 173
O'Neill, J. *see* O'Neil, Hugh
Oran, Tom 6, 7, 101, 207
Oriental BBC (Brooklyn) 86, 105–6
O'Rourke 6, 101, 162
O'Rourke, Jim "Orator" 9, 101–2, 113, 149, 151–53, 184, 186
Osceola BBC (Stratford, CT) 36, 184
Oswego BBC (Oswego, NY) 17, 70
Ottawa BBC (Ottawa, IL) 111

Pabor, Charlie 56, 102, 146, 148, 164–68
Pacific BBC (Rochester, NY) 91, 165
Parks, Bill 103, 201, 210–11
Pastime BBC (Baltimore, MD) 21, 77, 96, 106, 178, 180, 186, 187
Patterson, Dan 2, 103
Patterson, Tom 2, 103, 148, 162, 188, 190–192
Pavonia BBC (Jersey City, NJ) 108
Pearce, Dickey 10, 103–4, 145, 147, 190–91, 204–5
Peconic Club (Brooklyn, NY) 24
Penfield, Cal 175
Peoria, IL 92
Perry Park (Keokuk, IA) 212
Peters, John 7, 104, 160
Phelps, Nealy 104–5, 180, 192–93
Philadelphia, PA 5–8, 12–17, 19, 24–25, 31–32, 36, 43–44, 46, 49–51, 53, 55–57, 60, 64, 66, 68, 70–71, 75, 81–85, 87, 89–92, 94–96, 107, 109–10, 112–13, 115–117, 121, 126, 128–30, 139–40, 154–55, 184, 195; American Association Athletics 32, 46, 80, 81, 87–88, 107, 112, 114, 117, 130, 139; Arctic BBC 114; Athletic BBC 8–10, 12, 16–17, 22, 24–25, 27, 29, 36, 41, 44–45, 47, 51, 55, 57–58, 60–61, 64, 67–68, 70–71, 80, 84–85, 89, 92–94, 97, 105, 107–9, 111–12, 115, 121–22, 124, 127, 130, 135, 139, 144, 151, 154–56, 158–59, 166, 173, 177, 182–84, 186, 189, 191, 193–94, 196, 198–201, 205, 209; Eureka BBC 64; Geary BBC 15, 70, 93; Keystone BBC 13, 24, 43, 47, 53, 57, 59, 85, 92, 109, 139; National League Athletics 9, 10, 12, 14, 24, 30, 32, 45–47, 50–51, 55, 71, 74, 82, 84–85, 91–92, 94, 97, 102–3, 108, 113, 119, 127, 133, 136–37, 139–44, 148, 151–54, 156, 158–60, 164–65, 173–74, 183, 192–93, 198–201, 203; National League Quakers/Phillies 56, 68, 86, 109–10, 128–129, 135; Philadelphia BBC (White Stockings, Pearls) 9, 10, 12, 14, 24, 30, 45–47, 50–51, 55, 71, 74, 82, 84–85, 90–92, 94, 97, 102–3, 108, 117, 119, 127, 130, 133, 136, 139–44, 148, 152–54,

156, 158–60, 164, 173–74, 183, 192–93, 198–201, 203; Quaker City BBC 40, 57, 67, 85, 107; Union Association Keystones 61, 84–85, 107, 130; West Philadelphia BBC 24, 47
Phillips Academy 98
Pike, Lip 6, 105, 139, 145, 172–74, 176–77, 182–83, 205
Pinkham, Ed 105–6, 158
Pittsburgh, PA 42, 84, 113, 130; American Association Alleghenys 17, 22, 54, 60, 70, 77, 84, 104, 107, 112; National League Alleghenys 60, 72, 131; Players League Burghers 60; Union Association Stogies 23
Popplein, George 8, 106
Potomac BBC (Washington, DC) 194
Powhatan BBC (Brooklyn, NY) 24
Pratt, Albert "Uncle Al" 106–7, 166, 168
Pratt, Tom 107, 141, 145
Priam BBC (Troy, NY) 175
Providence, RI 19, 32, 70, 115; National League Grays 8, 16–17, 32–33, 38–39, 53, 55, 63, 66, 72, 80, 88, 90, 97, 100–1, 104–5, 121, 125, 134–36, 161
Putnam BBC (Troy, NY) 68

Quaker City BBC (Philadelphia, PA) 40, 57, 67, 85, 107
Quest, Joe 107–8
Quincy BBC (Quincy, IL) 65, 112
Quinlan 6, 108, 200
Quinn 108
Quinn, Patrick "Paddy" 7, 108, 110, 160, 179, 213–14

Radbourn, "Old Hoss" 63
Radcliff (Radcliffe), John 10, 108–9, 139, 141, 154, 156, 164–65, 182–83, 200–1
R.E. Lee BBC (New Orleans, LA) 42
Reach, Al 6, 9, 109, 121, 139–41, 144, 155, 161
Reach, Bob 109–10, 208
Reach, George 109
Reading, PA (Active BBC) 54, 70, 83, 111

Red Stocking Base Ball Park (St. Louis, MO) 206–7
Redmon(d), Billy 7, 110, 207–8
Reid (Reed), Hugh 7, 110
Reliance Amateur BBC (Williamsburg, NY) 73
Remsen, Jack 110–11, 147, 173–74, 192–93
Rensselaer Polytechnic Institute 13
Resolute BBC (Brooklyn, NY) 113
Resolute BBC (Elizabeth, NJ) 8, 12, 15, 18, 37, 42, 44–45, 53, 55, 82–83, 98, 113, 124, 133, 147–48, 156, 192, 201–3, 209
Ressler, Larry 6, 111, 126, 211
Reville, Henry 111
Rexter, William 8, 111
"revolvers" 9, 67, 136, 198, 200
Richfield BBC (Richfield Springs, NY) 82
Richmond, John 111, 144
Richmond BBC (Richmond, VA) 118, 123
Riley, "Pigtail Billy" 112, 213–14
Riverside BBC (Portsmouth, OH) 106
Robinson, Val 112, 198
Rocap, Adam 112–114, 144
Rochester, NY 32, 47, 74, 84, 87, 112, 118, 124, 127; Alert BBC 75, 79, 91, 124, 166; Excelsior BBC 42; Flour City BBC 75, 91; Hop-Bitters BBC 97; Pacific BBC 91, 165
Rockford, IL 11, 117; Forest City BBC 10, 14, 16, 19, 55, 57–59, 68–69, 113–14, 117, 122, 141–42, 158, 167–69; Rockford BBC 110
Rogers, Fraley 113, 151–52
Ryan, Johnny 113, 164–65, 183

Sager, Samuel "Pony" 113–14, 171
St. Louis 7, 11, 29, 42, 45, 47, 49, 56, 61, 70, 91–92, 96, 101, 104, 110, 116, 117, 203, 206–7, 212; American Association Browns 8, 36, 45, 47, 60, 62, 92, 118, 129; Elephant BBC (St. Louis) 206; Empire BBC (St. Louis) 7, 42, 101, 203–4, 206, 211; National League Brown Stockings 22, 31, 41, 45, 47, 58, 84, 90, 91, 100, 104, 117; St. Louis BBC (Brown Stockings) 7, 12, 22, 32, 40, 47–48, 55, 60, 66, 94, 104, 116, 120, 132, 143, 154, 174, 204–206, 208; St. Louis Black Stockings BBC 206; St. Louis Red Stockings BBC 3, 7, 8, 12, 28, 32, 42, 45, 49, 52, 56, 70, 92, 96, 101, 110, 125, 148, 154, 206–7, 212; Standard BBC 96; Stocks (Stockyard) BBC 203; Union Association Maroons 29, 92, 117; Union BBC 101, 206
St. Paul BBC (St. Paul, MN) 17, 77, 94, 108, 126, 128, 132
St. Paul School 50
Salaries 8, 9, 11, 33, 45, 105, 125, 129, 201
San Francisco, CA 23, 58
Say, Jimmy 114
Say, Lou 9, 113–14, 183, 188, 209, 211
Schafer, Harry 9, 115, 149–53
Scranton, PA 21
Sellman (Selman), Frank 67, 82, 108, 115, 178–79, 186, 188, 198
Sensenderfer, John "Count" 6, 25, 115–16, 139, 141–42
Seward, George 116, 205, 207
Shaffer 116
Shaffer, George "Orator" 116–17, 173, 192, 201
Shaffer, Taylor 117
Sheppard, John 117, 188
Sheridan 117
Simmons, Joe 7, 117–118, 158, 168–70, 213–14
Simpson, Marty 117, 188
Smiley, Bill 118
Smith, A. see Smith, Tom
Smith, Bill 118, 187–88
Smith, Charlie 118, 145, 191
Smith, John 119, 165, 188
Smith, Sid 145
Smith, Tom 6, 119
Snow, Charlie 119
Snyder, Charles "Pop" 9, 119, 183, 201, 209
Snyder, Jim 119–20, 162
Snyder, Josh 120, 161–62
Somerville, Ed 120, 156, 165
South End Grounds (Boston) 150
Spalding, Al 7, 9, 11, 55, 107,

Index

109, 120–21, 142, 149–53, 169–70, 191
Spanish-American War 51, 99, 122
Spencer 121, 195
Sportsman's Park (St. Louis) 47, 204 (See also Grand Avenue Grounds)
Springfield BBC (Springfield, MA) 17, 39, 94
Standard BBC (St. Louis) 96
Star BBC (Brooklyn) 24, 30, 46, 67, 71, 74, 100, 113, 126, 134, 139, 151, 191
Start, Joe 9, 44, 121, 145, 190–93
Stearns, William 122, 173, 195, 197, 208–9, 211
Stevens, Robert 122
Stires, "Gat" 7, 122–23, 171
Stocks (Stockyard) BBC (St. Louis, MO) 203
Stoddard 123
Stratton, Ed 123, 188
Studley, Seymour "Seem" 123, 195
Sullivan 6, 123, 165
Sullivan, Tom 96
Sutton, Ezra 124, 142–44, 166, 168
Swandell, Marty (Schwandel) 6, 124–25, 161–62, 203
Sweasy, Charlie 7, 10, 125, 148, 168, 196–97, 207
Syracuse, NY: American Association Stars 23; National League Stars 119, 133; Syracuse BBC 32, 40, 42, 70, 77, 118, 127

Taylor, "Big Bill" 53
Taylor, Z.H. 125, 183
Tecumseh BBC (London, Ontario) 20, 50, 65, 81, 120
Terry, Wallace 125–26, 211
Texas League 47
Thake, Al 6, 126, 147
Thompson, Andrew 89, 126, 211
Thompson, Frank 126
Tipper, Jim 127, 164–65, 173–74
Toledo, OH 92
Treacey, Fred 9, 10, 127, 142, 154, 156, 158–59, 199–200
Treacey, Pete 127
Trenton BBC (Trenton, NJ) 49, 125

Trenwith, George 127, 128, 155–56, 165
Tri Mountain BBC (Boston, MA) 22, 150
Troy, NY 10, 12, 13, 15, 24, 45, 58, 61, 73, 79, 87–88, 92, 98, 101, 105, 133, 136, 145, 158, 161–62, 176, 180–85, 191, 198–99; Haymakers BBC 13, 24, 43, 45, 56–57, 87–88, 92, 136, 162, 175–77, 182, 195–98 (see also Union BBC of Lansingburgh); National League Trojans 32, 39, 50, 53, 65, 68, 72, 74, 98; Priam BBC 175; Putnam BBC 68
Tweed, William "Boss" 190–91
23rd Street Grounds (Chicago, IL) 157

Union Association 9, 22, 47, 52, 61, 74, 84–85, 94, 98, 104, 107, 114, 117–18, 130, 132, 210
Union BBC (Lansingburgh, NY) 24, 45, 55, 57–58, 79, 88, 90, 92, 156, 171, 175–76, 179; see also Haymakers
Union BBC (Morrisania, NY) 18, 22, 23–24, 27–28, 61, 72, 78, 86, 102, 150, 166, 168, 194, 197
Union BBC of Rensselaer County see Union BBC of Lansingburgh
Union BBC (St. Louis) 101, 206
Union BBC (Washington, DC) 27
Union Grounds (Brooklyn) 146, 161, 189
United States Treasury Department 27, 44, 56, 71, 74, 85, 132, 194
University of Pennsylvania Dental School 36
Utica BBC (Utica, NY) 47, 82

Villanova University 84, 170
Vintage Atlantic BBC 146
Vintage Elizabeth Resolutes 202
Vintage New York Mutual Club 190

Waitt, Charlie 128, 205
Walker, Oscar 128
Wall, Howard 129, 209

Walte's Pasture 212
Ward, Monte 100
Warner, Fred 129, 156
Warren BBC (Warren, NY) 48
Washington, DC 6, 11, 12, 15, 27, 44, 51, 56–57, 65–66, 73–74, 84, 94, 100, 109, 112, 119, 122, 129, 132, 136, 195–97, 209; American Association BBC 72, 119; Astoria BBC 66; Capitol BBC 27; Jefferson BBC 112, 136; National BBC 8, 11, 12, 26, 28, 33, 44, 51, 56, 64, 71–72, 74, 82, 94, 96, 100, 120–23, 131, 135–36, 168–69, 183, 186, 188, 193–96, 100, 121–23, 131; National League BBC 21, 121; Olympic BBC 10, 12, 15–16, 21, 23, 26, 33, 35, 53, 57–58, 64–65, 67, 71, 74–75, 83, 95, 100, 109, 112, 115, 12, 125, 129, 131, 136, 141, 145, 151, 166, 168, 175, 177, 182–83, 186, 191, 195, 196–98, 208, 211, 213; Union Association BBC 91, 132; Washington BBC (1873) 12, 21, 23, 27, 50, 59, 62, 66, 72, 90, 119, 122, 129, 131, 147, 153, 159, 183, 187–88, 208–10; Washington BBC (1875) 12, 15, 32, 47, 49, 50, 52, 54, 63, 74, 84, 87, 103, 111, 115, 122–23, 125–26, 132, 154, 156, 165, 173–74, 208–11
Waterbury, CT 53, 112, 118
Waterman, Fred 7, 129, 196–98, 208–9
Waverly BBC (Baltimore, MD) 187
Waverly Fairgrounds (Elizabeth, NJ) 202
Weaver, Sam 130, 201
West, Billy 130
West Philadelphia BBC (Philadelphia, PA) 24, 47
Western BBC (Keokuk, IA) 8, 12, 37, 64, 76, 106, 141, 160, 193, 208, 211–14
Western tour 11, 56, 117, 169, 195
White, Elmer 7, 130, 166, 168
White, James "Deacon" 7, 9, 79, 95, 131, 151–53, 166–68
White, Warren 8, 131–32, 181, 183, 195, 197, 208–9
White, Will 131

White Lot (Washington, DC) 66, 194
White Stocking Grounds (Chicago, IL) 157
White Stockings Park (Chicago, IL) 158
Wilkes-Barre BBC (Wilkes-Barre, PA) 47–48, 85
Wilkins, Isaac 139
Williams, Alfred H. *see* Nichols, Al
Williams College 87
Williamsburg Yacht Club 111
Williamson, Ned 132
Wilmington, DE 96, 98, 118; Union Association Quicksteps 118
Witherow, Charlie 132
Wolters, Rynie 6, 7, 96, 132, 168, 189–91, 203
Wood 132
Wood, Jimmy 9, 133, 152, 158–62, 175–77, 199–200
Woodhead, Red 133
Worcester (MA): National League Ruby Legs 30, 36, 40, 42, 52, 61, 80, 98, 100, 105, 109
Worcester BBC 32, 100
Wordsworth, Favel 133, 203
Worth, Herb 133–34, 147
Wright, Al 140
Wright, George 7, 9, 20, 66, 75, 83, 134–35, 149–53, 164, 194
Wright, Harry 6, 9, 11, 66, 93, 113, 134–35, 139, 149–53, 169–70, 185, 196
Wright, Sam 30, 135, 164–65

Yale University 8, 49, 80, 98–99, 101, 163, 165
Yeatman, Bill 8, 135–36, 195
Yeatman, Sam 136
York, Tom 136, 173–77, 182–83, 200–1
Young, Cy 60
Young, Nick 196–98, 208

Zettlein, George 9, 10, 136–37, 145, 158–60, 162, 177, 191, 199–201

www.ingramcontent.com/pod-product-compliance
Lightning Source LLC
Chambersburg PA
CBHW060259240426
43661CB00060B/2841